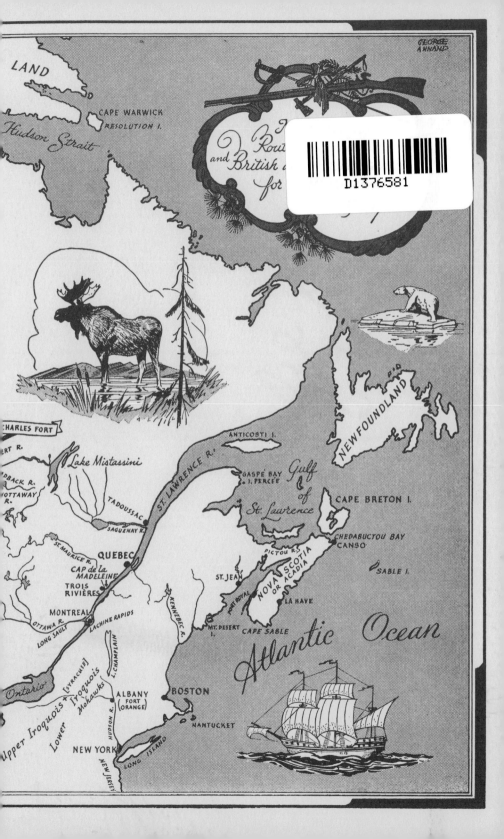

Publications of the

MINNESOTA HISTORICAL SOCIETY

RUSSELL W. FRIDLEY
Director

JUNE DRENNING HOLMQUIST
Assistant Director for
Research and Publications

Caesars of the Wilderness

MÉDARD CHOUART, SIEUR DES GROSEILLIERS
and PIERRE ESPRIT RADISSON, 1618-1710

by

GRACE LEE NUTE

Reprint Edition

MINNESOTA HISTORICAL SOCIETY PRESS
ST. PAUL · 1978

FIRST PUBLISHED IN 1943 BY D. APPLETON-CENTURY COMPANY, INC.,

AND THE AMERICAN HISTORICAL ASSOCIATION

LIBRARY OF CONGRESS CATALOGING IN PUBLICATION DATA:

Nute, Grace Lee, 1895–
   Caesars of the wilderness.

   (Publications of the Minnesota Historical Society)
   Reprint of the 1943 ed. published by Appleton-Century,
New York.
   Bibliography: p.
   Includes index.
   1. Chouart, Médard, sieur des Groseilliers, 17th
century. 2. Radisson, Pierre Esprit, 1620?–1710.
3. Explorers — France — Biography. 4. Hudson's Bay
Company. 5. Fur trade — New France. 6. New France —
Discovery and exploration. I. Title. II. Series:
Minnesota Historical Society. Publications.
F1060.7.C483N87 1978 971.01'6'0922   78-811

International Standard Book Numbers: 0-87351-127-1 Cloth cover
                                    0-87351-128-X Paper cover

Manufactured in the United States of America

TO THE MEMORY
OF MY FATHER
DEXTER ASBURY NUTE
(1860–1916)

Preface to the Reprint Edition

Thirty-five years have passed since the first edition of this book appeared. To my great satisfaction few changes in content need to be made for this reprint edition. Only one reviewer seems to have suggested that additional material should have been utilized. That reviewer thought that more attention should have been paid to the career of one of Radisson's fellow explorers, Diego Dionysius de Peñalosa. Indeed, it surprised me then and continues to amaze me that no one has picked up my hint that much needs to be done in French archives to bring out the true effects of two rather obscure priests in Paris on practically the entire exploration of North America in the latter half of the seventeenth century. I showed that these two men, Abbé Claude Bernou and Abbé Eusèbe Renaudot, were the center of a swirling sea of intrigue which shaped, in no slight degree, the course of exploration of De La Salle, D'Iberville, Jolliet, Hennepin, and many others. Yet to this day college students are still told the old stories of how and why those men opened the continent.

The book, so long out of print, did manage to come to the attention of a member of the Radisson family in Lyon (birthplace of Du Lhut). Monsieur J. P. Radisson wrote me that he had been motivated to try to confirm a family tradition that one of his ancestors had migrated to Avignon and so might well have caused that area to have been Pierre Esprit's birthplace, as I suggested. His efforts had not been crowned with success when he wrote, but he promised to continue them.

Despite the transfer of the archives of the Hudson's Bay Company from London to Winnipeg in 1974, and though a rumor circulated that they had been reclassified, the company assures me that my call numbers in footnotes referring to those documents are still valid.

ST. PAUL, MINNESOTA   *Grace Lee Nute*
JANUARY, 1978

Introduction to the Reprint Edition

During the period between the publication of Pierre Esprit Radisson's *Voyages* by the Prince Society of Boston in 1885 and the appearance of *Caesars of the Wilderness* in 1943, scholarly journals and books were often enlivened by the historical controversy surrounding Radisson and his fellow explorer, Médard Chouart, Sieur Des Groseilliers. Often referred to as the "Radisson problem," the controversy called into question almost every aspect of the two men's lives, from the authenticity of parts of Radisson's narrative to the exact itinerary the men followed in their travels.[1]

Throughout the sometimes acrimonious debate, hairs were split, fine points were delicately argued, and a great deal of ink was shed on the subject, but all in all the debate seemed nourished more often by speculation than by solid research. New theories occasionally took the place of new information and by the 1940s both the general reader and the uninitiated scholar were hard put to find their way through the web of misinformation.

With the publication of *Caesars of the Wilderness* in 1943, however, the historical debate came to an end. Based on many years of research in repositories throughout France, England, and North America, the book, with its skillfull presentation of new evidence, settled many of the questions that had long puzzled scholars. Where others had been content to speculate, Grace Lee Nute grounded her book in authentic though obscure manuscript sources and thereby managed to separate theory from verifiable fact.[2]

That *Caesars of the Wilderness* would become the definitive work on

[1] A listing of works relating to the Minnesota aspects of the controversy may be found in Michael Brook, comp., *Reference Guide to Minnesota History: A Subject Bibliography of Books, Pamphlets, and Articles in English*, 28 (St. Paul, 1974).

[2] Readers who are interested in retracing Nute's research can do so by examining the Grace Lee Nute Papers and the Radisson and Des Groseilliers Papers in the Division of Archives and Manuscripts, Minnesota Historical Society, as well as the Nute Papers owned by the University of Minnesota, Duluth. All three collections contain research notes and photocopies of many documents cited in this book.

Radisson and Des Groseilliers was evident from its publication. All those who reviewed it praised its exhaustiveness. Fulmer Mood called it a "splendid and important accomplishment in historical scholarship." W. Stewart Wallace said that it was "one of the most important contributions made to the history of North America in recent years." Lawrence J. Burpee noted that its author, "as the result of long and painstaking research and with the acute marshalling of a mass of hitherto unknown facts," had managed "to disentangle the threads and weave them into a clear and convincing story." Burpee seemed to express the opinions of most reviewers when he said that the book would "stand as practically the final word on Radisson and Chouart."[3]

He was right. Since 1943 little in the way of new research has been done on Radisson and Des Groseilliers. This may be due in part to changing historical interests, but major credit must certainly go to Grace Lee Nute for having finally explained a confusing subject to everyone's satisfaction.[4]

Another testimony to the value of *Caesars of the Wilderness* is the frequency with which it is used and cited by other scholars. E. E. Rich, for example, in his *History of the Hudson's Bay Company, 1670–1870* and in the volumes of company documents which he has edited for the Hudson's Bay Record Society, relied heavily on *Caesars* in discussing Radisson and Des Groseilliers. The same is true of other scholars whose works have touched incidentally on the lives of the two adventurers.[5]

For these reasons and because *Caesars* has long been out of print and difficult to obtain, the Minnesota Historical Society decided to

[3] *Minnesota History*, 24:151 (June, 1943); *Canadian Historical Review*, 25:68 (March, 1944); *Mississippi Valley Historical Review*, 30:256 (September, 1943). Summaries of other reviews of the book are in Mertice M. James and Dorothy Brown, eds., *Book Review Digest, Thirty-Ninth Annual Cumulation, March 1943 to February 1944 Inclusive*, 616 (New York, 1944).

[4] Arthur T. Adams, in his new edition of Radisson's *Voyages* entitled *The Explorations of Pierre Esprit Radisson* (Minneapolis, 1961), offers several theories on Radisson and Des Groseilliers which conflict with the evidence presented by Nute. They are expanded versions of the opinions he expressed in "A New Interpretation of the Voyages of Radisson," in *Minnesota History*, 6:317–329 (December, 1925), and "The Radisson Problem," in *Minnesota History*, 15:317–327 (September, 1934).

[5] E. E. Rich, *History of the Hudson's Bay Company, 1670–1870*, vol. 1 (London, 1958).

make the book available to a new generation of readers. No attempt
has been made to revise or update either the text or footnotes. However, some changes that have taken place in the location, organization, and accessibility of sources used by Nute should be mentioned.

Among the most frequently cited sources in this volume are letters
and record books in the Hudson's Bay Company Archives. This
impressive collection of fur trade materials, used by the author in
London, was moved in 1974 to Winnipeg, where it is now more
easily accessible to North American scholars. Moreover, it has now
been completely cataloged. Thus records from the Hudson's Bay
Company Archives referred to in this volume without catalog numbers have now been given numbers. For example, the earliest ledgers
of the company, dated 1667–76 and referred to in this volume as
ledgers 101 and 102, are now labelled A.14/1 and A.14/2. These
changes, however, need not disturb any scholar who wishes to re-
trace the author's steps, for the company's archivists have little trouble in identifying sources described by Miss Nute. It should also be
pointed out that a number of the sources cited, including company
minutes and letters, are now available in published form in volumes
5, 8, 9, and 11 of the Hudson's Bay Record Society series. Several of
these volumes also contain relevant excerpts from the company
ledgers referred to above.[6]

Also frequently cited in this book are various church and court
records and notarial contracts. Until 1972 they were housed in the
courthouses of Quebec City, Montreal, and Three Rivers (Trois
Rivières) where the author used them in the 1930s. Since 1972 the
records of each of these repositories have been consolidated into the
provincial system of archives branches known as the National Archives of Quebec. Many of these records have now been cataloged,
considerably facilitating research at each of the branches. In addition

---

[6] E. E. Rich, ed., *Copy-Book of Letters Outward &c* (Champlain Society, *Hudson's Bay Company Series*, vol. 11 — Toronto, 1948); Rich, ed., *Minutes of the Hudson's Bay Company, 1671–1674* (Champlain Society, *Hudson's Bay Company Series*, vol. 5 — To-ronto, 1942); Rich, ed., *Minutes of the Hudson's Bay Company, 1679–1684* (Champlain Society, *Hudson's Bay Company Series*, vols. 8–9 — Toronto, 1945, 1946); Rich, ed., *Hudson's Bay Copy Booke of Letters Commissions Instructions Outward, 1688–1696* (Hudson's Bay Record Society, *Publications*, vol. 20 — London, 1957).

published calendars of the records of notaries Severin Ameau, Guillaume Audouart, and Claude Lecoustre are now available.[7]

Although they found no flaws in Grace Lee Nute's scholarship, many early readers of *Caesars* criticized the inadequacy of the book's supplemental maps. To illustrate better the far-flung adventures of Radisson and Des Groseilliers, a new end-sheet map has been provided at the back of this reprint edition.

MINNESOTA HISTORICAL SOCIETY   *Bruce M. White*
JANUARY, 1978

[7] For the notarial calendars of Lecoustre and Audouart, see Archives de la Province de Québec, *Inventaire des Greffes des Notaires du Régime Français*, 1:24–28, 32–114 (Quebec, 1942). The calendar of Ameau is in vol. 11, pp. 50–137 of the same series (Quebec, 1948).

Preface

This book has been made possible through the kindness and coöperation of many persons and institutions. At various places in the footnotes I have indicated my indebtedness to individuals who have told me of data or who have assisted me to find material. It remains to acknowledge my indebtedness to the John Simon Guggenheim Memorial Foundation, which granted me a fellowship in 1934 enabling me to spend the year 1934–1935 in England, France, and Canada. During that year I was able to do extensive research in the Hudson's Bay Company Archives in London, in the Public Record Office, in the British Museum, in Somerset House, in the library of the Royal Society of London, in various libraries in Oxford and in London; in the Bibliothèque Nationale and several depositories of national archives in Paris; and in the judicial archives in Quebec and Three Rivers in Canada. To the officials and staffs of these institutions I hereby tender my grateful appreciation of all that they did for me.

Certain men entered into the spirit of my pilgrimage through Europe in quest of traces of two elusive Frenchmen of yesteryear and went out of their way to search with me. Such was a Dutchman, M. Henri Brugmans, who put his unique knowledge of many languages at my command and helped me find Les Groseilliers; such was a Frenchman, M. M. Giraud, who spent many weary hours in Paris, Avignon, and London, trying to locate certain information that I needed; such were two Englishmen of the Royal Society's staff in London, who were ever on the watch for data of interest for me, and one of whom found for me an unpublished diary of Hudson Bay explorations; and such were two Americans, Dr. Fulmer Mood and Dr. R. P. Stearns, who were very generous in sharing with me their greater knowledge of London and its treasures. Dr. and Mrs. Harcourt Brown similarly shared with me their zest for Paris and gave me information and showed me nooks and crannies that not only helped in the building of this book but that also left in me an undying love for Paris. To all of these persons and to many others who helped me in one way and another I give hearty thanks.

* * *

It should be stated at the outset that I have adopted a usage in this book that will be questioned by many. I have followed the French method of referring to Frenchmen who were entitled to the use of the title, "Sieur." Englishmen and Americans have not been consistent. We speak of La Salle and Du Luth. In one instance we use the "de" of the French name, similar to the German "von"; in the other we do not. I have tried to be more consistent and in this book the reader will encounter not La Salle but De la Salle. Some will point out, and with some little justice, that I mention Frontenac, not De Frontenac. The answer is that Frenchmen generally refer to him without the preposition, as they frequently do to persons with titles superior to "Sieur." I have also tried to follow the French usage in capitalization of family names based on places, that is, I do not capitalize the preposition or the particle when either follows immediately a title such as "Monsieur" or "Sieur."

Trifluviens will complain that their native place appears in this book as Three Rivers, whereas it appears on maps as Trois Rivières. The reason for the translation of the words is just that which prompts a Frenchman to say "Londres" and not "London." It is hard to pronounce the foreign word and there is an accepted translation of it. And while we are on the subject of pronunciation, it may be well to essay a pronunciation of the title of one of the subjects of this biography. Des Groseilliers cannot be pronounced adequately by persons unacquainted with the French language, but they can make themselves understood by pronouncing the words somewhat in this fashion: *day grow zay yay,* with a slight tendency to place the accent on the last syllable. Actually, all the syllables are accented equally, but to the ears of English-speaking persons, such a lack of accent has the effect of placing an accent on the last syllable. Les Groseilliers, it may be added, is the place from which Chouart took his title, and merely means "the gooseberry bushes." Radisson owned no fief and so was not entitled to the title, "Sieur."

G. L. N.

Minnesota Historical Society
Saint Paul, Minnesota

Introduction

This book tells the story of two French explorers, Médard Chouart, Sieur des Groseilliers, and his brother-in-law, Pierre Esprit Radisson. They explored North America in the seventeenth century, when Frenchmen discovered the Great Lakes, the Mississippi, the Ohio, the Missouri, Lake Winnipeg, and the Saskatchewan. Their names should be enrolled with Champlain's, Jolliet's, De la Salle's, Perrot's, Allouez', Hennepin's, and Du Lhut's. What a company of intrepid explorers called Quebec, Three Rivers, and Montreal their headquarters in that century of courage!

Many persons have attempted to tell the story of Radisson and Des Groseilliers. Most of them have actually told only a small part of it—the American, the Canadian, the English, or the French portion. This book is an effort to portray them as they were, now Frenchmen, now Americans, now Canadians, and now Englishmen.

It is a book of battles, but there is little bloodshed. The battles are engagements not of soldiers but of wits. Here is the wit of the Merry Monarch pitted against that of His Most Christian Majesty, each bent on stealing an American empire from the other. Here are Jesuit wits battling against Recollect, while each party solemnly lauds the Christian piety of the other. Men like the Recollects, who could outdo the Jesuits in the beaver trade and the establishment of new mission fields, were men indeed! Here is New England already outdoing Old England; and New France outmaneuvering Old France. And throughout the long yarn Radisson and Des Groseilliers slip nimbly between the Sun King and His Britannic Majesty, between Jesuit camp and Recollect clique, between New England and Old England, between

New France and Old France, and between Catholicism and Protestantism, giving merry chase to the wits of monarchs, fur-trading barons, governors, and churchmen.

Surely such men—who had not only wit to hold their own in the presence of royalty and churchmen, but also the physical stamina to recover from Indian torture, to command untamed savage tribes, to take an enemy's post single-handed, to survive the ice of Hudson Bay and the rocks of the Caribbean—surely such men deserve to be known better in that western world that they were the first white men to see, not only for what it was but also for what it might be.

Contents

Illustrations

ABBREVIATIONS

MANUSCRIPTS

AC . . . . Archives des Colonies

BN . . . . Bibliothèque Nationale
   MSS Fr. . . . . manuscrits français

H.B.Co. Archives . . . . . . Hudson's Bay Company Archives

PRO. . . . . Public Record Office
   CO. . . . . Colonial Office
   C . . . . Chancery Records
   S.P., Amer. & W.I. . . . . . State Papers, America and West
               Indies Series

   S.P., Dom. . . . . State Papers, Domestic Series

Three Rivers, prévôté records (Q) . Prévôté records of Three Rivers in
               the provincial museum at Quebec

PRINTED MATERIAL

Acts of the Privy Council, Col. Ser.   *Acts of the Privy Council, Colonial
               Series*

Cal. St. Pap., Dom. . . . . . *Calendar of State Papers, Domestic
               Series*

Cal. St. Pap., Am. & W.I. . . . *Calendar of State Papers, America
               and West Indies Series*

Caesars of the Wilderness

CHAPTER I

To the South Sea by the Bay
of the North

As the traveler of today journeys by car from Paris up the valley of the Marne toward Château-Thierry, he passes through Meaux and mounts a sort of bluff on the north bank of the river. When he turns the shoulder of this bluff, Charly-sur-Marne comes into view below him. It lies close to the river, but not really on its bank. A church dominates the little town—one of those churches with a tower like a little house superimposed athwart the nave, which are so typical of Normandy and quite occasional in southern England. This structure, dedicated to St. Martin, goes back to the thirteenth and fourteenth centuries. In the eighteenth century a slate flèche was added to the tower, but it has since been destroyed.

Charly is first met in history in 858, when it is mentioned in a charter granted by Charles II, le Chauve, to the Abbey of Notre Dame de Soissons. Tradition gives it a romantic origin, asserting that the little town derives its name from Charles Martel. Château-Thierry was his residence and Charly was part of the royal domain. It was called Charly-sur-Marne after 1552, but its Latin names were Carleium (1147), Challiacus (1261), and Carliacus. By 1481 it was known as Chaaly. Two fairs were granted to it in 1507.[1]

On July 31, 1618, a baby who was destined for fame was baptized in the church of Charly-sur-Marne. The name recorded in the parish register in Latin is Médard Chouart. He

---

[1] Dr. A. Corlieu's *Géographie du canton de Charly-sur-Marne* (Château-Thierry, 1879) gives a brief history of the place.

I

is more often recalled today by his title, Sieur des Groseilliers.[2]

The trip from Charly to Les Groseilliers is not long, if
one crosses the Marne at Charly by the bridge to Nogent
l'Artaud. In the seventeenth century Les Groseilliers was
included for administrative purposes in the bailiwick of
Charly. The route via the bridge takes one a few miles south
of Nogent l'Artaud to the bluffs. An easy, slanting road
mounts them. From the top one looks out over a pleasant
land. The man Chouart, returning in 1660 from a far country beyond Lake Superior, may well have compared the
scenes that lay before him with those that had so taken his
fancy south and west of the great upper lake. The two countries are strikingly similar today. Les Groseilliers itself, save
for the character of its buildings, might be a farm in Wisconsin or Minnesota. Arable land stretches away to the ho-
rizon, broken here and there by clumps of trees, farm buildings, and small ravines. The buildings of the farm are of
whitewashed stone and form a sort of hollow square. They
are farm houses of simple people and probably look much as
they appeared in Des Groseilliers' time. In May partridges
feed in the neighboring fields just as prairie chickens and other
grouse may be found on Middlewestern farms. Only the music
from the heavens is different, for Minnesota and Wisconsin
are not showered in May with the songs of skylarks, as is Les
Groseilliers.

Médard's father was also Médard Chouart. His mother
was Marie Poirier. He seems to have had a paternal uncle
named Antoine Chouart, and a cousin Médard Chouart,
to whom his own father stood godfather in 1622. Thus
there were at one time three Médard Chouarts. We know
little more about the family. In 1647, it would appear from
an old marriage record, the eldest Médard was still living

___

[2] The baptismal records of Charly-sur-Marne are now in the mayor's office
in that place.

in St. Cyr in the parish of Charly.[3] He is never mentioned as sieur. It is likely that the son became Sieur des Groseilliers through inheritance from his mother. As early as 1646 he is known by the name of this property rather than by his patronymic.

All that we know of his youth is contained in a letter by Mère Marie de l'Incarnation, the first mother superior of the Ursuline nuns at Quebec. On August 27, 1670, she wrote: "He was quite young when he came here, and he visited me often, both because of our native land and out of consideration for one of our mothers of Tours, with whose father he had lived." [4]

Just when Des Groseilliers passed up the "river without end," as the Indians described the St. Lawrence to its first known European discoverer, Jacques Cartier, is uncertain. Sometime between 1618 and 1645 a little seventeenth-century cockleshell of a French vessel carried the young man between the southern tip of Newfoundland and Cape Breton Island

---

[3] "Le 3 de Sept. 1647 les bans ayant este prealablement publies . . . le P. Barthelemy Vimont faisant L office de Cure en Leglise et paroisse de L'Imm. Concep. de N.D. a quebec a Interroge Medar Chouar fils de Medar Chouar demeurant a S. Cyre en brie de la paroisse de Charly et de Marie poirier sa femme. . . ." See a volume of the records of the parish of Notre Dame de Québec, 1621–1667, a copy of which is preserved in the Judicial Archives, Court-House, Quebec.

[4] The collected letters of Mère Marie appeared as early as 1681, edited by her son: *Lettres de la Vénérable Mère Marie de l'Incarnation, première supérieure des Ursulines de la Nouvelle-France,* edited by Dom Claude Martin. Since the Richaudeau edition of 1876 (3 vols., Tournai) is more readily accessible, reference will be made to it in this volume, rather than to the first edition, which is excessively rare. A new edition is just appearing—in the series, *Marie de l'Incarnation, Ursuline de Tours: Fondatriće des Ursulines de la Nouvelle-France—Ecrits Spirituels et Historiques,* edited by Dom Albert Jamet de la Congrégation de France. Thus far three volumes have appeared. Volume 3, *La Correspondance de Marie de l'Incarnation* (Paris and Quebec, 1935), carries the nun's correspondence into the year 1644. The letter of August 27, 1670, may be found in the edition of 1876, Vol. 2, pp. 447 and 448. The Canadian historian, Benjamin Sulte, states that the "Mother of Tours" was Sister Saint Bernard, whose family name was Savonnière de la Troche, but this seems to be merely a guess. Benjamin Sulte, *Histoire des canadiens-français, 1608–1880,* 5:7 (Montreal, 1882).

on his way to Quebec. Intrepid fishermen of Brittany had been frequenting the near-by cod banks since Cabot's visit and probably long before, and had given the "island" its name. Calm waters lay beyond—calm, at least, as compared with those outside the guarding islands. French fishing vessels dotted the blue water, especially about Percée Rock. The Gaspé Peninsula near-by stretched away in pleasant rhythms of forest and headland, cheering the weary sea traveler from Europe then as it still does. Only today neat little villages greet the eye, where Indians roamed on that day long ago. Soon the great island of Anticosti appeared. The boy or young man little thought as he passed slowly along the green shore of that fertile island, covered even now with primeval forests, that some day his title would be Seigneur d'Anticosti.

Beyond Anticosti the river began to narrow, and a few days later he must have passed the mouth of the Saguenay River, which enters the St. Lawrence from the north through giant portal rocks. This fjord of the Saguenay, long the hope of a way to the Sea of the West, comes down from a barren, mountainous wilderness that for years kept the French on the St. Lawrence from penetrating to the Bay of the North that figures so prominently in Des Groseilliers' career. At the junction of the two rivers was Tadoussac. When Des Groseilliers passed, it was already of respectable age. Some claim that its church is the oldest in all America. Today Tadoussac is a charming summer resort.

After Tadoussac, habitations became numerous even in Des Groseilliers' day. Away from the river, on both sides, in long narrow strips stretched the seigneuries of New France, feeble replicas of feudal estates in Old France. Their form, long parallelograms with a narrow side on the river, was determined by that river, which influenced New France in so many ways. It was the highway of the *habitant;* it supplied him with fish; it knit him to his fellows and united them all against Indian enemies; and it led him inexorably on to the great inland seas in the heart of the continent and made

The Lower Town of Quebec. Cartouche from J.-B. Franquelin's Manuscript Map of North America. Undated.

[Paris. Service Hydrographique, B 4040.10d.]

him either a great explorer or an invaluable, though humble
voyageur. Every *habitant* must have his dwelling close to
that great highway and so the frontage of any holder's estate
must be small, so that all may enjoy free transportation.

As Des Groseilliers neared Quebec, he saw the fair island
of Orleans, already settling with *habitants*. Two leagues beyond was Quebec itself on its rocky eminence. "We were still
more pleased at sight of the lower and upper towns of Quebec," wrote the author of the Jesuit *relation* of 1662–1663,
"beholding from a distance Churches and Monasteries that
had been built, and a Fortress perched upon a rock and
commanding the entire River." [5]

There is a persistent tradition that Des Groseilliers arrived
in Canada in 1641, but no evidence to establish the fact has
been found. Did news of New France reach the young man
in France, via the nun's family, through letters that the
Jesuits were sending about the Huron missions? It is by no
means unlikely. In any event, the next time that he emerges
from the obscurity that covers his youth, he is descending
to the lower St. Lawrence from the Huron missions in
modern Simcoe County, Ontario, in the area lying between
Lake Simcoe and Georgian Bay. He may have served there
either as a *donné* (a lay helper), or as a soldier or artisan—
probably in the first capacity.

Recollect missionaries had penetrated to Huronia as early
as 1615, but the last of their group, descending to Quebec
in 1625 to meet and instruct the Jesuits, who had been called
to assist the unsuccessful Recollects, lost his life in one of
the ever-dreaded rapids of the Ottawa route to the fur
country. His zeal and courage are enshrined forever in the
name of a rapid just back of Montreal, the Sault au Récollet.
So it was not until 1626 that the Jesuits entered the Huron
field; and they were obliged to abandon it in 1629, when the
English captured the tiny hamlet of Quebec. The last of

[5] Reuben G. Thwaites, ed., *The Jesuit Relations and Allied Documents*,
48: 159 (Cleveland, 1896–1901).

the Huron missionaries was captured there and taken to
England in 1629 by Lewis Kirke, one of the large family
of Gervais Kirke. The brothers of that family, especially
John and David, will be encountered often in the story of
Radisson and Des Groseilliers. After Canada had been returned to France by the treaty of St. Germain in 1632, the
active period of the Jesuits' greatest mission in New France
began. From 1634 to 1650 it lasted, through early failure,
later success, and final catastrophe. Twenty-nine missionaries, all told, served the Huron mission between 1615 and
1650. Seven of these lost their lives. The number of *donnés*
and other laymen and hired laborers is unknown, but it must
have been large.

It would be interesting and very enlightening from the
point of view of Canadian and American history, to know
the details of Des Groseilliers' life in Huronia. The arduous
toil of the missionaries, their long and difficult voyages to
and from Huronia, their interest in Indian languages and
western exploration, and their dispersion and, in some cases,
their martyrdom, have been told again and again. They form
one of the perennially absorbing chapters of American and
Canadian history. Des Groseilliers was a part of much of that
heroic chapter. It is thus a fitting, though an obscure prelude
to a heroic career. As in other missions, the Jesuits, once established in Canada, were soon a temporal as well as a spiritual factor. They aimed to extend their own sphere of activity,
that of the Catholic Church in general, and that of France.
Hence the discovery of more tribes to proselytize and more
territory to annex was a practical necessity. In addition,
the Jesuits were partly supported by the revenue of the
beaver trade; and the heart of the beaver country lay in yet
unknown lands west and north of Huronia.[6]

It is more than likely that this young man, Des Groseil-

---

[6] *Jesuit Relations,* 1: 21–27. The *relations* themselves give the best account
of the Huron mission.

liers, who later was to explore so many lands and tribes, began his explorations while at Huronia. The Jesuit *relations* hint at explorations in the 1640's made about the Great Lakes that nearly encircled Huronia. If men from the missions went out across Lake Huron, into Lake Michigan, up to Lake Superior, or elsewhere, it may be assumed that Des Groseilliers either was of the party or else a most diligent listener to those who returned. The ertswhile teacher of the Great Condé, Father Paul Ragueneau, who was the Jesuit superior at Huronia from 1645 to 1649, and the superior of all the Canadian missions from 1650 to 1653, wrote of Des Groseilliers in 1664: "He is a man capable of anything, bold, hardy, stubborn in his undertakings, who knows the countries [*of North America*], and who has been everywhere, to the Hurons, to the Ottawa . . . ." [7] Such a man was not twiddling his thumbs in Huronia during his sojourn in the interior.

It is the *relation* of 1646 that gives us our first definite news of the young man, then twenty-eight years of age: "Those who returned this year from the Hurons were Pierrot Cochon, Gilles Bacon, Daniel Carteron, Jean le Mercier, desgrosillers, racine, and Eustache lambert." [8] May we assume that it was Des Groseilliers himself who took to Mère Marie the letters that came down from Huronia with the

[7] Paul Ragueneau to ———, November 7, 1664, in Mélanges de Colbert in the Bibliothèque Nationale, Paris, No. 125, f. 181.

[8] See *Jesuit Relations*, 28:229. Mère Marie in a letter to her son of August 2, 1644, throws a little light on the kind of young men who went to Huronia. She writes: "Among those who have arrived [*from France*] this season, is a young man of excellent standing, aged twenty-two years, whom God has touched to serve in this country for the conversion of the Indians. You would be charmed to hear him talk on this subject and to see a young man, who has commanded in the armies of France, in such an unusual state of self-disdain. He is going to command in the Huron country, whither he will accompany three of the reverend fathers. . . . This young man would like to go everywhere to gain souls for Jesus Christ among the nations newly discovered and where none of our priests have yet been." She goes on to tell how he was studying the languages of these tribes in order to go among them. *Lettres,* 1:192, 193.

brigade of canoes, as well as some other information, which she relayed at once to her son in France in a letter dated September 10, 1646? She writes: [9]

The letters that we have received from Huronia tell us that a new country has been discovered and the gateway to it is found. It is the land of the people of the sea, called in Indian, Winnebago. This will be a fine mission, whither we hope to expand profitably, because these people are numerous and sedentary. The fathers are even planning to voyage on a great sea that is beyond that of the Hurons, by which they claim to find the way to China. By means of this sea, which is freshwater, they hope to discover many countries both on its shores and inland.

Father Poncet—whom Des Groseilliers' young brother-in-law, Pierre Esprit Radisson, was to encounter a few years later in New Holland and whom Mère Marie characterizes as her son's "bon ami"—seems to have attempted the contemplated voyage as early as 1649 and to have spent three months with the "Staring Hairs," as a translator has quaintly rendered the French words for the Ottawa Indians, the "Cheveux Relevés." [10]

Thus exploration west of Lake Huron stood when the Huron mission had to be abandoned because of Iroquois incursions in the late forties. The Hurons fled, some to Canada, some to the wildernesses of Wisconsin, some north, and some south. The neighboring tribes were also obliged to flee. The peninsula between Lake Huron and Lake Michigan was practically depopulated. If furs were to be obtained for New France, these terrified tribes must be visited in their new homes beyond Lake Michigan. It was to this task that Des Groseilliers soon set himself.

First, however, his own private affairs must be settled. A young man must marry and establish his family, especially in this new country. A wife was a true helpmate in New

[9] Marie de l'Incarnation, *Lettres*, 1:292.

[10] See a letter of Marie de l'Incarnation to her son of October 22, 1649, in her *Lettres*, 1:408, 409. It is an unknown English translator of a narrative by Radisson, who renders "cheveux relevés" as Staring Hairs. See *post*, p. 37.

France; sons have always been of prime importance on North American frontiers; and daughters brought family alliances that meant so much to Frenchmen of commercial bent.

On September 3, 1647, Des Groseilliers married Hélène Martin, the widow of Claude Etienne and the daughter of Abraham Martin. Here were family ties in abundance. The Martin family seems to have been Scotch and to have had connections with Samuel Champlain. Médard's wife is said to have been Champlain's godchild and to have been named for his wife. The Plains of Abraham, of tragic fame in Canadian and English history, were named for Hélène's father. Some tie, though now obscure, probably linked her first husband to a great pioneer in Canadian, Acadian, and Hudson Bay history, Charles de St. Etienne de la Tour, son of Claude de la Tour.[11]

Readers of Acadian history will recall how Claude de la Tour was associated with Jean de Poutrincourt in the founding of Port Royal in Acadia very early in the seventeenth century; how enemies drove them out of this colony, forcing the sons of both men in 1613 to flee to the wilderness and to learn the ways of the savages; how the De la Tours inherited De Poutrincourt's claims to Acadia; and how they fought and labored to make good their claim against a potent rival, Charnisay. They finally succeeded, after seeking aid from Sir David Kirke, the Governor of Newfoundland, and from Puritan friends in Boston. Chief among the New Eng-

[11] Parish records of Notre Dame de Québec, Volume 1621–1667. The Martin family had connections with two of the chief characters of this chapter: Des Groseilliers and Charles de St. Etienne de la Tour (see *post,* Appendix 1). Des Groseilliers' connections have been mentioned: a son of Martin, Charles Amador, had as godfather Charles Amador de St. Etienne de la Tour; Hélène, a daughter, married first Claude Etienne and secondly Des Groseilliers; she is reputed to have been a goddaughter of Samuel Champlain and a namesake of his wife. See Henry C. Campbell, "Radisson and Groseilliers. Problems in Western History," in the *American Historical Review,* 1:226–237 (Jan., 1896). There has been much speculation as to the origin of Claude de St. Etienne, father of Charles, and his title, Sieur de la Tour. Perhaps a closer study of the Martin and Etienne family genealogies might reveal interesting facts.

landers was Major General Edward Gibbons, who fitted
out young De la Tour with a vessel, men, and provisions with
which the latter started for Hudson Bay.

In 1653 Des Groseilliers visited De la Tour in his Acadian
home.[12] There, or earlier, the younger man may have learned
from De la Tour what the latter knew of that great Bay of
the North which figured so prominently in Canadian dreams
of a Northwest Passage in the second and third quarters
of the seventeenth century.[13] In 1683 that bay was to be the
cause of a hundred years' war between France and Great
Britain, started by the activities of Des Groseilliers and his
brother-in-law, Pierre Esprit Radisson. Till 1689 the eyes
of the readers of this book must be kept constantly on that
bleak region.

Thus Des Groseilliers in the later forties and in the early
fifties may well have been perfecting his knowledge of Hudson Bay preparatory to his opening of that region in 1668
and the founding of the Hudson's Bay Company in 1670.
In the middle fifties, however, his thoughts and purposes
took another turn. Land exploration toward the great Western Sea, the object of discovery of a Northwest Passage,
took up his time and energy. It is uncertain how much the
ruling passion in these years was exploration and how much
was love of gain, but in any event, the two soon became so
inextricably intertwined that he himself might not have
been able to say which motive predominated.

Perhaps his marriage made him realize that he must be
more practical, though that adjective could hardly be applied
to him in later life. Food for little mouths and land for his
home may have seemed necessary even to his impractical
mind. At least one son, Médard, was born of the union with
Hélène Martin, and lived to maturity. Another child died

---

[12] *Jesuit Relations,* 38 : 179.

[13] Appendix 1 speculates on De la Tour as the probable source of Des Groseilliers' information on Hudson Bay. See *post.*

in 1648. Its mother died early in the 1650's. In 1653 Des Groseilliers remarried. Soon there were many little mouths to feed.[14]

Here and there we can follow Des Groseilliers' trail in these mid-century years by the parish registers and the pré-vôté records of Quebec and Three Rivers. They are full of the minutiae of life in an outpost of the French empire.[15]

Tradition has it that Des Groseilliers went to France in 1649 or 1650. On August 24, 1649, the Jesuits record that "Medar" returned from France.[16] Possibly the reference is to their former assistant, Médard Chouart. Mère Marie also mentions a young man of her acquaintance who left for France in the autumn of 1649. As she gives no name, it is impossible to know whether she had in mind the young man who visited her often.[17] Since Des Groseilliers was constantly passing between France and Canada in the years of his life for which there are fuller records, he may even have made two trips at this period.

It is not known that Des Groseilliers had any close relatives in New France. A Pierre Chouard of Quebec was married to Marie-Madeleine Faye, but this event must have

[14] Cyprien Tanguay, *Dictionnaire généalogique des familles canadiennes,* 1:129 ([Montréal], 1871).

[15] A marriage contract of November, 1646, seems to have been signed by Des Groseilliers. M. Pierre-Georges Roy, however, in a letter of December 23, 1937, to the author, questions the accuracy of one important name in this document, as well as its date. On October 12, 1647, Des Groseilliers signed another marriage record in Quebec. The record of a transaction between him and Etienne Racine in October, 1648, has been preserved in the Gagnon collection in Montreal. Phileas Gagnon, *Essai de bibliographie canadienne,* 2:333 (Montréal, 1895 and 1913). On September 4, 1649, he signed a document in Quebec, "Ratification par Hélène Martin (Vve Claude Etienne) épouse actuelle de Médard Chouard d'une Vente faite par le dit Etienne à Mathurin Gai," in Judicial Archives, Quebec, *greffe* Claude Lecoustre, No. 8, Sept. 4, 1649.

[16] The Jesuits' journal under date of August 24, 1649, in *Jesuit Relations,* 34:59.

[17] Marie de l'Incarnation, *Lettres,* 1:411. It is impossible to tell from the French statement, whether it was a servant or the brother of a servant of the Ursulines, to whom Mère Marie has reference.

occurred late in the century, for the bride was baptized on October 27, 1676.[18] A niece migrated to Canada in 1661.[19]

[18] See Tanguay, *Dictionnaire généalogique*, 1:229.
[19] See *post*, p. 79.

CHAPTER II

The Governor's Two Men

On July 9, 1653, Des Groseilliers returned to Canada from De la Tour's home in Acadia. Thereafter we know the major events of his life in some detail. Every year is accounted for until 1685. His home now became Three Rivers. In 1653 that place was a little, fortified village of some thirty families. The date of its founding is generally given as 1634, twenty-six years after the establishment of Quebec and seven before the founding of Montreal. Its position, on the north shore of the St. Lawrence, about half way between Quebec and Montreal and at the mouth of the St. Maurice River, made it a favorite target for marauding Iroquois, who came up from the Hudson River by way of Lake Champlain and the Richelieu River. In this very year, 1653, they besieged the hamlet, whose fortifications, fortunately, had just been completed.

The Jesuits owned land in Three Rivers, both within and without the "ville" proper, as did also the thirty or so *habitants*. Jean Godefroy's concession was a large one, part of it fronting on the St. Lawrence. The rural land which Des Groseilliers acquired through marrying the widow of Jean Véron lay farther inland, to the northwest. The holdings of other persons to be mentioned in this chapter may also be noted: Elie Grimard's rural property was about the size of Véron's; within the walls Etienne Seigneuret and Elie Grimard dwelt close to the governor's home and the chapel of the Jesuits; outside the walls and to the west was the common mill, which served as a defense against the Indians as well as for its proper purpose.

THREE RIVERS, 1633–1657.

Dessiné par J.-G. Ecrement.

Three Rivers became a great nursery of valorous explorers and fur traders, partly, no doubt, because it lay on two of the main trade routes of the western Indians—the route via the St. Lawrence and Ottawa rivers, and the safer way via the St. Maurice River, whose three channels gave the place its name. It was the home of Jean Nicolet, who reached Green Bay, presumably, in 1634; of Nicholas Perrot, a famous coureur-de-bois and founder of French forts on the upper Mississippi, who has left us his memoirs; of the Pépins, for one or more of whom Lake Pepin on the upper Mississippi seems to have been named; and of the La Vérendrye family, great western explorers of the eighteenth century.

Across the St. Maurice, to the east of Three Rivers, lay Cap de la Madeleine, a later home of the Chouart family. Something of the amenities of life in Des Groseilliers' home villages may be gleaned from a description of 1662–1663: [1]

About thirty leagues above Quebec, the Habitans of Cap de la Magdeleine ran out of their houses, which are scattered over more than a league along that entire shore,—coming to meet us, and inviting us to land, that they might regale us in rustic fashion. But we were going down [*sic*] to the Town of Three Rivers, only a league distant from this Cape. There we were received with as much plenty, and the tables to which we were invited were nearly as well laid and furnished, as is possible in many parts of France.

In 1651 Des Groseilliers' first wife died, probably at the birth of a son, Médard.[2] On August 24, 1653, Des Groseilliers married Marguérite Hayet, the daughter of Sebastien and Magdelaine Hayet, sometimes recorded as Hayot, who became his bride in the parish church, Notre Dame de Québec.[3] Hierosme Lalemant was the officiating priest. It will be

---

[1] *Jesuit Relations,* 48:159.

[2] The census of 1681 for New France lists Médard Chouart as living with his father and as being thirty years of age. See Sulte, *Histoire des canadiens-français,* 5:64. A manuscript by Cyprien Tanguay at St. Paul Seminary, St. Paul, Minnesota, states that Médard Chouart, Jr., was born in 1651 and that his mother died soon thereafter.

[3] Quebec, parish registers, Notre Dame de Québec.

noted throughout the ensuing ten years that the records of births, deaths, marriages, and other events in Des Groseilliers' family indicate a close relationship between him and Jesuit priests of an exploring bent, such as Poncet, Lalemant, Allouez, Ragueneau, Ménard, Garreau, Albanel, Dablon, and Druillettes.[4] Lalemant, for example, had been long in Huronia. Father Leonard Garreau, who baptized Des Groseilliers' son, Jean Baptiste, on July 5, 1654, left in 1656 for the Ottawa country in the company of the traders of that year.[5] On April 15, 1659, Father René Ménard baptized Des Groseilliers' daughter, Marguérite.[6] In 1660 this priest, too, left for the Ottawa country. In May, 1662, Des Groseilliers started from New France for Hudson Bay. Just before he left, he borrowed money from Father Claude Jean Allouez.[7] In 1665 Allouez went to Lake Superior to begin the missions and the explorations that made him famous. He was the first to mention the Mississippi River by that name. Father Charles Albanel was to play a large part in the careers of Des Groseilliers and Radisson, as well as to become the first officially recognized discoverer of Hudson Bay among Canadian and French explorers. Father Gabriel Dreuillettes (Druillettes, Drouillet, etc.) went with Jean-Paul Godefroy on a delicate mission to Boston in 1651 and was the person who interviewed the "governor's two men" on their return from the far West in 1656. In 1661 he tried to reach the Cree Indians by a northern route, apparently suggested by the recently returned travelers, Radisson and Des Groseil-

[4] Sketches of these men may be found by consulting the index volumes to the *Jesuit Relations*.

[5] For the record of Jean-Baptiste's baptism, see the parish registers of Three Rivers. His godparents were Jean-Baptiste Legardeur and Catherine Leneuf.

[6] Three Rivers, parish registers. Her godparents were Jean Guérin and Françoise Radisson.

[7] See *post*, p. 82 for an explanation of Des Groseilliers' plans for 1662. The "reconnaissance" of a loan by Father Allouez is found in the Schmidt Collection of the Chicago Historical Society. It is dated May 15, 1662.

liers.[8] It has been argued that Des Groseilliers was a Protestant and that the Jesuits were not interested in his explorations. The facts do not bear out those arguments.

Des Groseilliers' wife, Marguérite Hayet, had been in New France for some time when she married her second husband. She had suffered from the Iroquois, who had massacred her first husband, Jean Véron, Sieur de Grosmesnil (Grandmesnil). A marriage contract between her and Véron gives the following information about her.[9] She was of the parish of St. Paul in Paris. At the time of the contract she was living in Three Rivers at the home of Jean Godefroy, Sieur de Lintot, who promised to bestow on her fifty arpents of land of his Lintot concession. This agreement was signed privately on November 25, 1646, and was registered by the notary on August 6, 1648. From the record of her second marriage we learn that she was the daughter of Sebastien Hayet and Madelaine Henaut. The residence of her parents is not given, though that of her husband's parents is mentioned in the same document. It was customary in a marriage contract of that period to refer to the residence of living parents. For that reason it is probable that Marguérite's parents were dead.

From other sources we know that she had two half-sisters and one half-brother in New France. Madelaine Henaut, it would appear, had married first Sebastien Hayet and secondly Pierre Esprit Radisson. By the latter she had Françoise, Elizabeth (Isabelle, a diminutive of Elizabeth, in

[8] *Jesuit Relations*, 46:179, 181. It is at least curious that Radisson's account of his first westward trip, supposed by many to have occurred from 1654 to 1656, tells of thirty Frenchmen and two priests starting for the western tribes and turned back by Iroquois. The references in the *relations* also tell how Fathers Dablon and Druillettes started from Three Rivers for the Cree, or for the Sea of the North, with thirty traders and how they were turned back in June, 1661, by the Iroquois. It is at least possible that Radisson was on that abortive expedition.

[9] Judicial Archives, Quebec, *greffe* Claude Lecoustre, April 26, 1648. The date on the face of the document is April 26; that on the reverse side is August 6, 1648.

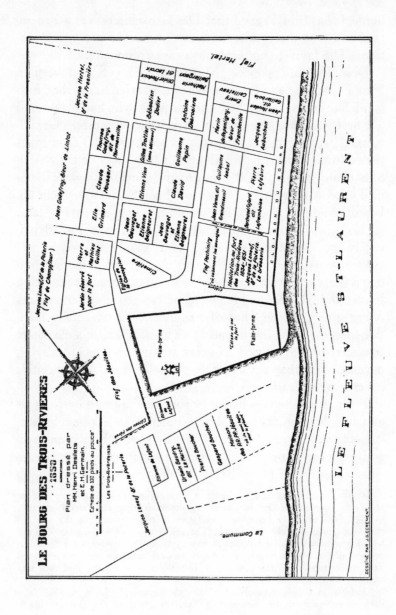

LE BOURG DES TROIS-RIVIÈRES
1650.

Plan dressé par
MM. Henri Desilets
et E. H. Germain.

Échelle de 100 pieds au pouce.
Les Trois-Rivières 1928

some documents), and Pierre Esprit. With this last child our story is even more concerned than with his brother-in-law, Médard Chouart, Sieur des Groseilliers.

Just why Marguérite Hayet was living in the home of Jean Godefroy is not known. The dowry that Godefroy gave her suggests that she was a servant or the daughter of a servant. Seigneurs in New France customarily gave marriage portions to their female servants or children of such servants. If she was a servant of this founder of Three Rivers, who had been taken to New France by Samuel Champlain and who had long been an interpreter and trader far into the interior, it is not strange that another great explorer met her, perhaps in Godefroy's home, and married her.[10]

With Des Groseilliers' marriage in 1653 records of his activities suddenly become very numerous. He appears to have decided on Three Rivers as his residence, perhaps because of the Godefroy connection of his wife, but more likely because of the land that he owned and the real estate that Marguérite brought him. She brought him more than lands, however. Two sons by her first marriage, Guillaume and Etienne, soon became a disturbing element in the lives of the newly weds. Reference is made to these children and their

---

[10] See Pierre-Georges Roy, *La famille Godefroy de Tonnancour* (Lévis, 1904) for a record of the importance of the Godefroy family in Canada and the United States from about 1626 to date. Both Jean and his brother Thomas, Sieur de Normanville, were accustomed to life among the Indians, both Iroquois and Algonkins. It was a relative of these men, Jean-Paul Godefroy, who was captain of the vessel that took Father Druillettes to Boston in 1651. Thomas Godefroy was captured by the Iroquois and tortured to death by them. When his estate was settled, ten livres were paid to Madame de Grandmesnil, in consequence of a "piece of writing of M. de la Potherie dated March 20, 1653." See a document dated July 5, 1653, in the *greffe* of Séverin Ameau in the Court-House, Three Rivers. Jean's sons were considered the best canoemen in the whole country. One of them accompanied Radisson and Des Groseilliers to Hudson Bay in 1682. The Le Moyne and Godefroy families seem to have been associated in various ways. Both families were accounted excellent linguists, especially of the principal Indian tongues. Jean Godefroy owned the earliest concession granted (and with a title of nobility) by the Company of New France. This was in 1633. See Dorothy A. Heneker, *The Seigniorial Regime in Canada*, 52 ([Montreal, 1927]).

parents in the records of several cases brought before the
authorities at Three Rivers in January, 1654.[11] By March 6,
1654, the situation was so tense that Des Groseilliers petitioned the Governor of Three Rivers, Pierre Boucher, to
appoint another guardian than himself for the two boys,
since his corrections of them had caused quarrels between
his wife and himself. Seigneuret was therefore made their
guardian once more.[12]

Neither Des Groseilliers nor his wife, however, was able
to keep out of court for long. On April 27, 1654, one Bar-
thelmy Bertaut, a master locksmith, haled Des Groseilliers
into court on the charge that Des Groseilliers had outraged
Bertaut's person, having struck him with the flat of his sword
to such effect that a surgeon had been obliged to treat his
wounds. Chouart was condemned by the court to pay the
court charges, the surgeon's fees, and three livres as a fine
for having taken the law into his own hands.[13]

[11] On January 14, 1654, Seigneuret, as former guardian of the minor children of the late Véron, appeared in court with Chouart and his wife in the
matter of an inventory of the effects of the deceased man; on the same day
the husband and wife also took up with the court the property of the Véron
children; on the twenty-first the couple, with others, replied to a charge that
they had not cut down the trees on their land on the islands at the mouth of
the St. Maurice River, where Iroquois might lurk unobserved, saying that
they would do so as soon as possible. They seem to have owned part of
L'Isle de la Trinité, Véron's former property. On the twenty-third of January
Chouart was ordered to pay the guardian of the Véron children 468 livres,
9 sols, 3 deniers that he owed them. Chouart replied that he would make it a
loan with interest and pay the principal when he could. *Query:* Was he
getting ready for his trip and procuring funds where he could? A document
of October 10, 1653, in the Gagnon collection suggests the same query. It is
an agreement notarized by Guillaume Audouart to the effect that Chouart
and his wife would pay 561 livres for a barrel of rum, 6 knives, a barrel of
raisins, 46 aunes of cloth, 4 pots of oil, 15 pots of cider "to be paid for in
beaver skins" of two kinds to Martin Grouvel of Beauport on or before
June 24, 1654. The same pair agreed to pay 37 livres in barley for cod and
salmon just bought. On the twenty-fifth of January, 1654, Seigneuret promised
for the Véron children that the woods on their part of the island already
mentioned should be felled. All of the documents cited, except that of October
10, 1653, may be found in *greffe* Ameau, or the records of the council, Court-
House, Three Rivers.

[12] Records of the council, Court-House, Three Rivers.

[13] Records of the council, Court-House, Three Rivers, under date of April
27, 1654.

Thus court records tell of certain events and ideas in the life of Des Groseilliers in the middle fifties. For another full year, however, they give no clue to the great scheme that must have been brewing in his mind even as he quarreled with his wife and neighbors.

*   *   *

Since the outbreak of the Iroquois wars against the Hurons in the late forties, New France had suffered great losses, both in men and in commerce. The Hurons and Ottawa, acting as middlemen in the fur trade between the French and the western tribesmen, had incurred the wrath of the Iroquois, who, too, coveted the lucrative rôle of middlemen. They attacked the western tribes with the fury that only Iroquois could exhibit. Huronia was abandoned, French missionaries fell martyrs to their zeal for souls, the Indians about the lower Great Lakes were sent in terrified flight to hiding places in the forests and along the streams of the regions known today as Wisconsin and Iowa, the beaver trade was interrupted, and the Jesuit *relation* of 1652–1653 states that not a beaver skin was brought to the warehouses of Montreal in that year.[14] If this state of things continued, New France would have to be abandoned.

The spring of 1653, however, brought to Three Rivers three canoes containing emissaries from the fleeing Hurons and Ottawa. To Trifluviens and other Frenchmen, who faced ruin if the beaver trade ceased, they brought very welcome news. "This was, that they were gathering together, to the number of two thousand men, in a very fine country about a hundred and fifty leagues farther away than the Hurons, toward the West; and that they were to come the next Spring in company." "Moreover," writes the chronicler, "all our young Frenchmen are planning to go on a trading expedition, to find the Nations that are scattered here and there; and

[14] *Jesuit Relations*, 40:211; also Marie de l'Incarnation, *Lettres*, 2:10–12, a letter of August 12, 1653.

they hope to come back laden with the Beaver-skins of several years' accumulation." [15]

Just why the company of young men did not go is uncertain. A document written many years later may contain the explanation.[16] In the nineties, Charles Aubert, Sieur de la Chenaye, who by that time had long been intimately acquainted with Radisson and Des Groseilliers, wrote a lengthy statement about the fur trade in Canada, in which mention is made of the fact that in 1656 two traders, who had been sent to the western tribes by Governor Jean de Lauson, returned to New France. There was a great deal of graft and jealousy in the fur trade then and later in New France, and it is more than likely that no one but a man sent by the Governor was permitted to set out.

In 1654 peace was made with the Iroquois. The western tribes were able to get to the French settlements once more. They appeared late in the summer bringing furs and news. The latter was "that above their country is a very large river, which empties into a great sea, which is believed to be the China Sea." When these Indians started back to their homes on August 6, 1654, the Governor's two men went with them.[17]

Prior to that time Des Groseilliers had been in court week after week. After that date only his wife's name is found in the court records relating to his immediate family. The two traders returned in the summer of 1656.[18] On September 29, 1656, Des Groseilliers' name reappears in the colony records, when he stood godfather to an Indian girl, whose godmother was Jeanne Godefroy.[19] This hiatus in the life of a man of a tiny place like Three Rivers in 1654 would make one suspect that Des Groseilliers was absent, even if

---

[15] *Jesuit Relations*, 40: 213, 215, 219.

[16] [Sulte], *Collection de manuscrits*, 1: 245–261. The date given by Sulte, 1676, is incorrect.

[17] *Jesuit Relations*, 42: 219. The quotation is from Marie de l'Incarnation's letter of September 24, 1654 in her *Lettres;* 2: 67.

[18] The *relation* states that "the two pilgrims" got back "toward the end of August of this year, 1656."

[19] Three Rivers, parish registers.

more definite evidence were not at hand. That evidence is found in several documents. On June 23, 1655, the sergeant of the garrison of Three Rivers appeared in court against "Margueritte Hayet wife of Médart Chouart des Groseillers absent," asking to be paid 598 livres in beaver skins due him. Another document is dated July 5, 1656, and in it Des Groseilliers once more is mentioned as "absent." Moreover, this document reveals that Des Groseilliers had planned his long absence with some care. It recites that when he departed, he left his wife's brother-in-law, Claude Volant, as his attorney, "to act and direct his affairs for him during his absence." An authoritative touch is added in the document of June 23, 1655, when Marguérite asked that time to pay the sum demanded of her be granted "until the return of her husband, des Groseilliers." She was granted her petition and the privilege of not being harassed by creditors "until the arrival of her husband or until word of him has been received." Interlined above the last clause is the statement: "People have lost hope of his return." [20]

It would be interesting to know who was Des Groseilliers' companion on the momentous trip to the West that saved New France from economic ruin and abandonment, brought a great flotilla of Indian canoes to Quebec, filled the warehouses with beaver, and opened the West to traders and missionaries. Radisson would have us believe that he was one of the two explorers, but a document signed by him in Quebec in 1655 shows that he could not have been in the West on a trip that required two years' time.[21] We may

[20] See a volume in the Provincial Museum of Quebec, Quebec, entitled "Prevote de Trois-Rivieres 1655–1667," under dates of June 23 and September 11, 1655, and of July 5, 1656.

[21] In 1885 or thereabouts a document written by Pierre Esprit Radisson was discovered in translation in England. It describes an expedition to the upper Great Lakes, as well as some other trips. It has led to the general belief that the governor's two men were Radisson and Des Groseilliers. It has been published as *Voyages of Peter Esprit Radisson, Being an Account of His Travels and Experiences Among the North American Indians, from 1652 to 1684*, edited by Gideon Scull, in *Publications of the Prince Society*

never know the name of the unknown hero, but the chances are that he was a Trifluvien. Indeed, all up and down the St. Lawrence, from Montreal to Tadoussac, were men capable of great daring and vision, men who later proved themselves worthy of such an undertaking. The names of Elie Grimard, Jean Péré, Jean Bourdon, and Charles Le Moyne come to mind immediately, but recorded facts are against the possibility that they were with Des Groseilliers in the West from 1654 to 1656.[22] Perhaps a document now lying unheeded in

(Boston, 1885). See *post,* pp. 29, 43 for proof that the manuscript is only a translation and that Radisson was in Quebec in 1655.

[22] One might suspect that it was Elie Grimard, who was granted land by the governor at the same time that Des Groseilliers received land upon his return, and whose son accompanied Des Groseilliers on a later trip to Hudson Bay, but a document in the prévôté records in Three Rivers shows that Grimard was there on May 15, 1656.

Was it Jean Péré? As early as 1669 Péré was sent by the intendant of New France to the Lake Superior country to discover a copper mine. Pierre Margry, *Découvertes et établissements des Français dans l'Ouest et dans le Sud de l'Amérique Septentrionale,* 6:19, note (Paris, 1886). In 1684 it was Péré who was chosen by Daniel Greysolon, Sieur Dulhut, to carry a message from Lake Superior to Jean Baptiste Chouart on Hudson Bay. See *post,* p. 237. Why was he chosen for both these tasks unless he had been in the Lake Superior country, especially as he took the very route to the Bay that Radisson claims for himself and Des Groseilliers when writing of the purported voyage from Lake Superior to Hudson Bay in 1660? Péré's route, now known as the Albany River, was long called Péré River on French maps after 1684. See especially the manuscript maps of Jean Baptiste Louis Franquelin. Several of his maps are to be found in the Archives de la Marine, Paris, Service Hydrographique, 4040, especially numbers 5, 6, and 9. Péré was a contemporary of Franquelin and seems to have been well acquainted with him.

Jean Bourdon would occur to any one's mind, for he was trying at that very time to find a route to Hudson Bay by sea. See J. E. Roy, "Jean Bourdon et la Baie d'Hudson," in *Bulletin des recherches historiques,* 2:2–9 and 21–23 (Jan., 1896), and also in booklet form (Lévis, 1896). One is tempted to believe that Bourdon, while with Des Groseilliers on this western trip, learned of the great beaver store north and west of Lake Superior and made his well-known trip toward Hudson Bay as a result. Bourdon, however, was in Quebec in 1656. See Roy, "Jean Bourdon et la Baie d'Hudson." It is significant, however, that Bourdon was aiming at the same objective, Hudson Bay, in 1657. It may signify a concerted attempt on the part of the Jesuits and the officials in New France to find the Northwest Passage; or, more likely, it represents the rivalry that existed between these two groups. See Bibliothèque Nationale, Fonds Français, Nouvelles Acquisitions, 9284 (the Margry Papers), folio 2, for a reputed "Lettre de la déclaration faite au greffe du Conseil Souverain de Quebec par le Capitaine Jean Bourdon." The date of the declaration is August 26, 1656, but there was no sovereign council in Quebec at

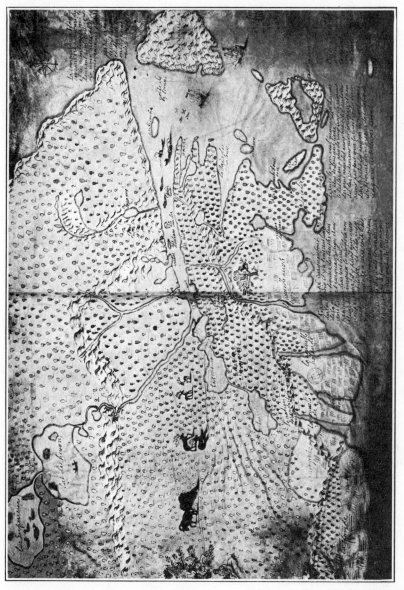

ANONYMOUS MANUSCRIPT MAP OF NORTH AMERICA. CIRCA 1658.

[Paris. Service Hydrographique, B 4040.1.]

Canada or France will some day bring to light the name of the unknown explorer.

that early date. Moreover, the journal of the Jesuits for 1657 (*Jesuit Relations*, 43:35) states as of May 2, 1657, "Monsieur bourdon weighed Anchor at quebec for the Voyage to the North." On August 11 of the same year he was back, having been turned back at 55°, where he encountered "un grand banc de glaces." *Jesuit Relations*, 43:53, 55, and 44:189. One might suspect that Des Groseilliers went with him in 1657, but court records show that Des Groseilliers was in Three Rivers on June 4 and July 18. See the parish records of Three Rivers for evidence that Des Groseilliers stood godfather to Jeanne Lafleur on June 4, 1657; and Three Rivers, prévôté records, entry for July 18, 1657.

Could Charles Le Moyne have been Des Groseilliers' companion? It was he with whom Des Groseilliers was associated in business in 1660. Le Moyne, who had been in the New World since 1641, was to give to his country eight famous sons, the Maccabees of New France as they were called. They are credited with having accomplished more for the expansion of the French empire than is any other single family, and were to be ennobled years later by Louis XIV. It is worth comment, perhaps, that it was these sons who undid for England, at least temporarily, the work that Radisson accomplished for her in Hudson Bay. The argument against Charles Le Moyne as Des Groseilliers' companion is the fact that his eldest son was born on December 10, 1656. Convenient studies of the Le Moyne family are Charles de la Roncière, *Une épopée canadienne* (Paris, 1930), with a bibliography, pp. 249–251; and Louis Le Jeune, *Le Chevalier Pierre Le Moyne, Sieur D'Iberville* (Editions de l'Université d'Ottawa, 1937).

These and other names of possible companions that might be mentioned suggest the ease with which Des Groseilliers might have found a kindred spirit for his enterprise in 1654.

Sometime between the abandonment of Huronia in the late forties and the year 1658 a crude map was drawn, which is here reproduced opposite page 24. It was first published in Grace Lee Nute's *The Voyageur's Highway* (St. Paul, 1941), opposite page 2. The first date is chosen as a limit because no mark of missions or habitations on the east shore of Lake Huron is to be found on the map. An earlier map would have shown the missions, without a doubt. The year 1658 is chosen as the other limit because of the fact that the words "du borgne" appear at La Have on the map. But the Sieur de Borgne was driven from La Have by the English in 1658. See Nicolas Denys, *The Description and Natural History of the Coasts of North America (Acadia)*, translated and edited by William F. Ganong, pp. 160, 161 (*The Publications of the Champlain Society*, Toronto, 1918). The entire map is not reproduced in that volume and the plate is not a facsimile, but only a copy of the original map, which is number B—4040 in Archives de la Marine, Service Hydrographique, Paris. For the purposes of this book the most significant part of the map is the note about Lake Superior, which reads in translation: "From Montreal to the Lake of the Hurons it is more than two hundred leagues. That lake is more than five hundred leagues in circumference. Some people [*des gens*] have told me of having gone around the upper lake [*le lac supérieur*] for twenty days without having accomplished half of its circumference. In the little lake close to the mountains, there are pieces of copper weighing five or six hundred pounds." It is obvious that the author of this map did not know of Lake Michigan as a separate lake and was unaware that Lake Huron emptied into Lake Erie. In other words, he (or his informant) had taken the usual route of subsequent years to Lake Superior by way of the Ottawa River, French River, Georgian Bay, and Sault Ste Marie. Recognizable on Lake Superior are several species of ducks. New Holland and New Sweden are represented and help to date the map. Three habitations of Nicolas Denys are shown.

CHAPTER III

The "Auxoticiat Voyage"

Father Druillettes, New France's envoy to New England
in 1651, interviewed the returned travelers in 1656.[1] "I send
you," he wrote to his superior, "some memoranda which I
have obtained, partly from two Frenchmen who have made
their way far inland, and partly from several Savages who
are eye-witnesses to the things which I am about to describe.
. . . In it [*a map accompanying the letter*] you will also
see the new routes for going to the North sea." After describing these new routes, he goes on to mention and describe
the following tribes: Pottawattomi, Kiskakon, Illinois, Winnebago, Menominee, Noquet, Mascouten, Fox, Poulak, As-
sinipoulak, Sioux, Cree, and some others. "The two Frenchmen who have made the journey to those regions say these
people [*the Makoutensak and Outitchakouk*] are of a very
gentle disposition." It is obvious that many eyes in New
France were turned toward the North Sea (Hudson Bay)
and the tribes that could give information about it.

Another mention of the two travelers is found in an account written in 1695 [2] by Charles Aubert de la Chenaye: [3]

[1] See *ante*, p. 4. The quotations are from *Jesuit Relations*, 44: 237, 239, 247.

[2] [Sulte], *Collection de manuscrits*, 1: 254, 261. See *post*, p. 156.

[3] It is worth a note in this connection that a similar case of appeal from
the tax of the "fourth" was made in 1663 after several Frenchmen, who had
been obliged to stay on Lake Superior for three years, returned with a great
flotilla of Indians and were required to pay a quarter of their furs as a tax
to the government. The language of their petition is strikingly like that of
De la Chenaye, especially "because they have exposed their lives to the risks
and hazards of their voyage, by which they have brought a notable profit to
the country, which would not have been possible without them." *Jugements
et délibérations du conseil souverain de la Nouvelle-France*, 1: 23, 24 (Quebec,
1885).

Only Monsieur de Lauson sent thither [*to the western tribes*] two individuals who returned in 1656, each one with from 14 to 15 thousand livres, and brought with them a flotilla of Indians with 100,000 écus worth of treasures. . . . I remember that those two individuals who brought back, in the time of Governor de Lauson, each 14 to 15 thousand livres, petitioned me to exempt them from paying the tax of one fourth, saying that the colony was under obligation to them for having caused a flotilla to descend which enriched the country.

A third account is found in the Jesuit *relation* of 1655–1656: [4]

On the sixth day of August, 1654, two young Frenchmen, full of courage, having received permission from Monsieur the Governor of the Country to embark with some of the Peoples who had come down to our French settlements, began a journey of more than five hundred leagues under the guidance of these Argonauts,—conveyed, not in great Galleons or large oared Barges, but in little Gondolas of bark. The two Pilgrims fully expected to return in the Spring of 1655, but those Peoples did not conduct them home until toward the end of August of this year, 1656. Their arrival caused the Country universal joy, for they were accompanied by fifty canoes, laden with goods which the French come to this end of the world to procure.

The narrative goes on with the colorful reception at Quebec, the request of the Indians for traders and priests, and the account of the two men's experiences during their "voyage."

First, it is well to note that the Huron language extends fully five hundred leagues toward the South, and the Algonquin more than five hundred leagues toward the North. . . . In the second place, there are in the Northern regions many Lakes which might be called freshwater Seas, the great Lake of the Hurons, and another near it, being as large as the Caspian Sea. In the third place, we were told of many Nations surrounding the Nation of the Sea which some have called "the Stinkards," because its people formerly lived on the shores of the Sea, which they call Ouinipeg [*Winnipeg*], that is, "stinking water."

Mention is then made of the Illinois, the Sioux, and the Cree. The last "surpass all the above in extent, reaching as far as the North Sea." A digression and an account of the baptiz-

---

[4] *Jesuit Relations,* 42: 219, 221, 223, 225–233.

ing of about three hundred Indian children follow. Then, at once, occurs the story that forms the beginning of Radisson's own account of this journey. A fourth account is given by Charlevoix: [5]

Fifteen days after this misfortune [*an Iroquois massacre of Hurons on the Island of Orleans*], thirty Ottawa, loaded with furs, landed at Quebec under the direction of two Frenchmen. . . . [*A description follows of the Iroquois raids on Western tribes and the breaking up of those tribes into wandering groups.*] It was one of these separated troops of Ottawa, which contained some Hurons, that the two Frenchmen, of whom I have just spoken, had brought from the shores of Lake Michigan to Quebec. . . . The two Frenchmen, who were good men, had baptized some of their children.

Radisson's account was written in French many years later.[6] He penned it while spending the winter of 1668–1669 in enforced idleness in London, waiting for the spring and a chance to follow Des Groseilliers to Hudson Bay. Des Groseilliers' ship had succeeded in reaching that place in 1668, whereas Radisson's vessel had failed. Business men at Court were backing the explorers. The men of affairs were also, most of them, members of the Royal Society, and hence interested in travel narratives *per se*. For them, for the King, or for both, Radisson wrote that winter the story of his own and his brother-in-law's experiences in exploring North America. Two chapters recount Radisson's experiences among the Iroquois in 1652–1654 and 1657–1658

---

[5] François Xavier de Charlevoix, *Histoire et description générale de la Nouvelle France avec le journal historique d'un voyage fait par ordre du Roi dans l'Amérique Septentrionale,* 1: 324, 325 (Paris, 1744).

[6] See the introduction to Radisson, *Voyages.* The author of the present volume has examined the manuscript of the first three "voyages" as found in the Bodleian Library, Oxford, England (Rawlinson MSS, 329) and notes that the volume that contains them is the exact counterpart of the early record books of the Hudson's Bay Company now preserved in that company's archives in London. The binding, the spacing of lines on the backbone, the paper, and the watermarks are identical. Therefore the author is prepared to say that this is the translation to which the Hudson's Bay Company's records refer on June 23, 1669, as made and paid for by them. See *post,* p. 121.

respectively. The third *appears* to be an account of the expedition of 1654–1656, though out of place chronologically. Radisson tells the story in such a way that he becomes Des Groseilliers' partner on the trip. It is easy to see why he did so: he felt that he must impress the Court group in order to keep their interest from lagging. Having doubtless heard Des Groseilliers recount many times his adventures on that expedition, Radisson felt that he could give the facts and so enhance his own fortune. It would simplify matters materially, he probably argued, to omit any reference to a third person. Moreover, he may have felt that the origins of his own knowledge of Hudson Bay went back to that trip and that therefore it was, in a sense, his own experience.

Late in the spring of 1669 the translation of this French account was finished and paid for. The French version has disappeared, but the translation, full of middle-class English expressions, is still in existence and has been published as *Voyages of Peter Esprit Radisson*. Though only a translation, it gives an account of the trip to the shores of lakes Huron and Michigan which identifies the explorers as the same men as those with whom Father Druillettes conversed. It is a very vague, incoherent account, just the kind that a man would write who must base his statements on something heard from another's lips. The only exact portion of it is the beginning, which, however, recounts the commencement of an expedition made not in 1654, but in 1656. *Query:* Was Radisson one of the party of 1656? That party never completed the trip, having been turned back by Iroquois hostilities. Radisson's story recounts how he and his companion refused to be turned back and went on to the West. Has Radisson combined accounts of his own incomplete trip and that of his brother-in-law? As far as can be judged at the present time, his narrative is a union of personal recollection and a résumé of what Des Groseilliers narrated when he returned to Three Rivers in 1656.

At all events Radisson did not accompany the expedition of 1654–1656, for he is known to have been in Quebec in 1655. Des Groseilliers did not go into the interior in the fall of 1656, since he was in Three Rivers in 1657. Therefore, it was an impossibility for the two men to have been absent together on a western trip at any time between 1652 and 1659, though Radisson's narrative seems to claim that they were. Hence Radisson in his narrative must either be recounting another's experiences of the trip of 1654–1656, or else manufacturing a tale. All things considered, it seems plausible that his narrative of the trip is what he had heard his brother-in-law describe.

The heading of the manuscript narrative by Radisson has been a puzzle to two generations of historians because of the strange word, "auxoticiat," in it. The title reads: "Now followeth the Auxoticiat Voyage into the Great and filthy Lake of the Hurrons, Upper Sea of the East, and Bay of the North." The puzzle need disturb no longer, since there is ample proof that what we have is only a translation of the original heading. In that heading one phrase has been left untranslated. The original French ran probably in some such fashion as this: "Ici suit le voyage aux Otouats dans le grand lac puant des Hurrons mer supérieure de l'Est et baie du nord." Radisson's French left much to be desired. No heading separates the third from the fourth voyage in Radisson's narratives, and so that title was doubtless intended to cover both voyages—as, in truth, it does. When Radisson completed his account of the third trip, he recapitulated by saying, in effect: Here endeth the first part of the trip described by the title, that is, the trip to the Ottawa (in French, *aux Otouats,* or a variant of that proper name). The translator merely made a bad guess when he encountered these two French words, "aux ottouats," concluded that they belonged together, misread the letters, and produced the exotic expression, "Auxoticiat." The word occurs twice, in two slightly different English forms, in the narrative. Hence the trip has come to be known as Radisson's Auxoticiat voyage.[7]

After his brief recapitulation Radisson proceeds without further explanation to tell of a trip that he and Des Groseilliers made into the West. The date of that trip is well known. It occurred in 1659–1660. On that expedition the two men explored Lake Superior (*la mer supérieure*) and the region west and northwest of it. Radisson claimed in his narrative of 1669 that the two men got even to Hudson Bay (*la baie du nord*), but this was merely another attempt on his part to persuade the London men of affairs that he and his brother-in-law were competent persons to head an expedition to find the Northwest Passage by going through Hudson Bay.

Radisson's story carries on the account from the point where he and his companion refused to be turned back and went on with the savages. They pushed on up the Ottawa River, crossed Lake Nipissing, descended French River, and entered Georgian Bay, an arm of Lake Huron. Thus far

---

[7] Edward C. Gale of Minneapolis seems to have been the first to conjecture that the word *auxoticiat* is a corruption of *aux Ottawas*. See his "The Radisson Manuscript" in *Minnesota History*, 7: 340–342 (Dec., 1926).

The "Auxoticiat" or Ottawa trip, as told by Radisson, begins with a well-known story, the one already mentioned as told by the Jesuits in the *relation* of 1656–1657. One might be led to suppose that Radisson had merely copied their story—in 1669 it was perfectly accessible in print in the Cramoisy edition of the *relations*—were it not for a few differences and some additions.

Both accounts mention that some thirty Frenchmen, two priests, and three young Frenchmen (two according to Radisson), set out late in August (the middle of June according to Radisson) to go with the Indians returning to the Great Lakes region. The Indians, too much engrossed in shooting their newly acquired guns to be watchful, were surprised by the Iroquois on the Ottawa River. Both sides made forts. The French and their Indians had been warned of the presence of the Iroquois by a friendly member of that tribe, but his advice had been disregarded. The whites (that is, all but the three young Frenchmen) turned back at Three Rivers, according to the *relation*. The three survivors went on till a fight occurred with the Iroquois (then, according to Radisson, two of the Frenchmen went on with the tribesmen), when the Frenchmen turned back and the Indians, escaping the Iroquois by night, returned unaccompanied by whites to their homes. The *relation* tells of the death of Father Garreau on this trip, but Radisson makes no mention of this important and tragic event.

the geography is clear. Moreover, as far as this point Radisson's later trip of 1659–1660 duplicated the route, which was the standard canoe route for all persons of all periods proceeding to Huronia, Lake Michigan, Lake Superior, and the far West. After Georgian Bay the route is undeterminable from anything that Radisson has written, despite much exegesis that historians have devoted to this translated text. Radisson himself never visited southern Lake Huron, Lake Michigan, or Green Bay, as far as can be learned. In trying to narrate what Des Groseilliers had told him of his experiences, therefore, Radisson could not be explicit. He recalled the names of some tribes, the general direction of the voyage, certain events, and the character of some parts of the country and of the island on which a landfall was made. The caption of the narrative is our only guide. According to that, as already given in the translated and the conjectured French forms, the travelers went to the Ottawa country (a general term used for many years to come to cover much of the middle of the continent), to Green Bay, and to Lake Huron.

Many readings of the translation of Radisson's narratives leave the impression that Des Groseilliers and his companion spent the years from 1654 to 1656 in the areas now known as southern Michigan and Illinois, and in the Wisconsin region about Green Bay. Again and again the contrast is made between the southerly range of this trip and the possibility of explorations in the North. Only once does it seem possible to identify any place surely. "In October we came to the strait of the 2 lakes of the stinkings and ye upper lake where there are little isles towards Norwest, few towards the southest, very small." Obviously the Straits of Mackinac are described in this passage, for the French term for "stinkings," as already mentioned, was *Puants*. Green Bay was known for years by the French as Baie des Puants, and Lake Michigan was not always clearly distinguished from Green Bay in early narratives. Lake Supe-

rior is merely a poor translation of the French words, *mer
supérieure*, or upper lake.

It is definitely stated by Radisson that the travelers did
not get to the Nadouessious (the Sioux or Dakota Indians,
then living both east and west of the upper Mississippi
River), nor to the country of the Christinoes, or Cree Indians. Consequently they must have confined themselves
between the Ohio country on the east, the eastern part of
the Wisconsin and Illinois country on the west, and Lake
Superior on the north. Radisson, to be sure, mentions a
trip to "Y^e great river that divides itselfe in 2, where
the hurrons wth some Ottanake [*Ottawa*] & the wild men
that had warrs wth them had retired." This may refer to
the Mississippi, to the Ohio, or to some smaller stream.
In any event, Radisson is quite explicit in stating that Des
Groseilliers did not go on this trip, explaining that his
brother-in-law remained on the island of the first landfall
(probably at the mouth of Green Bay) raising corn for the
return trip to New France.

Possibly Des Groseilliers' companion did get to the Mississippi, as many persons have claimed. Radisson expresses
the opinion that the river to which Des Groseilliers' companion (or was it only Indian friends?) went "has 2
branches, the one towards the west, the other towards the
South, wch we believe runns towards Mexico, by the tokens
they gave us." If he refers to the Mississippi, these were
the first Frenchmen, in all likelihood, who ever knew of
this great river in its upper stretches. Father Claude
Allouez, usually credited with being the first to report a
knowledge of it, did not go to the West until 1665.

It is fairly certain that Radisson knew nothing of the
upper Mississippi when he wrote his narrative in 1669.
Years later he wrote an article on suggestions for finding
the Sea of the West.[8] Three routes, he said, were avail-

[8] BN., Collection Clairambault, 1016, ff. 647, 648. It is printed in this
volume as Appendix 5.

able: (1) by way of Hudson Bay, where he had been; (2) through the country of the Sioux, where he had made several trips; and (3) by way of the Mississippi, where De la Salle was at the very moment of writing. In other words, in the early eighties, Radisson was careful to claim for himself a knowledge of the Hudson Bay and Sioux countries, but he had laid no claim at all to any knowledge of the Mississippi River. Is it likely that he would have let pass an occasion for saying that he had known of this river and its course since 1656?

For the return trip of Des Groseilliers and his companion the travel account becomes explicit once the Ottawa River is reached. Both the Calumet and the Long Sault rapids are mentioned by name. Radisson could be explicit in his description of a region that he knew from personal observation. His narratives of events in Hudson Bay in the eighties are detailed and exact. His story of the journey with Des Groseilliers on Lake Superior in 1659–1660 mentions several topographical features in such a way that identification is possible. In general, it should be said that that narrative is a clear, connected account by an intelligent, observant young man. The contrast between the accounts of later trips and the narrative of the expedition of 1654–1656 is striking.

One fact relative to the trip of 1654–1656 needs to be stressed. Obviously the journey's significance to Radisson was that information had been obtained about tribes to the north, and about a route to the ocean. "We had not a full and whole discovery, wch was that we have not been in the bay of the north, not knowing anything but by report of ye wild Christinos." Soon the two men will be testing the accuracy of this story of the Cree, and the result will be another colony on the mainland of North America.

* * *

Radisson tells us that Des Groseilliers had been to Lake Huron the year before he started on the Ottawa voyage. This statement is hard to reconcile with what has already been written of Des Groseilliers' life in Three Rivers. Probably this is as vague a remark as many others in this narrative. Doubtless the author had in mind Des Groseilliers' life in Huronia with the Jesuits before 1650. Indeed, Radisson goes on to say that Des Groseilliers had "made severall journeys when the Fathers lived about the lake of the hurrons, wch was upon the border of the sea."

A general outline of the confused narrative of the trip of exploration, 1654–1656, has already been given. Some little more needs to be said of the trip. It is possible to follow Des Groseilliers up the Ottawa, through Lake Nipissing, down French River to Georgian Bay, where the Indians separated. "Seven boats went towards west norwest and the rest to the South." "We that weare for the South went on severall dayes merily & saw by the way the place where the Fathers Jesuits had heretofore lived." There appears to have been a sojourn on an island—"the first landing isle"—a fight with the Iroquois, a rendezvous with the Pottawatomi and the "people of the fire" and with other Indians that had never seen bearded men before; the Frenchmen learned of the Sioux, the Cree, and Lake Superior; the Cree told the explorers of ships on Hudson Bay; and Des Groseilliers and his companion enjoyed a beautiful, rich countryside, saw pelicans, buffaloes, and turkeys, and arrived finally at Mackinac Straits, as already mentioned. Here they heard of the Chippewa's forcing the Sioux ever westward from Sault Ste Marie at the end of French guns and with French ammunition. The travelers appear to have spent a winter near the Sault, where moose were encountered. The Indians would not go down to Quebec with the Frenchmen the following summer, fearing the Iroquois; but the summer after that the Frenchmen's taunts of cowardice stung the natives into accompanying them.

Some have indentified the "first landing isle" as this and that island in the Great Lakes and the upper Mississippi. The concensus of opinion seems to be that it was either an island at the mouth of Green Bay, where the Indians fleeing from the Iroquois are known to have settled for a time, or an island near modern Detroit. Radisson says of this island: "After we travelled many dayes we arrived att a large island where we found their [*Indian allies'*] village, their wives & children. You must know that we passed a strait some 3 leagues beyond that place. The wild-men give it a name; it is another lake, but not so bigg as that we passed before. We calle it the lake of the staring hairs [*cheveux relevés*], because those that live about it have their hair like a brush turned up." The *cheveux relevés,* or Ottawa, are shown on Champlain's map of 1632 and on many later maps as occupying the area about modern Lake St. Clair, which is an expansion of the strait or "detroit" between Lake Huron and Lake Erie.[9] So it is possible that Des Groseilliers and his companion went south on Lake Huron, past his old home at Huronia, to the entrance of Lake Erie, crossed by the well-known por-tage route to Lake Michigan, and eventually reached Green Bay and Mackinac. Objections can be raised to all the conjectured routes that scholars have proposed for these Frenchmen and probably no one will ever know, with cer-tainty, where they wandered.

That they were pleased with interior America is shown by Radisson's ecstatic remarks: "The country was so pleasant, so beautifull & fruitfull that it grieved me to see y^t ye world could not discover such inticing countrys to

9 A reproduction of Champlain's map may be found on page 5 of Louis C. Karpinski, *Historical Atlas of the Great Lakes and Michigan* (Lansing, 1931), which also contains later maps illustrating the habitat of the Ottawa.

live in. This I say because that the Europeans fight for
a rock in the sea against one another, or for a sterill and
horrid country. . . . What conquest would that bee att
litle or no cost; what laborinth of pleasure should millions of people have, instead that millions complaine of
misery & poverty!" Here speaks the American frontiers-
man, though it was but the year 1669 when these lines
were penned.

CHAPTER IV

Des Groseilliers' Young
Brother-in-Law

To Marguérite Hayet Véron, the widow of the Sieur
de Grandmesnil, whom Des Groseilliers married in the
summer of 1653, there are many references in the unpublished annals of Three Rivers. They reveal her as a very
determined woman. Possibly her neighbors used a harsher
term. While her visionary husband was using up the family
means trying to discover the Northwest Passage, she was
bearing him five children, caring for her own three children
by an earlier marriage,[1] administering a little shop, raising
pigs and cattle, fighting her neighbors in court, and, in
general, running the family's affairs and, possibly, some of
the community's. Her half-brother, Pierre Esprit Radisson,
pays tribute to her on one occasion by calling her as good
a manager as her husband. "As good a Houswife as he"
is the quaint, middle-class Anglicism of the translation.
One has to sympathize with this stout-hearted pioneer
woman, who year after year appears in the court and church
records; losing her first husband to the Iroquois; quarrel-
ing with her second husband over the correct way of training her own children; looking in vain, month after month,
for a foolhardy husband gone to an unknown land from
which the neighbors say he will never return; standing
godmother to more than one little Trifluvien; renouncing

---

[1] Tanguay, *Dictionnaire généalogique*, 1:584, is authority for the statement
that there were three children of this union: Marguérite (1648), Etienne
(1649), and Guillaume (1651), but only the two boys are mentioned in the
numerous documents relating to the guardianship of Marguérite's children in
the 1650's and 1660's to which the author has had access.

her dowry rights to clear her husband's name and end the family debt, which he has created in order to go to Hudson Bay; welcoming him back after years of absence in Europe and elsewhere; outliving him many years; and finally dying, an old lady, in a new century and in a new country that had forgotten her husband's services and her own.

We have already speculated as to how and why and when the Hayet-Radisson family reached New France, but we have not considered where they came from. It has been stated that the Hayets were of St. Malo.[2] If Sebastien Hayet, the father of Marguérite Hayet des Groseilliers, was from St. Malo, however, it seems strange that his widow married a man of the south Rhone country, Pierre Esprit Radisson. Moreover, a thorough search of the extant archives of St. Malo reveals no such family as the Hayet-Radissons.

Three children are known to have been born of Madeleine Henaut Hayet Radisson's second marriage: Françoise, Elizabeth (Isabelle), and Pierre Esprit. The parish of St. Nicolas du Chardonnet, Paris, is mentioned by a modern scholar as the home of Elizabeth Radisson, who, he states, was born in 1638.[3] This fact, if fact it be, would seem to indicate that the family was Parisian. Marguérite's wedding contract with Véron states that she was "de la Ville de Parys paroisse de St. Paul."[4] Her birthdate is recorded in a standard modern genealogy as 1632 and that of Françoise as 1636.[5] In 1697 and 1698 Pierre Esprit swore that he was 61 and 62 years of age respectively.[6] This would mean that he, too, was born in 1636. Three

[2] Tanguay, *Dictionnaire généalogique,* 1:300.

[3] Tanguay, *Dictionnaire généalogique,* 1:330.

[4] The marriage contract is to be found in the *greffe* of Lecoustre in the judicial archives, Court-House, Quebec, under date of November 25, 1646.

[5] Tanguay, *Dictionnaire généalogique,* 1:300, 589.

[6] See *post,* Appendices 11 and 13, for the affidavits regarding Radisson's age.

censuses taken in New France, together with some few other documents, give the following conflicting data on the ages and deaths of the members of this family.[7]

	Census 1666	Census 1667	Census 1681	Interment Records	Other Data
Marguérite	34 [1632] *	38 [1629]	50 [1631]	Interred in 1711; age not given	
Elizabeth	28 [1638]	30 [1637]	48 [1633]	86 yrs. when interred, 1722 [1636]	
Françoise	30 [1636]	——	Dead	Died Oct. 3, 1677	
Pierre			41 [1640]	Will proved in 1710, but age not given	Affidavits show birth-date as 1636
Médard Chouart	36 [1630]		60 [1621]	——	Baptized July 31, 1618

* The dates inclosed in brackets are the years of birth, according to the preceding figure.

Though all other evidence points to Paris as Radisson's birthplace, four documents mention Avignon or neighboring places. Two documents by the Hudson's Bay Company

[7] The three censuses are printed in Sulte, *Historie des canadiens-français*, 4: 52–63; 4: 64–78; 5: 53–92. The census of 1666 is printed in more accurate form in *Rapport de l'archiviste de la province de Québec pour 1935–1936*, 1–154 (Quebec, 1936).

It will appear from this table how little faith one can put in the ages given in the several censuses of New France. However, it seems fair to deduce that Marguérite was the oldest child and that Pierre Esprit was one of the youngest in this family. Probably the order was: Marguérite, Françoise, Pierre Esprit, and Elizabeth. Marguérite seems to have been born about 1630 (she was married in 1646 and could hardly have been less than fifteen or sixteen at the time) ; Françoise in the middle thirties (she married prior to 1654) ; Pierre in the later thirties; and Elizabeth about 1640 (she married in 1657). Pierre's children were still being born in 1693. In his will of 1710 he refers to "my three small daughters." Probably, therefore, 1693 is not even the latest birthdate of his children. It is unlikely that he begat children after the age of sixty-five. If his last child was born in 1700, and his age were sixty-five at that time, the date of his birth would thus be the year 1635. If the last child were born in 1705, he could still be born as late as 1640. Until the actual record of his birth or baptism is found, it may be assumed that he was born not earlier than 1635 nor later than 1640. Had he been born later than 1640, he could hardly have been out on a shooting expedition in the early fifties, as we know

show plainly that Avignon or its immediate vicinity was the native city of this adventurous explorer.[8] In the records of births and marriages between 1584 and 1591 at Carpentras, a city near Avignon, are found entries giving what is without much question the birthplace and baptismal date of the explorer's father, the names of his paternal grandparents, and the fact that his father had moved to Avignon by the year 1607. All efforts to find the baptismal entry of Pierre Esprit Radisson, Junior, have proved unavailing, though the baptismal records in the Palace of the Popes have produced entries for eleven Radisson children, of three families, between the years 1615 and 1652. In 1606–1607 Anthony Radisson, the father of Pierre Esprit, Senior, is recorded as owning land in Moimoiron, near

he was. Moreover, it is unlikely that his brother-in-law would have asked a youth less than eighteen years of age to accompany him in 1659 on a dangerous and difficult trip among distant Indian tribes. See *post,* p. 58. Probably his own two statements of age may be considered correct, especially as they agree with each other. That is, he was probably born in 1636. For Elizabeth's marriage see Tanguay, *Dictionnaire généalogique,* 1:330; and page 589 of the same work for the statement that the year 1654 was the baptismal date of Françoise's son, Pierre.

[8] On January 26, 1676, the Hudson's Bay Company stated that Des Groseilliers was a Frenchman, but that Radisson was an Italian. See Public Record Office, Colonial Office, 134/1, Board of Trade, Hudson's Bay, ff. 21, 22. The explanation of this seeming misstatement appears about a decade later, when France was claiming the region about Hudson Bay. "The Case of the Adventurers of England Tradeing into Hudson's Bay in Reference to the French," a copy of which is entered in the Company's books as of May 6, 1687, states: "They [*the French*] cannot alledge that Radisson as a Frenchman acted any thing for the Advantage of France 1. Because hee is from Avignon and was Consequently a Subject of the Popes till made a Denizen of England by the Command of King Charles the Second of Blessed memory. . . ." Hudson's Bay Company Archives, A/6/1. Avignon and a small territory round about it did belong to the popes at the time of Radisson's birth and did not become a part of France until 1791. Hence Radisson, if born there, was an "Italian" and not a Frenchman. Since he was living and in the service of the Company when the second of the two statements by the Company was made, and since he had been in the Company's service for almost a decade prior to the issuance of the first statement (he had left the Company only a few weeks before it was made), the Company presumably had accurate data about him. Moreover, the officers of the Company would hardly have dared to make a remark which Radisson, in France at the time, could easily have proved false.

Avignon. Perhaps it was here that his grandson was born.[9]

Pierre Esprit Radisson, Junior, first appears in the records of New France, as far as can be determined, on November 7, 1655, when he signed his name to a deed at Quebec.[10] Nevertheless, it is possible to tell his story for at least three years prior to that time.

According to his own reminiscences, he went duck-shooting near his home at Three Rivers on May 24, 1651 or 1652.[11] The translation of his statement, which is all that we have, is ambiguous and it is impossible to determine whether he meant that he reached Canada in 1651 or that he went hunting in that year near his home at Three Rivers. Two comrades went with him, and all three were warned that Iroquois Indians were lurking in the vicinity. A youths' quarrel separated Radisson from his companions and he spent most of the day by himself.

[9] "The 21st of April, 1590, was baptized Pierre Esprit Radisson, son of Anthony Radisson. Godfather Monsieur Esprit Dabman, godmother Mademoiselle Lucretia de Maudeme. Poquet, priest." In the departmental archives of Vaucluse at Avignon, one finds, under date of April 6[?], 1607: "Emancipation of Pierre Esprit Radisson, son of Anthony and the late Honorade Barthoquine his first wife, of Carpentras, now residing in Avignon." M. Auguste Radisson of Lyons (d. 1939) was kind enough to look up this family record for the author through the courtesy of officials in Carpentras and Avignon. In Avignon the records are preserved in the Palace of the Popes; in Carpentras the municipal museum of the *archives communales* is in the Bibliothèque Inguimbertine. See in the latter, Régistre G. G. 2, "naissances et mariages de 1584 à 1591," folio 114, for the baptism of Pierre Esprit Radisson. The emancipation record is found in Etude de Beaulieu, nᵒ 1267, f. 88, Av. 6, XII, 1607. M. Radisson believed that the Radissons of the Avignon region may have descended from a member of his family, most of whom have been notaries at Tarare near Lyons since the thirteenth century. One member of the family was sent to Avignon on an important mission toward the end of the Middle Ages. See Achard and Duhamel, *Inventaire-sommaire des archives départmentales: Vaucluse,* 1: 62 (Paris, 1878), for evidence that Pierre Esprit Radisson, Senior, had moved to Avignon by 1607.

[10] A deed of sale by Pierre Soumandre to Jacques Boisel, signed by Henri Pinguet and Pierre Radisson, is to be found in Audouart's *greffe,* Number 435, in the judicial archives in the Court-House, Quebec. It is this document which proves that Radisson was not Des Groseilliers' companion on the western trip of 1654–1656.

[11] Most of the statements regarding Radisson's career between the dates of his capture by the Mohawks and the last events mentioned in this chapter are derived from his *Voyages,* pp. 25–134.

Toward sunset he stumbled on the bodies of his companions, who had been killed by the Iroquois. Hardly had he made the gruesome discovery than he found himself in the midst of the savage fiends, who threw him down, took away his gun and pistols, stripped him, and tied a rope about his waist. His youth probably saved him. The Indians treated him with leniency and kindness according to their lights. He was greased and painted, fed, untied, and allowed to spend the night lying between some of the braves. Next morning the party started for the home of these Mohawk Iroquois not far from the present city of Schenectady, New York. As the boy showed an interest in learning the Mohawk language, Indian whooping and singing; since he wrestled with an Indian boy and overcame him; and because he otherwise pleased his captors, he was allowed to sing in French, to use a knife, and to be adopted into one of the Mohawk families. The day on which he answered that he was a Mohawk, in reply to a question about his nationality, was made a period of rejoicing in his new family's history. A feast was given and three hundred guests were fed by his "father." His "mother" and "sisters" decked him out in Indian finery. His "brother" painted the lad's face, put feathers on his head, and tied his hair with wampum. Clearly the French boy had made a great impression on the simple dwellers along the Mohawk River.

After a bit he was invited to go on a hunting trip of some duration. All was going well when he encountered an Algonquian Indian, who had been captured by the Iroquois ten years earlier. This fellow persuaded Radisson, who was rather unwilling, to aid in the murder of their associates as the Mohawks slept before the camp fire. The grisly deed accomplished, the two men escaped and started to make their way to the St. Lawrence. Many harrowing experiences filled the two weeks that ensued. The two refugees pressed on till they were within sight of Three

Rivers, but on the opposite side of the great river from it. The Indian urged an immediate crossing, but Radisson counseled waiting until nightfall, lest some Iroquois be prowling near-by. The Indian's advice prevailed. A third of the crossing had been effected when the enemy was seen descending upon them. The Algonkin was killed and Radisson found himself a prisoner once more.

Torture followed such as no pen can describe adequately. It began immediately upon capture with the pulling out of a finger nail. The prisoners, of whom there were twenty-one besides Radisson, were shackled, unable to protect themselves against clouds of mosquitoes and big flies, forced to sing, and constantly tormented. One of the favorite diversions of the Iroquois was to put the ends of the captives' fingers into glowing tobacco pipes.

When the village was reached, a mob of Indian men, women, and children came out to make the last hours of the unfortunates unbearable, attached as they were in a queue by means of a rope controlled by an Iroquois. Before Radisson had to submit to this ordeal, his "relatives" sought him out, removed him from his place on the torture line, and took him to their cabin. Though this respite cheered him a little and saved him from the initial onslaught of the excited mob, it did not prevent him from further torture. Soon a contingent came for him, the slayer of three of the villagers. He was placed on the torture scaffold, where he was to remain for some sixty hours, tormented by mosquitoes and flies, pelted with hail, and at the mercy of fiends in human guise. Four finger nails were pulled out, a boy of less than four years was inspired by his mother to attempt to cut off one finger with a flint stone, an old man smoked three pipes at the end of one of the captive's thumbs, others burned the soles of his feet and his legs, a soldier ran a red-hot iron through his foot, and still others continued the pastime of pulling out his nails. Meantime Radisson saw his companions die, one by

one, having been deprived of this and that part of their
bodies, burned in flaming suits of birch bark, hacked and
splintered till only a breath remained, and then put out
of their misery.

Radisson's Indian family stood staunchly by him and
influenced the other Indians to spare the boy's life. His
"father," "a great Captayne in warrs," harangued an assembly at length; his "mother," a Huron captive, sang
and danced; and his "brother," already a veteran of two
killing parties, sang a war song. Finally Radisson's cords
were cut and he found himself at liberty, though in sad
physical condition as a result of his torture.

The following spring, entirely restored to health through
the tender ministrations of his Indian "mother" and "family," and dubbed Oninga, he went on a hunting trip with
a dozen or so young blades, including his "brother." It
is impossible to follow their route beyond the country of
the Cayuga Indians, in what is now western New York.[12]
Of the prisoners taken on this expedition Radisson says,
"none could understand them, although many Huron words
were in their language." Radisson is one of the first white
men who has left a travel account of the region beyond
the Appalachians. Moreover, his narrative is, for all practical purposes, an Indian's account of going on the war
path, since he indentified himself completely with his companions even to their psychology. For the moment, the
reader of his tale is back in primitive America, beneath
great trees in an endless forest, or on wide plains with

12 Hostile Indians were met and captured or slain. The general description
of the country explored and the stags and turkeys killed suggest Ohio, Indiana,
or western Pennsylvania, though an encounter with a peculiar reptile of
alligator characteristics might make one think of more southern regions. "You
must know yt as we past under the trees, as before mentioned, there layd on
one of the trees a snake wth foure feete, her head very bigg, like a Turtle, the
nose very small att the end, the necke of 5 thumbs wide, the body about 2 feet,
and the tayle of a foot & a halfe, of a blackish collour, onto a shell [skull?]
small and round, wth great eyes, her teeth very white but not long." This
creature fell into their boat or pirogue and frightened them severely before
they could get it out again.

possible enemies on the outskirts, sneaking up on unsuspect-
ing natives, who are quite unknown to the attackers, killing
ruthlessly in battle or mercilessly afterwards when captives
eat too much of precious food or when they cannot keep
up with the war party, and seeing one's companions die
from wounds of battle.

Back in the Mohawk village once more, Radisson decided to go on a trip of a few days' duration with nine
Indian friends to Fort Orange, a frontier settlement of
the Dutch, which was soon to be given its modern name
of Albany. There he was recognized as a Frenchman and
taken to the Governor. According to Radisson's reminiscences, the Governor offered to ransom him, but the offer
was rejected. However, a fortnight or so later, when the
return trip to the Indian village had been completed, Radisson repented of his decision and made his escape. Here
occurs one of the few dates in Radisson's entire account.
"I made my departure att 8 of the clock in the morning
the 29th 8bre, 1663," that is, October 29, 1653.[13]

It was only a short distance to a Dutch settlement.
Radisson found a little clearing some two miles from Fort
Orange, where a Dutchman was cutting wood. This man
was asked, to his utter amazement, to give the seeming
Mohawk a piece of paper, a pen, and some ink. "He won-
dered very much to see that, what he never saw before
don by a wildman." While the incredulous Dutchman
looked on, Radisson penned a letter to the Governor and
then dispatched it. Four "Flemings" were sent from the
fort to get the youth. "I was conducted to the fort of
Orange . . . where I have had the honour to salute the
Governor, who spoake french, and by his speech thought
him a french man."

[13] Obviously the date is wrong as it stands, probably because Radisson's
figures, being difficult to read, were wrongly transcribed by the English translator. It is worth a comment that Radisson's 5 looks like a 6 in the one extant
document that is known to be wholly in his handwriting. See his letter of
January 1, 1678, Appendix 4.

Now comes an episode in Radisson's narrative that can
be checked with the story of another captive. The Father
Poncet who is believed to have inspired Mère Marie de
l'Incarnation to venture to Canada, had been seized, in
August, 1653, near Quebec by the Iroquois and taken to
the same region where Radisson was a captive. Here the
priest was tortured, saw his French companion burned,
and finally was taken to Fort Orange. He arrived there
on September 20, 1653. He writes: [14]

A young man who had been captured at Three Rivers by the Iroquois, and ransomed by the Dutch, whom he served as interpreter, came
to find me, and, after some conversation, told me that he was coming
to make his confession on the next day, which was Sunday. . . . As
night was approaching, and I was going away to lie down on the bare
floor, without bed or supper, a Savage asked the Governor for leave to
take me to a family who were friendly to him. I was conducted thither,
and found there an old man who received me with much kindness. The
Frenchman whom I mentioned above was living in that house; and he
set his conscience in order during the three nights that I spent with him
under the roof of that worthy man.

Radisson mentions a Jesuit at the fort: "A minister that
was a Jesuit gave me great offer, also a Marchand [*merchant*], to whom I shall ever have infinit obligations, although they weare satisfied when I came to france att
Rochel. I stayed 3 dayes inclosed in ye fort & hidden."

The Governor sent Radisson to New Amsterdam, then
hardly to be recognized as the future largest city of the
world. Radisson remarks condescendingly that it was "a
towne faire enough for a new country." After some three
weeks in the city that was soon to change its name to New
York, Radisson embarked in a Dutch ship for Holland.
It took him about six weeks to reach Amsterdam. Here
occurs another date, January, 1654.[15] He next took sail
for La Rochelle, and after a cold passage reached it and
remained in that city or elsewhere in France till spring,

[14] *Jesuit Relations,* 40: 143, 144.
[15] The manuscript translation gives it as 1664.

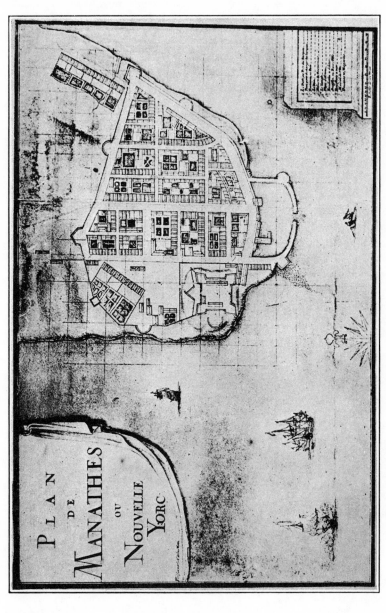

From J.-B. Franquelin's Manuscript Map of New England and New York. 1693.

[Paris. Service Hydrographique, 135-1-1.]

awaiting a ship for New France. La Rochelle was still in 1654 the great Protestant center of France and from it went most of the ships to New France. Finally a fishing boat took him across the Atlantic to the cod banks off Percée Rock. As this island played an important part in the careers of Radisson and Des Groseilliers, it may be well to identify it here. Today the Gaspé Drive affords one a view of this portaled rock in the Gulf of St. Lawrence close to the famous bird sanctuary, Bonaventure Island. Through its great arches the ocean pounds, and near-by, fishermen still probe the sea for their wares.[16] In Radisson's day it served as the quickest channel for information between Old and New France, for fishing boats were always going and coming. Here some Indian craft took him to Quebec. "I mean not to tell you the great joy I perceiv^d in me to see those persons that I never thought to see more, & they in like manner wth me thought I was dead long since."

Thus Radisson, still in his teens, was already embarked on that long life of adventure, danger, and travel that was to take him across the Atlantic twenty-four times, into the heart of a new continent, under the Arctic Circle, and into tropic seas.

* * *

[16] Nicolas Denys, who became the governor of all this gulf coast in 1654 and who was Radisson's host in 1662, wrote of this island in a book published in 1672: "Isle Percée is a great rock, which must be fifty to sixty fathoms in height, steep clear to the bottom on both sides. . . . At low tide one can go on firm ground, dry-shod, all around it. It must be three hundred and fifty or four hundred feet long. . . . I have seen it when it had only one opening, in the form of an arcade, through which a boat passed under sail. . . . There have since been formed two others, which are not so large; but these at present are growing every day. . . . All those which come here to make their fishery anchor under shelter of this island. . . . I have seen as many as eleven fishing vessels which have all loaded with cod. The fishery is very abundant." Denys, *Description and Natural History*, pp. 221, 222. On the same pages the editor gives interesting data relative to the geology, history, and modern status of Percée Rock. A recent photograph of the island in Leo Cox, "River Without End" in the issue of June, 1936, of the *Canadian Geographical Journal* (Vol. 13, No. 2), page 86, shows only one arch in the island.

His next account seems to tell of events that followed immediately on those of the preceding narrative. In reality nearly three years elapsed between his first and his second "voyage" into the Iroquois country. It is such disregard for details that makes his writing difficult to comprehend.

All that is known certainly of him in the interim is that he signed a document in Quebec on November 7, 1655.[17] He himself says of this period of the middle fifties: "In my absence [*in New Holland and Europe*] peace was made betweene the french & ye Iroquoits, wch was ye reason I stayed not long in a place." This obscure remark can be clarified. After fruitless beginnings, the Jesuits at last found a way to begin a mission among the upper Iroquois in what is now central New York state. In other words, a peace was arranged between the French and the Iroquois in 1654. Accordingly, in the summer of 1654 Father Simon Le Moine went on a tour of inspection. Returning in September to Quebec he reported very favorably on the reception accorded him by the Mohawks and Onondaga. The site chosen for a mission was among the Onondaga. In 1655 a beginning was made by Father Dablon and Father Chaumonot. In 1656 Dablon returned to Canada and secured two more priests, two lay brothers, and a party of French colonists. A fort and a settlement were made. Finally, in July, 1657, another contingent, including many Hurons, started west from Quebec, headed by Father Paul Ragueneau and Father Joseph Dupéron. With this group went Pierre Esprit Radisson.

The trip was marred for Radisson by the massacre of most of the Hurons. A party of Iroquois, sent to guide the expedition into the West, had suffered shipwreck on the eastward journey in the Lachine Rapids and had lost seven of their men. According to Radisson, who knew Indian psychology well, revenge for this misfortune was regarded as proper and even necessary. So the Iroquois decided to

---

[17] See *ante,* Note 10 of this chapter.

kill the French and the Hurons as soon as they should be in Iroquois territory. On reflection, however, the Iroquois decided that it would be unwise to murder any of the French. Therefore the Hurons were picked to suffer for all.

A landfall was made on a large island in the St. Lawrence. There all but one of the Huron men were killed in cold blood. Radisson tells us that he was bathed in the blood of the first victim, who fell at his very feet. (In Radisson's accounts he was always among the first, always on the winning side, and always the counselor of the course that later events proved wise.) Only the French youth's knowledge of the Iroquois language gave him any assurance, from the remarks that he could hear, that the Hurons alone were intended for the slaughter. Whether or not the French were merely being reserved for a later carnage is' unknown. At all events, the Jesuits helped buy the lives of the women and pacify the Iroquois, and the journey was resumed.

Other events made the journey unpleasant for Radisson. Again and again he trembled for his life. As he retold the story in his middle age in England, he still felt the poignancy of the fear that had consumed him. A reader cannot miss it: Radisson and an Indian stalk an eagle, which Radisson thinks is only a figment of his companion's mind and an excuse to shoot him; Radisson is ordered into a river, really to catch clams, but, the youth fears, merely a device to drown him; an Indian seizes Radisson's clothing and cuts a medal from the Frenchman's throat, to the consternation and terror of the youth.

Yet Radisson's sense of humor did not permit him in his narrative to omit a picture of himself and a young Iroquois canoemate, which apparently made the middle-aged Radisson chuckle in far-away London. The two were about of an age and quarreled incessantly.

The long familiarity we had wth one another breeded contempt, so that we would take nothing from one another, wch made us goe together by the ears, and fought very often till we weare covered in blood. The rest tooke delight to see us fight; but when they saw us take either gun or sword, then came they to putt us a sunder. When we weare in the boat we could not fight but wth our tongues, flying water att one another.

How well Radisson had learned the Iroquois tongue is implicit in this description of two lads, restrained from fighting because they were in an unstable canoe, and obliged to vent their emotion by calling each other names and taunting each other. How youthful they still must have been is also implicit in the description of how they wilfully sprinkled each other with water as they paddled. One day the Indian boy let the canoe slip. It was considerably injured. Immediately the two were at their battle, pommeling each other furiously: "there cuffed one another untill we weare all in bloode. Being weary, att last, out of breath, we gave over like 2 cocks over tyred wth fighting."

Shortly thereafter the voyagers pitched their wigwams beside some of the Lower Iroquois, just returning from their wars with the Eries. These recognized Radisson from his sojourn with them in 1652 and 1653. They "made much of mee." By them he sent gifts to his adopted "father," "mother," and "sisters." Of course, he was asked why he had left the Mohawks and he explained himself satisfactorily to them with a yarn about having traveled through the woods from the Mohawks' village to Three Rivers. After he had promised to visit his Indian "family" again, the returning warriors left for their home.

Always resourceful, Radisson now improvised a sail for the canoe in which he and his Indian companion were traveling on Lake Ontario. Soon lost in delight at the success of this scheme, he and the Indian failed to note that they were getting farther and farther into the lake and that a storm was upon them. A following sea threatened to overwhelm the light craft. Again the French youth's ingenuity came to the rescue. Taking a sack of corn, he tied it to the prow and let it fall into the lake. Thus the stern was forced up against the wind, and the waves no longer broke over the end.

After a successful landing from this escapade, a later shipwreck, and a journey inland, the little company arrived at the French fort near the site of the modern city of Syracuse, New York. Radisson tells us of acres of grain about it, fields of Indian corn and turnips, groves of chestnut and oak trees, and "a great company of hoggs so fatt that they weare not able to goe." Wild fowl and passenger pigeons were plentiful. "So this was not a wild country to our imagination but plentyfull in every thing."

Meanwhile the Huron who had been spared on the island of the massacre had escaped from the Upper Iroquois and had fled to the Lower bands. There he informed the credulous Mohawks how all the disasters that had been lately befalling the Iroquois had been due to the presence of the French. Nothing but destruction, he said, could be looked for from these intruders. Out of this situation developed very shortly a plan of the Iroquois to destroy the French and their new fort. The French, getting wind of the plot, resolved to escape. To do so, however, required boats, and the question was, how to build them. Finally deal boards were "contrived" to "make shipps wth large bottoms," "similar to those in use on our Loire River." [18]

One of the Huron slaves, Jaluck by name, noted these deal boards and learned of their destined use. The Jesuits had taught him Bible history, including Noah's biography, and now he "reflected soundly upon the structure that he thought verily . . . [was] to make an other arke to escape their hands, and by our inventions cause all the rest to be drowned by a second deluge." Jaluck forthwith spread the news of an approaching second flood. Ever willing to believe the incredible, the Indians were soon all in a mood to exterminate the whites. The Jesuits as they worked in and out of the wigwams doing missionary service noted

[18] Marie de l'Incarnation, *Lettres,* 2: 128.

the unrest and found its cause. Measures were resolved upon to ease the savages' minds. When next the Indians visited the fort to examine the building "ark," all was peace and serenity—for a false ceiling had been constructed, over which ship-building operations could go on unobserved by the tribesmen.

Two contemporary accounts of the stratagem used for escape exist, besides Radisson's narrative and Charlevoix' version, which was obtained largely from one of the others. The details vary, but the general outline of the story is the same. Radisson says that one of the Jesuits feigned a broken arm after an Iroquois feast at which he had been a guest. Any accident to a guest was a cause for grave concern among Indians, to whom bodily injury to a guest meant inevitable revenge. When he recovered, the Jesuit gave a feast, according to Indian custom, to celebrate his return to good health. This feast was set for the night in March when noise was necessary to cover up the embarkation of the French. All Indians were obliged by their fear of revenge to attend. All kinds of food were set before the guests. Indian manners required that everything set before a guest must be devoured. While the Indians were gorging themselves, the French kept them amused with games, dances, and, above all, with music. "There is a strife between the French who will make the greatest noise. But there is an end of all things; the houre is come, ffor all is embarked. The wildman can hold out no longer; they must sleepe. They cry out, *Skenon,* enough, we can beare no more." So they were given no more food, the fort was closed as usual, the Indians fell into a stupor induced by overeating—and, quite possibly, by drugs—and the French slipped silently away over their "little lake," barely free from ice. On the second day they reached Lake Ontario, and on April 3 they were in Montreal, having come without guides over a practically new and an extremely dangerous route partially obstructed by ice. Three men had been drowned, but the rest rejoiced in their escape from a cruel foe.

Mère Marie and the Jesuits give the credit for the success of the stratagem to an unnamed Frenchman. The former says: [19] "A young Frenchman, who had been adopted by a renowned Iroquois and who had learned their language, told his [Indian] father that he had had a dream that he must provide a feast, where everything must be eaten or he should die." Ragueneau writes: [20] "We invited all the Savages in our neighborhood to a grand feast, where we exerted our utmost skill and spared neither the drums nor the musical instruments, in order to lull them to sleep by an innocent charm. He who presided at the ceremony played his part with such skill and success that each one was bent on contributing to the public joy." One cannot refrain from wondering whether the young man was not Radisson himself. Charlevoix adds to Mère Marie's narrative the story that it was the young man, playing on the guitar, who lulled the natives to sleep.[21]

There is a strong hint in at least two contemporary accounts that some of the Frenchmen, including, perhaps, most of the garrison, commanded by Zacharie Dupuis, former commandant of the fort at Quebec, had played the craven in thus deserting their fort. Dollier de Casson, third superior of the Seminary of St. Sulpice, in his history of Montreal says that these soldiers "took such a fever that they were only cured of it by the sight of Montreal, which has on several occasions performed similar miracles." [22] However, De Casson was a Sulpitian and this was a Jesuit enterprise! [23]

[19] Mère Marie de l'Incarnation gives her entire account of this episode in her *Lettres*, 2: 128–137.

[20] *Jesuit Relations*, 44: 177, 179.

[21] Charlevoîx, *Histoire de la Nouvelle France*, 337.

[22] François Dollier de Casson, *Histoire de Montréal*, p. 124, in *Mémoires de la société historique de Montréal* (Montréal, 1868).

[23] But see also *Jesuit Relations*, 44: 159, for confirmation of De Casson's remark.

* * *

Meanwhile Des Groseilliers had been at his home in
Three Rivers, as certain records show. He stood godfather
to Jeanne Lafleur, a little half-breed, on July 14, 1657,
and on August 7 of that year his own daughter, Marie-
Anne was baptized.[24] On July 18 he brought suit against
Jerosme Langlois for a pistol left four months earlier with
the defendant to be repaired.[25] On August 19, 1657, he
was a witness to a marriage contract.[26] On February 9, 13,
and 23, and on March 2 and 9, 1658, Chouart was in court
at Three Rivers.[27] Radisson's narrative seems to say that
he and his brother-in-law started for the West immediately
upon the return of the Frenchmen from Onondaga in April,
1658. Yet Des Groseilliers is found in court or elsewhere
in Three Rivers on these dates: April 12 and 27, June 15,
and August 4, 1658; and May 15 and 19 and June 30,
1659.[28] On May 29 and 31, 1659, Radisson was in Que-

[24] A manuscript by Cyprien Tanguay at St. Paul Seminary, St. Paul, Minnesota.

[25] Three Rivers, prévôté records (Q), 1655–1667, under the date given.

[26] Médard Chouart signed the marriage contract of Jacques Ratté and Anne
Martin, according to the document now in Audouart's *greffe*, No. 576, in the
judicial archives, Quebec.

[27] See judicial archives in the Court-House, Three Rivers, under the first
three dates for the cases of Pierre La Rue, Maurice Poulin, Bertrand Fafard,
Sieur de la Framboise, and Robert de la Porte *versus* Des Groseilliers. On
March 2 and 9 Chouart and Poulin were prosecuting a case against Jean
Sauvaget.

[28] Chouart was godfather to Ignace Pellerin at Three Rivers on April 12,
1658. See Tanguay's manuscript at St. Paul Seminary and the parish register of
baptisms at Three Rivers. On April 27, June 15, and August 4 Des Groseilliers
was in court at Three Rivers. See Baston *versus* Médard Chouart, a suit for
264 livres' worth of merchandise not paid for; the Sieur de Godefroy *versus*
Médard Chouart, a suit to be paid for bricks; and Barthélemy Bertaut *versus*
Chouart a suit for payment of 14 livres. These three documents may be found
in the prévôté records at Three Rivers. On April 15, 1659, Father Ménard
baptized Marguérite Chouart, daughter of the Sieur des Groseilliers. See
parish records, Three Rivers. On May 15, 1659, Médard Chouart signed a
receipt in Three Rivers, given by Benjamin Auneau [?] to Christophe Crevier,
Sieur de la Meslée. The receipt is now owned by the Chicago Historical Society, Schmidt Collection, 1:33. On May 19 Chouart brought suit against
Pierre le Boulanger dit St. Pierre for a gun; and on June 30, 1659, Chouart

bec.[29] After June, 1659, there is silence in all the colony records for almost a year as far as these two men are concerned. In other words, they had gone together to the Lake Superior country.

was involved in two cases. See the prévôté records, Three Rivers (Q), 1655–1667, under dates of May 19 and June 30, 1659.

[29] A receipt of Denis Duquet to the widow Sylvestre of May 29, 1659, is signed by "Pre. Radisson"; and another of May 31 by Jean Juchereau de la Ferté to the same widow is signed in the same fashion by him. See Audouart's *greffe*, Nos. 763 and 764, Judicial Archives, Quebec.

CHAPTER V

"We Weare Demi-Gods"

Sometime in August, 1659, the brothers-in-law set forth.[1] Des Groseilliers seems to have spent at least a part of the preceding winter on a hunting expedition, for on May 19 of this year Pierre le Boulanger, Seigneur de St. Pierre, corporal of the garrison at Three Rivers, was sued by Des Groseilliers for a gun that the latter had lent, and which had been broken.[2] De St. Pierre replied that the gun had been lent on condition that if anything happened to it, the loss should be borne by all those going "a la chasse ensemble." There were four other members of the hunting party, one of whom was the Sieur de Normanville, the son of Jean Godefroy, Sieur de Lintot.

In his narrative Radisson indicates with what difficulty the two started on their trip. The Governor insisted that one of his servants go with them; the Jesuits tried to send a representative or two. Des Groseilliers, with his usual bluntness, told the Governor that he and Radisson knew what they were doing and that it was a case of "Discoverers before governors." Consequently it was necessary for

---

[1] A case of August, 1659 (see prévôté records of Three Rivers (Q), 1655–1667) involves Marguérite des Groseilliers and mentions "le Sʳ des Groseillers absent." The journal of the Jesuits for August 1, 1659, tells of news from Three Rivers that thirty-three canoes of western Indians had come from inland by interior routes and were asking for Frenchmen to return with them. *Jesuit Relations,* 45:105.

[2] The document relating this case and now in the prévôté records of Three Rivers (Q) is badly torn and many words are missing. Pierre Le Boulanger, Seigneur de St. Pierre, is mentioned by Tanguay in his *Dictionnaire généalogique,* 1:75. He married Marie-Reine Godefroy, daughter of the Sieur de Lintot and brother of the Sieur de Normanville. The Godefroys, a Protestant family of Rouen, may have been related to the family of Robert Cavelier, Sieur de la Salle, for Godefroy's mother was Perette Cavelier of Rouen.

the two men to slip away unnoticed. They were able to do so because Des Groseilliers was captain of the borough of Three Rivers. Radisson says,[3]

> That very night, my brother having the keys of the Brough as being Captayne of the place, we embarqued ourselves. . . . Being come opposit to the fort, they aske who is there. My brother tells his name. Every one knows what good services we had done to the countrey, and loved us, y[e] inhabitants as well as the souldiers. The sentrey answers him, "God give you a good voyage."

The flotilla of Indians from the interior, with whom the three men of the party (there was an unidentified companion at the outset) proposed to travel, had agreed to wait for them in the grass on Lake Saint Peter, an enlargement of the St. Lawrence above Three Rivers. When the Frenchmen reached the rendezvous, there was no one to be seen. Nothing daunted, they pressed on, and near the mouth of the Richelieu River the Indians were seen approaching. Each of the white men now went into a canoe with Indians. The unknown Frenchman cried out in a dream that night. Such an occurrence was considered a very bad omen by Indians and the Frenchman's companions obliged him to give up the journey.[4] Thus once more Des Groseilliers with a single companion was bound for the "pays d'en haut."

There were serious encounters with the Iroquois on the Ottawa River; Radisson and some of his companions explored beneath Chaudière Falls in the present city of Ottawa; the group suffered the pangs of hunger near Lake Nipissing; and, finally, with great joy, they found them-

---

[3] A document of October 10, 1661, corroborates Radisson's statement by referring to Des Groseilliers as "captaiñe du bourg des Trois rivières." See the *greffe* of Séverin Ameau, Court-House, Three Rivers, under the date given above. The case relates to a sale of land by Des Groseilliers and his wife to De St. Pierre. Radisson's statement is given on pages 175 and 176 of his *Voyages*.

[4] See *post*, p. 69 for a similar occurrence mentioned by the Jesuits. Indeed, it is so similar that one inevitably asks himself whether both authors are not referring to the same event. If so, was Radisson on the expedition to the upper country that left Quebec in 1660, and has he confused the two expeditions in his reminiscences?

selves on Lake Huron, where paddling was easier and danger of Iroquois very slight.

Radisson's narrative of this trip is as explicit as that of the former trip to the West is vague. He describes the Sault de Ste Marie, the famous white fisheries there, the great portaled cliffs on the south shores of Lake Superior, the River Ontonagon, Keeweenaw Point and Bay, and, finally, Chequamegon Point and Bay on the southern shore of Lake Superior, near its western end. In this area the two men decided to build, while their Indian friends should go to their families in the Wisconsin woods. A reunion was planned as soon as the natives could find their wives and bring them along to carry the two white men's baggage and trade goods.

Radisson and Des Groseilliers improved their time by building a small fort at the end of Chequamegon Bay.[5]

[5] The exact site may have been noted by a famous Catholic leader and author some two hundred and twenty-five years later. He writes: "Monday, Nov. 8th, I made an important archæological discovery five miles above Washburn, about two miles from the Southwestern end of Chequamegon Bay, near Mr. Wyman's place. He showed me two mounds, one of which we dug up a little and examined. The mound was about eight feet in diameter at the base and two feet high and almost entirely covered with a layer of boulders or stones, taken from the beach near by. After removing some of the boulders and clay we came upon a layer of ashes from four to six inches thick. In the ashes we found a long iron nail of wrought iron, hand made and bent, as if it had been clinched when driven into a board; it resembled somewhat a hook and was about 2½ inches long. It tapered down to a sharp point and the head was hammered rough. It was a regular old fashioned nail and was undoubtedly the work of civilized men, of whites. Besides we found part of a brass buckle, very artistically made, perhaps the shoe-buckle of some old French officer. Both objects had suffered from the fire. Besides we find what seemed to be a piece of clay-pipe stem, and pieces of bones of birds, fishes and animals. What do you think was this mound? It was not an Indian mound, for the objects found were decidedly of European make. It is located not far from the site of the ancient Jesuit Mission at the head of Chequamegon Bay. Near by can be seen three small holes, where the dirt was taken out, that covered the mound. It is at the very edge of a point of land and in a few years will disappear as the bank will cave in and destroy it." J. Chrysostom Verwyst, O.L.H., published in *American Antiquarian,* 9: 39–40 (Jan., 1887). This reference was kindly called to the author's attention by G. Hubert Smith. See also Guy M. Burnham, *The First House Built by White Men in Wisconsin* (Ashland, Wis. [1931]).

Then they ingeniously laid a snare of small bells, attached to a long cord, with which to be warned if intruders ventured too close to their habitation. Finally, before the natives returned, they cached part of their trading goods. Later they told the simple natives a cock-and-bull yarn about having sunk the treasure in the lake with the help of their Manitou, who would see that it was preserved and ready for use when they wished to recover it.

Almost a fortnight passed before the Indians returned. Radisson and Des Groseilliers were not alone during this period, however, for neighboring tribesmen came out of curiosity to see the visitors. Most of the natives were having their first glimpse of white men on this occasion. To them the Frenchmen made great display of their arms, which Radisson in his narrative lists with some pride: five guns, two muskets, three fowling pieces, three pairs of large pistols, two pairs of pocket pistols, two swords, and two daggers.

Finally the Indians of the interior returned with their families and the Frenchmen banqueted them with the wild fowl and animals that they had shot in the interim. The two strangers displayed their fort to their erstwhile companions with no little pride. "We were Cesars, being nobody to contradict us," is Radisson's summary of his contentment in this wilderness paradise. Finally it was time to move on into Wisconsin forests. Up went the Frenchmen's packs onto the squaws' backs. "We went away free from any burden, whilst those poor miserable[s] thought themselves happy to carry our Equipage, for the hope that they had that we should give them a brasse ring, or an awle, or an needle."

It is conjectured that the terminus of this trip was Court Oreille Lake in northwestern Wisconsin. At all events, the village to which they now proceeded was approached by boat across a "little" lake after a four days' march through a "beautifull" country "wth very few mountaines, the woods cleare."

A rousing welcome was given the strangers, who responded with sufficient gifts to stimulate friendship and respect but not so many that cupidity and contempt of prodigality should be aroused. This is one of many instances of that supreme gift of comprehending Indian psychology with which these two men were endowed. Few men, even of their own day and nation, approached them in their capacity to keep Indians' respect and good will while gaining commercial and other ends.[6]

At first Radisson stayed with one of his traveling companions, but later he was adopted into a Menominee family, and went with them in a smaller group to hunt in the forests. Runners were sent out during the winter to invite all and sundry to a great Feast of the Dead. Meanwhile Famine stalked the Wisconsin woods. A great snow fell and the hunters, obliged to use snowshoes, made so much noise stealing on their prey that animals got away before they

---

[6] In his narrative Radisson makes what appears at first glimpse to be a naïve statement. "We destinated . . . presents . . . to the end that they should remember that journey; that we should be spoaken of a hundred years after . . ." Two hundred years later, a descendant of these Indians, writing about the tradition of his people concerning the first white men to be seen on the southern shore of Lake Superior, stated that smoke was seen one early winter day coming from a supposedly uninhabited island (Madeline Island) off Chequamegon Point. Investigation revealed "a small log cabin in which they discovered two white men in the last stages of starvation." "These two white men had started from Quebec during the summer with a supply of goods, to go and find the Ojibways who every year had brought rich packs of beaver to the sea-coast. . . . Having come provided with goods they remained in the village during the winter, exchanging their commodities for beaver skins. The ensuing spring a large number of the Ojibways accompanied them on the return home. From close inquiry, and judging from events which are said to have occurred about this period of time, I am disposed to believe that this first visit by the whites took place about two hundred years ago." Since the manuscript of this account was written sometime between the year 1851, and its author's death in 1853, that is, before Radisson's manuscript had been discovered, it would have been impossible for the writer, William Whipple Warren, the half-breed son of a famous fur trader, to have gleaned his data from any other source than his Indian relatives. William Whipple Warren, *History of the Ojibways, Based Upon Traditions and Oral Statements,* pp. 121, 122 (*Minnesota Historical Collections,* Vol. 5, St. Paul, 1885).

could be killed. Finally, after many Indians had died and all had been reduced to killing their dogs and eating skins and powdered bones, a great crust formed on the snow, strong enough to bear a man's weight. From this the deer could not escape and they were easily caught and killed.

All through the famine period the Indians swore that some Manitou was bringing food to Des Groseilliers, for his countenance remained as usual, though the faces of the Indians became mere skin and bone. "But if they had seene his body they should be of another oppinion. The beard that covered his face made as if he had not altered his face." How young Radisson was is apparent from his next statement: "For me that had no beard, they said I loved them, because I lived as well as they." No Frenchman of Radisson's day would have been without his beard, especially in the woods, if he had been capable of raising one. Besides being difficult to shave off in the wilderness, a beard was a distinct protection against severe cold in winter and the hordes of mosquitoes that made life almost unendurable in spring and early summer. Hence it is obvious that Radisson was not yet of an age to grow a beard. Indians, who as a race could grow no beards, were, of course, unaware of the fact that there was any difference in this respect between the two Frenchmen. It is plain, therefore, that here is one of the best proofs that Radisson was a very young man in 1659.

Toward spring the Sioux sent representatives and gifts. Their weeping ceremony, so well described by Father Louis Hennepin, who visited the same Indians twenty years later, gives an authentic note to this part of Radisson's tale.[7] So does the description of the calumet, which quite obviously was made from catlinite of the red pipestone quarry from the region now known as southwestern Minnesota.

[7] See *Father Louis Hennepin's Description of Louisiana, Newly Discovered to the Southwest of New France By Order of the King,* translated by Marion E. Cross, pp. 89, 94 (Minneapolis, 1938).

Next in Radisson's narrative comes a vivid description of the great Feast of the Dead, to which "eighteen severall nations" came.[8] There was much feasting and ceremony at the rendezvous. Long speeches were made, gifts were exchanged, alliances were cemented, peace pipes were smoked, and games were played. Probably there is nowhere any better account than here of Indian customs before the natives had been influenced by white men's ways and goods.

During the rendezvous a delegation was sent to the Cree, or Christino, great enemies of the Sioux, to pave the way for peace between these rivals. Radisson says that he went with the delegation and that the journey was but of three days' duration. Earlier in his narrative he mentions an encounter with Cree on the south shore of Lake Superior. On the way back he, like most whites on their first winter trip in northern, snow-mantled regions, experienced the pain and inconvenience of snow blindness. Hardly an early traveler in the same region but had a similar experience.

After the feasting and mirth were over, Radisson and Des Groseilliers went, as they had promised, to visit the Sioux. Here, according to Radisson, they stayed six weeks. He describes the Sioux and their country in such a fashion that one easily recognizes the similarity between his account and that told by the Jesuit *relation* of 1660, purporting to summarize Des Groseilliers' report as made immediately upon his return to Quebec.

When spring came, the two men returned to Lake Superior with a company of Chippewa Indians. Some idea

[8] Much speculation has been wasted on the site of this great rendezvous. Just why it has been placed near Knife Lake, Minnesota, well within the Sioux territory of Radisson's day, is not clear to the present writer. The translation of Radisson's own account seems to exclude that possibility. His own words mention the "little lake" of the winter's sojourn as the rendezvous. Moreover, after the great feast, Des Groseilliers and he went "to the nation of y[e] beefe [*buffalo*], w[ch] was seaven small Journeys from that place [*the rendezvous*]." The nation of the buffalo were, of course, the Sioux. Hence one would assume that the rendezvous was outside Sioux territory and consequently well to the east or southeast of Knife Lake.

of the distance traveled by the two men in going to the Sioux after the rendezvous may be gleaned from Radisson's statement that it required twelve days for him to return to find those Indians who were going to Lake Superior. Here he seems to mean the band with whom he and his brother-in-law had spent the autumn and early winter about Court Oreille Lake. Arriving at Chequamegon Bay once more, the Frenchmen found their cache in good condition and built another fort on Chequamegon Point. Radisson injured himself seriously by trying to haul overloaded sleds on the rotten ice of Lake Superior off the end of the point. Much rubbing of his thigh and legs and several days of rest restored him to his former strength.

At last, with the spring, Radisson and Des Groseilliers planned to visit the country of the Cree, according to a promise that they had made to this people. A delegation of these Indians came to the Point, but the two men sent them ahead across the lake. Later the Frenchmen repented the loss of these guides, for they had to cross the western end of Lake Superior from La Pointe to (probably) Cross River or thereabouts, while the ice was breaking up.[9] On the other side, after their hazardous trip, they were given a fervent welcome by the assembled Cree.

Now comes one of the questionable parts of Radisson's story. He appears to tell of a trip from the north shore of Lake Superior, where the Cree were assembled, via a great river [*Albany River?*], to James or Hudson Bay. Needless to say, a trip of such length could not have been accomplished in the time at the men's disposal. Des Groseilliers was not absent from his home for more than

---

[9] Before the Indians of the north shore of Lake Superior had had much intercourse with whites, Father Friederich Baraga crossed from La Pointe to Cross River, Minnesota, in 1846, escorted by Indians of Grand Portage. There he set up a cross in gratitude for his safety duing such a hazardous *traverse*. Joseph Gregorich, *The Apostle of the Chippewas: The Life Story of the Most Rev. Frederick Baraga, D.D., the First Bishop of Marquette*, pp. 69, 70 (Chicago, 1932).

eleven months. It would have been impossible to reach the Bay from Lake Superior except in the summer months. The summer months of both years of the trip, however, are accounted for: the summer of 1659 was spent on the Great Lakes in reaching Chequamegon Bay; and that of 1660 in returning to Quebec.

Radisson doubtless had a motive for this falsification of his narrative. By 1668–1669, when he was writing it, he was in the service of the nascent Hudson's Bay Company. That company had believed the two Frenchmen when they told of a way from interior North America to that Sea of the West which was of so much interest to Europeans —a sea connecting Hudson Bay and the South Sea. Now, writing his story, Radisson must perforce account for his knowledge of that sea and the route thither and to do so he wrote of his explorations in its vicinity. A reading of this portion of Radisson's story reminds one, in its vagueness of style and lack of detail, of his account of the first western trip. Apparently Radisson betrays himself at once, through his general style, whenever he tries to invent or to recount something learned only by hearsay.

It may be asked where Radisson derived his knowledge of Hudson Bay and a canoe route to it from Lake Superior, when he wrote his narrative in 1669. Turn to the Jesuit *relation* of 1659–1660. There Father Druillettes (through Father Jerome Lalemant) tells of meeting Awatanik, an Algonkin who left Green Bay in June, 1658, passed that summer and the following winter on Lake Superior, covered a hundred leagues of territory the following spring and summer to Hudson Bay, and coasted along the bay and reached the Saguenay by a river connecting with Lake St. John. At a place thirty-two leagues from Tadoussac he met Father Druillettes and told him his story. Father Druillettes returned at once to Quebec and met the two Frenchmen, Radisson and Des Groseilliers. This was in the summer of 1660. Doubtless the three men exchanged

views and in all likelihood Father Druillettes told Radisson
and Des Groseilliers what he had learned from the Indian
of Green Bay. It is known that Druillettes got a vast
amount of information from Indians.[10]

Finally, after a false start, the two Frenchmen and a
great company of Indians were able to set out from Lake
Superior in the summer of 1660 for Montreal and Quebec.
All went well on the homeward trip. At the Long Sault
on the Ottawa River below the modern city of Ottawa,
this company saw the remains of a band of sixteen Frenchmen led by Adam Dollard, who had encountered a great
party of Iroquois at that point. Here, where Radisson
recalls the shipwreck of Des Groseilliers at the same spot
in 1656 and the consequent loss of the latter's diaries, a
small band of Frenchmen had broken the power of the
Iroquois and probably saved New France by giving their
own lives. There is now some question of Dollard's motive
in going to meet the Iroquois, but whether or not he acted
wisely, he cleared the way for Radisson and Des Groseilliers' return with great wealth for Canada. It is a famous
story. Every Canadian school child knows of the Dollard
Massacre of May, 1660. Radisson tells the story and ends:
"All the French though dead were tyed to posts along the
River side. . . . It was a terrible spectable to us, for wee
came there 8 dayes after that defeat, which saved us without doubt." Of course, he is wrong as to the number of
days. The last possible day of the Dollard Massacre was
May 11.[11] Radisson's party reached Montreal on August
20. Surely three months were not lost in a stretch of less
than a hundred miles.

A pause was made at Montreal while Des Groseilliers
made a business arrangement with Charles Le Moyne, a
merchant of that city. The document containing the agree-

[10] *Jesuit Relations*, 45: 217–227.

[11] See E. R. Adair, "Dollard des Ormeaux and the Fight at the Long Sault,"
in *Canadian Historical Review*, 13: 130–138 (June, 1932).

ment has survived and is now in the old court-house at Montreal, signed by both Des Groseilliers and Le Moyne. Radisson is not mentioned. A translation follows: [12]

Personally appeared &c Messieurs Charles le Moyne, merchant, a resident of this place, of the first part, and Medard Chouard desgrosellers, *habitant,* a resident of Three Rivers at present in this place, who in the presence of witnesses, hereinafter subscribed, have associated themselves and do now associate themselves by these presents for all and sundry the beaver whether greased, dry, or soft, which they shall trade with the Ottawa Indians and others at present in this place, not only on the St. Lawrence River, but also at Three Rivers and Quebec, in order that, the trade being finished, they may share alike, having first paid for the trade goods which shall have been bought by them, and to have equal parts of the principal and total of the said trade, all of which they have promised to do, and to work together in peace and harmony and not to do anything contrary to these presents under penalty of each one's property, both real and personal, now and for the future. Made at Villemarie in the said Island, in the forenoon of this twenty-second day of August of the year one thousand six hundred and sixty in the presence of the sieurs Le Ber and Jean Baudouin, witnesses to this, who have signed according to the ordinance.

[*Signed*]   C Le Moyne   Medar Chouar
              Le Ber [13]   Jean baudouin [14]
              Basset notary

If it were not for some other considerations, one would suspect that it was Charles Le Moyne, not Pierre Esprit

---

[12] This document was copied and supplied to the author by M. E.-Z. Massicotte, chief archivist, Old Court-House, Montreal. The family name of Des Groseilliers' partner, it will be noted, was spelled "Le Moyne." In modern French this becomes "Le Moine."

[13] The Le Ber family was a large and important one in New France. Probably the signer was Jacques Le Ber dit Larose, a merchant. He was the son of Robert and Colette Cavelier of Pitre in the bishopric of Rouen in Normandy. His wife was Jeanne Le Moyne, sister of Charles Le Moyne. Here is another branch of the Cavelier family of Rouen or its vicinity. There may have been strong family connections that led Robert Cavelier, Sieur de la Salle, to New France. See Tanguay, *Dictionnaire généalogique,* 1: 356. The Jesuit *relation* of 1661–1663 tells of Le Ber's arrest and the confiscation of his property in 1662, when sedition broke out in Montreal. See *Jesuit Relations,* 47: 289.

[14] Jean Baudouin was born in 1639, the son of Jean and of Jeanne (Bretel) Baudouin. He was married on November 27, 1663, to Marie-Charlotte Chauvin and their first child was born at Montreal on June 12, 1666. Tanguay, *Diction-*

Radisson, who accompanied Des Groseilliers on his trip to the West in 1659.[15]

* * *

The diary of the Jesuits records for August 17 to September 1, 1660:[16]

The Outawats had arrived there [*Montreal*] on the 19th, and left on the following day . . . reaching 3 rivers on the 24th, whence they

naire généalogique, 1:30. There was also a Jean Baudouin of Three Rivers, but probably the Montreal man was the witness.

[15] Now that we have had the story from Radisson's pen, let us see how others relate it. The Jesuits in their *relation* of 1659–1660 tell of the many new mission fields challenging their order. Second on the list are the Tobacco Hurons "on the Southwest," who have sent one of their captains. "He is making preparations here to conduct some Frenchmen, as soon as spring opens, to a spot sixty leagues beyond the lake of the people of the sea [*Winnebago Indians*], where his compatriots have taken refuge, and believe themselves safe in the midst of several Algonkin Nations, settled there from time immemorial." Here, then, is the general location of the Indians with whom Radisson and Des Groseilliers spent the winter of 1659–1660.

The *relation* goes on: "In the third place, on the west a great Nation of 40 Villages, called the Nadouechiowec [*Sioux*], has been awaiting us since the alliance which it only recently concluded with the two Frenchmen who returned from their country this summer. From what they have remembered of that Language" it is like the Algonquian.

"In the fourth place, on the Northwest, the Poualacs and other Nations . . . have formed together a league, offensive and defensive, against the common enemy."

"In the fifth place, farther toward the North, the Nation of the Kilistinons [*Cree*], situated between the upper lake [*Lake Superior*] and the sea-bay that we have mentioned, begins or ends that of the Poualac."

"This year, one thousand six hundred and sixty, . . . sixty canoes . . . [*of the upper Algonkins*], having arrived, two of our Fathers again joined them. . . . But one of them could not go beyond Montreal, owing to the whim of a Savage, who would not allow him in his canoe." "If the [*other*] father can escape their [*the Iroquois*] clutches, he will follow the Algonkins [*who came down with Des Groseilliers*] to a point midway between the Lake of the Sea People and Lake Superior, where those peoples promise us a residence on another Lake, three or four hundred leagues from here. Near it, they are to fell, this Winter, the trees for their abode, and to form a sort of center for several Nations who have already appeared there, and who will repair thither from different directions."

Here again is a reasonably clear location of the people with whom Radisson and Des Groseilliers passed the winter of 1659–1660. There tribesmen would normally be returning whence they had come, a point midway between the Winnebago (near Green Bay) and Lake Superior. *Jesuit Relations,* 46:69, 75, 77.

[16] *Jesuit Relations,* 45:161–163.

started on the 27th. They were 300 in number. Des grosilleres was in
their Company; he had gone to their country the previous year. They
had started from Lake superior in 100 canoes; 40 turned back and 60
reached here, loaded with furs to the value of 200,000 livres. They left
some to the value of 50,000 livres at Montreal, and took the remainder
to 3 rivers. They came down in 26 Days, and took two months to return. Des grosillers wintered with the nation of the ox [*nation du
bœuf*], which he says consists of 4 thousand men; they are sedentary
Nadwesseronons. Father Menar, father Albanel, Jean Guerin, and 6
other frenchmen went with them [*when the Indians returned to their
homes*].

Father Charles Albanel later played an important rôle
in the lives of Radisson and Des Groseilliers, in the affairs
of the Hudson's Bay Company, and in negotiations between
France and Great Britain. He must have become acquainted
with Radisson and Des Groseilliers at this time, if he had
not known them earlier. It was he whom the Indians refused
to have in their canoe "owing to the whim of a Savage."
So he did not go to Lake Superior with Father Menard
and Jean Guerin, both of whom died in the interior. These
two men had baptized Des Groseilliers' children before
they left.

It is obvious that Radisson and Des Groseilliers told
the Jesuits, on their return, of their geographic knowledge
of the regions beyond Lake Michigan. In the *relation* of
1659–1660, which tells of Des Groseilliers' return, appears
the evidence of this.[17]

The Savages dwelling about that end of the lake [*Superior*] which is
farthest distant from us, have given us entirely new light, which will
not be displeasing to the curious, touching the route to Japan and China,
for which so much search has been made. For we learn from these peoples that they find the Sea on three sides, toward the South, toward the
West, and toward the North; so that, if this is so, it is a strong argument and a very certain indication that these three Seas, being thus
contiguous, form in reality but one Sea, which is that of China. For,—
that of the South, which is the Pacific sea and is well enough known,
being connected with the North Sea, which is equally well known, by

[17] *Jesuit Relations,* 45:221, 223.

J.-B. Franquelin's Manuscript Map of a Part of Canada "Between the 44th and the 61st Degrees of Latitude and the 246th and the 297th of Longitude," September 10, 1681.

[Paris. Service Hydrographique, B 4040.2.]

a third Sea, the one about which we are in doubt,—there remains nothing more to be desired than the passage into this great sea, at once a Western and an Eastern sea.

It will be recalled that Radisson lists the "Sea of the East" in the caption to his joint account of his two western trips.

Now we know that, proceeding Southward for about three hundred leagues from the end of lake Superior, of which I have just spoken, we come to the bay of St. Esprit [*mouth of the Mississippi River, known from De Soto's explorations*], which lies on the thirtieth degree of latitude and the two hundred and eightieth of longitude, in the Gulf of Mexico, on the coast of Florida; and in a Southwesterly direction from the same extremity of lake Superior, it is about two hundred leagues to another lake, which empties into the Vermilion sea on the coast of new Grenada, in the great South Sea. It is from one of these two coasts that the Savages who live some sixty leagues to the West of our lake Superior obtain European goods, and they even say that they have seen some Europeans there.

Moreover, from this same lake Superior, following a River toward the North, we arrive, after eight or ten days' journey, at Hudson bay, in fifty-five degrees of latitude. From this place, in a Northwesterly direction, it is about forty leagues by land to Button Bay, where lies port Melson [*Nelson*], on the fifty-seventh degree of latitude and two hundred and seventieth of longitude; the distance thence to Japan is to be reckoned at only one thousand four hundred and twenty leagues, there being only seventy-one degrees of a great circle intervening. These two Seas, then, of the South and of the North, being known, there remains only that of the West, which joins them, to make only one from the three; and it is the fresh knowledge that we have gained from a Nation which, being situated at about the forty-seventh degree of latitude and the two hundred and seventy-third of longtitude, assures us that ten days' journey Westward lies the Sea, which can be no other than the one we are looking for,—it is this knowledge that makes us believe that the whole of North America, being thus surrounded by the sea on the East, South, West, and North, must be separated from Groeslande [*Greenland*] by some strait, of which a good part has already been discovered; and that it only remains now to push on some degrees farther, to enter nothing less than the Japan sea. In order to make the passage of Hudson strait, this is to be attempted only in the months of August and September; for, during these months only, the passage is less

blocked with ice. But enough of this for the present. If the Iroquois permit, we shall be fully able to go and enlighten ourselves more clearly
concerning this discovery, which being known to us only through the
medium of Savages, does not give us all the information we might
desire.[18]

Here then must be the story that the explorers told to
the Jesuits upon their return. In main outlines it is exactly
the story that the two men told later, first in New England
and later at Oxford and London. It was only from these
explorers, lately returned, that the priest writing the relation just quoted could have derived much of his account,
however much he says that his information came from
savages. Indians could not express themselves in degrees
of latitude and longitude. What the priest means to say,
no doubt, is that the two explorers, in their turn, got much
of this information, not from actual experience, but from
talking with western and northern tribes. It will be noted
that the natives farthest to the west with whom actual
contact has been made are recorded as living three degrees
of longitude farther east than Port Nelson, according to
the reckoning of the day. Contemporary maps show Port
Nelson about north of the western boundary of present-
day Minnesota. Here then, is the western limit of Des
Groseilliers and Radisson's personal explorations.

Creuxius' map, published in 1660, "Tabula Novae
Franciae Anno 1660," seems to embody most of this new
information.[19] It does not show the region west of Lake
Superior, but the 273rd degree of longitude, and the 47th
of latitude, by the scale of the map, would be a place in
eastern Minnesota or western Wisconsin. Perhaps the most

---

[18] *Jesuit Relations*, 45:223, 225.
[19] For a reproduction of this map and a discussion of its probable foundation on the Jesuit *relation* of 1659–1660, see Nellis M. Crouse, *Contributions
of the Canadian Jesuits to the Geographical Knowledge of New France, 1632–
1675*, especially Chapter V, "The Jesuits and the Overland Routes to the
Northern Sea" (Ithaca, 1924).

interesting new geographical information is the river flow-
ing from Lake Nipigon [?] to James Bay. Into the same
lake flows the River of the Assiniboines from a lake of
(presumably) the same name. Later maps denominate
Lake Winnipeg as the Lake of the Assiniboines. Radisson
in his narrative states that the Indians made a map of
the region which the Frenchmen had been unable to see
and gave it to them. With the help of this, the stories of
the Indians, and what the Frenchmen themselves had seen,
the two explorers seem to have gone straight to the heart
of the whole matter: they realized that the great fur center of the North American continent lay west and northwest of Lake Superior, and that the easiest route thereto
was not by the difficult canoe route through the Great
Lakes but on shipboard to Hudson Bay and thence by
canoe up either of two rivers, the modern Hayes and the
Albany, which empty into it. The rest of their actual exploring lives was spent in carrying out this idea. Though
they were also interested in finding the Northwest Passage
via Hudson Bay, that discovery was secondary in their
own minds. To some of their hearers, however, it was
paramount, and the two men knew how to make capital
of their listeners' interest.

In less than a year after Des Groseilliers and Radisson
returned from the West, the Jesuits tried to get to Hudson
Bay, almost certainly with the aim of carrying out the
two explorers' idea that in that direction lay the Northwest Passage. Both desire to be first in exploration and
interest in the fur trade would explain their haste.[20] On
June 1, 1661, Fathers Dablon and Druillettes started from
Tadoussac up the Saguenay to Hudson Bay. They reached

[20] Radisson's remarks are worth quoting on this point: "I have seen right-
minded Jesuites weep bitterly hearing me speake of so many Nations that
perish for want of Instruction. . . . I have seen also some of the same company say, 'Alas, what a pity 't is to loose so many Castors. Is there no way to
goe there?'" Radisson, *Voyages,* p. 240.

a point about half way, Necouba, and then returned.[21] The
following year another expedition was sent out under the
Sieur de Couture.[22] It, too, was unsuccessful in reaching
Hudson Bay. Thereafter the Jesuits gave over their attempts to reach the Bay until they learned that Des Groseilliers had taken an English company there in 1669.
Father Albanel's successful trip overland to the Bay immediately afterward was their answer to this move of their
former employee.[23]

[21] See *Jesuit Relations,* 46:179, 181, and Marie de l'Incarnation, *Lettres,*
2:202–210; also Louis Dablon's affidavit of May 3, 1662, in BN., Margry
Papers, 9284, ff. 2, 3.

[22] See a commission of May 10, 1663, to Pierre Couture in BN., Margry
Papers, 9284, f. 4, "Ordre de M. d'Avaugour au Sieur Couture pour aller au
nord"; and a "prise de possession" of "La Baie du Nord" by Sieur Couture
and Sieur de la Chesnaye, March 1, 1664, in BN., Margry Papers, 9284, f. 4.
This was Jacques de la Chesnaye, or Chenaye. See also Couture's own story
in BN., Margry Papers, 9284, ff. 5–10, as given on November 2, 1688. At that
time Paul Denis, Sieur de Saint Simon, gave his age as forty years and his occupation as "lieutenant de la maréchaussé."

[23] See *post,* 148.

CHAPTER VI

Papists as Puritans

Radisson tells us that the country would have been "undone" had not he and Des Groseilliers brought down the Indians and thousands of pounds of furs and skins from the interior in 1660. This might seem boasting, if we did not have the word of others to the same effect. Mère Marie, for instance, wrote to her son on September 17, 1660:[1]

Moreover, God has sent to the merchants more than 140,000 livres of beavers through the arrival of the Ottawa, whose sixty canoes were weighted with them. This heavenly manna has come just as those gentlemen were about to leave the country, believing that nothing further could be done for its trade.

Nevertheless, despite the fact that the two men were hailed as saviors of the infant colony, they were rather shabbily treated, if we may believe the story that Radisson wrote in the winter of 1668–1669, and a still later account that must have come in the first place from his own or Des Groseilliers' lips.[2] The story runs that the Governor threw Des Groseilliers into jail, fined both men, and confiscated a large part of their profits, presumably because they had gone to the West without the Governor's authority and consent. It would be interesting to learn the details of this affair. Unfortunately, Quebec records are silent on the point or are missing altogether. It was customary for

[1] Marie de l'Incarnation, *Lettres,* 2:173–177.

[2] Sir James Hayes of the Hudson's Bay Company got from Radisson and Des Groseilliers his information for a letter written to Sir Leoline Jenkins on January 26, 1683/4, and now in the PRO., CO., 1/66, document 129, ff. 315, 316. It refers to the two Frenchmen's complaints of hard usage by New France.

a tax of one quarter of the furs of any enterprise to be claimed by the farmer of the Company of New France.[3] Was more than this demanded of the two men? Radisson says yes.

Des Groseilliers and his wife, now as in 1656 after another successful trip to the West, acquired a large piece of land.[4] This he purchased on September 23, 1660, following his return from Lake Superior in August. The property was twelve *toises* in breadth and twenty in length and ran back from Rue Notre Dame, the main street of Three Rivers. For this he paid one hundred and fifty livres of Tours currency. On the land was a dilapidated house. By this time Médard and Marguérite were quite important and well-to-do persons of New France. Médard was still captain of the borough; they owned a good deal of real estate;[5] and they had both men and women servants. What Radisson's status was is less certain. However, he seems to have stopped in Three Rivers for a time after his western trip, since on September 18, 1660, he stood godfather to a little Trifluvien there.[6] Again, in 1661, a notarial document shows him in New France.[7]

By November 27, 1660, Des Groseilliers had left Three Rivers, presumably for France. On that day Marguérite

[3] The receipts for the "droit du quart" of beaver and other furs for 1660 were 55,140 livres, 7 sols, 4 deniers. For 1661 they were 26,930 livres, 16 sols, 3 deniers, besides 5,268 livres, 8 sols for "the eighth" at Tadoussac. *Jugements et délibérations,* 1:103. Thus Radisson and Des Groseilliers must have supplied a large part of the revenue of New France for 1660. The decrease in revenue for 1661 is noteworthy.

[4] See *Papier terrier de la Compagnie des Indes Occidentales, 1667–1668,* pp. 335–338 (*Archives de la province de Québec,* Beauceville, 1931).

[5] In 1668 Marguérite listed four pieces of real estate owned by herself and her husband: one of 30 square arpents adjoining the Godefroy lands, one of 40 square arpents on the so-called Fathers [*Jesuits*] Hill, one of 240 square *toises* on the other side of Rue Notre Dame, and one of 20 square *toises* at the foot of the hill by the fort. See Public Archives of Canada, transcripts, Actes de Foi et Hommage, Vol. 1, Part 1, pp. 91–96.

[6] Three Rivers, parish registers.

[7] Gagnon, *Essai de bibliographie canadienne,* 2:333. This is a receipt, dated October 28, 1661.

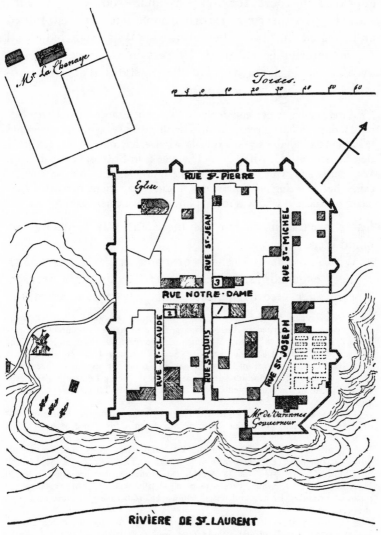

1. Marguérite Hayet des Groseilliers.
2. Claude Volant, Sieur de Saint-Claude.
3. Claude Jutras, Sieur de la Vallée.

appeared in court for her husband, who was "absent"
according to the court record.[8] Sometime between July 9
and August 29, 1661, he returned.[9] What had happened
in the interim is set forth by certain court records and
by Radisson's narrative. The latter states that Des Groseilliers

> . . . did resolve to goe and demand Justice in France. It had been bet-
> ter for him to have been contented with his losses without going and
> spend ye rest in halfe a year's time in France, having £10,000 [*livres?*]
> that he left with his wife. . . . There he is in France; he is paid with
> fair words and with promise to make him goe back from whence he
> came; but he seeing no assurance of it, did engage himselfe with a mer-
> chant of Rochell, who was to send him a Ship the next spring.

Later events show that his merchant was probably Arnauld Péré.[10]

While he was in France (probably in Paris), Des Groseilliers engaged Jeanne Godin, or Gaudin, as a servant.
The meager records indicate that she was an indentured

[8] Three Rivers, prévôté records (Q), November 27, 1660. Chouart, however, may have returned to Three Rivers, for a notarized document of October 10, 1661, ratifies a private arrangement between Chouart and the Sieur
de St. Pierre, dated December 22, 1660. Such a private document could have
been drawn up, however, on the high seas, in France, or elsewhere. See a sale
of land by Sieur and Madame des Groseilliers to Pierre Le Boulanger, Sieur
de St. Pierre, in Séverin Ameau's *greffe*, Court-House, Three Rivers, October
10, 1661.

[9] On the earlier date Marguérite Hayet "femme de Medard Chouar S^r
desgrosillers absen," sued the Sieur de St. Quentin for a pig of hers killed
in the grass near the water's edge, "where it was doing no harm." Three
Rivers, prévôté records (Q). On the later date Des Groseilliers made his
wife his attorney. See in the *greffe* of L. Laurant, Three Rivers, a sale of land
by Claude Herlin, Sieur de la Meslee, to Madame des Groseilliers, dated
November 5, 1662, which refers to a written power of attorney from her
husband produced by her and dated August 29, 1661. See also Note 14 of this
chapter.

[10] See *Jugements et délibérations*, 1:247, 248, 283; and the suit of Marguérite
Hayet *versus* Jean Bousquet and Jacques Joviel, February 14, 1665, in Three
Rivers, prévôté records (Q). In a document of July 2, 1663, in the same
prévôté records is a reference by Marguérite Hayet to the court concerning a
"composition between Arnauld Péré and herself dated 'April 27 last.'" Chouart is referred to in the document as still absent. The document of April 27,
found on page 24 of the same volume, is itself undated.

servant. He advanced money for her clothing and paid
her way from Paris to La Rochelle and from France to
Canada, as well as for a sojourn in La Rochelle and for
other expenses. When the young woman reached Canada,
however, she broke her engagement with the Des Groseilliers, and Médard sued her in the local court.[11] Godin
asserted in self-defense that she was willing to pay 102
livres for her passage and the advancement money, but
that, far from owing Chouart anything for the rest, he
owed her for her wages, especially for the long wait at
La Rochelle, when she could not embark because Des
Groseilliers' niece, also of the party, had not yet been
delivered of the child that was expected. All this took up
two months' time. The court gave a verdict for Des Groseilliers on October 1, 1661, and condemned Jeanne Godin
to pay one hundred and two livres for her passage money
and the advancement money, and, in addition, thirteen livres
as interest on the fifty-two livres of advancement money,
the rate, "à la grosse aventure," being that commonly
charged by merchants.

Again, on February 18, 1662, Des Groseilliers appeared
in court, this time against Jacques Besnard, claiming a
suit of clothes which Des Groseilliers had lent him in Paris
the preceding year, when both men were there, and which
Besnard was still wearing.[12]

[11] See two documents covering Des Groseilliers' suit against Jeanne Godin,
or Gaudin, in Three Rivers, prévôté records (Q) under dates of September
23 and October 1, 1661. An article signed "Berneval" and entitled, "Les filles
venues au Canada de 1658 à 1661," in *Le bulletin des recherches historiques,*
47:96–119 (April, 1941), mentions Jeanne Godin, daughter of the deceased
Laurent Godin of Aunay in Normandy and Marie Haude, his wife, and states
that her marriage contract of October 10, 1661, was annulled on November
19, and that she eventually married Pierre Larue.

[12] Three Rivers, prévôté records (Q). A Jacques Besnard is mentioned
by Tanguay as having married Catherine ——— and having a daughter,
Marguérite, who was baptized at Three Rivers on August 9, 1658. Tanguay,
Dictionnaire généalogique, 1:49. In the prévôté records a Jacques Besnard
is recorded as having been captured by the Iroquois in 1659. See those records
(Q) under date of March 18, 1662.

During Des Groseilliers' absence a fourth child was born
of his union with Marguérite. Little Marie-Antoinette was
baptized on June 7, 1661, by Father Claude Jean Allouez,
soon to be famous as an explorer of the Lake Superior
country and the first white man to mention the Mississippi
River, as far as extant records prove.[13]

The court records of the winter of 1661–1662 reveal
certain facts about the Chouart family. Des Groseilliers
had at least one man servant; owned oxen; lent or sold
food to neighbors; secured Indian corn—presumably for
his anticipated trip to the West—by making arrangements
to take Jean Le Moine's man, Réné Ouré, to the Indian
country with him; and was reported en route down the
St. Lawrence River with ten men, bound for the "North
sea."[14]

[13] Three Rivers, parish registers, baptism of Marie-Antoinette Chouart.

[14] One Antoine Daunay was a servant in the household, probably an indentured one, for a court case mentions the fact that he was obliged to get
his master's consent to a certain course of action that he wanted to follow.
See the suit of Guillaume Pépin *versus* Anthoine Daunay for payment for a
wound suffered from the shooting of a pistol believed to be unloaded, in the
prévôté records of Three Rivers (Q), under date of February 4, 1662. Tanguay
records an Antoine Daunet, who was baptized in 1641, married Marie Richard,
and was the father of eight children, all born at Boucherville. *Dictionnaire
généalogique,* 1:159. On February 11, 1662, Chouart was in court against
Martin Foisin, who had injured one of Des Groseilliers' oxen while cutting
down a tree. Three Rivers, prévôté records (Q). On the eighteenth of the
same month Des Groseilliers prosecuted Guillaume Pépin, for ten pounds of
lard lent by Madame des Groseilliers to Madame Pépin, who swore that in
return she gave her neighbor eggs, milk, and "other articles." Three Rivers,
prévôté records (Q). On March 20 an agreement was made between Des
Groseilliers and Jean Le Moine before Claude Herlin, the notary at Cap de
la Madeleine near Three Rivers, whereby Des Groseilliers was to get sixty-
six livres' worth of Indian corn for making a trip to the Ottawa Indians and
taking Le Moine's man, Réné Ouré, with him. See the record of the suit of
Jean Le Moyne against Marguérite Hayet for wheat and for twenty livres'
worth of beaver delivered to Des Groseilliers according to an agreement of
March 20, 1662, in the prévôté records of Three Rivers (Q), under date
of August 5, 1662. René Houré (Ouré, Auré, Houray, etc.) was born in 1630
and buried in Champlain, June 12, 1706. He married Denise Damané and
their nine children were born at Champlain. Tanguay, *Dictionnaire généalogique,* 1:309. The census of 1666 lists Houré and his wife as living in Three
Rivers, aged 36 and 25 years, respectively. Census of 1666 (1936 ed.), p. 148.
Jean Le Moine, or Le Moyne, was borne in 1634 near Rouen and married
Madeleine de Chavigny at Quebec on July 24, 1662. He was living in Three

It would appear that Des Groseilliers left Three Rivers in the spring of 1662 stating that he intended to go to Hudson Bay. He did not go, and the explanation, such as it is, of his reason for not carrying out his original

Rivers with his wife, two children, and two servants when the census of 1666 was taken. Tanguay, *Dictionnaire généalogique,* 1:379; and the census of 1666 (1936 ed.), p. 142.

Thirty livres' worth of goods were known to have been paid over to Des Groseilliers at the time of his agreement with Jean Le Moine. On August 5, 1662, Le Moine sued Marguérite for the entire sum. She asked the court for time, saying that by the end of October her husband might be back or that she would have news of him. The court gave her a month of grace for the payment of the thirty livres, and "considering the fact that the time in which a voyage to the Ottawa can be made is not yet expired," placed the burden of proof concerning the rest of the contract on the Sieur Le Moine, pending Des Groseilliers' return.

By April 27, 1663, Marguérite had given up hope of her husband's return. On that date she appeared before the magistrates of Three Rivers and made a request, "saying that her husband had undertaken an extremely dangerous voyage upon the Bay of the North from which it is to be feared that he will not return." Three Rivers, prévôté records (Q), Vol. 1, p. 24. Before looking into the details of her request, it will be well to look at certain preparations for this journey that were made and for which records are preserved.

Des Groseilliers was in Three Rivers at least as late as the end of April, 1662. On April 16 and 22 he was in court, where he is described as "capitaine du bourg des Trois rivières." On April 16 the case of Des Groseilliers' servant, Antoine Daunay, was taken up again. See the *greffe* of Ameau, Court-House, Three Rivers. Des Groseilliers is mentioned in this document as "Sieur desgroseiller capitaine du bourg des Trois rivieres." On April 22 three cases were before the court concerning Des Groseilliers, two of which were for "35 livres de pois livrés a ses gens." See the prévôté records of Three Rivers (Q). Des Groseilliers' plans for his trip were well advanced at that time, apparently, for he had been buying peas for his men for the journey. Chouart claimed to have paid Eustache Lambert of Quebec for the material, but the Pépin already mentioned wrote a letter in which he said that he had had a letter from Lambert denying this statement. It may be added that dried peas constituted for generations the staple food of voyageurs on their long canoe trips. They were cooked in salted water, with grease, till a sort of porridge resulted.

Apparently Des Groseilliers left Three Rivers in a birch-bark canoe, for on May 29, 1662, Jean Seipin [?] was in court suing Marguérite for a "canot descorce," which Des Groseilliers had borrowed and taken away with him. Three Rivers, prévôté records (Q). Marguérite offered Seipin the use of her wooden canoe until she could get him another bark one or the value of such another. According to the journalist of the Jesuits for 1662–1663, Hierosme Lallement, Des Groseilliers' canoemen numbered ten. The priest wrote: "I left Quebek on the 3rd [*of May, 1662*] for 3 rivers. On the way I met des Grosillers, who was going to the North sea. He passed Quebek during the night, with 10 men; and when he reached Cap Tourmente he wrote about it to

plan is to be found in Radisson's narrative. Radisson writes, after the passage already quoted, which explains how Des Groseilliers made an agreement with a merchant of La Rochelle for a ship:

In that hope he comes away in a fisher boat to yᵉ pierced Island, some 20 leagues off from yᵉ Isle d'eluticosty [*Anticosti*], the place where the ship was to come; that was to come whilst he was going in a shallop to Quebucq, where I was to goe away with him to yᵉ rendezvouz, being he could not do anything without me; but with a great deel of difficulty it proved, so that I thought it possible to goe tast of yᵉ pleasures of France, and by a small vessell that I might not be idle during his absence. He presently told me what he had done, and what wee should doe. Wee embarked, being nine of us. In a few days wee came to yᵉ pierced Island, where wee found severall shipps newly arrived; & in one of them wee found a father Jesuit that told us that wee should not find what wee thought to find, and that he had put a good order, and that it was not well done to distroy in that manner a Country, and to wrong so many Inhabitants. He advised me to leave my Brother, telling me that his designs were pernicious. Wee see ourselves frustrated of our hopes. My Brother told me that wee had store of merchandize that would bring much profit to yᵉ french habitations that are in yᵉ Cadis [*Acadia*]. I, who was desirous of nothing but new things made no scruple.

Radisson's translator has done such a poor job of this bit of the narrative that it is hard to determine exactly what the author intended to convey. The gist of his re-

monsieur the Governor." *Jesuit Relations*, 47:279. It was characteristic of Des Groseilliers to let the Governor know his plans after it was too late for the latter to make any protest or take any action.

Before Des Groseilliers left Three Rivers he made Marguérite his attorney, feeling, no doubt, that he was undertaking a risky business. On May 15, 1662, she gave the forge, tools, and other things as surety for five hundred livres loaned by Father Claude Allouez, superior of the residence of the Jesuits at Three Rivers, to Des Groseilliers for the "pensions" of their children at the Jesuit school in Quebec, "as well as for other things to them delivered." Marguérite promised repayment in two months. The act of attorney was dated August 29, 1661, according to a receipt given by Marguérite Hayet to Father Claude Allouez on May 15, 1662, and now in the Schmidt Collection, Vol. 1, p. 33, in the Chicago Historical Society; and also according to a document already cited in Note 9 of this chapter, concerning a sale of land by Claude Herlin.

marks seems to be, however, that Radisson went to France
for a time, bought a small vessel, and returned to Quebec,
where Des Groseilliers was to pick him up, go to Percée
Rock to meet the Rochelle ship there, and proceed to
Hudson Bay to the appointed rendezvous with the western
Indians.[15] At all events, Des Groseilliers' plans went awry,
for at Percée Rock he and his company found in one of
the ships newly arrived from France a Jesuit, who tried
to prevent the explorers from carrying out their plan. This
Jesuit may have been Fr. André Richard, who had known
Des Groseilliers some ten years earlier in Acadia. Richard
was on Percée Rock in 1662. Again, it may have been
Father Henri Nouvel, who arrived in Canada on one of
the first ships from France in 1662.[16]

What that plan of Des Groseilliers' was, which this
Jesuit called pernicious, is doubtless explained by the letter
of another Jesuit, Paul Ragueneau. He wrote late in 1664
that Des Groseilliers was in New England, where he was
inciting the English to make an outpost among the Iroquois
at Onondaga, in order to anticipate the French in the
trade and conquest of the West.[17] It would seem likely,
therefore, that Des Groseilliers, like many another Canadian who found the fur trade and exploration hampered

[15] It has been conjectured by some persons that Radisson's allusion to the
fools of Paris, who saw "enter their King and ye Infanta of Spaine, his
spouse" (p. 198) means that he was in France and himself saw the royal
entry. Louis XIV was married to the Infanta, Marie Therese, in June 1660,
and the pair made their triumphal entry into Paris on August 26. Therefore
Radisson could not have seen the event with his own eyes, but he may well
have heard the Paris populace still buzzing over the pageantry of that splendid
spectacle when he arrived there a little later. Radisson was with Des Groseilliers at Montreal on August 21, 1660, and at Three Rivers on August 24, 1660,
as already mentioned; he was in Quebec on September 18, 1660; and he was
apparently somewhere in New France on October 28, 1661, for on that date
Des Groseilliers gave him a "reconnaissance." See Gagnon, *Essai de bibliographie canadienne,* 2:333; and Three Rivers, parish registers, under date of
September 18, 1660.

[16] *Jesuit Relations,* 47:221, 285.

[17] See *post,* p. 92.

by the graft and favoritism in New France, was planning henceforth to deal with the residents of the Hudson Valley. He knew from his own and Radisson's experiences that he could market his western furs through the Iroquois, either to the Dutch or to the English.

It is likely that Péré brought out in his ship the merchandise that Madame des Groseilliers mentions in her request to the court already mentioned. At any rate, Péré soon sued her for payment for clothing and other articles and deprived her of many of her possessions in order to get satisfaction. Péré's ship arrived at Quebec on June 16, 1662.[18] On April 27, 1663, Marguérite asked the court to save her and her children from ruin by allowing her to renounce her dowry rights and have an inventory made of all the property owned jointly by herself and husband, so that it might be sold and the debts paid. She mentioned particularly a debt to "Sᴿ Peré," merchant, of almost two thousand livres.[19]

That Marguérite believed fully that her husband's intent was to go to the Ottawa Indians by way of Hudson Bay is revealed by this episode. The abandoned wife states in her petition "that her husband has undertaken a very dangerous voyage on the Bay of the North and that it is greatly to be feared that he will not return. Yet he has created several debts by his poor management and bad conduct, with which she is just now being disturbed." She also asked to be made the guardian of the children. The court ordered a permission to her to renounce her right in the joint holdings of herself and her husband as provided by French custom; an inventory, under careful legal supervision, of all the Chouart possessions, with ultimate provision for a sale; and a gathering of all the Chouarts' relatives to learn their feeling with regard to having Marguérite made the legal guardian of her children. Such

[18] *Jesuit Relations,* 47:285.
[19] Three Rivers, prévôté records (Q), 1:24.

a family assembly was customary in New France when a husband or wife died.

The brothers did not go back to Quebec as they would doubtless have done if the Jesuit had really changed their plans. Instead they went to visit a famous man, Nicolas Denys, or Denis. A decade later their host was to publish one of the earliest works on New France, *Description géographique et historique des costes de l'Amérique Septentrionale.* Denys had come out to Acadia in 1632 with De Razilly. Troublous times followed, with De la Tour and Charnisay fighting for control of the region. In 1650 Charnisay died and Denys established himself at Saint Peters in Cape Breton, an admirable station for the Indian trade and the fisheries. There, in the winter of 1653–1654, Denys bought from the Company of New France all the great territory comprising the coasts and islands of the Gulf of St. Lawrence from Canso to Gaspé, and was made governor and lieutenant-general thereof by the King. The English conquered the region during the Cromwellian wars with France, but left Denys undisturbed, perhaps because of his friendship with De la Tour. Denys resided at Saint Peters till 1669, when he moved to Nepisguit. He, like so many others with whom Radisson and Des Groseilliers had contact, was a native of Tours.

"We arrived at St Peter, in ye Isle of Cape Breton," writes Radisson, "at ye habitation of Monsr Denier [*sic*], where wee delivered some merchandizes for some Originack [*moose*] skins; from thence to Camseau, where every day wee were threatned to be burned by the french; but God be thanked, wee escaped from their hands by avoiding a surprize." Guerilla warfare was the order of the day, and though Radisson's reference here is obscure, it fits the facts about the uneasy days of the sixties in Acadia and its environs. Denys himself describes an attempted sack by De la Giraudière, who [20]

[20] Denys, *Description and Natural History,* p. 103.

. . . brought out a hundred men to the country, who arrived at Camp-
seaux, where they knew that my ship must arrive, as it did soon after.
. . . [Strategy] to enclose and fortify all my dwellings with two little
bastions, which, furnished with eight pieces of cannon and some swivel-
guns, with an enclosure of barrels filled with earth, put me in a state of
defence. . . . Some time afterwards La Giraudière and his brother
with all their man . . . came with the intention of forcing me to give
up. . . . They contented themselves with remaining three days in
sight of the fort without doing anything more than to move about from
place to place, after which they went back.

It is known that this event described by Denys occurred
in the 1660's, but heretofore no exact date has been assigned it. Possibly Radisson's narrative proves that it
occurred in 1662.

At Canso, Denys was just erecting a new and important
station, Chedabouctou, now known as Guysborough. This
was a great rendezvous of the fleets to and from France.
Apparently, till this time, Radisson thought that Des Groseilliers was planning to go to France, but here

. . . my Brother told me of his designe to come and see new England,
which our servants heard, and grumbled and laboured underhand
against us, for which our lives were in very great danger. Wee sent
some of them away, and at last with much labour & danger wee came to
Port Royall, which is inhabited by ye french under ye English Government, where some few dayes after came some English shipps that
brought about our designes, where [in New England] being come wee
did declare our designes.

Thus, via Denys' hospitable forts at Saint Peters and
Canso, and probably via De la Tour's fort at Saint John,
across the bay from Port Royal, the two exiles reached
New England. If, as seems likely, Des Groseilliers renewed
his earlier acquaintance with De la Tour while stopping
at Port Royal, his visit may well have had two profound
results: De la Tour would have an opportunity to give
him details of his own experiences in Hudson Bay; and
De la Tour would probably give Des Groseilliers letters
of introduction to his friends and financial supporters in

New England. Was one of them that Captain Shapleigh, or Shapley, whose ship had been reported in Hudson Bay in 1640 by a Spanish naval officer? [21] The Shapleigh family of York and Kittery in Maine and of Charlestown in Massachusetts was an important one in colonial New England. Major General Edward Gibbons of Boston, the owner of Shapleigh's vessel (according to the Spanish account) was the man with whose money De la Tour had saved his property at Port Royal.

At all events Radisson and Des Groseilliers now spent nearly three years in New England, probably in Boston. Merchants of that place put reliance in the newcomers' tales of furs in the far interior and of a route to the Western Sea. They fitted out a vessel, which actually got into the straits leading into Hudson Bay. Radisson, in the *Voyages*, gives a version of the story, which is also substantiated by Sir James Hayes.[22] Radisson says:

Wee were entertained, and wee had a ship promised us, and ye Articles drawn, and wee did put to sea the next spring for our discovery, and wee went to ye entry of Hudson's streight by ye 61 degree. Wee had knowledge and conversation with ye people of those parts, but wee did see and know that there was nothing to be done unlesse wee went further, and the season of the yeare was far spent by ye indiscretion of our master, that onely were accustomed to see some Barbadoes Sugers, and not mountaines of sugar candy [*that is, icebergs*], which did frighten him, y^t he would goe no further, complaining that he was furnished but for 4 months, & that he had neither Sailes, nor Cord, nor Pitch, nor Towe, to stay out a winter. Seeing well that it was too late, he would goe no further, so brought us back to ye place from whence wee came, where wee were welcome, although with great losse of goods & hope.

[21] See *post*, p. 283 for references to Shapleigh and Gibbons.

[22] Sir James Hayes, writing in 1684 as the ex-secretary of Prince Rupert says: "Des Groziliers and Radison . . . with draw themselves to New England and offered there their Service for the discovery of the greate Beaver trade of Canada, and were on y^t Account entertained by Some Merchants of Boston who Sett out a Ship under their direction & Conduct for Hudsons Bay, but when they had proceded as far as the mouth of Hudsons Streights they were discouraged to proceed on their voyage & so returned rē infectā." Sir James Hayes to Sir Leoline Jenkins, January 26, 1683/4, PRO., CO., 1/66, document 129, ff. 315, 316.

Radisson continues his story with an account of the promise of two ships for a second voyage. While the merchants were awaiting the proper season for a start to Hudson Bay, they filled their time by sending one of the vessels to Sable Island, which, much worn away by the elements since Radisson's time, is still well known to mariners of the North Atlantic. It was famed for its wrecks, its wild cattle, and its walrus, seal, and other fisheries. Sir Humphrey Gilbert's ship is thought to have been wrecked on the island. Even today it is one of the most dangerous spots known to mariners the world over. Here the vessel was lost, though its crew was saved. The merchants waited too long for the return of this vessel and the Hudson Bay voyage could not be made that year—probably the year 1664. Radisson continues:

They went to law with us to make us recant the bargaine that we had made with them. After wee had disputed a long time it was found that the right was on our side, and wee innocent of what they did accuse us. So they endeavoured to come to an agreement, but wee were betrayed by our own Party. In ye meantime ye Commissioners of the King of Great Brittain arrived in that place.

The King's commissioners who arrived in Boston on July 23, 1664, were Colonel Richard Nicolls and George Cartwright, Esquire, of the four men sent by the King to see that Manhattan should be captured from the Dutch and to get information on the New England colonies, the charter of Massachusetts, and the disputes then rife in New England. The other two commissioners were Sir Robert Carr and Samuel Maverick.[23]

Radisson goes on:

In ye meantime ye Commissioners of the King of Great Brittain arrived in that place, and one of them [*Nicolls*] would have us goe with

[23] A vast amount of information regarding the King's commissioners may be found in *Records of the Governor and Company of the Massachusetts Bay in New England,* edited by Nathaniel B. Shurtleff, particularly in Vol. 4 (Boston, 1854).

him to New Yorke, and ye other advised us to come to England and offer our selves to ye King, which wee did. Those of New England in generall made profers unto us of what ship wee would if wee would goe on in our Designes; but wee answered them that a scalded cat fears ye water though it be cold.

Radisson's remarks add a little to a chapter in New England history that remains to be written, that is, New England interest in the beaver trade of the continent and expeditions that were made in the early and middle portions of the seventeenth century to find the "beaver lakes," to the west, which Indians reported in glowing terms. Captain Walter Neal of New Hampshire was one of the leaders of this movement in the thirties, much of whose time went to exploring and surveying. Another leader was that Captain Young who is reported to have taken three men with him about 1640 and to have gone on a quest for the "great beaver lake." He went up the Kennebec River, thinking it might be the route to that lake and the South Sea. Over the height of land he portaged and emerged finally in the St. Lawrence. There he was captured by the French and sent to France. The Jesuits report the story in their *relation* of 1640 and their remarks show that their captive, whose name they nowhere mention, was none other than Sir Thomas Yonge, or Young. Among other stories he told the Jesuits of his previous explorations up the Atlantic Coast and of his hope to reach the "sea of the North" via the Saguenay River. It is significant that De la Tour, Des Groseilliers, and others to be mentioned in this book looked to New England for encouragement and financial assistance in their schemes for the beaver trade and the discovery of the Northwest Passage. New England scholars have not done full justice to their own history in letting this absorbing chapter go unwritten.[24]

[24] *Jesuit Relations*, 18:235. For Neal and Young see Samuel A. Drake, *The Making of New England, 1580–1643*, pp. 133, 137, 223, and 224 (Boston, 1886); and for Young see Edward D. Neill, *English Colonization of America*, pp. 261–263 (London, 1870); *Calendar of State Papers, Domestic Series, 1635–1636*, p.

Another account of Radisson and Des Groseilliers' sojourn in New England was given at a later time by Radisson.[25]

> On or about the yeare one thousand six hundred sixty and two your
> Orator and his Brother . . . intending to goe into France to give the
> French King an Accompt of their discoverys there did goe into New
> England in their Way to France and there discoursing with Colonell
> Nicoll (who was then Governour of New Yorke) and severall other
> Englishmen of great Esteeme there your Orator and his said Brother
> made knowne to them their design of goeing to the French King and
> to Informe him of the great discoverys they had made in the said parts
> of the West Indies and of the Easinesse of setling Factorys there . . .
> whereupon the said Collenell Nicolls and the other persons there
> (haveing some wild Notion before of that part of the World) hearing
> your Orator talke soe distinctly and give such particular Accompts of
> the places persons languages and Commoditys thereof did at length
> prevaile on your Orator and his said Brother to quitt their designe of
> goeing into France and instead thereof to come for England.

It is odd that two Frenchmen of such character as Radisson and Des Groseilliers could have spent some three years
in Boston and leave no trace in her records. Diligent search,
however, has revealed no reference to them. Perhaps they
assumed other names; perhaps they lived elsewhere than
in Boston. Even the lawsuit that Radisson describes cannot
be determined, for there seems to be no reference to it in
the voluminous records of the period.[26] The sole report

446; Maryland Historical Society Fund *Publications,* 9:315; and Raphael
Semmes, *Captains and Mariners of Early Maryland,* p. 139 (Johns Hopkins
Press, 1937), where Young is referred to as "a life-long friend of the Calverts."
Young was related to John Evelyn, the diarist. Robert Evelyn accompanied
Young, his uncle, to America in 1634; and other members of the family also
migrated about that time to America. See the *Evelyns in America,* edited by
Gideon D. Scull (Oxford, 1881).

[25] This is a part of Radisson's petition to Sir John Somers, Lord Keeper
of the Great Seal of England, dated May 22, 1694, PRO., C6/303. It is
printed in the *Beaver,* the organ of the Hudson's Bay Company, for December,
1935, p. 42. See also *post,* p. 263.

[26] In 1664 the vessel, *The James and John,* owned by Edward Tyng, John
Saffin, and other merchants of Boston was "bound for ye Isle of Sables," "Richard Hickes Master," according to manuscript court records in Boston. A lawsuit developed which is reported in *Records of the Court of Assistants of the
Massachusetts Bay, 1630–1692,* 3:168, 169 (Boston, 1928). It is possible that

in English comes from a rare book, John Josselyn's *New Englands Rarities,* published in 1672 and written by a man long resident in New England. He writes: "The discovery of the Northwest passage (which lies within the River of *Canada*) was undertaken with the help of some Protestant *Frenchmen,* which left *Canada* and retired to *Boston* about the year 1669." [27] This must refer to Radisson and Des Groseilliers. If so, it indicates that the two men passed themselves off for Protestants while among the Puritans.

Two contemporary French accounts have been found. Father Paul Ragueneau wrote at Paris on November 7, 1664, in a letter to Colbert already quoted in part: [28]

I have received a letter from Mr. Destrades from The Hague written on October 27 stating that the English with an army of ten thousand men have taken all of New Holland together with the fort and the city called New Amsterdam. They have driven out the inhabitants, granting permission to them to take away their property within the space of three months—a thing that cannot be done. Mr. Destrades adds that if the King could make arrangements with the English to carry on war against the Iroquois, those savages would soon be totally destroyed. He advises me to take up the matter with you, stating that he has always noticed that you have a deep interest in that country and in the advancement of the Catholic Relgion. But, hope as I may for the destruction of the Iroquois by means of the English, yet I fear that the latter will be of no more help than the Dutch. For the English will have the same reason for preserving the Iroquois, that is, the great quantity of skins that they will secure from those Indians. It is even to be feared that the English will anticipate us and make an outpost at Onondaigua in the heart of the Iroquois peoples, in order to make themselves master of all New France, at least of the best parts of it, and of all the upper

this is the ship to which Radisson refers. The author has searched diligently, but with no success, the manuscript court archives of Massachusetts in Boston.

[27] This reference was found for the author by Fulmer Mood, then a research fellow in the Henry E. Huntington Library, San Marino, California, where the author subsequently read the passage in one of the few copies of this volume that have survived.

[28] This letter is to be found in BN., Mélanges de Colbert, document 125, f. 181. Count Godefroy D'Estrades (1607–1686) was a French diplomat and Marshal of France, who had just negotiated the restitution of Dunkirk by the English (1662), was ambassador at the moment in Holland, and held the title of Viceroy of America.

tribes. A man named Des Groselers, a fugitive from Quebec, who has left his wife and children there, and who is now with the English in New England, had the plan to push them to that undertaking. He is a man capable of anything, bold, hardy, stubborn in what he undertakes, who knows the country and who has been everywhere, to the Hurons, to the Ottawa, and who has testified of his animosity towards the French. I have believed it necessary to inform you of this, for you will see more clearly than I what ought to be done in this matter.

Thus early and with rare penetration the Jesuits perceived the economic and political significance of Des Groseilliers. He had the key to the future development of the North American continent; and he was giving it to the English. No wonder that such Titans in their respective spheres as Ragueneau, D'Estrades (of whom more will be heard shortly in Des Groseilliers' career), and Colbert, began to correspond about him. How would the English respond to Des Groseilliers' offer? Thereby would New France and consequently Old France win or lose. Ragueneau was fearful that they would accept, since it already appeared that they had acted on Des Groseilliers' advice to get control of the Iroquois by capturing New Holland.

Another of the French believed that the capture of New Holland was due in part to this man. Though Mère Marie mentions no name in her letter of July 28, 1665, to her son, she undoubtedly was referring to Des Groseilliers when she wrote: [29]

This conquest [*of New Holland*] was made by men from New England, who have become so strong that they are said to number forty thousand. They recognize the king of England as their ruler, but they do not like to pay taxes to him. A *habitant* of this country, but one who was not regarded well here because of his rebellious nature and bad disposition, withdrew himself to the English some two years ago, and, according to report, gave them information about many things in the Iroquois country and of the great profit they could derive from its fur trade, if they were in control of it. It is believed that this is the reason for their attack on New Holland.

[29] Marie de l'Incarnation, *Lettres,* 2:293.

Thus did Radisson's experience in the Iroquois country serve his brother-in-law.

It may be added here that Mère Marie seems to have kept in close touch with Des Groseilliers as long as she lived. She writes on August 27, 1670, of their acquaintance, as already quoted; so it is certain that these two persons knew each other. On August 20, 1663, she wrote to her son of events and conditions in Acadia and Port Royal, of the Sieur Denys, and of an attempt to reach Hudson Bay.[30] Presumably she had just had a letter from Des Groseilliers or had talked with persons who had had such a letter, for the news was recent. Where better could she have got such information than from Des Groseilliers himself, who, as we have seen, had just been to Acadia, Port Royal, and the home of Sieur Denys, and who was then en route to or had just made a sea voyage to Hudson Strait? "They have discovered a thing that has been sought for a long time," she writes, *"viz.,* the entrance to the great Sea of the North, about which are many peoples who have never heard a mention of God. . . . It is believed that this sea leads to China and Japan." It is even likely that the letter she wrote linking Des Groseilliers with the conquest of New Holland was based on a letter from him.

One other person refers to Des Groseilliers in New England at this time. This was his long-suffering wife. On July 2, 1668, she gave to the Seigneurs of the Company of the West Indies, the successors of the Company of New France, who were making a reconnaissance of all real estate held of them in New France, the amount and location of her lands and those of her husband. She refers to him as "absent for six years since he started for New England." [31]

[30] Marie de l'Incarnation, *Lettres,* 2: 242, 447, 448.
[31] *Papier terrier,* 335–338.

CHAPTER VII

The Best Present

Radisson's narrative accounts for the years from 1665 to 1669 in a page and a half of printed text. Fortunately other documents are fuller. Radisson disposes of his trip to England and his early weeks there in one sentence: "Wee are now in ye pasage, and he y^t brought us, which was one of the Commissioners called Collonell George Carteret, was taken by ye Holanders, and wee arrived in England in a very bad time for ye Plague and ye warrs." Thus easily does he dispose of a sea voyage, a capture by the enemy, a landing in Spain, a trip from Spain to England, the ghastly effects of the bubonic plague on stricken London in 1665 and 1666, the war with the Dutch that was absorbing England's attention and changing the course of empire throughout the world, the gay court of Charles II at Oxford, and the great fire in London.

Many of the events and personalities that Radisson omits or deals with quite casually are of the utmost importance for the lives of himself and his brother-in-law. It was not George Carteret, but George Cartwright, who took the men to England. Small wonder it is that Radisson became confused between the names of the two men who now led him to a new country and a new life. The names Carteret and Cartwright were pronounced identically in England in 1665.[1] Sir George Carteret received the two men at the

[1] See Fulmer Mood, "The London Background of the Radisson Problem," in *Minnesota History*, 16:391–413 (Dec., 1935). John Evelyn's diary for June 21, 1671, affords a bit of information on Colonel Cartwright. Evelyn writes: "To Council again, when one Colonel Cartwright, a Nottinghamshire man, (formerly in commission with Colonel Nicholls) gave us a considerable relation of that country [*New England*]." William Bray, ed., *Diary and Correspondence of John Evelyn, F.R.S.*, 2:60 (London, 1857).

hands of Colonel George Cartwright, who thus explained his motive in writing to Lord Arlington, chief secretary of state, on December 14, 1665: [2]

> Hearing also some frenchmen discourse in New England of a Passage from the West Sea to the South Sea, and of a great trade of Beaver in that Passage, and afterwards meeting there with sufficient proofe of the truth of what they had said concerning the Beaver trade, conceiving great probability for the truth of the Passage, and knowing what great endeavours have been made for the finding out of a North West Passage, I thought them the best present I could possibly make to his sacred Ma[jes]tie, whereupon I perswaded them to come to England.

On August 1, 1665, the good ship *Charles,* whose master was Benjamin Gillam of Boston, sailed from Nantucket, its last port of call in the New World, on her way to England.[3] She carried the two Frenchmen, Colonel Cartwright, probably other passengers, and a cargo of 547 beaver skins, 96 moose skins, 154 otter skins, 10 fox skins, and some Brazil sugar, the total valued at £540.7.0.[4] A rather large amount of Nevis and Barbados sugar that was also in the cargo has not been reckoned in these figures.

The war between England and the Dutch states was

[2] This letter is printed in *Documentary History of Maine,* 4: 201, 202, 299. An abbreviation of Cartwright's name in the original manuscript is responsible for Scull's error on page 12 of Radisson's *Voyages,* where the letter is quoted and its author's name given as George Carr.

[3] Edmund B. O'Callaghan, *Documents Relative to the Colonial History of the State of New York,* 3: 106–108, and an endorsement not given there but printed in *Cal. St. Pap., Colonial Series, America and West Indies, 1661–1668,* p. 334.

[4] See the case of Phillip French, October 4, 1666, where Samuel Bulstrode's deposition of that date is given, in *Suffolk Deeds,* 5: 69, 70 (Boston, 1890); and *The Winthrop Papers,* Part IV, in *Collections of the Massachusetts Historical Society,* Fifth Series, 8: 104, 129–137 (Boston, 1882) quoting John Winthrop's letter of November 12, 1668; and a letter of October 29, 1666 (p. 104) by Winthrop: "I am out of hope you had any letters frō my selfe last yeare, for I heare since I came to this towne that Mr Gillam ship in wch Col: Cartwright returned being taken by the Duch all letters lost in [the] sea." The author is indebted to Raymond P. Stearns of the University of Illinois for the last reference, which he found originally in the papers of the Royal Society, London. French's deposition lists the goods as shipped "in the moneth of July 1665 . . . from the sayd Boston upon the good shipp called the Charles of sayd Boston whereof Mr Benjamin Gilham was Master . . . bound for London."

waging for the supremacy of the seas. Every English merchantman was good prize for the industrious, energetic
Dutch seamen, who often preferred to keep what booty
they found on a vessel and release the ship itself in Spanish
waters rather than get only their allotted share of prize
money for the transaction in a Dutch court of admiralty. So
it happened in the case of the *Charles*. Captain Gillam had
royal orders to keep with Captain John Pierce's vessel,
Lady, which carried masts and deal boards and therefore
was a slow sailer.[5] Thus delayed at least ten days in his
schedule, Captain Gillam found himself, not unnaturally,
facing a Dutch caper. For two hours the *Charles* defended
herself, but the odds were against her and she finally capit-
ulated.[6] All her papers were thrown overboard.[7] From Cartwright's remarks, it would appear that the crew and passengers were landed in Spain. By December Cartwright,
and probably his two Frenchmen, were in London.

The London in which Radisson and Des Groseilliers now
found themselves was the mediaeval city that perished
within a year in the flames of the Great Fire of September,
1666. It was still a walled town dependent on its great
river, the Thames, for most of its character and prosperity.
In that respect it was not unlike Paris, which both men

[5] See *Documentary History of Maine,* 4:201, 202, Cartwright's letter of
[December 14] 1665; and PRO., S.P., Domestic, Entry Book 29:141, f. 223,
the Navy Board Records for 1665; "Whereas Sr Wm Warren has brought home
amongst his New England masts in ye shipp Lady Jno Peirce commander . . ."
under date of October 14, 1665. See also John Winthrop, Jr., to Henry Oldenburgh, Nov. 12, 1668, *Winthrop Papers,* 8:129, 130. This letter states definitely
that Colonel Cartwright was in "Capt. Gillams ship" which "was taken in
the tyme of the warre." A letter of August 18, 1668, by Winthrop may possibly
indicate that he knew of Radisson and Des Groseilliers' plans. He writes:
"the full discovery of something that possibly would have beene of better
worth . . . in these pts of America." See pp. 126 and 127. "Discoveries," he
writes, cannot be made during the Indian wars then raging. Since he was so
conversant with Colonel Nicolls, could it be possible that he, too, was interested in exploration to the West?

[6] "We mett the Dutch Capn [*Caper*], who (after we had defended our
selves two howers) took flight, & landed in Spayn." *Documentary History of
Maine,* 4:201, 202.

[7] See Note 4 in this chapter.

doubtless knew well. In other respects there were wide contrasts between the cosmopolitan French capital and the provincial trading center of England of five or six hundred thousand souls; just as there was a vast difference between the cultured, sophisticated Parisians and the bluff, untutored Londoners. Perhaps nothing emphasizes the difference more readily than the reputation of a certain French abbé, who in this period was considered an astoundingly erudite man because he understood English. To learn the language of such a second or third rate country as England was too much to expect of any but the most scholarly Frenchmen. On the other hand, all Englishmen of any education or social standing spoke French. Radisson in later years always couched his letters to his English employers in French.

It is unlikely that the two Frenchmen stayed long in London after their arrival, for all who could had fled the plague-afflicted metropolis. A few brave souls, like Samuel Pepys —he who preserved Radisson's manuscript reminiscences —and the Duke of Albemarle—who helped finance Des Groseilliers' first trip to Hudson Bay—had stayed on, but the King, court, professional men, and hundreds of others had fled to the country or to towns in the provinces. The noisy rattle of coaches and carts on the cobbles of the narrow streets was not so great as usual that autumn; and the low, one-family, oak-framed houses of lath and plaster with overhanging stories painted and richly carved were not the scene of London's usual bustle and activity, for a large part of their inhabitants were either dead of the plague or in exile from their homes. Even the great noble houses—Somerset, Essex, Worcester, and the like—along the southern side of the Strand and fronting on the river, were largely deserted. Now and again that summer of 1665 a great social event occurred, like the marriage of Sir George Carteret's eldest son to Lady Jemimah, daughter of Lord Sandwich, but even that event was spoiled for some of the participants by glimpsing a ghastly female figure in a passing coach, "in a silk dress and stunk mightily," who was being borne to the pest house. Near Greenwich, by which the ship bearing Radisson and Des Groseilliers from France to London may well have passed on its way up the busy Thames bordered with shipyards, human bodies lay unburied. By September, 1665, Londoners to the number of over six thousand a month were perishing of the plague.[8]

Cartwright and his two protégés proceeded to Oxford, probably by barge up the Thames. That was the usual route between the two cities at the time. On December 30, 1665, the secretary of the Royal Society in London wrote to a fellow member then at Oxford, the celebrated scientist, Robert Boyle:[9]

Surely I need not tell you from hence, what is said here with great joy of ye discovery of a North-west-passage, made by 2 English and one French man, lately represented by ym to his majsty at Oxford, and answered by a royall graunt of a vessell, to sayle into Hudson's bay, and thence into the South-Sea, these men affirming, as I heare, y[t] w[i]th a boat they went out of a Lake in Canada, into a river, w[hi]ch discharged itself North-west into the South-Sea, into w[hi]ch they went, and returned North-East into Hudson's Bay. I hope, if this be truth, I shall receave the favor of y[ou]r confirmation.

At Oxford Sir George Carteret took the explorers in hand, and, it would seem, arranged an audience with the King. Carteret was a loyal councillor, treasurer of the navy (1660–1667), vice-treasurer (1667–1673), and a commissioner of the board of trade (1668–1672) in the course of a busy official life.[10] It may be added that he was also a "one-time pirate and 'the richest man in England.'"[11]

[8] Arthur Bryant, *Samuel Pepys,* 1:257–263 (New York, 1933); and Arthur Bryant, *The England of Charles II,* Chapter 2 (London, 1934).

[9] Printed in Grace Lee Nute, "Radisson and Groseilliers' Contribution to Geography," in *Minnesota History,* 16:418 (Dec., 1935).

[10] Mood, "The London Background of the Radisson Problem," p. 396; and Mood, "Hudson's Bay Company Started as a Syndicate," pp. 52–58, in *The Beaver* (March, 1938). Samuel Pepys's diary and other papers afford a picture of Carteret, the man, rather than the official. See Bryant, *Samuel Peyps,* Vol. 1.

[11] See William E. Dodd, "The Emergence of the First Social Order in the United States," in *American Historical Review,* 40:217–231 (Jan., 1935).

He had an equity in Carolina, of which he was a lord pro-
prietor, as well as in New Jersey. He was financially interested in the African trade. In due time he became a heavy
shareholder in the Hudson's Bay Company. Such a man
would be awake to the trade possibilities both in the beaver
traffic of interior North America and in a veritable Northwest Passage.

Radisson in later years gave a slightly fuller account of
his Oxford experience. He writes: [12]

> Whereupon severall of the Lords of his said Majesties Privy Coun-
> cell did carry your Orator and his said Brother to the said King Charles
> the Second who was pleased to Command your Orator to give him an
> Accompt of the Manners Languages Scituacon and of the severall parts
> of that Country and his said late Majestie was soe well pleased with
> the relacon given him by your Orator thereof . . .

Thus in all probability came into being Radisson's auto-
biography, of which the Oxford manuscript already mentioned is a translation. The translation was preserved in
the papers of that astute and "curious" diarist, Samuel
Pepys. It could not have been completed for many months,
for it refers to events in 1669, but this order from the King
seems to have been the reason for its inception.

A recent biographer of Pepys shows without question
that Pepys made a point of gathering narratives of voyages,
especially of those undertaken in an attempt to find the
Northeast and Northwest passages. "Of such voyages Pepys
delighted to accumulate records, binding them nobly as
they deserved and placing them among his treasured books
and manuscripts." In 1676 he even induced the King to set
out a frigate under Captain John Wood to find a Northwest Passage, and Pepys himself, along with the Duke of
York, Lord Berkeley, Sir Joseph Williamson, Sir John
Bankes, and three others, became the owner of the pink,
Prosperous, and a "joint adventurer" in the enterprise.

[12] Grace Lee Nute, "Two Documents from Radisson's Suit Against the
Company," in *The Beaver,* pp. 41-49 (Dec., 1935).

Though no evidence has been found proving without question that Pepys was acquainted with Radisson and Des Groseilliers, it is highly probable that he met and knew them at this time or a little later. Pepys was so much a man about town and beginning to wield so much influence with king, royal duke, and courtiers, that it would be passing strange if the three men did not become fairly well known to one another.[13]

Other persons whom the two explorers must have met in Oxford were Prince Rupert and Sir Peter Colleton. The former, a Bavarian cousin of the King, had become famous for his exploits in the Civil War and his interest in scientific and artistic research. He was another of the outstanding

[13] Bryant, *Samuel Pepys*, 2:174–175. The author of the present book has made careful comparison between the books of the Hudson's Bay Company for the late 1660's and the 1670's and the volume in the Bodleian Library at Oxford which contains the manuscript of Radisson's *Voyages* (Rawlinson MS 329). The binding, the lines on the backbone, the size, the paper, the watermarks are all so similar that the conclusion of a common origin is inescapable. The Radisson volume, in folio, begins with a fly leaf on which is written: "a la plus grande gloire de Dieu," followed, in another handwriting, by: "M. S. Pepys." One watermark is a cross, below which are the letters IHS. Below that is LM on the first page, a large crown on certain later pages, a lily of France on still others. Another watermark may be described as a crown below which is a fleur de lys, from which is pendant a small triangle marked: "WR"; see a similar watermark in H.B.Co. Archives, A/1/1, f. 2. Pepys, as a member of the Royal Society and as the Clerk of the Acts in the Navy Office, could easily have come into possession of a translation of Radisson's manuscript. Arrangements were made "to procure an order from his Royal Highness to Trinity house, importing, that every Captain and Master of a ship, should take along with them in their Voyages, a Copy of such printed Books, and make observations . . . . wherof they should upon their returne, give one to Trinity-house, and another to the [*Royal*] Society." Royal Society Archives, Journal 3, 1666–1668, under date of November 7, 1666. On March 12, 1680, the president of the Royal Society spoke "againe about the usefullnes of Collecting all the Journalls of Voyages that had been made & had not been yet published, and urged that some care might be taken to make such a Collection. . . . The President Desired Mr Perkins would make that collection wch he undertook to doe." On March 18, "Mr Perkins . . . gave an account that upon enquiry he found, that the greatest number of Journalls of Voyages were in the Navy Office, that there were very few or none either in the East India or Trinity House . . . . he was desired to proceed with his Enquiry." Royal Society Archives, Journal 6:234, 235. William Blathwayt, Sir John Narborough, and Captain Anthony Wood were mentioned as persons likely to have records of voyages.

members of the Royal Society, which, even as the Frenchmen arrived in London, was publishing "Directions for Sea-men, bound for far Voyages." [14] The directions were, in part, as follows:

It being the Design of the *R. Society,* for the better attaining the End of their Institution, to study *Nature* rather than *Books,* and from the Observations, made of the *Phaenomena* and Effects she presents, to compose such a History of Her, as may hereafter serve to build a Solid and Useful Philosophy upon; . . . [*and as*] they formerly appointed . . . Master Rooke . . . to think upon and set down some *Directions for Sea-men* going into the *East* & *West-Indies* . . .

The said seamen were now desired to keep an exact diary, later to be perused by the Royal Society. They were asked to observe declination of the compass, mark longitude and latitude, use dipping needles, note ebbs and flows of tides, make plats and draughts of the prospect of coasts, promontories, islands, and ports, mark bearings and distances, indicate the depth of water and the nature of the bottom of the sea, and, in general, report on what they observed. Later a set of these inquiries was put in the hands of the captain of the vessel on which Des Groseilliers finally reached Hudson Bay.[15]

Prince Rupert's home at this time was Windsor Castle, where his unique laboratory and his library were housed. Much is known of his scientific and artistic achievements. His reading predelictions also bear on the interest he might be expected to take in Radisson and Des Groseilliers. In November, 1677, his library contained, among the 1,195 items that are listed: Blaeu's "New Atlas in Dutch"; many other Dutch maps and books of value to mariners; *Purchas his Pilgrim;* a book on navigation by "Bapt^a Remusio [*sic*], 1663"; "Journall of Ship Levant"; "Journal of Mary & Martha," by Captain John Butler, 1672; invoice of the

---

[14] Royal Society, *Philosophical Transactions,* 1:140–143. The date was January 8, 1665/6.
[15] See *post,* p. 118.

Shaftsbury Pink "for Hudson Bay, 1674"; "Journall for
Hudsons Bay Jo. Thompson 1676"; "Journall ye Speedwell
to find ye N. East Passage 1676 Capt Wood"; many of
Sir Walter Raleigh's works; the history of the Royal Society by Thomas Sprat, 1667; "Voyage a Canada S^r de
Champlain Paris 1632"; and "Journall in Written hand." [16]
A man of such a library must have found the two Frenchmen's conversation highly interesting and their hopes
worthy of encouragement.

Radisson writes of the next step in his career merely this:
"Afterwards ye King came to London sent us to Windsor,
where wee stayed the rest of ye winter." It was January
27, 1666, when Charles II with his court left Oxford for
Hampton Court. He had allowed forty shillings a week for
the maintenance of the two explorers in Oxford and, writes
Radisson, "wee had chambers in ye Town by his order,
where wee stayed 3 months." From Windsor they moved
"up" to London.

A London that appealed so much to Pepys must also have
had charms for the two Frenchmen—a river teeming with
freight, passenger, and pleasure craft; open fields and
rural England within easy reach of all Londoners; a sophisticated and much-traveled king, who spoke French as
easily as English and who was accessible, without much ado,
to most of his subjects; a walled "city" proper which the
explorers may well have seen burn in 1666 and rise again in
succeeding years with the aid of the great Wren; play-
houses from which Pepys's Puritan conscience tried in vain
to keep him; coffee houses by scores that were an integral
part of all Londoners' lives, and one of which saw the turning point in Radisson's life in 1684; music a necessity of
the soul and not an adornment as in modern London; citizens who did not find it effeminate to appear clad in rich

[16] See a manuscript, "Catalouge [sic] of all the Bookes In his Highnesse
Prince Ruperts Library," in the British Museum, Royal MSS, CXIX:23.

colors, fine lace, great velvet capes, befeathered hats atop wigs of prodigious size and no great cleanliness; modern business methods on the eve of dividing England into two great political camps; and a fundamentally democratic country in which a man like Pepys could rise from poverty and obscurity to great wealth, power, and influence.

As spring navigation opened, the Frenchmen were "sent for," to quote Radisson's own account, and "put into ye hands of Sir Peter Colleton," the son of Sir John Colleton. The baronet died shortly "and Peter succeeded to one of the lord proprietorships in Carolina, to which in the year following he added an interest in the Bahamas. The Colletons, a numerous clan from Devonshire, were well connected, and their ample fortunes were broadly based on the sugar loaves of Barbados." [17] It was this man, apparently, who made arrangements for the ship that had been promised at Oxford the preceding autumn. On June 1, however, the Dutch appeared off the North Foreland, and major naval engagements took place on the following days. This was just the period of the year to sail for Hudson Bay. So it is of a disaster of major consequence to him that Radisson writes, "soe wee lost that opportunity. So wee were put off till ye next yeare." In the meantime the vessel, probably Colleton's, was sent to America to get news of the fate of Barbados, but she was captured and taken to Holland.

Disasters were not ended. The next year, 1667, "Wee lost our second voyage, for ye order was given to[o] late for ye fitting another ship, which cost a great deale of money to noe purpose." Something of this ship can be gleaned from the records of the Hudson's Bay Company. On January 4, 1668, in the ledger, under the name of Sir George Carteret and on the Per Contra side for 1667, is recorded: "By Cash paid for the Discovery Ketch (which was bought for the Companyes use & sold by their Order) more than

---

[17] Mood, "The London Background of the Radisson Problem," p. 398.

she produced upon Sale £70.0.0." ¹⁸ Captain William Stannard was in command of this ketch. This was in all probability the vessel to which Radisson has reference.

¹⁸ H.B.Co. Archives, Ledger 101, f. 31.

CHAPTER VIII

The Struggle for the Bay Begins

Meanwhile, what of the two explorers in London? Men of less faith and energy would have been utterly discouraged at the continual failure of their plans. To add to their discomfiture, they were marked for service by spies in the employ of foreign governments. Once Holland and France realized that England was going to follow the two Frenchmen's suggestions, the plans of these two men became of interest to those governments. D'Estrades has been observed in Holland corresponding with the Jesuit, Father Paul Ragueneau. Now this French ambassador's name is mentioned again in connection with Des Groseilliers and his plans.

Late in the year 1666 a man who gave his name as Elie Godefroy Touret (or La Tourette) was arrested and placed in the Gatehouse, a famous prison in Westminster, "for corresponding wth his Maties Enemyes." [1] His examination, which took place on November 17, revealed that, according to his own statement, he was a native of Picardy; that he had been five months in England; that prior to his removal to England he had been at The Hague for three weeks; that for the ten and a half years prior to that pe-

[1] PRO., S.P., Dom., 23/279. This is a warrant for Touret's arrest and is dated November 21, 1666. On November 12, Sir John Colleton wrote to Lord Arlington that "the Frenchman he named to him, lives at the house of one De Marrye, a footman of the Duke of York, who lives in a yard leading from King Street to Westminster Abbey. He came into England with a pass from the States of Holland, as he confessed to Mr. Gresellyer, the person whom he tried to entice into Holland and carry to De Witt." Cal. St. Pap., Dom., 1666–1667, p. 256. Since Touret saw so much of Des Groseilliers at this time, it is likely that the two Frenchmen were living in the same neighborhood near Westminster Abbey.

riod, he had been living with the son of the Rhinegrave; and
that he had gone to England to seek employment as a
valet.[2] Apparently he was questioned closely as to his relations with D'Estrades, De Witt, and others in the Dutch
states, for he denied categorically that he had had any conversation with them or that he had been closeted with
D'Estrades in the latter's office. He admitted that he knew
Des Groseilliers and that he had called him uncle, but only
from good will. He denied attempting to entice Des Groseilliers into the Dutch service or that he had ever quarreled
with Des Groseilliers or had himself ever considered service with the Dutch.

On November 12 Sir John Colleton wrote to Lord Arlington that "Captain Goosberry" would wait upon "your
Lords[hi]p this afternoon—hee is now gone to seek the
other witnesses." [3] One of these was a man named A. de
l'Heurre, who swore: that "M^r de grosilier" had always
suspected Touret, because the latter had called him uncle
and, though a man without means, had been able to live in
England without working; that Des Groseilliers had tried
to avoid Touret; that Touret had said that Des Groseilliers if he were in the Dutch service, would be rated higher
than in London, but that in England his merits were not
recognized; and that if his "discoveries were under the protection of Holland," it would be more advantageous to Des
Groseilliers.[4]

In the meantime Touret, close prisoner in the Gatehouse,
was petitioning Lord Arlington for release, for pen and
ink, for the privilege of having Madame de Marrye "provide him necessaries," and for pity.[5] When flattery, cajolery,

---

[2] PRO., S.P., Dom., 29/178, No. 100, "Examination de soy disant Tourette
&c prise le 17. Nov. 66."

[3] PRO., S.P., Dom., 29/178, No. 147. It is hardly necessary to explain that
"Gooseberry" is an attempted translation of "Groseilliers."

[4] PRO., S.P., Dom., 29/178, No. 99.

[5] PRO., S.P., Dom., 29/181, Nos. 41, 42, and 43.

and abject submission had failed, he tried turning state's
evidence. On December 23, 1666, he wrote, in his very il-
literate French, that he would explain Des Groseilliers and
his deceits to Arlington, namely, that Des Groseilliers had
caused Touret to pass himself off as his nephew till the
latter learned of the explorer's falsity. This came about
through an inquiry to Des Groseilliers' servant, Moreau,
relative to the distance that separated Des Groseilliers'
home in New France from the country to which the explorers were bound. Moreau had replied that it was only
fifty leagues, and that the French always went there to get
furs; that Madame des Groseilliers had told him that her
husband would return to his home when his fortune was
made; that Des Groseilliers was harboring a thieving, dishonest priest at his lodgings, a man who had fled from his
convent at Lyons, having stolen fifty thousand écus from
the Marquis de Chateauneuf, the nephew of Marshal La
Ferté; that the three men—Des Groseilliers, his brother,
and the priest—showed him (Moreau) how they were
coining money, with which they would buy goods for the
fur trade, and, once in the far country of the Indians, Des
Groseilliers would keep well away from the English and
would get furs cheap with his coins; and that the priest had
told him in Des Groseilliers' presence that the Duke de
Bouquicans had offered him two hundred pieces per annum
to have him secure Des Groseilliers for the duke's service
and to tell the latter his secret; that Des Groseilliers tried to
induce Touret to go with him on the expedition, but when
Touret refused and asked to be taken to Colleton, Des
Groseilliers had replied that he saw that Touret wanted
to ruin him and that he would prevent such a catastrophe;
that therefore Des Groseilliers had presented charges
against Touret; that the Frenchmen said that they would
present the gold to the King as though coming from unex-
plored countries; and that these things Touret had learned

from Des Groseilliers' own mouth and "from his book which I have given to Your Lordship." [6]

It would be interesting to know the fate of this spy, but no further record of him has been found. It is at least suggestive that Lawrence Van Heemskerk, a native of The Hague, was shortly commissioned captain of the *Nonsuch* (that is, in 1668) by the Duke of York; that it was the *Nonsuch,* though under another master, on which Des Groseilliers sailed to Hudson Bay in 1669; and that in 1670, when Colbert de Croissy, the French minister in London, proposed to Colbert that Radisson and Des Groseilliers should pass to the service of Louis XIV, Colbert replied that Van Heemskerk had already asked for ships for the same discoveries as those Des Groseilliers and Radisson promised. Three ships were granted the Dutchman. [7]

That D'Estrades was actively interested in finding the Northwest Passage is evidenced by a letter that he wrote to Colbert on February 12, 1665, from The Hague: [8]

Those who have proposed to me a way to the Indies by the Sea of the North have returned from Amsterdam, their partners not wishing to undertake this enterprise, at least until they are furnished with fifty thousand livres for the purchase of a vessel of twenty pieces of cannon, and three *galecottes* of a hundred tons each. I sent them back as deceivers, there being no chance of their obtaining such an advance.

It is likely, in the face of all these hints and bits of evidence, that the plans of the two French explorers had become known through one or more of the following channels: (1) the Dutch mariners, who had captured them; (2) Van Heemskerk's position in the English navy; or (3) direct correspondence between the explorers and the French court or ambassador. D'Estrades, aware as early as 1664 of Des Groseilliers' interest in a Northwest Passage, would be

[6] PRO., S.P., Dom., 29/182, No. 106.

[7] See *post,* p. 125.

[8] BN., Margry Papers, 9284, f. 10. Since this is only a copy by Margry, it is possible that the date has been misread, and that it should be 1666 instead of 1665.

watching the explorer's every move. The third method of obtaining the information is not unlikely in view of Colbert's letter of May 2, 1670, to Colbert de Croissy, which refers to "two Frenchmen who offer to place the King in possession of the countries which they have discovered in Hudson Straits, provided that His Majesty would grant them one of his vessels." [9]

Despite all the foreign interest so suddenly aroused in Radisson and Des Groseilliers' plans, the English court and merchants were successful in retaining the two men in their interest. At last it was possible to make plans for a voyage that prospered. On December 31, 1667, a so-called *gazette-à-main* (a manuscript newsletter or newspaper) was issued in England with this announcement: [10]

There have been for some yeares last past some overtures made by two or three Frenchmen for the discoverey of the so long looked for Northwest passage. . . . These men have much praised those Northerne parts of America and pretend they can shew a passage out of some of those lakes and bayes about Hudsons bay quite to the South Sea. The Prince, the Generall and Severall other persons are entring into the Adventure as associates and The King besides the Commission he gives them for impowering them to undertake the Voyage lends them a small Fregatt into the Bargain and will give them the sole trade of what Countryes they shall discover.

The books of the "adventurers," or, as we should say today, the investors, begin with the late months of 1667. They and other documents show that the following men were financially interested: Prince Rupert, the Duke of Albermarle, the Earl of Craven, James Hayes, Sir Peter Colleton, Sir George Carteret, John Portman, and John

---

[9] P. Clément, *Lettres, instructions, et mémoires de Colbert,* 3:239 (Paris, 1865), quoting Archives de la Marine, Depêches concernant le commerce, 1670, f. 181.

[10] This is to be found in a bound volume of printed and manuscript newsletters classified as No. 160, folio 26, in All Souls College MSS, at All Souls College, Oxford. The author wishes to express her appreciation for the use of this excerpt.

Kirke. These men were already investors in other trading ventures.[11] For example: on December 18, 1660, a charter was granted to the Royal Adventurers into Africa, among whom were Lord Craven and Sir George Carteret; early in 1663 the Royal African Company was reorganized and two more of the above list became shareholders, Prince Rupert and Sir John Colleton; on March 24, 1663, a charter was granted to the lords proprietors of Carolina, who numbered in their membership Craven, Carteret, Colleton, and Albermarle.

James Hayes, soon to be Sir James Hayes, was the secretary of Prince Rupert. John Portman was a famous goldsmith in London. John Kirke, soon to be Sir John Kirke and Radisson's father-in-law, was one son of the large family of Gervais Kirke, a mercer of London long resident in Dieppe, where his eight children were born.[12] With his sons he had been interested in the trade of Canada since the 1620's.[13] Some of these brothers had captured Canada

[11] Mood, "London Background of the Radisson Problem," and "Hudson's Bay Company Started as a Syndicate."

[12] See page 28 in *Letters of Denization and Acts of Naturalization for Aliens in England and Ireland, 1603–1700,* edited by William A. Shaw (Publications of the Huguenot Society of London, Vol. 18, London, 1911), where are listed the eight children of George [*sic*] Kerke: David, Lewis, Thomas, John, James, Peter, Catherine, and Mary. A bill for their naturalization passed both houses of Parliment on May 7, 1621. The father is listed as an "Englishman and citizen and mercer of London." He was the son of Thurston Kirke of Greenhill in Derbyshire, who was the son of Arnold Kirke. On December 1, 1631, a grant of arms was made by Sir Richard St. George to Captain David Kirke, eldest son of Jervas Kirke of London, merchant, which added the arms of the French Admiral De Rockmond, whom David, Lewis, Thomas, John, and James captured, to their paternal coat. See *Cal. St. Pap., Dom., 1631–1633,* p. 195; and *Grantees of Arms Named in Docquets and Patents to the End of the Seventeenth Century,* edited by W. Harry Rylands, p. 145 (Publications of the Harleian Society, 66, London, 1915).

[13] Gervais Kirke was listed in 1612 as one of the Company of Merchants of London, Discoverers of the Northwest Passage. This company had promoted Sir Thomas Button's trip of 1612–1613 and Gibbons' of the next year to Hudson Bay. See Miller Christy's edition of Luke Fox, *North-West Foxe* which he published as *The Voyages of Captain Luke Foxe of Hull, and Captain Thomas James of Bristol, in Search of a North-West Passage . . .* (Hakluyt Society Publications, London, 1894).

from the French in 1628. In 1632 it was restored to France, with the proviso that the Kirkes should be reimbursed by the French court for their outlays and losses. Again and again in the intervening years the family had endeavored vainly to have payment made them, applying now to France, now to England for redress. All that they secured, however, was the grant of a coat of arms in England and knighthood for some of the brothers.[14] In 1628/9 stock was made out for a company similar to the one now forming in 1667–1668.[15] This earlier charter granted to Sir William Alexander, "Jervice" Kirke, Robert Charleton, and William Berkeley, "of London Merchantes," the right to form "one jontte stocke and body" for having "discovered a trade like to prove verie commodious . . . for the providing of Beaver skyns furres hides skins of wild beastes masts and other materialls." By the time Radisson and Des Groseilliers had reached England in 1665 John Kirke, who was paymaster and receiver of the Band of Gentlemen Pensioners, was appealing to the newly restored King to see justice done his family.[16] The Cromwellian wars had seen many captures of Acadian ports by the English. The

[14] David was knighted early. No record has been found of the knighting of Lewis and John, both of whom used the title, "Sir." The Hudson's Bay Company records begin to speak of "Sir" John Kirke in June, 1674. See *post,* pp. 143, 169, 175, for further references to the Kirkes and their petitions.

[15] PRO., Patent Roll, No. 2485, m2d, 4Charles I (1628/9), "Commission to William Alexander, Knight etc. . . . to incorporate your selves . . . in one jontte stocke and body . . . for the making of a voyage jontly into the saide Gulfe of Canada and Ryver of Canada and partes adjacent for further discoverie of the trade aforesaid. . . . By Writ of Privy Seal."

[16] See *Calendar of Treasury Books, 1660–1667,* edited by W. A. Shaw, p. 670 (London, 1904) ; and *Documentary History of Maine,* 4 : 195–199. The latter reference shows the connection between the Kirkes, Charles Etienne, Sieur de la Tour, Major-General Edward Gibbons, and so forth. It also gives a history and the amount of the Kirkes' claims. In the same volume, pp. 232–240, is a translation of the "Representation of Sr Lewis Kirk & Mr John Kirk . . . concerning Accadie." The translation is dated September 10, 1667, but internal evidence shows that the original petition must have been made prior to 1664 and merely brought out, translated, and submitted again at the time of the Treaty of Breda.

treaty of Breda between England and France in 1667 restored them—in fact, all of Acadia—to France. In antic-
ipation of that treaty Kirke entered his plea once more.[17]
It is probable that he was permitted to be a member of this
new "adventure" because the King realized the cogency
and validity of his claim and wished to propitiate him. In
addition, Kirke held a shadowy claim to the territory itself,
which the King was granting to the new body of adventurers. This fact is made clear by a document of January, 1684,
entitled "The title of the Kirkes to Canada." [18] Therein
occurs this statement: "But the Territories w[hi]ch belonged to the Kirks lying on the North Side of the Said
River [the St. Lawrence] were never mentioned in the
Treaty [of Breda], but they have still a standing Right
thereunto w[hi]ch remaines entire." Since this document
was the British government's official denial of a French
claim to the Hudson Bay area, it expresses the government's
recognition of the Kirkes' claim. It is readily apparent,
therefore, why in the months of the Breda treaty negotiations the government should be willing to include Kirke
in the nascent Hudson's Bay Company.

The King now granted to this group of men one of his
naval vessels, the *Eaglet*. Charles II in his warrant for using the ketch, characterized it as "one of Our small Vessells," and specified that the rigging and victualling should
be the adventurers' concern.[19] This vessel had been built at
Horselydowne by a man named Higgins in 1655. Its length
by keel was forty feet; its breadth by beam sixteen feet;
it was seven feet deep in the hold and it had a draught of
eight feet of water. Its burden was fifty-four tons and in
peace its crew, officers, and gunners numbered twelve men.
In war its complement was thirty-five men abroad and forty

---

[17] See *ante,* p. 10, Note 13.

[18] PRO., CO., 1/66, ff. 271, 272. On the back of the document is the date,
January 26, 1684.

[19] This document is printed in Nute, "Radisson and Groseilliers' Contribution to Geography," p. 419.

at home. It carried eight guns. It was sold by the naval authorities in May, 1674.[20]

Its sister ship on this expedition was the ketch *Nonsuch,* which had been built at Wivenhoe in 1650 by a man named Page. It was thirty-six feet in length and fifteen feet in breadth, drew six and a half feet of water and was seven feet deep in the hold. Its burden was forty-three tons and it carried six guns in peace. Its ordinary complement of men was twelve, but in war time it could carry thirty-five men at home and twenty-four abroad. It was sold in November, 1667, by the navy,[21] apparently to Sir William Warren, for an entry in the archives of the Hudson's Bay Company under his name is as follows: "March 30, 1668 By the Nonsuch Ketch bought of him & by him delivered for the use of the Company . . . valued at £290." [22] Warren was deeply involved in trade with British colonies in North America and was the owner of that vessel of Captain Pierce's with which Cartwright's vessel in 1665 was ordered to keep company on the way to England.[23]

In such cockleshells as these the explorers set forth on their momentous journey in 1668. Radisson was assigned to the *Eaglet,* Captain William Stannard commanding; Des Groseilliers to the *Nonsuch,* whose master was Captain Zechariah Gillam. The latter's brother was that Benjamin Gillam who had commanded the vessel in which the two explorers had set sail from Nantucket in 1665. Zechariah Gillam had also a son and a nephew named Benjamin Gillam. All were captains; all were involved in the traffic between Old England and New England. It is almost impossible to disentangle the Gillams in New England history. In the eighties Zechariah's son Benjamin was to play almost as

[20] *A Descriptive Catalogue of the Naval Manuscripts in the Pepysian Library,* 1:290, edited by J. R. Tanner (Navy Record Society Publications, Vol. 26, 1903–1923).

[21] Tanner, *Catalogue of Naval Manuscripts,* 1:290.

[22] H.B.Co. Archives, Ledger 101, f. 33.

[23] PRO., S.P., Dom., 29/141, f. 223, the Navy Board Records for 1665, a document signed by Samuel Pepys and dated October 14, 1665.

large a part in the fortunes of Radisson and Des Groseilliers as Zechariah occupied in earlier years.[24]

Through the records of the Hudson's Bay Company it
is possible to watch the excitement and eager interest that
attended the preparations for the journey. On March 7
there was a dinner; on March 30 another dinner was held,
this time at the Sun Tavern; on April 8 James Hayes carried a chine of beef to the Pope's Head Tavern; on April
15 another dinner was held in the same place at a cost of
six pounds seven shillings. On May 2 there was a bill, presumably for food, at the Exchange Tavern. Meantime
the vessels were being repaired, fitted, and provisioned.
Mr. William Mason, sailmaker, made several sails for the
Eaglet and repaired several others, to the total amount
of forty-eight pounds. Peter Romulus, the ship's surgeon
and an old Three Rivers acquaintance of the two explorers,
fitted up his chest of medicines and implements, which, with
his service, amounted to twenty pounds and sixteen shillings.
Malt, paper, quills, ink, 18 barrels of shot, 8 gallons and
a quart of lemon juice to prevent scurvy, 5,000 needles,
blunderbusses, muskets, pistols, beer, raisins, prunes, anchors, peas, oatmeal, tobacco for both captains amounting
to thirty-seven pounds, cables, cordage, pitch, tar, axes, saws,
hammers, other carpenters' tools, shirts, hose, mittens, other
slops, beef and pork worth £162.1, compasses, stands of
colors, ship lanterns, medicines, scrapers, spears, hatchets,
wines and spirits, and a thousand and one other items—
engaged the attention of those responsible for the success of
the trip.[25]

[24] For the Gillam family, see *Records and Files of the Quarterly Courts of
Essex County, Massachusetts,* volumes covering 1662–1667, 1667–1671, and
1672–1674; the Ninth Report of the Record Commissioners of Boston, *Births,
Baptisms, Marriages, and Deaths, 1630–1699* (Boston, 1883); and Robert
Boyle, "Experiments and Observations Touching Cold," 2:228–403, in his *His-
tory of Cold* (in his *Works,* London, 1744).

[25] The information in this paragraph is gleaned from many items in the
first ledger book of the Company, which covers the years from 1667 to 1674,
especially folios 33, 34, 36, and 40. H.B.Co. Archives, Ledger 101.

From December, 1667, to May 25, 1668, Portman, Colleton, and Kirke doled out week by week to Radisson and Des Groseilliers ("Mr. Gooseberry" in the records) one pound sterling, two pounds, occasionally five pounds. From May 25 until November, 1668, there are no further entries. Both men were absent. Radisson began to receive his weekly allowance again on November 6 and continued to get it until May 7, 1669. On February 1, 1670, Des Groseilliers' salary entry reappears, and on February 17, 1670, Radisson received another amount.[26]

One document that has special interest for this period is the "Instructions" to Captain Stannard and Captain Gillam, delivered to them at the outset of the expedition.[27] It states that great deference is to be shown Radisson and Des Groseilliers, "they being the persons upon whose Credit wee have undertaken this expedition." The main interest for the first season was to center about trade with the Indians. Wampum, bought from the two Frenchmen "for our money," was to be delivered by small quantities in trade. The result of the first winter's trade was to be put in the spring into the smaller of the two vessels, the *Nonsuch,* and to be taken back to England by Captain Stannard and "Mr Gooseberry." Radisson, Thomas Gorst (a sort of supercargo), and Gillam were to stay a second season, for which provisions should be sent on the *Nonsuch* on her second trip to the Bay in 1669. In case no cargo could be secured and it seemed wise to return, Captain Gillam was to guide the *Nonsuch* home, taking Radisson and Des Groseilliers with him; and Captain Stannard was to go to Newfoundland, there to sell his provisions. Thence he was to depart for New Jersey or New York, for in the former place Phillip Carteret, kin of one of the adventurers, was governor.

"You are to have in yo[u]r thoughts the discovery of

[26] See H.B.Co. Archives, Ledger 101, ff. 32, 70.
[27] Nute, "Radisson and Groseilliers' Contribution to Geography," pp. 419–423.

the Passage into the South sea and to attempt it as occasion shall offer." Radisson and Des Groseilliers were to be the advisers concerning such an expedition, for, the document adds, these men say that by paddling seven days from the river where they intend to trade they will reach the Stinking Lake, which is but seven days from a strait leading into the South Sea. It is clear, therefore, that the ships were bound for the mouth of a river in Hudson Bay—undoubtedly that river which Radisson says in his narrative was descended by the two explorers on their Lake Superior trip to the West. Later events show that the river sought was either the Hayes or the Nelson, to which Radisson made his way in 1670. The lake is obviously Lake Winnipeg, for this Indian word means "stinking." It is reasonable to assume that the two Frenchmen had either traveled to Lake Winnipeg from the Sioux country, or, more probably, had learned of it from the Indians west of Lake Superior. It is true that from Lake Winnipeg went practically all the expeditions of much later date that did reach the Pacific by way of western Canada. However, more than seven days were required, even for Indians, to cover the hundreds of miles that lay between Lake Winnipeg and the western ocean. A vessel for a trip of discovery, the instructions continued, would be sent in 1670, if the information obtained on the first trip seemed to warrant it.

A newsletter of June 9, 1668, states: "The design set on foot some months since by Prince Rupert, the Lord General, and several other undertakers, for the discovery of the North-West Passage, being now brought to maturity, two small ketches, the *Norwich* [*sic*] and the *Eaglet,* set sail this week to Breton's [*Button's*] Bay." [28]

The vessels sailed from Gravesend. The committee of the Company went to that place by barge to see them off. On June 6 Isaac Manychurch was paid five pounds

[28] Historical Manuscripts Commission, 12th *Report,* Appendix VII, "The Manuscripts of S. H. Le Fleming, Esq., of Rydal Hall," p. 56 (London, 1890).

J.-B. FRANQUELIN'S MANUSCRIPT MAP OF JOLLIET'S DISCOVERIES. 1681.

[Paris. Service Hydrographique, B 4040.11.]

for piloting the *Eaglet* and the *Nonsuch* out of the Thames. The voyage had begun.[29]

* * *

In fact, Captain Gillam's journal of the voyage shows that the *Nonsuch* weighed anchor at Gravesend on June 3.[30] For ten days it bore north. On the fourteenth of June the Orkneys were in sight. The captain then steered "westerly" and on August 1 he saw land bearing west from him. By this time he had sailed 524½ leagues. Great flocks of small birds flew about. The latitude was 59° 35'. On August 3 there were "20 Islands of Ice then in sight at once and no Ground at 120 Fathom." On August 5 he saw Resolution Island and Cape Warwick. On August 11 he noted Cape James. On August 16 Digges Island came into view. Polar bears were sighted on August 21. On September 1 he went on shore on one of the innumerable islands, among which he was trying to find his way. He noted traces of Indians and on September 22 he saw smoke on the mainland. A gun was fired and the Indians came and began trading with the party. The natives told Gillam of a river on the East Main, for which he made and at whose mouth he arrived on September 29. This was the estuary into which Rupert, Broadback, and Nottaway rivers empty. The ketch entered, touching twice on a rocky ledge; but getting farther in, it anchored in two fathoms of water. "The River is a mile broad, and lieth in E. by S." By December 9 the river was frozen so that

---

[29] H.B.Co. Archives, Ledger 101, ff. 33, 36.
[30] This "journal" is really an abridged paraphrase of the log of the *Nonsuch* as published under the title of "A Breviate of Captain Zechariah Gillam's Journal to the North-West, in the Nonsuch-Catch, in the Year 1668," as published in *The English Pilot The Fourth Book*, pp. 5 to 9. Published at London for William Fisher "at the Postern on Tower-Hill, and John Thornton at the Plat in the Minories MDCLXXXIX." John Thornton later became the map maker for the Hudson's Bay Company. See also Joseph Robson, *An Account of Six Years Residence in Hudson's-Bay, from 1733 to 1736, and 1744 to 1747*, Appendix 1, p. 5 (London, 1752).

he walked on it to an island. "April, 1669. The cold
Weather almost over, the *Indians* began to resort to them;
June, calm and hot Weather, they begin to work on their
Vessel, and sent his Boat to sound the River, who found
it flowed eight Foot Water, and now only wait for Wind
and Tide to carry them down the River and over the
Shoals."

Further facts about the first winter on the shores of
Hudson Bay can be gleaned from the questions which
Captain Gillam answered for the Royal Society.[31]

1. What time of ye year they set out from hence? june 5th.
2. What time they arrived at ye place proposed? Aug. 22th [*sic*].

.   .   .   .   .   .

8. What kind of people they met with at their harbour, their manners, way of living, language? The people somewhat tawny in-
clin'd to thieving, using bows and arrows, living in tents, wch
they remove from one place to another, according to the seasons
of hunting, fowling, fishing. As for their meat, they live on veni-
son, wild foule, as geese, partridges, and rabbats, wch both are as
white as snow, and of wch there is great abundance, the Captain
affirming, to have kill'd above 700 such white partridges. Their
fish are Sturgeon, brave pikes, Salmon-troutes taken by ym with
nets. . . .

9. How the Captain and his company order'd their way of living,
whilst they stay'd there? When they came a shore, they built
ymselves a house of wood, and dugg a cellar 12. foot deep into ye
ground, where they putt some barrels of good bier, wch at their

---

[31] In the Robert Boyle papers in the Royal Society, London, are four forms
of the questions put to Gillam by Henry Oldenburgh at various times, together with Gillam's answers after his return from Hudson Bay. The Journal
Book of the Royal Society for May 19, 1670, Vol. 4, pp. 141, 142, mentions the
reading of the questions and answers. Probably the original form is the manuscript filed in the Society's Classified Papers for 1660–1740, XIX, "Questions
and Answers" No. 19, "Queries proposed to ye Captain, yᵗ went to ye place
of the Bevertrade." The author is indebted to R. P. Stearns for first calling
this document to her attention, and to the Royal Society for their kind permission to use it and quote it. A much fuller form of the queries is to be found
in the Register Book, 1668–1675, No. 4, pp. 190–193. It contains data on the
first trip and also on the trip of 1670–1671. The difference in dates between
Gillam's log and the form quoted in this book suggests that there is some
mixing of these two trips in Gillam's purported reply of 1670.

time of coming away being taken out, after it had layn there 8.
or 9. months, prov'd very excellent liquor; they in ye mean time
brewing all the winter long of the provision of malt, they had
taken with ym. They went hunting with their guns, and kill'd
dear, and fowle.

. . . . . .

13. How they had their health? Very well, lost not one man; only
in returning they found some trouble of the Scurvy in their mouths.

. . . . . .

18. What time they came away? june 14th; but they could not, having sailed on to the North, goe on in the month of july; but
were forc'd to turn back, so yt it was ye 12th of August, till
they were clear of the ice.

. . . . . .

21. . . . . . They traded with 300 Indians.

* * *

Meanwhile Captain Stannard and Radisson in the *Eaglet*
were having trouble enough. Radisson writes: "Wee went
together 400 leagues from yᵉ North of Ireland, where a
sudden great storme did rise & put us asunder. The sea
was soe furious 6 or 7 houres after that it did almost
overturne our ship, so that weè were forced to cut our
masts." On August 13, 1668, the *London Gazette* carried
this news item: "Plymouth, Aug. 7. On Wednesday last
[*August 5*] came in the *Eagle*—Ketch, having in her way
for Newfound-land been severely handled by storm, in
which she spent her main Mast, and with some difficulty
put back again to refit." [32] On October 8 James Hayes
wrote to the Commissioners of the Navy: "His Maᵗⁱᵉ was
pleased some months since to lend the *Eaglett* Ketch unto
his Highnesse Prince Rupert, the Duke of Albemarle and
others, who had designed an expedition for Hudson's Bay."
Contrary winds, he continues, have damaged the vessel,

[32] The file of the newspaper which was consulted is in the Harvard College
Library.

for which he wants an order to send her to Deptford to "ye hands of the Master of Attendance." [33] The damage to the *Eaglet* was considerable, as the record for repairs at Deptford in 1668 show. At that place the "Eaglett Ketch" was repaired to the extent of £113.0.0.[34]

It is even possible to explain in nautical terms why the vessel did not succeed in her voyage. On December 16, 1668, "Sir Robert Vyner, Sir Edward Hungerford, Sir John Robinson & other Adventurers to Hudson's Bay" petitioned the King for another vessel, the pink, *Hadarine,* "Rigged and fitted, shee being a Vessell of less worth to his Majesty and much more fitt than" the *Eaglet,* which has returned "and is since delivered to the Commissioners of His Majesty's Navy, shee being by reason of the deepness of her Wast [*waist*] unable to endure the Violent Stormes they mett with." [35]

The petition was granted. It has another significance than that already mentioned. It will be observed that three new members of the party of "advanturers" are mentioned, all well-known residents of London. Sir Robert Viner had lent large sums to the King. He was a nephew of Sir Thomas Viner, who had been Lord Mayor of London in the year 1653–1654. Sir Robert himself was an alderman in 1666, a sheriff in 1672, was knighted June 24, 1665, was created a baronet in June, 1666, and was goldsmith, or banker to Charles II. Sir Edward Hungerford was a brother-in-law of James Hayes. Sir John Robinson was Lieutenant of the Tower of London.[36]

It would be interesting to know why these men now took the responsibility of the second venture toward Hudson

[33] PRO., S.P., Dom., 1668, 247/126.

[34] PRO., S.P., Dom., 1668, 29/251, f. 23, "An Estimate of the repaire of Severall of his Matie Ships."

[35] *Acts of the Privy Council of England, Colonial Series, Vol. I, A.D. 1613–1680,* p. 497 (Hereford, 1908), edited by W. L. Grant and James Munro. The document is dated December 16, 1668.

[36] Mood, "Hudson's Bay Company Started as a Syndicate," p. 56.

Bay. Had the others become fearful that the *Nonsuch* would not return? Was Radisson able to present such a convincing picture of what he alone could discover that new men took up the burden? It seems apparent that Radisson wrote his now famous *Voyages* just before this venture began, for he describes events up to June, 1669, and hopes for success in his imminent fourth attempt to reach the Bay. That attempt began in June, 1669. The manuscript was translated prior to June 23, 1669, since on that date James Hayes, for the adventurers, paid five pounds for the "translating a Booke of Radisons." [37] It may be that this narrative influenced the new investors to attempt the second adventure.

The *Hadarine* was destined not to go to Hudson Bay. On January 8, 1669, the Duke of York reported that the vessel was employed in His Majesty's service and so was not available.[38] Another ketch, therefore, was ordered fitted and rigged to be placed at the disposal of the adventurers. This was the *Wivenhoe,* built by Page at Wivenhoe in the years 1665 and 1666.[39] It was much larger than the *Eaglet* and the *Nonsuch.* Captain Stannard again commanded.

Again Radisson was on the losing side. We lack information on the reason for Captain Stannard's second failure. From another would-be discoverer of the Northwest Passage, Lawrence Van Heemskerk, it seems fairly certain that the vessel, carrying Radisson, the Dutchman, Captain Stannard, and others went to Greenland and got into Hudson Straits, for Van Heemskerk states that with him on a northern trip of this period was "a man who had lived five or six years with the Iroquois and who spoke their language well. He told me that the Indians had assured him that there was a passage, though a distant one, by way

---

[37] H.B.Co. Archives, Ledger 101, f. 33.
[38] *Acts of the Privy Council, Col. Ser., 1613–1680,* p. 499.
[39] Tanner, *Catalogue of Naval Manuscripts,* 1:286, 292.

of the Californias to the South Sea." [40] This is the only information we have on the voyage, and it indicates that Stannard as a mariner was not the equal of "Old Zack," as the New Englander, Gillam, was called.

Between June 23, 1669, and January 20, 1670, the books of the Company carry no accounts for the *Wivenhoe*. Presumably, therefore, she was absent during most of that period. On January 20, 1670, custom duties were paid for the ketch herself and for seven hogsheads of sugar.[41] So Radisson was back in London for another winter.

Just as Radisson and his company were setting sail for Hudson Bay, the adventurers took steps to get a charter. On June 23, 1669, the King granted to Hungerford, Robinson, Viner, Sir Peter Colleton, James Hayes, and John Kirke the sole trade of the northern part of North America, the limits of which were carefully specified.[42] He also granted the "sole Trade and comerce wth the Christianoats [*Cree Indians*] Nadouseranohs [*Sioux*] and all other Nations inhabiting the Coasts adjacent" to the area thus specified.

Two points in this grant are noticeable: the personnel of the adventurers in June, 1669, as compared with the investors of June, 1668; and the reference to two tribes of Indians encountered by Radisson west of Lake Superior on his expedition of 1659–1660. Only two of the original adventurers, and the son of a third, are recognizable, but Hungerford, Robinson, and Viner appear for a second time in the annals of the expedition of 1669–1670. What had happened to Prince Rupert, Lord Craven, and the other noble adventurers? Or were they concerned only with the *Nonsuch?*

The *Nonsuch* appeared again in the English waters in

[40] BN., Margry Papers, 9284, ff. 10, 11. See *post,* p. 127.
[41] H.B.Co. Archives, Ledger 101, an item in "Incident Charges of Capt Gillam's first & Capt Stannards first & second Voyages."
[42] This document is printed in Nute, "Radisson and Groseilliers' Contribution to Geography," pp. 423, 424.

October, 1669, for on the nineteenth of that month the adventurers "paid Custome of the Nonsuch Ketch" and her cargo to the amount of £34.1.10.[43] The *London Gazette* for October 14, 1669, carries this item:

Deal. October 11. This last night came in here the Nonsuch Ketch, which having endeavoured to make out a passage by the North-West, was in those seas environed with Ice, which opposing her progress, the men were forced to hale her on shoar and to provide against the ensueing cold of a long Winter; which ending, they returned with a considerable quantity of Beaver, which made them some recompence for their cold confinement.

Excitement must have prevailed among the adventurers when the great success of their undertaking on the *Nonsuch* was apparent. Two days after the paying of customs duties, a royal grant was made out to the same group of men as those listed in the grant of June 23, 1669.[44] The earlier document was now canceled and the new grant refers to the discovery as an accomplished fact: "[They] have made such discoveries as doe encourage them to proceed further in pursuance of their said Designe." It is significant that no reference is made in this later document to the Christianoats, Nadouseranohs, or other tribes.

A sale of beaver appears to have been held on February 28, 1670, for on that day some three thousand pounds of beaver were sold to five purchasers at a total price of £1379.6.10.[45] Not a bad cargo for a vessel of forty-three tons to bring home in the year 1669!

By this time Radisson and Des Groseilliers were reunited in London, doubtless with many a yarn to swap, and all was preparation for a repetition of Des Groseilliers and Gillam's success. Little did they suspect, apparently, that the erstwhile master of the *Nonsuch* was struggling to

[43] H.B.Co. Archives, Ledger 101, an item in "Incident Charges of Capt Gillam's first & Capt Stannards first & second Voyages."
[44] Printed in Nute, "Radisson and Groseilliers' Contribution to Geography," pp. 424–426.
[45] H.B.Co. Archives, Ledger 101.

get to the Bay before the Frenchmen. Still less did they know that their own remarks to Van Heemskerk were persuading Louis XIV to do for the Dutchman what France had consistently refused to do for her own two explorers.

CHAPTER IX

Competition from France

While the adventurers made preparations for another voyage and went about the weighty business of securing a charter, Van Heemskerk obtained from Louis XIV on April 27, 1670, a concession of "all the lands which have been and shall be discovered by him in all North America entered from above Canada towards the North Pole, and extending to the South Sea as much and as far as he can reach." He was empowered also to form a company and was given vessels for his purpose. On the same date he received naturalization papers, which state that he was a Protestant and a native of The Hague, who, being charged with interesting duties in the service of the King, could no longer reside in his native city, but wished to establish himself at Dunkirk.[1] The Count d'Estrades was mentioned at this time as forming a partnership with Van Heemskerk.[2] It was just at this time also that Colbert wrote to the French ambassador regarding the Dutchman:[3]

He has given a similar story to the King, of a country that he also has discovered at 51° 22'. His Majesty has recently granted him all the countries that he has discovered or shall discover . . . so that you must inform yourself diligently whether the Frenchmen have made the same discovery and, however that may be, you must see that they pass at once into France, I being sure that the King of England, if he learns of this knowledge of theirs, will grant them what they demand. That would be a serious injury to the Sieur Van Heemskerk.

[1] BN., Margry Papers, 9284, ff. 16, 17, copied from Archives de la Marine, Registre des Expéditions Concernant les Indes Orientales et Occidentales, 1670, f. 65 1/2. See also BN., Manuscrits Français, 6652, ff. 184, 185.

[2] BN., Margry Papers, 9284, ff. 16, 17.

[3] Clément, *Lettres de Colbert*, 3:239. See also *ante*, p. 108.

On May 12, 1670, Van Heemskerk wrote a remarkable letter to Colbert from Portsmouth, England, describing his experiences in England and his trip to Hudson Bay.[4] It leaves small doubt that Van Heemskerk had been in touch with either Radisson or Des Groseilliers. The latitude of his discoveries is exactly what the two men had named. Moreover, there is just enough accuracy to the description of the Hudson Bay region and just enough advocacy of the plan outlined by the two Frenchmen in England to suggest the true source of the Dutchman's hazy ideas. There is further evidence that it was Radisson with whom he had talked, probably during the ill-starred voyage of 1669–1670 about which so little is known.

In 1697 France and England each was trying to keep the other from the Hudson Bay area and to win it for herself—the area so hotly contested by these two countries from 1686 to the negotiations for the Treaty of Ryswick. The French minister De Pontchartrain recalled, or had recalled to him, the claim that France held to Hudson Bay through Van Heemskerk and his family. The Dutchman was still living in Brest. A dispatch was sent to him at once. The old fellow replied on July 1, 1697:[5]

I have received the letter with which you honored me relative to a passage into the South Sea by way of Hudson Bay and the Californias. The Sieur Ollivier Van Nord, my great-uncle, made a voyage for Holland to the East Indies, entering by way of Formosa in the South Sea and departing to the north of California, reaching Holland by way of Hudson Bay.

He terms the newly discovered area the "Florida of the North."

I remember that trip and I myself made one to Greenland. I entered Hudson Straits. There was with me a man who had lived five or six years with the Iroquois and who spoke their language well. He told me that the Indians had assured him that there was a pas-

[4] BN., Margry Papers, 9284, ff. 11–15.
[5] BN., Margry Papers, 9284, ff. 10, 11.

sage, though a distant one, by way of the Californias, to the South Sea.

He goes on to tell how at Dunkirk in the year 1670 he was ordered by Colbert to go to the French court and how Louis XIV granted him letters patent for the formation of a company and gave him three vessels. He then relates briefly the ill-success of his journey, but swears that, despite his sixty-five years, he could still make the Northwest Passage for the King.[6]

* * *

On August 14, 1670, Van Heemskerk began his journey from Brest to the "Florida of the North" for the discovery of the Northwest Passage for the honor of His Most Christian Majesty.[7] He had with him three vessels, the *St. Jean Baptiste*, the *St. Pierre,* and the *St. Jean Evangeliste*. About latitude 57° 50′ a terrible storm separated Van Heemskerk's vessel from the other two. He arrived back in Brest on September 30 ignorant of the fate of the two other vessels. They, meanwhile, were safe in the harbor of Pendennis. The issue of the *London Gazette* for October 3 has this to say of them:

Pendennis, Sept 26   Here lately put in Two French men of war, of Three which were sent out with a Commission for the discovery of a Northern passage to the East-Indies, but meeting with extraordinary colds and ill weather were forced to return, having lost company of their other companion which they suppose to have perished. These two are of *Dunkirk,* carrying only Eight or Ten Guns apiece.

Meantime Radisson and Des Groseilliers, whose knowledge with Captain Gillam's seamanship had succeeded where all others had lost the way and failed, were starting again for Hudson Bay. The English Company, which

[6] For De Pontchartrain's reply, see BN., Margry Papers, 9284, ff. 30–34.
[7] BN., Margry Papers, 9284, ff. 18–24, "Registre journalier du voyage du Nord de Florida pour découvrir le passage du Nord Ouest pour l'honneur et réputation de sa Majesté très-Chretienne."

had received its charter on May 2, 1670, protested the
French invasion of their territories. Colbert replied, in
answer to this protest, which apparently was sent through
the French ambassador in London: [8]

> With regard to the navigation of Hudson Straits, it is true that
> Van Heemskerk, a Dutchman, is in the King's service and has pro-
> posed to His Majesty to go to discover seas and countries which have
> never been and are not now inhabited by any European nation, be-
> tween 52° and 54° north latitude, under certain concessions granted
> him. There is nothing therein that can injure the king of England
> or his subjects. But if, in the execution of this enterprise, the country
> claimed by Van Heemskerk is found to be occupied by the English
> —in that case the King will not permit it and will satisfy the King
> of England without trouble. You will perceive quite readily by this
> statement that no contest or difficulty will arise in this matter.

While the Hudson's Bay Company was protesting the
French invasion of their rights and the two monarchs were
smoothing over all difficulties because of the Secret Treaty
of Dover, then being negotiated,[9] Colbert was receiving
word from a correspondent in Dunkirk that the English
were aiming to anticipate Van Heemskerk. Now for the
first time, apparently, the French court learned of the return of the *Nonsuch* with its great cargo of rich furs.[10]

> I have just learned from Mr. Hariford, an English merchant of
> this city, recently returned from London, that a ketch of 25 to 40
> tons had arrived from Florida of the North, where Sr Heemskerk
> plans to go; that the said ketch wintered there and returned laden
> with beaver skins as half its cargo. These skins, he says, were very
> fine, and, he adds, since the vessel's arrival, two London bankers
> have made a company in which Prince Robert [*Rupert*] is inter-
> ested and which has a charter from the king of England. They have
> equipped two little merchant vessels and a royal frigate of ten pieces

---

[8] G. B. Depping, ed., *Correspondance administrative sous le règne de Louis
XIV*, 3:430, 431 (Paris, 1852). The last letter is dated August 5, 1670.

[9] One can follow the events of 1670 conveniently in the correspondence between Charles II and his sister in France in Cyril Hughes Hartmann, *Charles
II and Madame* (London, 1934).

[10] A copy of a letter of September 4, 1670, sent in a letter by Hubert to
Colbert, September 8, 1670, in BN., Margry Papers, 9284, ff. 24, 25.

and set out a week before Sr Hemskerk set sail, planning to follow
him or to wait for him, to enter Hudson Bay with him. . . . The
wind always favors him. He may be at his destination as I write,
but this news is not agreeable. Hemskerk talked much about Prince
Robert. I fear he has communicated his plans to him. Time will tell.

Meanwhile Prince Rupert was lending his aid to the
English adventurers. On April 12, 1670, an entry was made
in the Treasury Book that "The Prince's docquet about
the Hudson's bay is to be offered to-morrow." [11] The privy
seal docquet book kept by Sir Edward Dering (later deputy
governor of the Hudson's Bay Company) during the
absence in Ireland of Lord Roberts, keeper of the privy
seal, has an entry for April 18, 1670, that helps to tell
the story of the nascent company.[12] Seemingly it is the
first draft of the charter that was to go into effect, all
properly sealed, on May 2, 1670:

> An Incorporacion of Prince Rupert, Duke of Albemarle, Earl of
> Craven, Lord Arlington, Lord Ashley, Sir John Robinson, Sir Robert
> Vyner, Sir Peter Colleton, Sir Edward Hungerford, Sir Paule Neile,
> Sir John Griffith, Sir Phillip Carteret, James Hayes, John Kirke,
> Francis Millington, William Prettyman, John Fenne, John Portman,
> into one body politique by the name of Governours and Adventurers
> trading to Hudsons baye.

It granted them and their successors all the lands and the
sole trade of the seas and creeks lying within the entrance
of Hudson Straits.

On May 2 the charter of the Company passed the great
seal and there came into being a corporation that has survived to this day, one of the oldest in the world. It is usually
called simply the Hudson's Bay Company. It has not been
without its struggles and adversities in the 270 years of its
existence. This volume will carry its story, at least in outline,
to 1710, and will tell of wars, sieges, and attempts to revoke
its charter. In the middle of the eighteenth century and again

[11] *Calendar of Treasury Books, 1669–1672*, p. 401.
[12] British Museum, Additional MS 38,862.

a century later it had to fight for its existence. Yet it has survived, and in so doing it has proved how sound economically were the views of the two men who first dreamed of the exploitation of the fur resources of northern North America.

CHAPTER X

"Where Poor Hudson Ended His Dayes"

As soon as the charter had been secured, a governor of the new colony was selected, vessels were obtained, and a new adventure was begun.

For Governor the adventurers chose Charles Bayly. To minds of the twentieth century this choice seems an odd one. Bayly's qualifications were: one incarceration after another in English, French, and Italian jails, mainly for fanatical proselytizing for the Quaker faith; eight or more religious-political pamphlets that he had written and published; a colonial birth, or, at least, residence in a colony; backsliding as a Quaker; and prosecution by John Robinson, Lieutenant of the Tower, by whose recommendation Bayly was now called to the attention of the new Hudson's Bay Company.[1]

In the early sixties Bayly called himself "a Foreigner," the place of his abode being "in *Mary-Land* in *Virginia*." He seems to have been a resident of Severn in Anne Arundel County, Maryland, though local records have little to say of him. A letter of November 14, 1657, apparently written by the Quaker, Robert Clarksonne, to a Quaker missionary, Elizabeth Harris, mentions several Quakers at "Severon . . . in Virginia," including "Charles Balye, ye yonge man who was wth us at o^r parting," and who "abides convinced

[1] Most of the facts concerning Charles Bayly were found at the Library of the Society of Friends, London, to whose librarian the author wishes to extend her grateful acknowledgment. The Swarthmore Manuscripts, Vol. III, No. 7, contain the letter to Elizabeth Harris mentioned in the next paragraph. *A Descriptive Catalogue* of *Friends' Books* by Joseph Smith, 1:212 (London, 1867), gives information on Bayly, as does also the *Journal . . . of . . . George Fox*, edited by Norman Penney (Cambridge, 1911), under date of 1660. See also *Cal. S.P., Dom., 1666–1667*, pp. 530, 531.

& severall others in those pts. where hee dwelt." The names
are of Talbot, Anne Arundel, and Kent county residents
of Maryland. Among them was John Perrot, or Parratt,
with whom Bayly later went to Rome in order to attempt
to convert the Pope. Perrot was submitted to the Inquisition,
put in Bedlam, and finally released in May, 1661, through
the intercession of Bayly and a woman missionary. Bayly
meantime had been in prison in Rome, but had been released.
Perrot and his followers returned, at least part of the way
barefoot, through France, where Bayly was again thrown into
prison. One of his pamphlets was issued in 1661 "From the
Common Goal [sic] in Burkdou [sic] in France, about thirty
leagues from Dover, where I am a Sufferer for speaking
the Word of the Lord to two Priests." Later he was in
prison in Dover (1662), Bristol (1663), and the Tower
(1663). The charge against him in 1663 was "seditious
practices." In the Tower he was "on His Majesty's allowance." On July 7, 1669, he signed a bail bond guaranteeing
that he would leave the kingdom fifteen days after his release
from the Tower. Another bond of even date and signed by
him guaranteed that he would leave the kingdom within eight
days, proceed to France, and give himself up to the Tower
once more upon his return.[2]

In France he was noted by the English ambassador, Henry
Savile, upon whom he made no such impression, it would
seem, as upon the Hudson's Bay Company. Savile wrote to
Viscount Halifax on September 4, 1669:[3] "My lady [*Lady
Lexington*] has made some kind of will here, by which she
has left the care of her children to Sir Anthony Sellenger
as I am told; here is at present nobody with them but an
old quaker with a long beard, one Bayly, who I think was

---

[2] See a letter in Hudson's Bay House, London, written by the Governor of
the Tower, October 18, 1933, relative to Bayly and giving the text of the two
bonds to which reference is made.

[3] *Letters to and From Henry Savile, Esq., Envoy at Paris, and Vice-Chamberlain to Charles II and James II,* 24, edited by W. D. Cooper (Camden Society Publications, London, 1857).

prisoner in the Tower when I was, and a Frenchman that served my Lord Chesterfield, who is the only one that speaks French in the Company." Bayly returned to the Tower late in 1669. On December 23, 1669, it was ordered that he again be released on condition that he

. . . will betake himselfe to the Navigation of Hudsons Bay, and the Places lately Discovered and to be Discovered in those parts, which Sir John Robinson, Lieutenant of the Tower hath undertaken he shall doe, Provided the Adventurers in the said Navigation will assure unto him the said Charles Bayly such conditions and Allowances as may be agreeable to reason and the nature of his Employment.[4]

It would be interesting to know more of what went into the choice of the new Governor. Governors of English colonies were usually men of standing and power, often titled gentlemen. Bayly fulfilled the dreams of the Company and under his guidance the Hudson Bay colony grew and prospered and the adventurers received ample financial returns from their investments. When he died, on January 6, 1680, the Company gave him a signal honor.[5]

Mr. Baily came well home, but within a month of his arrivall fell sick and dyed, by whose unexpected death wee lost much of the light & assistance we expected from him. But the Company bestowed an honourable buryall on him and have now sent over an Escutcheon, which we should have you set up for the observation of the Indians, that they may be made to understand he is dead, and y[t] the Company used him kindly.

He was buried "in the Church of S[t] Paules Covent Garden in which Parish he was borne." [6] These are the principal facts thus far available for a man who deserves a fuller fame.[7]

[4] *Acts of the Privy Council, Col. Ser., 1613–1680*, 1: 540, 541.

[5] Letter of instructions to Governor John Nixon, May 29, 1680, in H.B.Co. Archives, A/6/1. It is signed by Prince Rupert, Hayes, Wren, Yonge, and other members of the Committee.

[6] H.B.Co. Archives, A/1/2, entry of January 6, 1679/80.

[7] The inscriptions on the fly leaf of a portolan atlas of 1583 by Giovanni Martines of Messina and now in the Ayer Collection of the Newberry Library

On May 31, 1670, the *Prince Rupert,* a frigate just completed and commanded by Gillam, and the *Wivenhoe* under
Captain Robert Newland's direction, set sail from Ratcliffe
for the Bay. There had been the usual round of tavern din-
ners. Besides the new governor, the captains, and the two
Frenchmen, there were on board the vessels Thomas Gorst,
who kept a diary of the journey, Nehemiah Walker, Thomas
Davis, Paul Mercer, a Mr. Foster, and a Mr. Manning, besides many others whose names are unknown. Radisson went
on Newland's ship with Bayly, and Des Groseilliers and
Gorst were assigned to the frigate. The two vessels kept
company along the Downs, past Land's End, the Scilly Isles,
across the North Atlantic, through the straits, and past Cape
Charles Island (now Charles Island) and Cape Wolsten-
holme, till on August 17, 1670, Digges Island was sighted
and passed. The next day the *Wivenhoe* sailed west for Port
Nelson to found a settlement that was planned to be the
Company's chief factory. The *Rupert* steered southeast for
the wintering ground of the previous year. About fourteen
leagues from their destination they saw Point Comfort and
anchored there. Gorst writes: [8] "The Capt Mr Foster, M^r
Gooseberry & I went ashore killed some Fowle & stayd all
night." Here trade was begun with the natives. After some

in Chicago read as follows: "14 Augusti 1595. This Book is gyven to me W. L.
Burghly by ye Lo. Charles Howard high Admyral of England." "Ce livre mest
donné par Charles Bailly gouverneur de la Bay d'udson En 1673 J'apartiens
a pierre Esprit Radisson serviteur du Roy de la Grande Bretaigne a tous qui
ces presents." "Ce livre ma Este donne par le nomme cy dessus Nomme Radisson pour la mour duquel Je le gardere toute ma vie jusquē a ce que Je trouve
a man defaire un faveur dun autre. 1675. [*signed*] Morpin [*?*]." "Il la rendu
a Radisson a qui il appartenant [*?*] 1680 [*?*]." Grateful acknowledgment for
the use of this atlas is hereby made to the Newberry Library.

[8] "Gorst's Journal to Hudson's Bay in 1670 n° 11" is a hitherto unpublished
manuscript in the Guildhall Library, London. It was generously called to the
author's attention by Henry W. Robinson, librarian of the Royal Society.
Permission to publish it has been received from the Library Committee of the
Guildhall Library, owners of the copyright. On the last sheet Paul Mercer
recounts the story of the *Wivenhoe* after she parted company with the frigate
and until Newland's death. It is plain that the "journal" is a mixture of diary
and reminiscences. It is printed *post,* Appendix 2.

preliminary scouting the vessel started for Fort Charles on Rupert River, the establishment made by Gillam and Des Groseilliers on the preceding trip. She grounded on the bar but got free in an hour. On September 8 "By sailing and warping wee got up the River & Anchored before Charles Fort in 2½ fathom at low Water."

The cargo was taken ashore, the vessel was unrigged, wild geese gathering for the fall migration in thousands, as they still do at this spot, were killed in great numbers, and a dock was begun near the house of the previous season. Timber was cut and a new house was built for Captain Gillam. By this time the Indians were coming "apace" and were "willing to Trade." As soon as the dock was finished, a high tide was utilized to "get in yᵉ ship." The hold was "rummaged" for beer, which was taken out and buried to "preserve it from freezing that wee may not want for our homeward bound Voyage." Since malt had been brought in the cargo, more beer was brewed for the winter's consumption. The house was thatched, the captain and Foster being the "Principall artists" in this task. Others fetched clay for mortaring the chimney that was now constructed with bricks brought from England.

The houses, made of upright logs chinked with moss, consisted of two stories besides the cellar. In the latter were kept the beer, brewed there for daily consumption, the beef, the pork, and the butter. The "chamber," or second floor, held the dry provisions, such as bread, flour, dried peas, and oatmeal. "On the ground floore was our kitchin, Dyining roome & Lodgings—which were Standing Cabbins such as are used in his Maᵗⁱᵉˢ shipps." The large chimney was kept roaring, for "wee spared not ye wood, that Country affording enough to keep always Summer within while nothing but Ice & snow are without doores." Outside was "a good Oven" in which "ven[i]son pasty" was cooked.

On October 12 the houses were so nearly prepared for the winter that several men were sent to the woods to cut the

winter's fuel. In the afternoon a ship's boat was seen making
for Rupert River. It was soon recognized as the *Wivenhoe's*
longboat, in which Radisson and three companions were
discerned. They came ashore and told sad news. Their captain was dying after an attempt to get into Port Nelson.
After the *Wivenhoe* had parted company with the *Rupert,*
it struck upon some rocks near Mansfield's [*Mansel ?*] Island on August 19 and was in great danger of foundering.
However, the crew managed to keep it afloat and took it
into Port Nelson, where they arrived on August 31. Bayly,
Walker, and others went ashore on the north side of the
river and spent the night there in an Indian lodge.[9] The next
day the Governor took formal possession of "all the Lands
and Territoryes" of Port Nelson "for his Matie and in tocken
thereof, nayled up the Kings Armes in Brasse on a Small
Tree there." A storm now came up and forced the vessel
from the river, "and they could not gett her back againe."

It was noted while at Port Nelson that Indians had been
living there recently. Wood could be obtained easily, and
the men had seen "great store of wild fowle Rabbets &
Deeres." Strawberries, gooseberries, large red currants,
huckleberries, and cranberries were seen. "The weather beginning to grow cold apace & ye men being tired & disheartened with fruitlesse labour, Upon a Consultation it was resolved on as most fit, to saile to Ruperts River." Radisson
and his comrades also reported that two men had already died
and that the captain and several men were lying sick in the
ship now riding at anchor at Point Comfort.

The next morning after the arrival of Radisson and his
companions at Charles Fort, Captain Gillam, Foster, and
six others went out in the *Rupert's* boat and Gorst with four
men went in the *Wivenhoe's.* "Wee run aground upon y^e
barr & were forced to stay till the Flood brought us off,

⁹ Affidavit of Nehemiah Walker, Mariner, in PRO., CO., 134/1, f. 203, June 14, 1687.

though it were bitter freezing weather, so cold that ye Water
thickned & stuck to Our Oares while wee were rowing."

Captain Newland died the following morning at ten
o'clock. Scurvy seems to have been the cause of his death.
Two days later, under Gillam's direction, the *Wivenhoe*
came safe to anchor a half mile below the place where the
Prince Rupert lay in dock. On the eighteenth a military funeral was accorded Captain Newland, with guns from both
vessels and a company of men following him in arms to his
grave beside the new house. On the twenty-fourth his possessions were sold before the mast.

Now it was necessary to build a dock for the *Wivenhoe*
and to erect wigwams for her crew, since it was too late in
the season to build another house. Old sails were used in
lieu of skins. That winter could not have been a pleasant
one for the *Wivenhoe's* crew. Food did not lack, however.
The Indians began at once to bring in deer and barter them
for dried peas, "which they love extreamly but hate beef
& pork & every thing which tasts of ye salt."

On Christmas day "wee made merry remembering our
Freinds in England, having for Liquor Brandy & strong beer
& for Food plenty of Partridges & Venson besides what y^e
shipps provisions afforded." Nevertheless vitamins were
lacking in the bountiful diet, for on January 16 Captain Gillam fell sick of the scurvy, "which is there the onely disease."
He recovered quickly. Radisson and Des Groseilliers seem
never to have suffered from this malady. Doubtless their
years with the Indians in earlier times had taught them the
proper diet for such a country.

At the end of January Radisson went to "Moose Cebee"
[*Moose River*], on the southwest side of James Bay, where
he found tall, straight pines and spruces nearly sixty inches
in circumference, admirable for masts for the royal navy.
He did not return until March 14, but even then he could
not tell much about this new river's depth, since it was still

thick with ice. The next statement in the diary refers, apparently, to a later expedition of the same season: "That [*Moose River*] was yᵉ place where afterwards yᵉ Governoʳ went along with him & traded with yᵉ People of that place & from thence had all yᵉ Beaver which was brought home in yᵉ Wivenhoe, which neverthelesse wee beleeve would have been brought to Ruperts River if no body had went thither to fetch it." Already jealousy was raising her head!

There had been some plan for Governor Bayly and several men to remain in the country over the next season, probably at Port Nelson, but it appears, at least from Gorst's remarks, that not enough men followed his own example and volunteered for the period.

On March 31, in true English fashion these denizens of the Artic planted peas and mustard seed, "which came up well enough for yᵉ time wee stayed there & no doubt but all sorts of rootes would have grown very well if Wee had been furnished with seed." The hogs and hens, he adds, "lived & did well enough." By April 18 wild geese and ducks were returning in great numbers from the South and Mr. Manning and Mr. Walker were deputed to kill as many as they could. By May 16 the weather was "hot" and the mosquitoes "very busy." The river was clear of ice on May 22 and by the thirtieth a new shallop, the *Royall Charles,* could be launched.

Anchor was weighed for the homeward journey on July 1, but first wood must be cut. So a stop was made at Point Comfort. While there Governor Bayly, Gorst, and some others took a shallop "to make further discoveries." "Upon an Island wee found an old wigwam not built by Indians, but suppose it rather to bee yᵉ place where poor Hudson ended his dayes." They also landed on Charlton Island, "yᵉ place where Capᵗ James of Bristoll wintered, wee found severall barrell boards, Trees sawne, & ye bones of some persons supposed to be yᵉ same he buryed there."

On July 24 the journey homeward was actually begun.

The two ships parted company on August 17 and Gorst writes that he did not see Gillam again "untill wee found him in ye River of Thames." Gorst's vessel sighted the Scilly Isles on September 30 and on October 2 the vessel "arrived safe at Plymouth."

Years later—in 1687 and again in the late nineties—England and France were both striving to prove first occupancy and formal taking possession of Port Nelson. Had Gorst's diary been available, there could have been no question, for this document proves conclusively that Radisson, Newland, and the crew of the *Wivenhoe* actually went to Port Nelson in 1670 and took possession of the region for England. The journey of 1670–1671 was to serve Radisson in good stead twelve years later, when he occupied Port Nelson for the French. Though attempts at settlement did not cease with this first, abortive one by the Hudson's Bay Company, nothing came of them till the very year that Radisson returned thither in French employ. Then his knowledge of the place, gained from this first visit, enabled him to get ahead of his rivals, who were unacquainted with the Port Nelson region. Throughout his active exploring career he never ceased to believe that one of the major routes to the South Sea lay through the river that emptied at Port Nelson. For this idea he had gone to New England. He had told it in Old England. It seemed likely to succeed when he got to Port Nelson in 1670, but others, who could not stand what he could endure in the wilderness, forced him to leave almost at once. Finally, in 1682, he and Des Groseilliers occupied it for the French and thus began the wars for possession of Hudson Bay that were to continue until the end of the American Revolution.

With that keen insight which always characterized him, Radisson saw at the outset of his career that Port Nelson was the key to the fur trade of inland North America. From 1778 to 1821 the North West Company of Canada tried to prove that his earlier route, via the Great Lakes, was just as good as the one by way of Port Nelson. In the end, however, the Bay route won, and the North West Company coalesced with its rival, the Hudson's Bay Company, largely for the sake of the economies of cheaper transportation by way of Hudson Bay. We shall see Radisson trying to impress upon the French court that his route to the Western Sea was better than De la Salle's. De la Salle, however, had more powerful friends at court than Radisson.

CHAPTER XI

The End of Eight and a Half Years' Service

Little is known of the trips that Radisson and Des Groseilliers made after 1671 and prior to the severance of their connections with the Company late in 1675. In 1671 they got back to England in October.[1] They were employed during the succeeding winter as advisers upon such points as the number, kind, and sizes of kettles, hatchets, French knives, arrowheads, fowling pieces, powder horns, shot, and guns, which were to be shipped to Hudson Bay for barter with the Indians; upon the grading of furs for the great sale of seven thousand pounds of beaver that took place on January 24, 1672;[2] upon the quantity and kinds of provisions to be taken on the next trip; and upon similar matters. Records of the money doled out to them from time to time are all conveniently summarized in one of the Company's books.

It was decided by the Committee of the Company that a settlement should be made at "Moussebee," presumably at Radisson's suggestion, since he had introduced the place to Governor Bayly. Two vessels were to proceed to the Bay in 1672, the *Employ* and the *Prince Rupert*. Later a third, a dogger, seems to have been included in the plans. The *Rupert* was to return the same year, if possible, with Captain

---

[1] "Our merchants have news of the safe arrival of 'their other ship very rich from the North-west passage.'" Newsletter of October 17, 1671, in the Le Fleming MSS, summarized in the 12th *Report* of the Historical Manuscripts Commission, Appendix VII, p. 84. "All the newes is that Zecharyah Gillum is returned from the norwest passage with aboundance of bever." Wait Winthrop to John Winthrop, Jr., Boston, December 11, 1671, in *Winthrop Papers*, 8:388.

[2] H.B.Co. Archives, A/1/1, ff. 8, 10, and 11, entries of January 16 and March 4, 1671/2.

Gillam, who "upon his returne" was "to have a reward for his good services according to his merit." The bark, *Employ,* was to "stay in the country." [3]

The departure was later than usual, about June 22, according to the expense account then kept by the Company for barge hire to Gravesend, for pilotage, lighterage, and so forth. It may be that one of the vessels returned that season, for Gillam is recorded as having received money in October, 1672.[4] Radisson and his brother-in-law were paid on June 10, 1672, and no further payment is mentioned till November, 1673. Captain Thomas Morris commanded the dogger, Captain Gillam the *Rupert,* and Captain Samuel Cole the *Employ.* The first two were reported in English waters once more on October 9, 1673.[5] One of the gunners of the *Employ* was William Bond of Rederith, who testified years later that he sailed from London in June, 1672, with Samuel Cole as master of the vessel, and arrived at the Company's factory at Rupert River in the following October.[6] There he spent the winter. In July, 1673, he was sent by Governor Bayly to Port Nelson. The *Employ* arrived there in September. It remained about fifteen days, the men noting Sir Thomas Button's wintering grounds. There were no Indians to be found, but goods were left "that the Indians finding the Same might be Induced to be there the next year." The vessel returned to Rupert River in October to give the Governor an account of what had been accomplished. Though Governor Bayly intended to follow up this second attempt to settle Port Nelson, nothing could be done the following season for want of provisions.

Radisson returned to England in 1673, but Des Groseilliers remained in the Bay with the *Employ* and her men. The

---

[3] H.B.Co. Archives, A/1/1, ff. 13, 14, and 15, entries of April 12 and 15, 1672.

[4] H.B.Co. Archives, Ledger 101, f. 36, debit side of the account with "Capt Zachariah Gillam" under dates of October 16 and 25, 1672.

[5] H.B.Co. Archives, A/1/1, f. 19, entry of October 9, 1673.

[6] PRO., CO., 134/1, f. 205, May 20, 1687.

experiences of the ensuing winter in the Bay are known in some detail. Before they are recounted, however, it may be well to observe the little that is known of Radisson from 1673 to 1676.

Sometime before Radisson left England for France in 1675 he married one of Sir John Kirke's daughters. His own statement is that he married her in 1672.[7] Sir James Hayes has a little more to remark: "Radisson . . . had before his flight deluded & privately married a Daughter of S[r] John Kirk (a Gentleman of his Majesties band of Pensioners & a member of the Hudsons Bay Company)."[8] No record of the marriage has been found. As the Kirke girl was a Huguenot and Radisson a Catholic, some unusual wedding arrangement may account for the lack of formal record. Kirke at the time of his death in 1685 was a parishioner of St. Martin's in the Fields, and the parish records afford data on him and other members of his family.[9] Even this daughter's Christian name has not been found, however, though some writers on Radisson's career have confused her with Mary Kirke, a notorious courtesan of the period. Persons named Kirke were so common in Restoration England that one must thread his way gingerly among the records of them.

When Radisson returned to England in October, 1673, in Gillam's vessel, shipping was so dangerous on account of the third Dutch War that Captain Gillam was ordered by the Committee of the Company to remain at Portsmouth, where he had docked, until he should have a convoy to London. Radisson, however, was to "take the first opportunity of comeing up to London," and Gillam was ordered to supply

[7] See *post,* Appendix 11, for an affidavit by Peter Espritt Radisson annexed to a letter of the Hudson's Bay Company addressed to the Lords Commissioners, June 5, 1699.

[8] Sir James Hayes to Sir Leoline Jenkins, January 26, 1683/4, PRO., CO., 1/66/129, ff. 315, 316.

[9] Sir John Kirke's will is filed in Somerset House, London, and is dated June 12, 1685. It was proved June 24, 1685.

him with four or five pounds of expense money.[10] The Company seems to have been appreciative of Radisson's special knowledge in the Indian trade and to have consulted with him time and again on the kind of articles that should be purchased for the next voyage. On December 11 the Committee ordered: [11] "That Mr Hawkins accept & pay . . . to Sr James Hayes £4:1 for charges obtayneing a gold chayne & meddale for Mr Radisson." This medal was a signal honor and Radisson refers to it with pride in later years. Some historians have referred to trouble at this time between Gillam and Radisson. If trouble developed, it probably had to do with Radisson's informing the Company that its captains and others were trading on their own account with the Indians. On January 15, 1673/4, at a Committee meeting, it was "Ordered That a bill be prepared & Exhibited in Chancery in the name of this Company against Captain Guillam Captain Morris, & the rest of the seamen & others imployed in this last voyage for discoverye of private trade." [12]

It would appear that Radisson's reason for not going to the Bay in 1674 was failure to receive from the Company what he thought was due him. A general court took up the matter on June 29, 1674, after the departure of the ships to the Bay, and came to the decision to allow

. . . Mr Raddison one hundred poundes per annum from the time of his last arrival at London, in consideration of services done by him, out of which to be deduced what hath bin already paid him since that time, & if it shall please God to blesse the Company with good successe hereafter that they shall come to be in a prosperous condition, they will then reassume the consideration hereof.[13]

The Company continued Radisson and his brother-in-law on their payrolls until well into the year 1676. The records

[10] H.B.Co. Archives, A/1/1, f. 19, entry of October 23, 1673.
[11] H.B.Co. Archives, A/1/1, f. 23.
[12] H.B.Co. Archives, A/1/1, f. 25.
[13] H.B.Co. Archives, A/1/1, f. 42.

show payments to Radisson on January 22, July 8, and November 7, 1674, and on April 12 and July 29, 1675; and on April 7, 1676, the entry is for "Interest of money lent upon his medall £7..0..0." Des Groseilliers was to receive twenty pounds by an order of October 11, 1675. Another entry for 1676, but without information as to the day of the month, is, "By cash paid Groselier & Radison £127..0..0." As a statement of what had been received from the two men in exchange for these sums there is the entry: "Per Contra. By eight years & ½ service at home and abroad in the Companyes Employment." [14]

Meanwhile, the effect of the two explorers' deeds was being felt in New France. By November 10, 1670, the intendant of New France, Jean Talon, a man of energy and vision, had become aware of the threat to the French control of the fur trade in northern North America. In fact, he must have known of it much earlier in the year, for Mère Marie de l'Incarnation in Quebec wrote of Des Groseilliers' exploits in Hudson Bay in a letter of August 27 to her son. We have already noted that portion of the letter that describes Des Groseilliers' youth. It is pertinent here to quote another portion of the letter as showing the current Canadian opinion of Des Groseilliers and his discovery: [15]

He led the [New] English to expect that he would find the Northwest passage and accordingly they sent him to England, where he was given a vessel, a crew, and everything necessary for the voyage. Thus outfitted he put to sea, where, instead of taking the customary route, whereon others have always failed, he went off on a tack and hunted so well that he found the great Bay of the North. There he found a numerous tribe and filled his ship or ships with furs of immense value. He returned to England, where the king gave him twenty thousand *écus* as a reward, and he was made a Knight of the Garter, which is said to be a very great honor. He took possession of this great country for the king of England. As for

[14] See the records of committee meetings for the dates given; and Ledger 101, ff. 32 and 70, and Ledger 102, ff. 33 and 51.

[15] Marie de l'Incarnation, *Lettres,* 2:447, 448. An *écu* was worth four *livres* in Canada in 1666; ten *livres* made a pound sterling.

himself, he became rich in a very short time. A gazette was issued for this French explorer in England.

It is not credible that Des Groseilliers was made a Knight of the Garter, but evidently he wrote back to Quebec a story that did not hide his light under a bushel. The gazette story is probably true, for the only printed newspapers of the day in England were court inspired. Other news was passed about in *gazettes-à-main,* or handwritten "extras" that circulated more or less surreptitiously. One of them, mentioning the two Frenchmen and their plan, has already been quoted.

Talon, then, in his letter of November 10, 1670, was only repeating to Colbert what was current knowledge in Canada: [16]

> I learn by the return of the Algonquins, who will winter this year at Tadoussac, that two European vessels have been seen very near Hudson's bay, where they "cabanent," as the Indians express it [*the meaning is that they built dwellings*]. After reflecting on all the nations that might have penetrated as far North as that, I can light only on the English, who, under the guidance of a man named Des Grozeliers, formerly an inhabitant of Canada, might possibly have attempted the navigation, of itself not much known, and not less dangerous. I intend dispatching thither over land some man of resolution to invite the Kilistinons [*Crees*], who are in great numbers in the vicinity of that Bay, to come down to see us, as the Ottawas do, in order that we may have the first pick of what the latter savages bring us, who, acting as pedlars between those nations and us, make us pay for a round-about of three or four hundred leagues.

Other portions of Talon's dispatches by the same fleet from Canada tell of a project by a man named Poulet, of Dieppe, to find the Northwest Passage by sailing northeastward from California; of De la Salle dispatched to find the passage to the South Sea; of Péré, sent the preceding year to find a copper mine on or beyond Lake Superior; of De Saint Lusson sent to find "a communication with the South Sea which

[16] This letter has been published (in part) both by Margry and by O'Callaghan. See Margry, *Découvertes et établissements des Français,* 1: 87–92; and O'Callaghan, *New York Colonial Documents,* 9: 67–70.

separates this continent from China"; and of similar matters. If royal medals would not thereby be rendered too common, Talon suggests, a dozen should be sent him with which to reward useful discoveries, either of new countries or of mines. It is quite clear that the news of Des Groseilliers' successful trip of 1668–1669 was bringing things to pass in New France.

Des Groseilliers had at last stung the Canadians into action, but it required a little while and more threats of competition before the scales fell from Colbert's eyes. He replied to Talon's statesmanlike letter on February 11, 1671 : [17]

> Your action in sending Sieur de la Salle to the southward and Sieur de Saint Lusson to the northward to discover the passage to the South Sea is very good; but the principal thing to which you must look in these kinds of discoveries is to find copper mines, in order that many Frenchmen may be drawn from old to New France. . . . I will look into Captain Poulet's proposition.

Unemployment in France was of more concern to Colbert at that moment than the loss of an American empire.

The Jesuits, on the other hand, had no intention of losing an American empire. Their keen brains recognized at once what Des Groseilliers' actions meant for them. It was their aim that all possible discoveries should be made under their aegis. It was for that reason, no doubt, when Péré reached their Ottawa mission in the course of his explorations of 1669–1670, that he seems to have been detained and his letters either censored or scrutinized so closely that he dared not write freely to Talon. The intendant complained in his dispatch of 1670 that "This Péré has not returned and is living with the fathers who keep the Ottawa mission, whence he writes only ambiguously. This makes me fear that they have kept back the knowledge that he was to get of this mine and prevented him from communicating his discoveries in their entirety." [18]

[17] Colbert to Talon, Archives des Colonies, B3: 22.
[18] Talon's letter to Colbert, November 10, 1670.

Mère Marie's undated letter of the early part of 1671 tells of two Jesuits gone to explore the region north and west of the Great Lakes and of De Saint Lusson's colorful pageantry at Sault Ste Marie, where amid the singing of the *Vexilla Regis* and the reverberations of musket volleys he took possession of that north country for France.[19] Father Allouez, she writes, has gone to even more distant peoples than has been his wont in his Lake Superior mission. Father Charles Albanel has gone to Hudson Bay. On the way to the Bay, she writes, Indians told Albanel's party of the arrival in James Bay of two large vessels and three small pinnaces from England, with the intent of taking possession of the country. She adds that the two large vessels have returned to England, loaded with furs, but that the pinnaces are wintering in the Bay. "Here we have a set-back of consequence to our temporal progress," she writes. "If only someone had been sent thither by France, as the court had been warned to do, this loss would not have occurred. Those who have gone thither on this exploration will perhaps not leave without planting the Cross there with the fleurs des lys in the face of the English." Unfortunately for France, there were few at the court of Louis XIV equal in statesmanlike vision to this nun in Quebec, or Des Groseilliers would have been heeded a decade earlier.

Talon wrote again to Colbert with the fall fleet of 1671.[20] In this letter there was much about De Saint Lusson and the route to the South Sea. De la Salle was not yet back. "Such discoveries must be the work either of time, or of the king." A clear-headed man, this Talon, and the pity is that his words were not heeded. He goes on:

Three months ago I dispatched with Father Albanel, a Jesuit, Sieur de Saint Simon, a young Canadian gentleman, recently honored by his Majesty with that Title. They were to penetrate as far

[19] Marie de l'Incarnation, *Lettres*, 2: 529–539.
[20] Talon to the King, November 2, 1671, in O'Callaghan, *New York Colonial Documents*, 9: 71–73.

as Hudson's bay; draw up a memoir of all that they will discover; drive a trade in furs with the Indians, and especially reconnoitre [*to learn*] whether there may be any means of wintering ships in that quarter, in order to establish a factory that might, when necessary, supply provisions to the vessels that will possibly hereafter discover, by that channel, the communication between the two seas—the North and the South sea.

He then tells of news from Father Albanel regarding English vessels in the Bay, and goes on:

If my letters, in reply, are safely delivered to the said Father, this Establishment will be thoroughly examined, and his Majesty will have full information about it. As those countries have been long ago [*anciennement*] originally discovered by the French, I have commissioned the said Sieur de Saint Simon to take renewed possession, in his Majesty's name. . . . It is proposed to me to dispatch a bark of sixty tons hence to Hudson's bay, whereby it is expected something will be discovered of the communication of the two seas.

De Saint Simon's own account of this winter's jaunt to Hudson Bay is extant.[21] It states that in 1671 Paul Denis, Sieur de Saint Simon, then twenty-three years of age, left Quebec with Father Albanel, a man named Sébastien Pennara [?], and eight Indians. They followed the Saguenay–Lake St. Jean–Nemiskau route to the Bay, where they found two houses. No one was in them and the houses were in disrepair, having no windows or doors and being constructed only of upright logs and thatched roofs. The Frenchmen explored along the Bay till they found a great number of Indians. Father Albanel baptized the chief of this band and the party returned to Rupert River. Father Albanel nailed up the king's arms at three places, thus taking possession of the country for France.

Years later France was to make much of this *prise de possession* in her claims against the English occupancy of

---

[21]"Enquête faite par le Lieut. générale en la prévôté de Québec," November 2, 1688, a copy of which was made on November 12, 1712, and signed by Vaudreuil and Bégon. BN., Margry Papers, 9284, ff. 5–10, affidavit of Paul Denis, Sieur de St. Simon.

Port Nelson. Had Des Groseilliers been in the Bay during the winter of 1671–1672 instead of the season of 1673–1674, he might well have left the English interest two years earlier than he actually did. For Father Albanel, reputedly the son of English parents resident in France, was more than a match for the explorer and his English employers, as events were to prove.

Albanel did not find Des Groseilliers in 1672, but in 1674 he was successful. In October, 1673, Radisson returned to England in Gillam's ship, as already related, but Des Groseilliers remained in the Bay. A diary kept that season by Thomas Gorst shows that Des Groseilliers was one of those who went in the *Employ* in July, 1673, to Port Nelson.[22] An attempt was also made the same season to find the Severn River, which the Indians had probably described to the English party. On October 10 ice began to form on the shore of the Bay and on the twenty-third Indians arrived, one of whom was from Quebec. By November 6 Rupert River was frozen over. February was marked by a thaw and by scurvy among the men. Geese were seen on the first of April the following year and word came that a party of Frenchmen were eight days' journey up the river.

On May 20 it was learned from Indians that the "upland" Indians of the hinterland would not arrive for trade, having been intercepted by the French.

In May, 1674, the Governor sent Des Groseilliers, Cole, Gorst, and others to trade at Moose River, apparently at Des Groseilliers' recommendation. They returned in June, having got only about 250 skins. The Governor himself then went to "Moosebee" and got 1,500 skins from inland Indians who came to trade with him. By June 24 all the Indians had left. The Governor took this opportunity of

[22] See John Oldmixon, *The British Empire in America,* 1: 549–558 (London, 1741) ; the diary is also quoted in J. B. Tyrell, ed., *Documents Relating to the Early History of Hudson Bay,* pp. 384–396 (Champlain Society Publications, Vol. XVIII, Toronto, 1931).

going to find Albany River and exploring Port Nelson further. He reached Albany River on July 18, "where no
Englishman had been before." He stayed till July 21 and
tried to reach Port Nelson, but was unsuccessful. He got
back to his base just before Albanel arrived on August 30
in a canoe. En route the latter had been stopped by Indians,
but he had managed to get through once more to the Bay.
This time he found the man he was seeking, Des Groseilliers.

By the fall of 1673 Frontenac was in Quebec and Talon
had left. The new Governor on November 13, 1673, sent
word to Colbert by the returning fleet: [23]

> Des Groseilliers is seducing all our Indians and by means of
> presents is drawing them to the Bay, where he is established. So I
> have decided to make use of the zeal which Father Albanel, a Jesuit,
> expressed to go thither on a mission in order to turn the Indians
> away from that route, which would injure the trade of Tadoussac
> and even that of the Ottawa. To these Des Groseilliers, according
> to what is told me, has also sent presents, but as yet he has had no
> reply and I shall use every effort to prevent him from so having.
> The said Father Albanel is to sound out Des Groseilliers, if he en-
> counter him, and try to see if he can make him return to our inter-
> ests. Father Albanel wanted to take Des Groseilliers' son, who is
> here with us, but I believed that was not fitting for the trip.

Father Albanel took with him not only letters for Des Groseilliers, but also one for the Governor from Frontenac
recommending the priest to Bayly.[24] Gorst relates that the
letter to Des Groseilliers "gave jealousy to the English of
his corresponding with the French." He also states that Des
Groseilliers' son-in-law [stepson?] lived in Quebec and had
accompanied the priest part way with three other Frenchmen, who returned, fearing the Indians.[25] Gorst then proceeds to tell how Albanel and his party were ready to depart
from Fort Charles when seven guns were heard. Unfortu-

[23] *Rapport de l'archiviste de la province de Québec pour 1926–1927*, p. 50
(Quebec, 1927).
[24] PRO., CO., 134/1/217. The letter is dated October 8, 1673.
[25] Oldmixon, *British Empire in America*, 1: 556. The word *jealousy* meant
suspicion in seventeenth-century English.

nately for Albanel, it was the ships from England, the *Prince Rupert* and the *Shaftsbury,* bringing out a new Governor, William Lyddal. Bayly determined to send the priest as a prisoner to England.

Captain Gillam and Governor Bayly were supposed to return to England with the *Prince Rupert* in 1674, but the weather forced Gillam and his crew to winter in the Bay. So the provisions that were intended for the new Governor and the men who were to stay with him were used up. In 1675, therefore, every one left the Bay except four men, who were left to guard the property there and to hold possession for England. With the Englishmen went Father Albanel, his men, and two Indians. One of the natives died en route, but the other, "Prince Attash," arrived in England and was given to Prince Rupert.[26] Captain Shepard in the *Shaftsbury* arrived at Deal on September 24, 1675. Captain Gillam arrived in the same port the following day. One of Sir Joseph Williamson's news agents boarded the *Rupert* and interviewed Gillam. "I see the french Jesuit, which is a little owld man: and the other Indian that is livinge is a very Losty man," he reported.

The Jesuit, Albanel, utilized his knowledge of English and England to good advantage. Though he was charged with seducing the Indians of Hudson Bay to popery, a French allegiance, and a French market, and with inciting Des Groseilliers to treacherous designs, he was soon allowed to go to France with every mark of favor. Almost ten years later Prince Rupert's former secretary, Sir James Hayes, wrote to Sir Leoline Jenkins:[27]

One Pere Albanell a Jesuit and missionary of Canada and another french man who were in that Expedition, and in the same Fray [*an Indian assault en route from Canada to Hudson Bay*], fled from the

---

[26] Morgan Lodge in letters of September 24 and 25, 1675, from Deal, reported to Sir Joseph Williamson, Secretary of State, all the information given in this paragraph. PRO., S.P., Dom., 373/174 and 175.

[27] Sir James Hayes to Sir Leoline Jenkins, January 26, 1683/4, PRO., CO., 1/66/129, ff. 315, 316.

dang^r & came to our Factory to Rupert River, and dissembling the accident y^t brought them thither, desired to be receaved as freinds in distress But one Mr Charles Bayly, who at y^t time governed for the Company in the Bay being informed by some freinds—Indians, y^t ye said Pere Albanell had been sometime before at our Fort at Rupert River & findeing the armes of his Maj^tie of greate Brittain there sett up, and the men who belonged to that factory absent, hee had pulled downe the Kings Armes with Indignity, Mr Bayly thought it his Duty to send him for England, there to receive the pleasure of the Company. But at his arr[i]vall hee was used with more Gentlenesse then he had reason to Expect, for after a Short Stay here, he was (upon his request and other more powerfull applications) dismissed with a Certificate of the Comittee of the said Company, setting forth in what manner hee was brought over—to the End he might not fall into disgrace wth his Superiours at his returne, as if hee had fled from his mission, wch hee pretended to be apprehensive off; and some money they also gave him in Charity towards the defraying of his Voyage for France, for which kindnesse he soon made ungratefull returnes, for in the time of his sejour here, he found the way to dispose our said Servants Grozilier & Radison to Leave our imploym^t and soone after his arrivall in France their peace was made there, and such Invitations made from thence as tempted them to breake their faith and privately to withdraw themselves from the Service of the Company.

The "more powerful applications" were probably those of Charles II and the Catholic Duke of York, soon to be the Governor of the Company, who was the brother of the King and an ardent friend of the Jesuits.

* * *

So, after a little more than ten years from their arrival in plague-stricken England, Radisson and Des Groseilliers slipped quietly across the Channel to a France that had never understood their ideals and objectives and from which, under the protection of the Jesuits, they now expected much. For the second, but not the last time, they were doomed to disappointment.

CHAPTER XII

Black Robe Versus Gray Gown

Neither man could have been totally ignorant of the attitude of Louis XIV and his chief ministers toward the Jesuits. They must have sensed, what was common knowledge in New France, that the King was favoring the Recollects and Sulpicians there as a means of checking the power of the Jesuits, and that one of Frontenac's strongest assets in royal eyes was his leaning toward the Recollects. In the King's memorial "to serve as instructions to M. de Frontenac" of April 7, 1672, it is specifically stated that the new governor "must treat the Jesuits, who deserve it for their zeal, with a great deal of consideration; but if they should attempt to carry ecclesiastical authority too far, he must reprehend them with gentleness. He is to protect in like manner the Sulpicians and the Recollects, so as to counterbalance the authority of the Jesuits." [1] The next year Frontenac's instructions were that the court would send Recollect priests that year and every succeeding year, in order to counterbalance the excessive authority of the Jesuits. Unlike the ordinary clergy, the letter continues, the Jesuits do not appear to wish to attract the Indians to live with the French and become civilized. Frontenac must strive, in concert with the Recollects, to work a change in this matter. [2]

On November 10, 1674, Frontenac wrote very plainly to the provincial of the Recollects at Paris regarding the attitude of the Jesuits in Canada toward the Recollects; of attempts to prevent the Recollects from entering the mission

---

[1] *Rapport de l'archiviste de la province de Québec pour 1926–1927*, pp. 3–6.
[2] *Rapport de l'archiviste de la province de Québec pour 1926–1927*, pp. 25, 26.

field in New France; of the need for fourteen or fifteen Recollects, eight for Quebec, two for De la Salle's post on Lake
Ontario, two for Three Rivers, and two for Percée Rock;
and of the wisdom of sending the provincial's reply to Frontenac's letter to Madame de Frontenac, so that she might
send it to her husband, without interference, for "there are
people here very curious to know what instructions others
receive." [3] The inference is clear that the "curious people,"
the Jesuits, had their own successful devices for securing and
reading the instructions from the King to the Governor.

The day after this document was penned, an equally frank
letter was addressed to Colbert by the Recollect leader in
New France, Eustache Maupassant.[4] It tells of the Jesuits'
attempts to thwart the Recollects' activities in New France,
of the Governor's kindness in building a home for the expected Recollects, of the jealousy of "certain people," and
of other conditions.

If I had wished to enter into the cabals here formed against the
governor, I would have found much favor with the "ones" who have
a great deal of power in this country; but I am too good a subject
of the King to separate myself ever so slightly from the obedience
that I owe to him that is the king's personal representative.

Thus clearly did the Recollects ally themselves with the King
in his struggle with the Papacy for temporal power in France,
a struggle of the 1670's and 1680's in which the Jesuits, as
watch-dogs of Church authority, took the opposite side. Nevertheless, the Jesuits felt, and rightly, as Bishop Laval's
agent, Jean Dudouyt, writes, that "this Pontificate . . . is
not favourable to the Jesuits." "This creates an uneasy feeling among the Jesuits of France against the Bishops and even
against the Seminary, which finding itself obliged to support

---

[3] BN., Mélanges de Colbert, 171, ff. 54–56. This letter, written by Frontenac
to Father Germain, the provincial of the Recollects at Paris, was received by
his successor, Hyacinthe le Febvre, who inclosed it in a letter of March 9, 1675,
to Colbert, together with a letter of November 12, 1674, from the superior of
the Recollects at Quebec. The enclosure forms folios 57 and 58.

[4] See above, Note 3 of this chapter.

the Bishops, cannot do so without giving trouble to the Jesuits in several things." [5]

It was to this situation that Radisson and Des Groseilliers now returned at the instigation of the Jesuits. Letters of "grace, pardon, and remission by His Majesty to Médard Chouart Des Groiselliers and Pierre-Esprit Radisson" were issued immediately after Albanel got back to France in December, 1675.[6] Lured by these and probably with promises of the grant which was actually signed on April, 6, 1676, permitting the two men to establish a seal fishery for twenty years off the coast of Anticosti and a porpoise fishery from Anticosti to Montreal, Radisson and Des Groseilliers left London for Paris late in 1675.[7]

The letter of Dudouyt already quoted throws some light on the failure of Radisson and his brother-in-law to elicit anything worth while for their exploration schemes from Colbert: "M. de Comporté is [made] grand provost at 500 livres salary. . . . He owes the appointment to M. de la Chesnaye, for M. de Frontenac had worked strongly for M. Lemoyne. The Sieur Ratisson has obtained nothing, and Jolliet's proposition has not been agreed to, to go to the Illinois and form a settlement, the expense of which M. de la Chesnaye had offered to defray." De la Chenaye, already encountered in the annals of Radisson and Des Groseilliers, was a powerful fur merchant in New France.[8] He was a great friend of Abbé Eusèbe Renaudot, the grandson of Thé-

[5] A letter signed J. D. D. [*Jean Dudouyt*] to Mgr. Laval, Paris [1677], and published, from the original in Laval University, in Canadian Archives, *Report*, 1885, Note C, pp. xcix–cxxxi. Jean Dudouyt was sent by Bishop Laval, as his grand vicar, to France in 1676. He remained there till his death in 1688.

[6] *Inventaire des insinuations du conseil souverain de la Nouvelle-France*, edited by Pierre-Georges Roy, p. 51 (*Archives de la Province de Québec*, Beauceville, 1921). It is also copied in BN., Margry Papers, 9284, ff. 40, 41.

[7] O'Callaghan, *New York Colonial Documents*, 9:794; BN., Margry Papers, 9305, f. 278. The author is indebted to M. M. Giraud for the second reference.

[8] See his memoir on Canada, printed in [Sulte], *Collection de manuscrits*, 1:245–261, as of the year 1676, though actually its date was October [31], 1695. On page 252 in the printed version, De la Chenaye states that he went to Canada first in 1655. The original document is to be found in AC., C11, 13:440, and a copy is in BN., Margry Papers, 9274, ff. 48–55, where the date is given as 1697.

ophraste Renaudot, the founder of the press in France. Renaudot now became the decisive factor in the two explorers' careers.

Théophraste's son, the father of Eusèbe, had been the dauphin's physician. Both of these Renaudots had been great powers in France. Their descendant, Eusèbe Renaudot, was noted for his linguistic abilities and his zeal for religion, though of the Jansenist flavor. He stood high in the esteem of Louis XIV and Colbert. The latter relied upon him for information to direct the policy of the court in its relations with England, especially after James II mounted the throne and Louis XIV saw his chance to return England to Mother Church. Renaudot was also consulted in matters touching Rome and Spain. He was one of the few Frenchmen who could speak English at a time when that language was not one of the social graces. He was *habile*, as the French said. Moreover, he was greatly interested in the new "science," and corresponded with important "scientists" of the day. One of his special friends was François de Callières, whose attachment to the Matignon, Condé, and De Longueville houses gave him immense political power. Besides this powerful politician's aid, Renaudot could count on that of Colbert, of the two princes of Conti, of Condé, of Bossuet, and of the Marquis de Montausier.[9] He was not in sympathy with the Jesuits, favoring instead the King's Gallican principles. He and De Callières were especially interested in De la Salle's explorations.

Closely connected with Renaudot was Abbé Claude

[9] For data on Renaudot, see his own papers in BN., Nouvelles Acquisitions, 7483–7497; also 9294, ff. 12–16; the *Journal des Sçavans*, 1748, p. 581; and the Historical Manuscripts Commission, 7th *Report*, Appendix, p. 392. For the De Callières family see *Nouvelle biographie générale*, published by Firmin-Didot & Cie (Paris, 1878); J. Edmond Roy, *Rapport sur les archives de France relatives à l'histoire du Canada*, p. 909 (Ottawa, 1911); H. Moulin, "Les deux de Callières (Jacques et François)" in *Mémoires de l'Académie de Caën*, XXXVIII (1883); and Benjamin Sulte, in the Royal Society of Canada [First Series], *Proceedings and Transactions*, Vol. 8, Section 1, pp. 91–112 (Ottawa, 1890).

Bernou, of whom little is known. In 1686 Bernou wrote that he was then forty-eight years of age; and describes himself at another time as "bachelor in theology of the faculty of Paris, Rue St. Honoré." On still another occasion he describes himself as

. . . Abbé Bernou, come to Rome from Paris to aid in defending the just rights of the Crown of Portugal in the colony of St. Sacrement [*in South America*] against the Spanish. He has the advantage of having been born in the vicinity of the lands of the illustrious house of Némour. He represents with profound respect to Your Serene Highness that when Sieur Taborda, Portuguese envoy to the court of France, chose him for this work . . . to serve the crown of Portugal he . . . quitted a post to which he cannot return and which gave him an honorable living.[10]

It will be noted that Bernou refers to the "house of Némour." In 1666 César d'Estrées, Bishop of Laon and later Cardinal, conducted Marie Elizabeth Françoise of Savoy, daughter of the Duke of Nemour, to Portugal to marry King Alphonse. In his train went Nicolas Thoynard, one of the outstanding "scientists" of the day. Thoynard's correspondence was with such men of genius as Abbé Hautefeuille, John Locke, Melchisedech Thévenot, Abbé Renaudot, the nephews of Blaise Pascal, the Danish scientist Oläus Römer, Bernard de la Monnoye, Abbé Claude Nicaise, Bossuet, Du Cange, André Morell, the great numismatist, and many others. He was especially interested in navigation, astronomy, and geographical discoveries. He returned to Paris in 1668 in the train of César d'Estrées.[11]

[10] Bernou to Renaudot, January 1, 1686, in BN., Renaudot Papers, 7497, f. 285; and BN., Clairambault Collection, No. 848, ff. 363, No. 1016, f. 651, and No. 1017, f. 191. Pierre Clairambault (1651–1740) held positions under Colbert, De Seignelay, De Pontchartrain, and De Maurepas. He was a great collector and administered the estate of Abbé Bernou, wherefrom he got many documents of interest for North American history and geography. See also Margry, *Découvertes et établissements des Français*, 1:428, 429.

[11] Thoynard's manuscripts form Nouvelles Acquisitions, 560–563, in the Bibliothèque Nationale, Paris. He was a friend of Abbé de la Gallinée, of De la Salle, of De Longeuil, and of D'Iberville. He was a cousin of De Beauharnois and related to De Pontchartrain.

César d'Estrées came from one of the most interesting and powerful families of seventeenth-century France. His father was François Annibal, Marquis de Coeurs, "duke, peer, and marshal of France." His brothers were François Annibal II, duke and peer of France and ambassador at Rome; and Jean, Vice-Admiral of France. To get money on one occasion the father of these three famous brothers borrowed 45,000 écus from "Mr du Housset, Maistre Antoine Legoux, Mr Ollier, and others," among whom was Esprit Cabart de Villermont. This last was a correspondent of Abbé Renaudot and Abbé Bernou, a friend of Madame de Maintenon, a relative of the Canadian explorer-priest, Père Thierry Beschefer, and a "councilor of the king." [12]

Of the names mentioned, those of Cardinal D'Estrées, Abbé Bernou, Abbé Renaudot, Nicolas Thoynard, Cabart de Villermont, and De Callières are of special significance. D'Estrées seems to have been the center and focus of the entire group. In his service in Rome was Bernou, who worked hand in hand with Renaudot. Thoynard was also in D'Estrées' service, as we have seen; Thoynard has preserved some important records of explorers in American by means of his papers. De Villermont had loaned money to the Cardinal's father and so the Cardinal felt some obligation to him. We shall see Radisson in the service of the Cardinal's brother, Admiral D'Estrées.

Other bonds united all these men. Chief among them was an interest in geographic explorations, especially in America. Most of them were backers of De la Salle. Most of them favored the Recollects as against the Jesuits, and the King of France as against the Pope in ultramontane disputes.

---

[12] For the D'Estrées family, see BN., Collection Clairambault, 879, ff. 140–145, a memoir of Marshal d'Estrées against the Duchess d'Estrées, February 7, 1705; also ff. 146 and 149. For De Villermont, see Bernou's long correspondence with Renaudot in BN., Renaudot Papers, many of which seem to have been preserved by De Villermont. The latter, also a "newspaper" man, annoyed Renaudot by publishing some of the information that Renaudot's clique received from explorers, and which in their eyes should have been kept secret.

Much of their correspondence has survived and reveals the enthusiasm of these men and their kind in France, England, Germany, the Netherlands, Denmark, Sweden, and Italy for "curious" phenomena such as explorers would note in the flora and fauna of newly discovered lands; for the relatively new organizations, like the Académie des Sciences in France and the Royal Society in England, that furthered the interests and enthusiasm of these men; for new gadgets to make life "comfortable" and agreeable; and for new machinery and implements to make science exact.[13]

As early as 1679 and perhaps earlier Abbé Bernou became De la Salle's agent. One letter of Bernou to Renaudot gives a full account of how this situation came about and how De la Salle later complained of the retaining fee that Bernou felt was a reasonable one. Bernou wrote that he felt this complaint of De la Salle was unjust, "but I will not serve him with less exactitude, since I am still possessed of the desire I have had all my life, and of which I am not the master, for the French colonies, having served many others similarly without any hope of recompense." [14]

Among these others were Radisson and Des Groseilliers. To understand what happened to these men in the next few years, it becomes necessary to explain the relations of De la Salle with Bernou, Renaudot, De Callières, and De Villermont.

De la Salle evidently sent detailed letters or accounts of his trips of the years from 1678 to 1682 on the Great Lakes

[13] The best source of information for all these men is the archives of the Royal Society, London. These archives were put at the author's service through the kindness of that venerable and famous organization. The author is especially indebted to the librarian, H. W. Robinson. Another source of information is the organs of such societies as the Royal Society, the Académie des Sciences, and so forth. The author is also indebted to Harcourt Brown, Professor of Romance Languages at Brown University, who introduced her to Thoynard, Nicaise, and many of the other French scientists of the seventeenth century, and whose Scientific Organizations in Seventeenth Century France (History of Science Society, New Series, 1934) was of great service to her.

[14] Bernou to Renaudot, April 11, 1684, in BN., Renaudot Papers, 7497, ff. 116, 117.

and the Mississippi River to Bernou, who wrote up a *relation* and made a map from them.[15] The letters seem to answer the charge, made by certain historians, that Bernou deliberately falsified De la Salle's *relations* and maps in order that that explorer might have the credit for having discovered the Ohio River and other topographical features in the Mississippi Valley.[16] Bernou was a match for the Jesuits in intrigue, but he appears to have had a genuine regard for geographical truth. In one letter he refers to his reputation for being a great politician, and the inference is that his services in that domain were in great demand.[17] Thus, in 1685, a certain memoir that aimed at securing a large part of the New World for a new bishopric, the "island of Louisiana," for the Recollects, was Bernou's, according to his own statement, though it was accepted everywhere as Cardinal D'Estrées' handiwork.[18]

As one browses through the manuscript remains of the latter seventeenth century, one gradually becomes aware of many documents in a very precise handwriting. Usually they inclose a memoir presented to the French, Portuguese, or Papal courts. Usually, too, there is no signature, and the intent of the paper is to present the petition of an explorer or churchman. If one bothers to compare the writing with Abbé Bernou's signed letters, the conclusion of a common author-

---

[15] The evidence on this head is found in Bernou's letters to Renaudot in the latter's papers, especially BN., Renaudot Papers, 7497. A recent study of De la Salle's relations to Bernou and Renaudot, though incomplete and somewhat biased in favor of the Jesuits, is nevertheless the best presentation of that relationship that has yet appeared. It is Jean Delanglez, S.J., *Some La Salle Journeys* (Institute of Jesuit History Publications, Chicago, 1938). The author appears unaware of De Callières' influence on Renaudot and Bernou and the part De Villermont played. See also other publications by the same author.

[16] Grace Lee Nute, introduction to Marion Cross's translation of *Father Louis Hennepin's Description of Louisiana* (Minneapolis, 1938), particularly pp. xii and xiv; Delanglez, *Some La Salle Journeys,* pp. 21 and 22; and BN., Renaudot Papers, 7497, ff. 89–91, 116, 117.

[17] Bernou to Renaudot, February 22, 1684, in BN., Renaudot Papers, 7497, ff. 97, 98.

[18] See Bernou to Renaudot, April 3, 1684, May 22, 1685, and June 19 and July 3, 1685, in BN., Renaudot Papers, ff. 113, 220, 221, 224, 226, and 227.

ship is inescapable. Such a petition representing the desires of Pierre Esprit Radisson has been found.

It exists in two forms, one of which begins: "Sieur Radisson having acquired a special knowledge of the larger part of North America by his voyages in New France and by the sojourn he made both north of it and south of it among the English, whom he has left in order to obey the orders he has received and to satisfy the desire he has always had to serve his own country . . ." It goes on to exalt New France and her possibilities and to explain why she is, at present writing, slipping backward. Reference is made to the peace made with the Iroquis, to "the present population of New France, which is close to ten thousand souls," and to the slump in beaver prices that forced the formation of a fur company, about three years earlier, whose purpose was to be conversant with the amount of furs proper to market. The author then proceeds to summarize the possibilities of the two other occupations open to *habitants,* that is, the fisheries and agriculture. As the document is incomplete, the author never reaches the discussion of agriculture, but he spends a good deal of ink on the (*sedentary*) fisheries.[19]

The second form of Radisson's petition, similar up to this point to the first, goes on expatiating at length on the fisheries, adds a list of other native products that would enhance France's commerce, and mentions minerals. The author then divides New France, for agricultural purposes, into east and west. The dividing line is Montreal. The western part can again be divided—north and south. The north is richer in furs and probably so in mines. The documents end with the very beginning of the discussion of the southwest.[20] Its date was probably 1677.[21]

[19] BN., Collection Clairambault, 1016, ff. 649–650. See Appendix 3, this volume.

[20] BN., Collection Clairambault, 1016, ff. 390, 391. See Appendix 3, this volume.

[21] The reasons for assigning it to that period must be given. Radisson and Des Groseilliers were interested in fisheries at that time, as evidenced by the

Almost certainly Bernou either found something that he needed in Radisson's memoir and copied it for his own use, or he himself shaped that memoir for presentation to the court. The draft form of the petition seems to indicate the second course. It is in Bernou's handwriting and it is full of changes and erasures. Thus, like so many of his compatriots, Radisson put his case into the hands of a man who was famed

concession granted them in 1676. In 1676 Des Groseilliers returned to Canada, where he remained for several years (see *post,* p. 169). Hence he is not mentioned in the documents. Radisson, too, was in Canada in 1676 and left France in 1677 to be absent till well into 1678. Therefore 1677 was the year for Radisson to pen such a petition in France. Moreover, the fur-trading company mentioned in Radisson's petition was organized in 1674. In 1677, as we have already noted in Dudouyt's letter, Radisson was urging something before the court at the same time that Jolliet was planning a colony among the Illinois. A letter of instructions from Colbert to the intendant of New France, Duchesneau, dated April 28, 1677, and apparently taking up most of the points treated by Dudouyt's letter, mentions Sieur Jolliet's request for permission to go and settle the Illinois country with twenty men, and the proposal of erecting a fort at Percée Rock. [Sulte], *Collection de manuscrits,* 1:262, from AC., 1676–1678, Series B, Vol. 7, f. 1. Neither request was granted. Dudouyt likewise states that neither Jolliet's nor Radisson's request was granted. Thus we have a clue to the object of Radisson's petition. Percée Rock was the center of the cod and other fisheries; and was closely associated with Radisson's career. Later an attempt was made by him and his associates to use it as an entrepôt for furs obtained in the Hudson Bay trade of a certain Canadian company. His friend, Nicolas Denys, has much to say about the sedentary fisheries in his book published in 1672. In 1672 Pierre Denys, a nephew of Nicolas, began an active attempt to establish sedentary fisheries there. BN., Collection Clairambault, 1016, ff. 295, 337; P.-G. Roy, *Inventaire des concessions en fief et seigneurie,* 2:127 (*Archives de la Province de Québec,* Beauceville, 1927); and Denys, *Description and Natural History,* pp. 222, 223, Footnote 2. Thus it would seem that Radisson's petition dates from 1677 and that it aimed at a possible monopoly of fishing rights at Percée Rock.

We have still more evidence that 1677 was the date of the petition. In 1682 [?] a document was written by Bernou entitled, "A friend of Cavelier de la Salle presents the official relation of the undertaking of 1679–81." Margry, *Découvertes et établissements des Français,* 2:277–288. Much of it is reminiscent of the Radisson memoir already discussed and of another Radisson memoir of 1681 [?]. The document of 1681, found in both the Clairambault Collection and the Margry Papers, is headed, "Mémoire sur les découvertes et Commerce de Lamerique septent[riona]le." It is concerned with the possible routes to the mines of North America, which are assumed, *a priori,* to be in the "west and southwest." References to De la Salle and to his departure for Lake Michigan and the Mississippi date the manuscript. BN., Margry Papers, 9284, ff. 50–53, and Clairambault Collection, 1016, ff. 647, 648. Since this document is of unusual interest for Radisson and for De la Salle's and Peñalosa's proposed expeditions (see next footnote), it has been translated and printed in

for the success of his petitions. Probably this was the beginning of Bernou's long association with the fortunes of Radisson and Des Groseilliers. It is important to add that Bernou
was thus the chief link between these two men and De la
Salle. Radisson's experiences and conclusions were drawn
upon to further De la Salle's plans for a great colony in
the Mississippi Valley.

If Radisson's petition dates from 1677, Bernou, when he
penned it, was already interested in the career of a strange
person, whose story gets inextricably mixed with that of De
la Salle. This man was Diego Dionysius de Peñalosa.
Peñalosa's purpose in the middle seventies in France, or
rather the purpose of his patron, one of the D'Estrées,
representing no doubt Louis XIV, was to humiliate Spain
and acquire for France some of the American territory
claimed by Spain and from which came much of Spain's
yearly revenue in treasure ships that were the targets of
English, Dutch, and French privateers and of the buccaneers
of the Caribbean.[22] Bernou was aware of this royal French

Appendix 5. In the document of 1682 the author uses the same numerical figures as Radisson's memoir of 1677, both with regard to beaver skins that may
be profitably marketed and the number of families that can subsist thereby. In
this connection the later document (1682) mentions that the population of New
France is gaining and cites for proof the recent censuses: 1671, seven thousand
persons; 1677, nine thousand persons; "last year" (there was a census in 1681)
nearly twelve thousand persons. Now it happens that the earlier document
(1677) states that "the inhabitants have multiplied there [New France] up
to eight to ten thousand souls."

Here, then, is further reasonably good proof that the earlier document was
written in 1677, especially as Louis XIV wrote on April 16, 1676, protesting
that 7,832 persons were far too few for the census of the year and that there
must be some mistake in the figures. Louis XIV to Frontenac, in [Sulte],
Collection de manuscrits, 1:236. Sulte, Découvertes et établissements des Français, 5:37, 47, gives the population figures for Canada as follows: for 1675,
7,832; for 1676, 8,415; for 1679, 9,400; and for 1680, 9,719.

[22] See post, p. 282. For further data on Peñalosa, see C. W. Hackett, "New
Light on Don Diego de Peñalosa," in Mississippi Valley Historical Review, 6:
313–335 (Dec., 1919); E. T. Miller, "The Connection of Peñalosa with the
La Salle Expedition," in the Quarterly of the Texas State Historical Association, 5:97–112 (Oct., 1901); William E. Dunn, Spanish and French Rivalry
in the Gulf Region of the United States, 1678–1702; the Beginnings of Texas
and Pensacola (Austin, 1917); Dictionary of American Biography; and the

interest in "New Biscay" and found Peñalosa his ready and willing tool to make the purpose become a reality. For Peñalosa claimed to have traveled widely in New Biscay, and to have seen the fabulous riches of Quivira and Teguayo. An undated "Memoire pour la decouverte et la Conqueste des Pays de Quivira et de Theguaye dans l'Amerique Septentrionale," though in Bernou's handwriting, was obviously to be presented in Peñalosa's name, since it describes him and his career.[23] It concerns itself not alone with the Southwest, but with Acadia, which the author couples ingeniously with the western proposition. The memoir does not mention De la Salle and refers to the recent discovery of the Mississippi. Thus it can be dated as shortly after 1673. Again the statements and arguments of Radisson's petition of 1677 appear. It would seem, therefore, that Bernou wrote more or less "model" petitions for the different explorers, all of which contained the same facts and arguments. By 1682 he was cleverly combining four projects: De la Salle's, Radisson's, the Recollects', and Peñalosa's. For that reason one must study the careers of the two other explorers and realize the schism in the Catholic Church in France in order to comprehend Radisson's and Des Groseilliers' lack of success in France.

From Bernou's correspondence with Renaudot in later years, it is apparent that Bernou was personally more interested in Peñalosa's scheme than in De la Salle's.[24] By 1684 De Seignelay was also greatly interested in Peñalosa's plan. How far Bernou was interested in Radisson's plan *per se* is hard to estimate from available data. It is certain, however, that he made use of Radisson's geographical informa-

index to Waldo G. Leland, *Guide to Materials for American History in the Libraries and Archives of Paris* (Washington, 1932). For the buccaneers, see Clarence H. Haring, *The Buccaneers in the West Indies in the XVII Century* (New York, 1910), and A. O. Exquemelin, *The History of the Bucaniers of America*, 2 vols. (London, 1741).

[23] BN., Fonds Français, 9097, ff. 171–178.

[24] This statement is made after many careful perusals of Bernou's letters to Renaudot in the latter's collection in the Bibliothèque Nationale, Paris.

tion in numerous ways. As Des Groseilliers is never mentioned in these earlier documents by Bernou, they were
probably penned after Des Groseilliers' return to Canada
in 1676.

CHAPTER XIII

Disappointment Once More

Radisson and his brother-in-law did not remain long in France after their defection from the Hudson's Bay Company. As soon as they had left England, representations were sent to the French court by the English government warning against them and the plans that they were hatching. On January 26,1676, there was presented in England "To the Kings most Excellent Matie The humble Peticoñ of ye Governo^r and Company of Adventurers Trading into Hudsons Bay." [1] It recites that

There hath been of Late some attempts made from Canada to ye prejudice of y^r Peticoners by a Father Jesuit one Charles Albanel, who not only used his Endeavo^rs by Letter to draw from theyre service a French man one De Grosilier and one Radison an Italian who had been for severall yeares Employed by y^r Peticone^rs and to seduce them to Canada, But also in ye absence of y^r Peticoners ships pulled downe yor Ma^es Ensignes wch were set up in Hudsons Bay.

After Albanel's enforced sojourn in England, the petition continues, he

. . . tooke his Journey for France. And soon after his departure the sayd De Grosilier and Radison having Recd a summe of money from y^r Peticoñers secretly w[i]thdrew themselves and are now together with the sayd Father Jesuit at Paris. From all wch y^r Peticoñers have great reason to suspect some farther Ill designe ag[ains]t theyre Colony & Trade in Hudsons Bay.

The petition asked that the English crown present a memorial to the French ambassador on the subject. On the same day the petition was read at Whitehall and the Privy

[1] PRO., CO., 134/1, Board of Trade, Hudson's Bay, 1:21, 22.

Council ordered that Secretary Coventry represent the case, as desired, to the French ambassador, Monsieur Henri de Massue, Marquis de Ruvigny.[2]

The relations between the French and English crowns in the seventies and early eighties were such that neither side cared to offend the other needlessly. Charles II depended upon his cousin Louis XIV for money so that he need not call a session of the English parliament. Louis XIV, on the other hand, wanted Charles II to acknowledge his Catholic faith openly. Charles played a very ingenious game, tantalizing his cousin, getting his money from Louis, supporting English commerce and imperialism, and never losing the trust of his own subjects by offending them with his religion. Again and again Radisson and Des Groseilliers were to run afoul of the accord between the two monarchs. In 1676 it was now their misfortune to encounter it. Whatever Albanel had planned for or promised the two renegades was not carried out. We have Radisson's own statement of what Colbert offered as an inducement.[3]

He states that he and his brother-in-law, seeing their advice rejected "with contempt" by the Hudson's Bay Company, and "the Councill of other Persons imbrac'd and made use of, which manifestly tended to the ruin of the setlement of the Beaver Trade," accepted Colbert's offer and resolved, "though with Very great reluctancy, to return back into France." The bait, he says, was a promise "unto us of paying us 400 Lewi-Dors [*louis d'or*] redy money, of discharging all our Debts, and of giving us good Employments."

As soon as they reached Paris, they presented themselves to Colbert. At first he blamed them for preferring England's service to France's. However, letters of pardon and reinstatement were given the two men. Radisson admits that

[2] PRO., Privy Council Register, 2:65 (1 Oct. 1675—27 April, 1677).

[3] The author on occasions has made her own translation of the French version of Radisson's narrative of 1682–1683, as given in French in Canadian Archives, *Report*, 1895, Note A (Ottawa, 1896); on other occasions she has used the contemporary translation printed in Radisson, *Voyages*.

"all was done as promised, except in the matter of employment, wherein we dallied for a long time uselessly." Then, Radisson adds, he perceived the cause for this delay. His wife was still in England. Colbert himself one day gave that as the reason and added that Mrs. Radisson must come to France. Radisson explained that he was not master of that situation, for his father-in-law would not allow his daughter to leave England. Colbert then recommended that Radisson and Des Groseilliers make a trip to Canada to consult there with the Governor relative to what could be done.

It is apparent from Radisson's narrative of what occurred in Canada that Frontenac considered him and Des Groseilliers as tools of the Jesuit party and a threat to his own hopes for De la Salle and the other explorers of the Recollect party. In addition, the intendant, Jacques Duchesneau, took a step that seems to have decided the two men that Canada could offer them little. On October 19 he called a meeting of the leading fur traders of New France for the purpose of fixing the price of beaver. At the meeting, which seems to have taken place the next day, there were present, among others, Robert Cavelier de la Salle, Charles Le Moyne, two of the Godefroys of Three Rivers, Louis Jolliet, Des Groseilliers, his stepson, Etienne Véron de Grandmesnil, and Radisson.[4] Immediately after this meeting Radisson left for France and Des Groseilliers returned to his family in Three Rivers.[5]

[4] See AC., Collection Moreau St.-Méry, Vol. 2–1, ff. 32–43.

[5] Another document of the period mentions Radisson and Des Groseilliers. On October 27, 1676, the Sieur D'Auteuil, the procureur general of the Sovereign Council of New France, wrote and dated his conclusions regarding Radisson and Des Groseilliers' petition to the Council requesting that their pardon paper be registered. Since the Council had begun its "customary holidays after the departure of the fleet" for France, regular action could not be taken by the Council. Des Groseilliers, moreover, was mentioned as having gone to the "regular abode of his family" at Three Rivers, while Radisson had gone back to France with the fleet. So D'Auteuil wrote that he could do nothing but write out his own conclusions, which were that the pardon papers should be registered. He then signed and dated his conclusions. It may be

Late in 1676, therefore, Pierre Esprit Radisson must have found himself back in France looking for employment. As the later seventeenth century was a period of widespread unemployment in France, his task could not have been easy. Nevertheless, by September, 1677, he was sailing from France, a marine guard in the fleet of Vice-Admiral D'Estrées. It would appear that Abbé Bernou, failing to get action on the petition already discussed, had helped Radisson find employment.[6]

Vice-Admiral D'Estrées had had difficulties in getting his naval expedition against the Dutch approved. The Dutch War was pressing France rather hard. Besides the United Provinces and Spain, she had much of continental Europe against her. England had already withdrawn from the combat, a blow to France. A Messina revolt was occupying most of the French navy when D'Estrées proposed to Colbert an attack on the Dutch colonies. Colbert, fearing any new expense to the King, could not aid his friend at the moment, but promised to do what he could. So D'Estrées got his own friends and acquaintances to outfit the vessels he needed and to provide for the men. The plan was to

added that when Des Groseilliers and Radisson returned to Quebec in 1683 after a trip to Hudson Bay, they found that the paper was still unregistered. Action was then demanded of the Council and obtained, and the document at length was duly recorded. *Jugements et délibérations,* 2: 907, 908.

[6] In that portion of the Clairambault papers in the Bibliothèque Nationale which consists of the Abbé's manuscripts is a long letter entirely in Radisson's handwriting and signed by him. It is written from the island of Grenada in the West Indies and is dated January 1, 1678. There is no salutation except the word, "Monsieur," which for the seventeenth century indicates that the letter was written to a person of standing. In the text of the letter reference is made to the aid received by the writer from the recipient of the letter and to the hope that something in the letter, which had been requested by the addressee, would prove worthy of being read to "the noble souls to whom I am, as to you, the humble and grateful servant, P. E. Radisson." All these indications point to Bernou as the recipient of the letter; for he was connected, as already stated, with the D'Estrées; he was forever requesting travelers to write to him about the peoples and scenes they observed; and it was his practice to read aloud such letters and narratives to Cardinal D'Estrées, to Abbé Renaudot, to De Callières, and to others of their group. Bernou's letters in the Renaudot Papers make these facts very obvious.

attack all the Dutch forts on the Guinea Coast, commencing
with the island of Gorée. If successful there, the Vice-
Admiral would pass to America and the West Indies, especially to Surinam, a very rich and powerful colony.

D'Estrées' enterprises in this field of operations in the
early part of 1676 were not very successful, but he sailed
again late in September, 1677, from Brest. This time Radisson becomes our chronicler: [7]

> We left Brest the twenty-seventh of September, whence I had the
> honor to write you the list of the vessels that compose this squadron.[8]
> Bad weather forced us back again the following day. We set sail
> again on the third of October. Until the tenth of that month we
> tacked down the coast of France. The wind being uniformly favor-
> able, we caught sight of the island of Porto Santo on the eighteenth
> and, the following day, of Madeira. Without anchoring we continued
> our route, south-southwest.

They passed Gomera and other islands and crossed the
tropic of Cancer on the twenty-sixth. "All who had never
before crossed that line were baptized there." Presumably
Radisson was among them and watched Father Neptune
clamber over the side of the vessel and suffered the usual
rather severe hazing and "baptism" of all who had never
before crossed the tropic.

On the twenty-ninth flying fish were all about the vessels
and some even fell within them. On the last day of the
month Cape Verde was sighted, from which the island of
Gorée was distant only seven leagues. Flying English and
Dutch flags the vessels approached this object of their
travels. Two forts guarded it, one on higher ground than the
other. Some firing occurred and then the French demanded
surrender. The Dutch pretended to reject this demand. So

---

[7] P. E. Radisson to [Bernou], autograph letter signed, BN., Collection Clairambault, 1016: ff. 376–377. See *post*, Appendix 4, for the text of the letter and
a translation.

[8] There were, in all, 18 sail: 10 men-of-war, 3 fire ships, and 5 victuallers.
See Sir Jonathan Atkins to the Lords of Trade and Plantation, November 28,
1677, in *Cal. St. Pap., Am. & W. I., 1677–1680*, No. 498.

an attack was planned. "I petitioned Count D'Estrées to permit me to—go with this party as a volunteer, although at Brest he had granted me the favor of speaking for me—more favorably than I deserved—to the intendant, who ordered me the post and rations of the marine guards. He answered now to the same end, that he was keeping me for bigger things." The lower fort having been abandoned already by the Dutch, the French attacked the upper fort. "Not 300 cannon shots were fired when a white flag was run up," for a shot had reached the powder magazine and caused the Dutch to fear that another such missive would not be so favorable to them. The pillage was good and much booty was secured. The forts were burned and the French set sail to do further damage.

On the twelfth of November their fleet was in sight of Santiago. On December 6, Tobago was sighted.[9] On December 7 the fleet anchored three leagues from the fort of this island. After some preliminaries the French attacked. The third shot fell on the brick powder magazine and blew into bits the Dutch commander, Admiral De Binkes, and the officers who were dining with him at the moment. Radisson says that a conservative estimate of the dead from the explosion and resulting fire was two hundred men, but many, he said, claimed the figure to be as high as four or five hundred.[10] "I saw the bomb fall and had the honor to be the first to cry, 'Long live the King.' " Jesuit and other priests

[9] For other accounts of the movements of this fleet, see *Cal. St. Pap., Am. & W. I., 1677–1680,* Nos. 559, 603, 642, 665, 689, and 690.

[10] The correspondence cited in the two preceding footnotes estimates that 250 men and most of the officers were killed and that five or six hundred prisoners were taken. See especially No. 559. Another account of the taking of Tobago is given in Exquemelin, *History of the Bucaniers of America,* 1:258, 259. Vice-Admiral Jacob Binkes is mentioned: "the *French* began their Attack, by casting Fireballs into the Castle with main Violence; the very third Ball that was cast in, happened to fall in the Path-way that led to the Storehouse, where the Powder and Ammunition was kept; in this Path was much Powder scattered, thro' the Negligence of those that carried it to and fro, for the necessary Supply of the Defendants, which by this means taking Fire, it ran in a Moment to the Storehouse, which suddenly was blown up, and with it Vice-

THE WEST INDIES CAMPAIGN, 1677–1678.

gave comfort to the dying. "I was of use to some of these as an interpreter, explaining to them what the priests were saying to them." Did Radisson, then, know Dutch as well as French, Iroquois, Algonquian, and English?

After the inevitable pillage and seizure of ordnance the fleet again put to sea for Grenada. Here Radisson's account ends, at the beginning of the new year in that island, when he penned his last letter to Bernou. Some of his comrades, however, wrote later letters that have survived. From them many of the details of the rest of the story can be pieced together. All the French were in high spirits and looked to complete their conquests. One of them writes to his father from Grenada on January 4, 1678, mentioning "the good

Admiral *Binkes* himself, and all his Officers, only Captain *Van Dongen* remained alive. This Mischance being perceived by the *French*, they instantly ran with 500 Men, and possessed themselves of the Castle." This author confirms Radisson on the dates of the departure from France and the arrival in Tobago. He gives the number of captured men as three hundred.

wine and fine turkeys that are very cheap in this country, as well as the little pigs." Beef and mutton were very dear. "Wine is cheaper than in France. Bread that would be worth a sol in Paris costs 15 sols here. In fine, to live well here one ought to have a good purse." [11]

In May Count D'Estrées weighed anchor again and set sail to take Curaçao, the last important stronghold of the Dutch. Perhaps the vivid and jubilant letter of an Englishman of Barbados will tell better than any paraphrase the story of the great disaster that followed.[12]

The French it seems desirous to attempt some what more either upon the Dutch or Spaniard, or both, made their first designe upon Carassao, the Governor whereof sent out 3 Ships to discover and to take such care that they attended the French Fleet and to keep out of Danger of being taken. The French Discovering of them it seems gave them chace with their whole Fleet; the Dutch better acquainted with those Seas then the others drew them on amongst some Islands where there was neither water for those Great Ships nor possibility of avoyding the Shelves and Rocks there. The first Ships that Struck gave Guns according to the Sea custome to give notice to those that followed to stand off, which they tooke for an Engagement and pursued more egarly to their ruine. . . . Monsᵣ D'Estree and most of his officers are saved, and not many men lost, though all their Great Ships are ruined and gone. But for all this as my Intelligence sayes D'Estrées lost not his Courage, but with the Ships he had left would have attempted Carassao. But his Buckneers (which are only beasts of Prey) seing there was little to be gott but Blows left him and would not hazard any farther with him.

The island on which the wreck occurred is "the Isle of Aves, or Birds; so called from its great plenty of birds . . . especially Boobies." [13]

Thus Radisson's career as a marine guard ended suddenly on the rocks of the Island of Aves in the Caribbean Sea. At a later time he valued his losses as "more than 2000 livres

[11] BN., Fonds Français 20,625, ff. 444, 445.

[12] Copy of Sir John Atkins' letter to Secretary Coventry, Barbadoes, August 1, 1678, in PRO., CO., 1/66, f. 248.

[13] John Masefield, ed., *Dampier's Voyages by Captain William Dampier,* 1:77–81 (New York, 1906).

by shipwreck."[14] He returned with the remnant of the fleet to Brest, "having lost all my Equipage in this disaster."[15]

The Vice Admirall & the Intendant wrote to Court in my favour, & upon the good character they were pleas'd to give of me, I receav'd a gratuity of 100 Louis D'ors upon the King's account, to renew my Equipage; & these Gentlemen also were pleased to tell me I should ere long have the command of a Man of Warr; but thinking that could not so easily bee, I desired leave to make a turn over into England under pretext of visitting my wife & to make a farther Tryall of bringing her over into france, whereupon I had my pass[port] granted, with a further gratuity of 100 Louis D'ors towards the charges of my voyage.

He was told that if he succeeded in getting his wife to France, he would be given employment.

Sir John Kirke, however, was not to be won over. He positively refused to let his daughter go to France. On the other hand, he asked his son-in-law to write to his friends in France in an endeavor to get the sum of money that had been owing the Kirke family since 1633. Radisson says that he did as his father-in-law requested and that De Seignelay was not well pleased.

On this visit to London Radisson put out feelers to learn what was the status of the Hudson's Bay Company, their attitude toward him, and the prospects of reëmployment by them. The outlook proved to be not very hopeful, and so he returned to France to the chidings of De Seignelay. "Hee revil'd me, & told me hee knew very well what an Inclination I had still for the English Interest, saying with all that I must not expect any confidence should bee put in me, nor that

---

[14] Radisson's petition to the Marquis de Belleroche at Paris, undated but later than December, 1683, and prior to May, 1684, is partly published in [Sulte], *Collection de manuscrits*, 1:319. The entire petition is copied in BN., Margry Papers, 9284, ff. 61, 62. See *post*, Appendix 6.

[15] The disaster occurred at 8 P. M. on the evening of May 3 or 4. D'Estrées stayed off the haunt of buccaneers till May 28, when he sailed with seven vessels, all he had left, to France, leaving five hundred men behind. See the relation of Thomas Wigfall in *Cal. St. Pap., Am. & W. I., 1677–1680*, No. 718. Radisson writes that he reached Brest in July.

I shold not have the least Imployment, whilst my wife stay'd in England." Nevertheless, De Seignelay promised to speak to his father, Colbert, in Radisson's behalf. Colbert also upbraided Radisson, but told him to go to see the minister's right-hand man in trade matters, the notorious Bellinzani.[16]

Hee told me that Mons[r] Colbert thought it necessary that I should conferr with Mons[r] De La Chesnay,—a Canada Merchant who mannadg'd all the Trade of thos parts, & who was then at Paris, that with him some mesures should bee taken to make the best advantage of our Discoveries & intreagues in the Northern parts of Canada, to advance the Beaver Trade, & as much as possible . . . . to hinder all strangers from driving that trade to the prejudice of the French Collonies.

The decade that had elapsed since Des Groseilliers brought back a rich cargo of pelts from Hudson Bay had established the Hudson's Bay Company firmly in the Bay. Its success finally led the Canadians to realize bitterly that what the English were gaining the Canadians and French were losing. De la Chenaye, as a Canadian and as the director of the beaver trade in New France, had reasons enough to be in France in 1681 complaining to Bellinzani and to Colbert of a carefully maintained harmony between the English and French crowns that was working havoc with the livelihood of himself and most Canadians. Radisson writes,

The said Mons[r] Belinzany also told me I could not more oblige mons[r] Colbert, nor take any better cours to obtaine his friendship by any servis whatsoever, than by using all my skill & industry in drawing all the natives of thos Northern parts of America to traffick with & to favor the French, & to hinder & disswade them from

[16] Father François Bellinzani, originally of Mantua, went to France in 1658 and was naturalized. He was employed first in Mazarin's house, was ennobled in August, 1679, and later was made director of the companies of the East Indies, of the North, and of the Levant. See Clément, *Lettres de Colbert,* 1 : 369 and 7 : 135. He was disgraced at Colbert's death and died in 1684. See also De la Salle's accusation of Bellinzani's extortions from him in Margry, *Découvertes et établissements,* 1 : 338–340. It appears to have been Bellinzani's rôle to require a douceur in such cases as Radisson's and De la Salle's in return for aid from Bellinzani and Colbert.

trading with strangers, assuring me of a great reward for the servis I should render the state upon this account, & that M^r De La Chesnay would furnish me in Cannada with all things necessary for executing what dessignes wee should conclude upon together to this intent.

Thus Colbert would not himself, as for the crown, sponsor any scheme inimical to the English, but he could wink at the same scheme when undertaken by De la Chenaye. For Colbert and Louis XIV never saw eye to eye in matters of trade and overseas colonies.[17]

Radisson's next move was to spy out the plans of the Hudson's Bay Company. So, early in 1681, as far as we can judge from available evidence, he arrived once more in London and conferred with the officers of the Company. The letter of instructions that the Committee of the Company addressed in June to Governor John Nixon in the Bay stresses the importance of settling Port Nelson. Despite numerous attempts to colonize that area, it was still practically unknown and completely untenanted. A postscript to the letter indicates that after the main body of the letter had been composed, Radisson appeared and gave the writer fear that in the Bay, "our dangers from the French doe approach." [18]

Whether or not Radisson learned then of the proposed English fort and colony at Port Nelson is not known, but in the light of subsequent events it seems likely that he found out this bit of news at that time. For his own plan, as finally worked out from Quebec, was to do the self-same thing for the French and to do it before the English could do it.

Having learned all he could in London, Radisson returned to France. He had hoped to see De la Chenaye again, but that gentleman had returned to Quebec. Radisson prepared to follow him. First, however, he had an interview with

---

[17] See also Radisson's statement in 1697 in PRO., S.P., America and West Indies (transcript in Public Archives of Canada, M394B, pp. 61–70).

[18] H.B.Co. Archives, A/6/1, ff. 11, 12.

Colbert and that hardheaded official "wished me a good voyadge, advising me to be carefull." Well did Radisson need that caution, as events were to prove.

Radisson's next move is a very significant one and refutes to no slight degree the claim often made, especially by churchmen, that the Jesuits had little or no interest in the beaver trade. "I went to visit the Society of the Jesuits at Paris, as being also concern'd with La Chesnay in the Beaver Trade. They gave mee some money for my voyadge." One can anticipate readily enough, therefore, that Frontenac, foe of the Jesuits, would oppose Radisson's plans.

CHAPTER XIV

Canada Again

Frontenac's objections should have been foreseen by De la Chenaye and Radisson. With the autumn fleet to France went a dispatch from the Governor dated November 2, 1681.[1] It refers at length to Radisson, mentioning his marriage, his West Indian experiences, his proposal to go "to make establishments along our coasts in the direction of Hudson Bay" in one of De la Chenaye's boats, and the Governor's refusal to countenance such a project without specific permission from France. Radisson, too, tells of the refusal, which was apparently expected by De la Chenaye, for the latter had an alternate project completely ready for the Governor—that Radisson should be given a passport to return to London via New England in a boat then ready to sail from Quebec. Radisson intimates that Frontenac only appeared to refuse the first request and fully understood that the second was really the first in another guise. This request was granted and, according to Radisson, its very nature was such that the Governor could not have misunderstood it, especially as it permitted Radisson to take three men with him. The men's names alone should have warned the Governor of what was brewing, he said. One of them was Des Groseilliers' second son, Jean Baptiste Chouart, then a man of twenty-seven years. Radisson knew him as an expert woodsman and trader, who had "frequented the Indian countries all his life." This young man invested five hundred livres of his own money in the venture. The second man was Pierre Allemand, a famous pilot in New France

[1] *Rapport de l'archiviste de la province de Québec pour 1926–1927*, p. 136.

and an early cartographer.[2] The third was Jean Baptiste
Godefroy, of the pioneer family that we have encountered
earlier in Three Rivers. This young man was one "who understood the Indian language perfectly and whom I knew to
be able as a trader," as Radisson explains.

Again one of our venturesome explorers spends a season
in Acadia. Nicolas Denys was still alive, though an old,
poverty-stricken, disillusioned man. Was it at his home (or,
more likely, at that of his son Richard) that Radisson
passed the winter of 1681–1682? Or did he go to Boston
and see young Benjamin Gillam? By spring he was again at
the renowned center of the fisheries, Percée Rock. A vessel,
probably ordered by De la Chenaye from La Rochelle, arrived for Radisson, but it was "only an old craft of about
50 tons, with 12 men of a crew, including those who were
with me." Provisions were low. Radisson was downhearted.
Then Des Groseilliers arrived on board the vessel that had
been supplied to him, probably in France. The fact that Des
Groseilliers was already aboard her when she arrived at
Percée Rock suggests that he had spent the winter in
France. What had he been doing since Radisson left him at
Quebec in 1676? Briefly, he had been getting acquainted
once more with his wife, after years of separation.

*   *   *

Marguérite had much sorrow and trouble to report for
the decade and a half since Médard had departed down the
St. Lawrence in a borrowed bark canoe for which she had
been obliged to compensate the owner. In 1666 her husband
was still regarded as a resident of Three Rivers and listed
with her in the census of that year,[3] along with his two sons,
a servant, and one of his stepchildren. The other was at-
tending the Jesuits' school at Quebec.[4] The following year,

---

[2] See *post*, p. 225 for Allemand's later exploits in Hudson Bay.
[3] *Rapport de l'archiviste de la province de Québec pour 1935–1936*, p. 141.
[4] Gagnon, *Essai de bibliographie canadienne*, 2: 333.

however, Des Groseilliers was not listed in the census; and Marguérite was recorded in such fashion as to suggest that there was some doubt about her status—whether she was a wife or a widow.[5] By 1668 the neighbors had settled the question in their own minds, one of them even referring to her as Des Groseilliers' widow.[6] These two censuses afford considerable information on members of the Chouart family, their possessions, and their relatives, the Jutrats and the Volants—Marguérite's two sisters and their families.

These must have been hard years for Marguérite. She can be glimpsed now and again leasing or selling parts of her property, receiving assistance from the government, suing in court and being sued, and fighting her children's little battles fiercely.[7] Just after her husband had gone on his ostensible trip to Hudson Bay in 1662, she had appeared before the local governor and other officials as already described, and begged to be allowed to renounce her dowry rights in order to be able to satisfy Péré.[8] This was a desperate step for a French woman of the seventeenth century to take. She also asked to be made once more the guardian of her children.

On April 27, 1663, she made a "composition" with Péré, which gave her a breathing space,[9] but on July 30, 1664, she was in court again, complaining of his conduct.[10] Shortly she found it necessary to have her brother-in-law appointed

---

[5] Sulte, *Histoire des canadiens-français*, 4:70. By this time Marguérite was a resident of Cap de la Madeleine, just across the St. Maurice River from Three Rivers.

[6] See Jean Pépin's statement of June 28, 1668, in *Papier terrier de la compagnie des Indes Occidentales*, edited by Pierre-Georges Roy, p. 314. *Estienne Vien* in the printed version is probably a misreading of *Estienne Véron*.

[7] Most of the information on these episodes is to be found in the prévôté records of Three Rivers (Q). See also documents of 1668 and 1669 in Ameau's *greffe*, Court-House, Three Rivers, by which Marguérite leased and sold lands.

[8] See *ante*, p. 84.

[9] Three Rivers, prévôté records (Q). Jean and Arnauld Péré, both of whom are mentioned in these documents, were brothers. Arnauld was a merchant of La Rochelle; Jean served as his attorney in New France. See a document of December 20, 1664, in the above-mentioned prévôté records.

[10] *Jugements et délibérations*, 1:247, 248.

the children's guardian so that she could leave Three Rivers
to attend to matters between her and Péré; [11] and to have
reimbursement for the expense that he had caused her.[12]

She lost one of her youngest children in November of this
year, 1664, when Marie-Anne Chouart died.[13] Another untoward event was Arnaud Péré's seizure of her shop and
forge, which he closed for three days.[14] On November 17,
1675, her sister's daughter, Madeleine Jutras, married Jean
Amador *dit* Godefroy, the son of that Jean Godefroy at
whose home Marguérite had lived during her early years in
the country. The "acte de mariage" bears the names of a
host of witnesses, including, curiously, those of the bride's
uncles, Pierre Esprit Radisson and Médard Chouart. They
were described, however, as "absent." [15]

On August 21, 1677, Marguérite's sister, Françoise
Volant, made her will. She died on October 3. The following May 11 a meeting of the family was called, as was customary when either parent of minor children died, to appoint a guardian for them.[16] "Medard Chouart S^r des
Groseilliers who is also a brother-in-law by virtue of his
wife" was present. Thus the wandering husband took his
place once more in the family circle after fourteen years on

[11] *Jugements et délibérations*, 1:273.

[12] *Jugements et délibérations*, 1:276.

[13] See the parish registers, Three Rivers. There is some confusion about this
record. The interment entry states that the child was Marie Anne [*Maria Anna
in the Latin*], and that she was four years of age when buried on November
31 [*sic*], 1664. Yet Marie Anne was baptized on August 7, 1657. Marie Antoinette was baptized on June 7, 1661, but Tanguay mentions her marriages:
in 1679 to Jean Jalot and in 1695 to Jean-Baptiste Bouchard. *Dictionnaire
généalogique*, 1:129. Probably it was Marie Antoinette who died in 1664 and
Marie Anne who married. An officiating priest at a funeral could distinguish
between a four-year-old and a seven-year-old child.

[14] Three Rivers, prévôté records (Q), February 14, 1665, a suit by Marguérite Hayet against Jean Bousquet and Jacques Joviel. The census of 1666
lists these men as gunsmiths.

[15] Acte de marriage de Magdeleine Jutras et Jean Amador dit Godefroy,
Ameau's *greffe*, Court-House, Three Rivers.

[16] See a document in the prévôté records of Three Rivers (Q), dated May
11, 1678, as well as following documents. See Françoise's will in Ameau's
greffe, Court-House, Three Rivers.

ocean and land, in Europe, in New England, and under the Arctic Circle.

Between the time of his return to Three Rivers and the beginning of the trip to Hudson Bay in 1682 little else is known of Des Groseilliers' activities. In the summer of 1677 he is known to have been in Quebec;[17] on September 3, 1678, he was living at Champlain;[18] by April 10, 1680, he is described as the "Seigneur d'Anticosti"; on August 30, 1681, he gave his residence as Sorel.[19] On March 21, 1678, Des Groseilliers appeared before the sovereign council to protest that the royal license granted him and Radisson on March 23, 1676, for the white porpoise fishery of the St. Lawrence and the sea otter trade of the island of Anticosti had not been registered by the council. He added that he had been to Anticosti the preceding summer and learned that it was only in winter that he could secure sea otter. As the letters patent stipulated that the enterprise must be begun within a year and he still must find an associate to share expenses with him, he begged for an extension of time. The council granted him an additional year.[20]

Sometime between 1676 and 1682 Des Groseilliers met a well-known character, who, fortunately, has left an account of their intercourse. Father Louis Hennepin arrived at Quebec in 1675. Shortly this Recollect friar was to leave for Fort Frontenac and the Illinois country with De la Salle. Early in 1680 Hennepin began the trip up the Mississippi River on which he found and named the Falls of St. An-

---

[17] Two agreements of partnership between François Guyon, Sieur des Prez, and Médard Chouart, Sieur des Groseilliers and Seigneur de l'Isle d'Anticosti, conveying the bark, the *Ste Geneviève,* owned by Guyon and Jean-Baptiste Chouart, June 8, 1677; and the breaking of the contract by legal action on August 20, 1677. Copies of these three papers were kindly made by the archivist of the Province of Quebec from the originals in the Judicial Archives, Court-House, Quebec.

[18] See Gagnon, *Essai de bibliographie canadienne,* 2:333.

[19] See Gagnon, *Essai de bibliographie canadienne,* 2:333.

[20] *Jugements et délibérations,* 2:184, 185.

thony. He spent some time with the Sioux along the river and about Mille Lacs Lake, now in Minnesota, and thus became acquainted with the very tribe to whom Des Groseilliers had gone twenty years earlier. What caused Hennepin to want to go to the Sioux country? His own remarks give a clue: [21]

> The great Hudson Bay . . . . was discovered by Sieur Desgroseliers Rochechoüart, with whom I often canoed while I was in Canada. . . . While I was in Quebec the Canadians said that the Sieur des Groseilliers was trying to dupe them when he assured them that it was difficult getting into Hudson Bay because the ice was seven or eight feet deep. . . . I cannot vouch for these facts, but the aforementioned Sieur desgroseliers and others have assured me that they had passed between blocks of ice "as high as the towers of big cities."

He adds that Des Groseilliers was still (1697) in England, according to William III's secretary, Blathwayt.

Later Des Groseilliers was slated by men in the French court to accompany De la Salle on his sea voyage to the mouth of the Mississippi.[22] It is known that the colony planned by De la Salle was to include the Sioux countries north and west of the Mississippi. It is at least possible that Hennepin's chats with Des Groseilliers between 1676 and 1678 led the friar, and through him De la Salle, to want to explore the country—and its beaver resources—of which Des Groseilliers told him. If Des Groseilliers also mentioned his belief that through the Sioux country lay a route to the Western Sea, it is small wonder that De la Salle and Hennepin were agreed as to the need of exploring that country, even while the journey *down* the Mississippi waited.

When the census of 1681 was taken, both Radisson and Des Groseilliers were back in Canada.[23] Médard Chouart gave his age as 60, though he was actually 63. Mar-

---

[21] Louis Hennepin, *Nouveau Voyage,* pp. 290–292 (Utrecht, 1698). See *post,* p. 272 for William Blathwayt.

[22] See *post,* p. 215.

[23] Sulte, *Histoire des canadiens-français,* 5: 55, 64.

guérite is listed as 50, and her stepson, Médard Chouart, who was living with the couple, was put down as 30 years of age, which is at least approximately correct. This family's possessions are listed as one gun. No land and no cattle are recorded, and one wonders whether the whole family was not living with Marguérite's son, Etienne Véron, who seems to have been prosperous, if not affluent, and who comes immediately after his mother's family in the census list.[24] Radisson is recorded, probably at a tavern or boarding-house, in the lower city of Quebec. His age is given as 41 and his possessions are listed as one gun.

[24] The Collection Moreau St.-Méry in Archives des Colonies has many references to the Sieur de Grandmesnil (Etienne Véron), showing that he was a daring trader and important man in New France. See *Supplement to Dr. Brymner's Report on Canadian Archives*, by Edouard Richard, in Canadian Archives, *Report*, 1899, pp. 39–101 (Ottawa, 1900).

CHAPTER XV

Rivals Meet

The great portaled island off the Gaspé Peninsula, Percée Rock, which was such a feature in Radisson's life, again becomes important in the year 1681. Nearly all of the fishing vessels from France touched there early in the spring fishing season. If a message was to be sent *sub rosa,* or an illegal venture begun, here was the place for rendezvous. It is not strange that De la Chenaye's illegal operations center at this island.

The King's farmer general (*fermier*), after the dissolution of the West Indies Company in 1674, was permitted to have three sources of revenue: the fur trade of Tadoussac, a quarter of all beaver skins brought to New France by her traders, and a tenth of all moose hides. In addition, a duty was charged on all goods entering the country. To avoid payment of these tithes and other duties, De la Chenaye and his companions—who in 1682 formed themselves into a company composed of Pierre de Saurel [*or Sorel*], Guillaume Chanjon, Jean Gitton, and Joseph Petit [*Bruneau*]—arranged a rendezvous at Percée Rock in the spring of 1682.[1] They agreed that their two vessels, after leaving Hudson Bay, should return, not to Quebec, but to Percée Rock. There Radisson and Des Groseilliers were to get the equivalent of the "quarter"—presumably the furs themselves—instead of seeing them turned over to the

[1] "Ordonnance de M. de Meulles au sujet des prétentions des intéressés en la société de la ferme du Canada sur le produit de la traite d'une expédition à la Baie d'Hudson organisée par MM. de la Chesnaye, Gitton, Bruneau et la dame veuve de Sorel" in *Ordonnances, Commissions Etc. Etc., des Gouverneurs et Intendants de la Nouvelle-France, 1639–1706,* edited by Pierre-Georges Roy, 2:49–53 (*Archives de la Province de Québec*), Beauceville, 1924.

fermier at Quebec. At Percée Rock a vessel, the *Black Eagle*, was to meet the venturers, take their cargo of furs and skins, and market them in Holland or Spain. How much of this scheme for disobeying the law was known to Colbert, Bellinzani, De Seignelay, and the Jesuits, when the scheme was hatched in Paris, is hard to estimate. All of them knew at least something of it. It is perhaps significant that Bellinzani was utterly discredited upon Colbert's death, which occurred during the international negotiations consequent on the Hudson Bay episode of 1681–1683.

What the company planned must have been based on Radisson's representations to them of the river that he and Des Groseilliers had been trying for twenty years to see utilized. Both men saw clearly from the start what it took the Hudson's Bay Company and the French court a generation to perceive, namely, that the great storehouse of beaver skins was in the region north and west of Lake Superior; and that the really effective avenue thither was not the Great Lakes but the river that empties into Hudson Bay at Port Nelson. At least twice they themselves had been there, only to be obliged to return before anything constructive had been accomplished. Now, just as the two pleaders for this route saw themselves in a way to be successful, Fate in her ironical fashion produced two other sets of persons from whose eyes the scales had recently fallen. Port Nelson became suddenly very desirable in the year 1682.

One chapter of colonial history which remains to be written is that of the interlopers. Charters granting exclusive trade of certain areas to specified groups like the Hudson's Bay Company had become common by 1682. However, frontier conditions in the English and French colonies, particularly in Massachusetts, were not producing respect for such monopolies, or even for theories of monopoly. Consequently interlopers like those who now appeared in Hudson Bay took matters into their own hands

and traded where they would, thumbing their noses deri-
sively at distant companies, courts, parliaments, and officers
of the law. The early records of the Hudson's Bay Company are full of charges against New England interlopers.
One of them was Benjamin, son of Zechariah Gillam, who
appeared in Hudson Bay in 1682. He must have got at
least part of the information necessary for his venture from
his father. There have even been hints that Radisson was
in league with both of them.[2] At all events, the two barks
of the Frenchmen, young Gillam's *Batchelor's Delight,*
manned by "14 men all Batchelors & very resolute Fel-
lowes," and the great ship of the Hudson's Bay Company
in "Old Zack" Gillam's charge, arrived more or less si-
multaneously at Port Nelson late in the summer of 1682.[3]

Radisson always contended that his party was the first
to arrive. Des Groseilliers, writing to a prominent person
in France, probably De Seignelay, stated late in 1683 that
his party had been at Hayes River for fifteen days when
the others arrived.[4] On the other hand, Benjamin Gillam,
John Bridgar, and others of the English party asserted the
priority of young Gillam's arrival. It is to be observed
how quickly the Hudson's Bay Company dropped charges
of interloping against young Gillam when it realized that
the English claim of priority of arrival, as against a French
claim, must depend solely on the interloping colonial. He
represented the Company there in no way—in fact, he was
opposing it—but everything else had to be overlooked when

[2] "This was not done neither without some Jealousey [*suspicion*] that Old
Gillam & his son & Radison had Laid this plott Togeather in Old England to
frustrate the Comp[ies] Intentions" in "The Comittees Answer to Esq[r] Yonges
Letter," March 8, 1692/3, H.B.Co. Archives, A/6/2, ff. 68–71. See *post,* Appendix 10. In the same letter the committee states that Radisson probably got
his information from the report of Captain John Abraham, of the Company's
service, recommending a post at Port Nelson.

[3] H.B.Co. Archives, A/6/1, f. 39, the Company to Edward Randolph, Aug.
13, 1683.

[4] An unsigned letter, but certainly written by Des Groseilliers, in AC., C[11],
Vol. 6, f. 203. See *post,* Appendix 7.

it became a question of English versus French ownership
of the region about Port Nelson.

John Calvert, who as surgeon went on the *Prince Rupert*
to Port Nelson in 1682, swore in 1687 that even Radisson
and Des Groseilliers, while still in the Bay, acknowledged
that young Gillam arrived at Port Nelson on August 19,
1682.[5] The Canadians, he said, got there only on August 23. Perhaps the full truth of the matter will never
appear, since all the material witnesses saw the cogency of
arguing for prior possession for their own party. It is
worth noting, however, that Benjamin Gillam, before he
had opportunity to be influenced by the Hudson's Bay Company, presented a petition in Quebec in 1683, which says
nothing of his having been on the ground before the French
arrived.[6] He does give August 18 as the date of his landfall
at Port Nelson but by the French calendar that would have
been August 28. The diary of Gillam kept on this expedition was long in the possession of the Hudson's Bay Company, but it was never cited in any of the controversies
growing out of this affair.[7]

Fundamentally Gillam's and Radisson's accounts do not
differ in describing the course of events in the dramatic
year 1682–1683 in Hudson Bay, though Radisson's narrative, being much the longer of the two, is consequently
much more detailed.

The Nelson River empties into Hudson Bay from the
west only a short distance north of the mouth of the Hayes
River. A narrow spit of land is all that separates the
two rivers at their mouths. Here Frenchmen and British

---

[5] PRO. CO., 134/1/ f. 213, June 10, 1687.

[6] PRO., S.P., Amer. & W. I., 64/115, under date of October 15/25, 1683. Both
the French version of the letter and a contemporaneous translation are extant.
The Committee acknowledges Radisson's priority of arrival in its letter of
March 8, 1692/3. See *post,* Appendix 10.

[7] See "A True State of the Case Betweene the Hudson's Bay Company and
the French of Canada in the West Indies," in H.B.Co. Archives, A/6/1,
ff. 100–102.

subjects established themselves in 1682, each company ignorant of the others' presence. Benjamin Gillam established his post on an island in the mouth of the Nelson River; Radisson and Des Groseilliers began to build on the north shore of the Hayes, mooring their two small vessels in a little stream near their houses. While Des Groseilliers supervised building operations, Radisson went up Hayes River toward Lake Winnipeg, accompanied by his nephew, Jean Baptiste Chouart, and a member of the ships' crews. Radisson's object was to find Indians and make arrangements for getting peltries from them. This move of itself reveals how much cleverer the two Frenchmen were than their Anglo-Saxon opponents, whose first thought was for their own physical comfort during the Arctic winter. Well up the river Radisson encountered Indians, impressed their simple minds by means of his thorough knowledge of Indian psychology, and made very satisfactory arrangements with them for future trade with them, their relatives, their friends, and their allies. Thereupon the Frenchmen fell down the river to their post. They arrived there about the middle of September.

Both Radisson and Gillam agree in naming September 17 as the day on which a meeting of the Frenchmen and the New Englanders occurred. Radisson says that the very day on which he got back to his fort a noise of cannon surprised him. After some unsuccessful attempts to learn the source of such a noise in a region supposedly uninhabited by white men, the Frenchman discovered a tent on an island in the mouth of the Nelson. Some reconnoitering produced the information that there was a vessel in that river and that a house was being constructed on the island. Radisson decided to interview these interlopers. Approaching in a canoe in such fashion that they would be taken for natives, Radisson and his three companions were noticed by the New Englanders. Attempts were made by Gillam's party to address the newcomers in Indian, "which they

Read in a Book." Radisson replied in Indian, then in French, and finally in English. Thus he learned that they were New Englanders, that they had no license or commission to trade in the Bay, and that they were planning to get beaver skins from the natives. Thereupon Radisson announced French priority there and claimed the area for his sovereign, forbidding the others to trade there.

Gillam and Radisson were old acquaintances and soon made out each other's identity. They settled on a course of action for the winter, whereby the French would protect the New Englanders by means of the former's superiority in numbers, a superiority which Radisson deliberately fabricated in order to win his ends. He and his men then set off in a canoe down the Nelson to return to their post. A few miles from the island they spied a vessel under sail entering the river. The Frenchmen put hurriedly to shore on the south side, but not before they were perceived and followed. To gain time for observation and to screen himself temporarily, Radisson built a smudge. The vessel anchored and spent the night near him but no one ventured ashore because of the smoke. Next morning a boat was sent from the vessel. In it were John Bridgar, the newly appointed Governor of the proposed Hudson's Bay Company colony at Port Nelson, and six sailors. As they approached, Radisson, who had hidden his men, addressed the Englishmen in Indian, both to embarrass them and to learn whether any one of them was competent to deal with the Indians thereabout. No one answered, but the boat grounded and the men prepared to land. At that point Radisson presented arms and addressed them in English, commanding them to stop till he knew who they were. They told him their mission and named the captain of their vessel—Zechariah Gillam, the father of the New Englander already established on the island near-by. Gillam, it will be recalled, had been the captain of the first vessel of the Hudson's Bay Company to reach the Bay, and his family had been acquainted with Des Groseilliers even earlier in New England. About the time that the two Frenchmen had left the Company and gone to France in 1675, Gillam had been sued by the Company for trading on his own account in beaver skins from the Bay.[8] For some years, therefore, he had not been employed by the Company, but had had a rather eventful period in Carolina, where he had espoused the cause of the colonists in an uprising.[9] He had become unfriendly to the two Frenchmen in the early seventies, perhaps because it was they who revealed his private trading proclivities to the Company. Radisson even says of him, "I distrusted Captain Guilliem, who had declared himself my enemy in London, being the tool of those who had caused me to abandon the English service."

Radisson now made his position clear. He told Bridgar that this was French territory about them, for he had taken possession of it for Louis XIV. The others, he said, were too late. Of course the Company's men protested this claim and advanced their own. After considerable parley Bridgar and three men were allowed to land to talk with Radisson. Bridgar soon showed that he believed that he was in Hayes River, but Radisson corrected him and showed him the place where Sir Thomas Button had wintered. Bridgar invited Radisson on board his vessel and against the advice of his own people Radisson accepted the invitation, taking the precaution, however, to leave two Englishmen as hostages with the other Frenchmen. This visit gave Radisson an opportunity to refer casually to the big establishment and the fort that the French were making, to the large number of men they had, to their two vessels already in the Bay and the third that was expected, and, in general, to impress the credulous Englishmen. Then Radisson departed promising a future visit.

[8] H.B.Co. Archives, A/1/1, f. 25, entry of January 15, 1673/4.
[9] For this chapter in Gillam's life see Charles M. Andrews, *The Colonial Period of American History: The Settlements*, 3:226, 227, 254 (New Haven, 1937).

Instead of returning to his brother-in-law, Radisson hid two days in the woods and observed the preparations of Bridgar's party for making a fort. Then Radisson went to tell Des Groseilliers all that he had discovered. The two men laid careful plans: Radisson should handle both sets of interlopers; Des Groseilliers was to manage the fort; and young Jean Baptiste Chouart was to go up into the interior with one companion to find the natives and make sure of their trade. A portion of the plan was to keep Bridgar and his party ignorant of the New Englanders' presence. Young Gillam's fear of the Company, on whose preserves he was poaching, fitted admirably into Radisson's strategy. Nevertheless, when Radisson next visited young Gillam, the latter was carefully informed that it was his father who commanded the English vessel and that the elder Gillam was ill. Benjamin was distressed at this news and wanted to go at once to see his father. Radisson agreed to effect a reunion of father and son and did bring them together very cleverly soon afterwards without Bridgar's becoming aware of the relationship of the two men.

For a long time Bridgar remained in ignorance of the presence of the third group at Port Nelson. When he did send two men to spy out Radisson's fort (about whose position Radisson had deliberately deluded the English) and they arrived instead at the New England post, they were frightened away by young Gillam's actions, which, though friendly, were misinterpreted by the spies. So the latter reported only the finding of a fort, which they and Bridgar naturally concluded was Radisson's. This event, however, led to young Gillam's undoing. Zechariah Gillam and some of his men were lost on October 21 in the wreck of the *Prince Rupert,* when that vessel was forced off shore by ice. Now Radisson realized that Bridgar and the few remaining men were completely at his mercy unless the two Anglo-Saxon groups should combine forces. Benjamin Gillam had promised Radisson to receive no one into his island fort without Radisson's knowledge. Yet he had been on the point of receiving the two English spies who had stumbled upon his fort. Radisson's spies were all about and they did not fail to inform their master of Gillam's action. So Radisson saw his opportunity for seizing the New England vessel and taking the young commander himself captive to the French fort. Radisson's strategy in both these actions was very clever and it was not till success had crowned his efforts and young Gillam had been in Radisson's fort for a month that the New Englander even realized that he was a captive. Then, when he boasted of New England's defiance of all monarchical control, Radisson (never loath after his return to his English allegiance to inform the English of his regard for King Charles and the English cause) "treated him as a worthless dog for speaking in that way." Gillam, resentful of such treatment, threatened to return to his fort and Radisson informed him that he was a prisoner. Radisson then withdrew to allow an Englishman to tell Gillam that Zechariah Gillam and the Company's vessel had been lost in the ice and that Bridgar was actually at Radisson's mercy, though unaware till now of that fact. Radisson then skilfully seized the New England vessel and fort without bloodshed and put his own men in charge of them.

One of Gillam's men escaped in the mêlée and ran to inform Bridgar. Now for the first time the Governor learned of the colonial interlopers. He complained to Radisson that if he had been told, he, too, would have helped take the men poaching on his Company's preserves. He even went further and asked for some of the spoils! By this time Radisson could afford to be lenient to Bridgar, who had lost his only ship, his captain, several of his men, and some of his provisions.

Meantime spring came and with it the freshets that neither Englishmen nor Frenchmen were prepared for on those strange rivers, where ice, driven by rising water, could inflict unsuspected damage. Though the Frenchmen had taken what they believed were unnecessarily great precautions, their two vessels were sheared off by the ice, which the freshets forced up the little stream in which their hulls lay frozen. Only the bottoms were left and these, Radisson noted, were evidence of how much they owed to a kind Providence, for one of the vessels was rotten when thus opened up to daylight, and the other had never been bolted. After some deliberation, the bottom of one of them was chosen for rebuilding. Great fears were entertained meantime for the safety of the New England vessel, but here Bridgar's advice, given unwittingly, but heeded by the ever alert Radisson, saved the day. In the autumn Bridgar had told how he had once saved a vessel in Hudson Bay by cutting the ice about it down to the keel. Radisson had wisely ordered this course to be followed after he had acquired young Gillam's vessel. When the ice fields moved in on her, therefore, she was simply pushed up on shore and not badly injured.

Bridgar continued to live in his fort, losing several more of his men from illness, and remaining more or less dependent on the French for the wherewithal to subsist. Such at least is Radisson's version of the story; and the sequence of events seems to corroborate it. Radisson's aim was to remain rather friendly but to prevent Bridgar from getting any furs and to make him plan to leave in the spring, thus preventing any English settlement from developing in the Port Nelson area. However, Bridgar's conduct finally led Radisson to a complete declaration of what he required from the Englishman: the latter was not to go again to the island fort, where the New Englanders were located; and he was to go to the Bottom of the Bay to the other English posts as soon as navigation opened. Bridgar finally comprehended his situation, but he chose to state that only one of three things would oblige him to abandon the place: the order of his masters, force, or famine. Finally, by ruse,

Bridgar was lured to the island fort and held captive. Both forts of the interlopers were then burned, after men and goods had been removed, and preparations were made for sailing—Bridgar and his men in a boat to the Bottom of the Bay, Radisson and his party in Gillam's vessel for Quebec and France. Young Chouart and seven other men were to remain to hold the French post and to prepare for further trade with the Indians till a vessel could be sent to them from France or Canada.

When the time came for Bridgar to set out with his men in a ship's boat (he had preferred it to Radisson's offer of one of the two remaining vessels) for the English settlements in James Bay, he realized his danger and asked for Des Groseilliers' bark. His request was granted, but at the last moment the Frenchmen learned of some treachery on Bridgar's part in planning to go back to Port Nelson and he was obliged to remain with the vessel bound for Quebec, though his men were all allowed to proceed toward the Bottom of the Bay in the bark.

After some harrowing experiences, the *Batchelor's Delight,* now carrying the original crews of the *St. Pierre* and the *Ste. Anne,* as well as Pierre Allemand, Radisson, Des Groseilliers, and Bridgar, reached Quebec on October 20, 1683. There the Governor released Gillam and his ship, an act that played directly into the hands of the Governor's enemies in France.[10]

In September the *Black Eagle* from France lay at Percée Rock awaiting the explorers from the Bay. To the island came agents of the *fermier,* who reported later in Quebec what they had found. On September 18 the *fermier* presented a petition to De Meulles, the intendant, asking action against the originators of the plan for trading in the Bay without paying tribute to the *fermier.* De la Chenaye and Chanjon appeared in reply, acknowledged

[10] The Governor's ordinance is printed in *Ordonnances, Commissions Etc. Etc., 1639–1706,* 2: 56.

that they and their associates had sent out the expedition, and said that they would yield all to the *fermier* in return for the cost of their disbursements. The *fermier,* they said, had no claim on furs taken outside the area of the farm, the Bay being certainly outside its jurisdiction. De la Chenaye and Chanjon agreed to bring the vessels to Quebec, having always planned, they added, to exchange their furs there for good letters of exchange, exempt from the quarter tax.[11] On November 5, De la Barre, the new Governor, who had succeeded Frontenac, issued a decree forbidding the *fermier* to continue to confiscate the furs brought from Hudson Bay. The case, he said, was to go to Colbert for decision, "being of the first importance." Later, on November 8, the case came before De Meulles. His decision was

. . . that the beaver from the Bay, which has been taken to the warehouse of the *fermier,* shall be exchanged by the said Chalons to the said Sieurs de la Chesnaye, Chanjon, and their partners for letters of exchange for their full value and without deduction of the quarter tax. Nevertheless, a quarter of the value of the letters of exchange shall remain in the hands of Sieur Héron, agent of the *fermier* at La Rochelle, not to be drawn upon until other orders are received from His Majesty and the Lords of His Council.

As regards the confiscation of all the beaver, as demanded by the *fermier,* "we have already sent the parties to His said Majesty to have justice done." The "parties" thus sent to France were, among others, Radisson and Des Groseilliers.[12]

[11] *Ordonnances, Commissions Etc. Etc., 1639–1706,* 2:49–53, 57.
[12] *Ordonnances, Commissions Etc. Etc., 1639–1706,* 2:57–59.

CHAPTER XVI

The ''Jawes of ye French Leviathan''

The autumn of 1683 found Radisson and Des Groseilliers en route to Paris. Again their plans had miscarried, but they remembered their instructions from Colbert and apparently had faith that he would settle the affair in their favor. To their consternation they learned, when their vessels docked at La Rochelle, that Colbert was dead. Nor were they long in discovering that the Hudson's Bay Company, through its Governor, the Catholic Duke of York, brother of Charles II, was already complaining of their conduct and that Louis XIV was giving heed. The "Jawes of ye French Leviathan," as Sir James Hayes quaintly refers to the situation in his letter from Great Tew, Oxfordshire, on December 27, 1683, were ready to seize the two explorers.[1]

As early as January 10, 1683, the French ambassador had presented the English court with a protest against English settlements in Hudson Bay.[2] De la Barre, who had succeeded Frontenac as Governor of New France and who had become deeply involved in the fur trade with De la Chenaye, had written to France on November 11, 1682:

On the north there is an English company, trading in Hudson Bay, that is beginning to make establishments in the territory proclaimed as French by the King, our Master, full twenty years ago. I will not trouble their sea-borne commerce, but if they advance into the interior, as they are doing by means of poor little forts, and seduce our Indians, I shall have them expelled. Such a course will be easy enough, for they are weak. However, I shall be glad to have

[1] Hayes to John Werden, Secretary to the Duke of York, PRO., CO., 1/66, ff. 299, 300.
[2] De la Barre to [De Seignelay], November 11, 1682, *Cal. St. Pap., Am. & W. I., 1685–1688*, No. 2072; also H.B.Co. Archives, A/6/1, ff. 26, 27.

His Brittanic Majesty apprised that I wish to do nothing to displease him.

De la Barre's letter was presented by the French ambassador on January 10, 1683, and Sir James Hayes, Deputy Governor of the Hudson's Bay Company, was asked to draw up a reply.[3] Thus began the formal contest for America between the two nations. It had been brewing for a generation, but it had been kept well out of sight till De la Barre reached Canada. As the Recollect faction were wont to remark gleefully in these years, "the old Onontio [*Frontenac*] managed better." The hostilities that now began as Canadian trade insurgency were recognized as a war by France and England only in 1689, but warfare had begun on the shores of Hudson Bay in 1682 and continued, almost without break, till 1713.

On April 27, 1683, the Hudson's Bay Company's letter of instructions to Governor Henry Sergeant in the Bay warned him of the French jealousy of the English in Hudson Bay, recommended choosing strong young men who knew the Indian language, who should be sent "to penetrate into the Country to Draw downe the Indians by fayre & gentle meanes to trade wth us," and told him of Benjamin Gillam's plans to go to Hudson Bay in the *Batchelor's Delight,* as well as of several other interloping schemes from New England.[4] On the same day a letter was written to Captain Zechariah Gillam, mentioning the "Intelligence" lately received that Gillam's own son, after his father had been chosen for a trip to the Bay, had left England and concocted an interloping design.[5] The elder Gillam was, of course, long dead, but news of his tragic end had not yet reached London. The Company also set on foot schemes to

---

[3] H.B.Co. Archives, A/1/2, entry for January 20, 1682/3. For Sir Leoline Jenkins' official reply to the French King, see also the entry for March 3, 1682/3, A/6/1, f. 36, and PRO., CO. 1/66, ff. 275, 276. It was couched in French and based on Hayes's draft.

[4] H.B.Co. Archives, A/6/1, ff. 27–31.

[5] H.B.Co. Archives, A/6/1, f. 32.

thwart young Gillam by enforcement of the Navigation Acts and the appointment of Edward Randolph in Boston to "seize on Young Gillam . . . and Capt Zachariah Gillam and Capt Ezbon Sandford if they arrive there." [6]

All the summer of 1683 the Company was uneasy. Then, late in the fall, a ship arrived from Hudson Bay bearing news of Radisson and Des Groseilliers' actions there. Reality proved even worse than any possible surmise. No time was to be lost. A petition by the Company to the King asked for immediate action at the French court on the part of the English ambassador; the punishment of Radisson was demanded; and damages and restitution of property were claimed. By January 11 Lord Preston, the English envoy extraordinary in Paris, was presenting a memorial to Louis XIV.[7]

Like many others interested in Hudson Bay, Richard, Viscount Preston of Haddington, was closely attached to James, Duke of York. Yet, like Pepys and others who recognized the Duke's ability and essential honesty, while deploring his religious fanaticism, Preston had no intention of subverting the Protestant religion in England; and, though ambassador to France, he had a deep distrust and dislike of France and the French. In an age of strange contradictions both the Duke and the Viscount played as paradoxical rôles as any one. James, though an ardent Catholic, was chary of receiving money from Louis and resisted with some force Louis' schemes for increasing the French empire both in Hudson Bay and in the Gulf of Mexico.[8]

[6] H.B.Co. Archives, A/1/2, entry of June 27, 1683.

[7] H.B.Co. Archives, A/6/1, ff. 42, 95, 96; also in *Cal. St. Pap. Am. & W. I., 1685–1688*, Nos. 2085, 2088–2095.

[8] The papers of Lord Preston are preserved by a descendant in collateral line, the Hon. Sir Fergus Graham, M.P., of Netherby, Cumberland. Even the great box, in which they were shipped from France, when the envoy returned to England, still contains some of them. The author is much indebted to the present owner for his kindness in letting her browse through them at her leisure. Though they were calendared by the Historical Manuscripts Commission (7th *Report*, London, 1879), the most important volume of dispatches for the purposes of this study of Radisson and Des Groseilliers was over-

By January 25, 1684, Viscount Preston had presented still another memorial, this time stating that Radisson had arrived at La Rochelle since the petition of January 11 had been presented, and that by the time of writing must be in Paris.[9] Meantime on January 19, Preston laid the whole situation before Sir Leoline Jenkins, Secretary of State, by letter. It is perhaps the most explicit letter available on Canadian-French affairs at this period. Preston writes:[10]

I find the great support of Mons[r] de la Barre, the present Governor of Canada, is from the Jesuits in this Court, which order hath always a great number of missionaries in that country, who besides the conversion of the infidel have had the address to engross the whole castor [*beaver*] trade, from which they draw considerable advantage. The late Governor, the Marquis de Frontenac (in whose time this [*Radisson's*] enterprize was proposed and rejected by him as a thing which must prejudice the good correspondence which subsists betwixt the two Crowns), did ever oppose himself to their designs and exerted the King his Master's right to that traffique, but they found the means by the interest of Father de la Chaise to have him recalled, and the present Governor sent, who complyeth with them wholly, and giveth them no kind of trouble in their commerce. By this, sir, you will see that we are like to have those Fathers our enemies in this affair, and they are very powerful solicitors in this Court.

The letter breathes the ideas of De Callières' party and probably he or his Recollect supporters had been consulted before it was written. For it was they who solved the problem in large measure for the English company and court.

De la Barre, acting for the Jesuits, must naturally oppose De la Salle, whose known purpose was to erect a new government in the Mississippi Valley, which should be entirely without the jurisdiction of the Jesuits. Accordingly it is not strange that De la Salle returned from his explorations to

looked in that inventory. It contains practically all of the letters of Gédéon Godet. It is entitled "Godet's Letters." As the Preston collection is referred to in the *Report* of the Historical Manuscripts Commission as the papers of Sir Frederick Graham, they will be cited hereafter as Graham MSS.

[9] H.B.Co. Archives, A/6/1, f. 96.
[10] Graham MSS.

the mouth of the Mississippi in 1682 only to find himself without funds, hounded by creditors, despoiled of his fort at De la Barre's command, and without authority to return to the Illinois country. He was in Quebec when Radisson and Des Groseilliers returned from Hudson Bay in 1683, and he went to France in the same fleet with these men, perhaps even in the same vessel with one of them. Awaiting De la Salle impatiently in Europe was his attorney, Abbé Claude Bernou, who had just left Paris for Rome to take up the cause of the Portuguese as against the Spanish claims to the colony of Saint Sacrement in South America. Fortunately for history, Bernou was thus absent from Paris when De la Salle arrived, for Bernou had to depend on his friend, Abbé Eusèbe Renaudot, for information. It is the correspondence between these two men that gives us the complete story of what was passing behind the scenes in the French court.[11]

Bernou was attached to the train of Cardinal D'Estrées in Rome. Since D'Estrées was greatly interested in geographical discoveries, Father Marco Vincenzo Coronelli was just completing for him to present to Louis XIV the now famous Marly globes and certain maps embodying the most up-to-date geographical information available at that time. Bernou had long been interested in geographical exploration and had supplied Coronelli with material on Peru (supplied to Bernou in part by Peñalosa), on Mexico, on the Mississippi River (supplied by De la Salle and Hennepin), and on Hudson Bay (probably supplied in part, at least, by Radisson). Bernou now tried to get from De la Salle, Radisson, Des Groseilliers, and, indirectly, from the Hudson's Bay Company itself the latest facts about American geography, in order that he might make the globes and maps as perfect as possible. This fact explains to some ex-

[11] The Bernou correspondence is found in the Renaudot Papers in the Bibliothèque Nationale, as already cited in previous chapters. Hereafter in this chapter, letters by Bernou to Renaudot will be assumed to be in Volume 7497 of those papers.

tent the mention of Radisson and Des Groseilliers in the
Bernou-Renaudot correspondence. The two abbés were willing to do something for the two explorers in order to have
a chance to learn geographic facts from them. However, De
la Salle came first in the priests' plans, for he would pull
their chestnuts out of the fire. It is doubtful whether Radisson and Des Groseilliers sensed their own secondary importance on their arrival, for they soon appealed to Renaudot
for help against the English complaints against them. They
could hardly have made a more fatal mistake, for it was the
aim of the De Callières-Renaudot-Recollect group to keep
England friendly until certain other plans had come to maturity.

Bernou's correspondence with Renaudot opens at this period with derogatory remarks on De la Barre as compared
with the "old Onontio" already quoted and with consola-
tory messages to Renaudot because of Colbert's death.[12] It
is obvious that behind Colbert, working with him and expecting place rewards from him, were such men as De Callières and Renaudot. Another letter, in which jest and serious
intent commingle, reveals some of the plans for America:
the Sieur Tarin De Cussy has been appointed through
Bernou's efforts to the governorship of Santo Domingo;
this Governor is to help De la Salle establish a new colony
right down the length of the Mississippi Valley, the buccaneers of De Cussy's jurisdiction fighting and ousting the
Spanish; and a new archdiocese is to be established in this
part of the New World, whither the scholarly recluses,
Renaudot and Maubuisson, can retreat, under Bernou's be-
neficent rule as archbishop or intendant. "It is to you and
Monsieur de Callières that I owe all this," he writes in effect, and now all that is left to be done for "my navigators"
is to see De la Salle made governor of the colony, when he
shall have returned to France, "as I have advised him to

[12] September 28, 1683, f. 50.

do." [13] In Bernou's next pertinent letter, that of December 14, 1683, De Callières is again mentioned: "Please give my best thanks to Monsieur de Callières for his goodness in interesting himself in my affairs. You are my two polar stars, who prevent me from suffering shipwreck in the sea of negotiations on which you have embarked me."

It was not till February 1, 1684, that Radisson and Des Groseilliers were mentioned in the correspondence. Bernou's letter of that date is a long one and takes up, first of all, De la Salle's affairs, urging that De la Salle join his plans to those of Peñalosa and return to the Mississippi by its mouth rather than risk detection of his plans by the Jesuits by returning through Canada as usual.

> As for my two other nephews, what a great difference there is between them and De la Salle, as you recognize rightly. If their exploit is as you describe it, I recommend them to Milord Preston and do not want to get mixed up in the matter. Only, I beg you, by means of Marshall D'Estrées or any one else, get from them the map of Hudson Bay. Mr. Radisson carried off an English map . . . and you will oblige the Cardinal and Madame Geography.

By February 22, 1684, De Villermont had written about Radisson and Des Groseilliers. Bernou writes:

> I have just received Mr. de Villermont's long letter admitting that Mr. de la Barre's and Mr. Radisson's maneuvres were unwise. He tells the latter's escapade as you do and regards it as a bad matter that Radisson will have to smooth out for himself. . . . I second everything you say about him [De Villermont]. I know him as well as you do and I am surprised that you have so bad an opinion of such a great politician as I am, or as I am supposed to be. Have no fear; he shall learn nothing of American affairs from me. Yet he could be made use of in a certain matter. . . . I beg you to enlighten me on two points. First, whether Mr. Radisson and his brother-in-law came knocking at your door; and what you did with your *chien de tendre*,[14] for, I must confess, had it been my affair, I should have been greatly embarrassed. The second point is, whether Count de

---

[13] October 19, 1683, f. 54.
[14] This is a clever, seventeenth-century pun.

Frontenac is not planning to profit by this affair to mount his steed once more [*that is, return to Canada as governor*]. The recall of the other [*De la Barre*] would be a fitting compensation and the change would greatly please me as well as Mr. de la Salle.

How little Radisson and his brother-in-law must have realized that the men to whom they were appealing for help were the very ones who were snatching at every straw to effect De la Barre's recall; and that their escapade in Hudson Bay was just what this group needed to oust the Governor! Renaudot would not hesitate to sacrifice Radisson and Des Groseilliers for a chance to get Frontenac back to Canada, so that De la Salle's project might go forward.

The same letter gives an inkling as to the hand that wrote most of the successful "American" petitions of the period:

You make fun of the old abbé [*Bernou*] by saying that they [*De la Salle's backers*] need his American pen. I know that De la Salle's affairs are in better hands than mine, being in yours and Monsieur de Callières'. But when it comes to the Grand Project, don't despise it. I should not be useless to you, I think. . . . If you think proper, I will send you two or three little memorials for your use: one regarding the objection that France will be depopulated by the plan [*of settling a colony in the Mississippi Valley*], another regarding the utility of this project, a third touching the means for making it a success, another concerning the remedy for the inconveniences that may be feared in its execution or later, and, finally, one on the subject of the practicability of the scheme.

What are these but echoes of Radisson's memorials?

By March 21 Renaudot's advice in the Hudson Bay affair had been rejected by those persons who were handling the matter in the French Court, for Bernou wrote on that day,

The road that you wanted to follow in the affair of Messrs Radisson and Des Groseillers seems to me longer but also surer than that which Mr. Thévenot [15] wants to take. For even if he proves that the English had abandoned their colonies in Hudson Bay, he still can-

[15] Melchisédech Thévenot, another French scholar interested in American exploration and the author of works on that subject, may be studied by consulting the index volumes of the *Jesuit Relations*.

not prove that they had not reëstablished them, since they have been taken and pillaged. I wish him success.

Bernou knew by March 28 that Renaudot had succeeded in getting the map of Hudson Bay, since he wrote on that date,

As for the map of Hudson Bay, have it copied as quickly as possible, if you have not already done so. You will give pleasure to the Cardinal as well as to Father Coronelli. If you lack helpers, you can employ Mr. Peronel, Father Coronelli's friend and mine, who lives with Sir [————] Penne. . . .

You ask what it matters, provided he [De la Salle] return to his explorations. . . . Signor, it does matter. It matters greatly to me. I knew his proposed route even before you wrote me, and as it is my diocese, I know that he can run many risks in this navigation. Wherefore, I should like him to make use of one of the nephews of our friend the Dominican [De Cussy]. . . . As for my so-called godsons [Radisson and Des Groseilliers], if they distrust you, so much the worse for them. If you can help them, very well. If not, I wash my hands of them.

The same letter carries regrets that De la Salle's affair has not been united with Peñalosa's.

Meanwhile De Villermont must have learned of plans not mentioned in the Bernou-Renaudot letters, for his chief French correspondent in England, the famous Henri Justel, wrote on April 2 to a friend at Oxford that Count Peñalosa had been given a frigate "for a great expedition towards America, in which the Santo Dominican buccaneers are to be employed," and that "Mr. de la Salle is to return to the Mississippi." [16] In his letter of April 4, Bernou writes that De Villermont is complaining that he has not all of Bernou's writings. "He is the friend of our lords [probably De Callières and De Seignelay at court and possibly Cardinal D'Estrées]," writes Bernou, "for some reasons of weight that I cannot disclose to you, and he will elicit a command

---

[16] Justel to Thomas Smith, Bodleian 361, Smith MSS, 46, Bodleian Library, Oxford; this letter was called to my attention by Dr. Harcourt Brown.

to me to see these documents, which I must avoid carrying out."

Again on April 11 Bernou returns to the topic of Radisson and Des Groseilliers:

As for the two Iroquois, I believe that you are right, for, in addition to what you say, it cannot be said that we were established there [*Hudson Bay*], nor can it be denied that the English were. That settles the matter as far as I am concerned, without all these rhetorical questions. I hope all will go well and that the old Onontio may return to his flock. I have nothing more to tell you about the map. Remember that of Hudson Bay. Mr. De Callières and you will use it as you think best in these affairs of the New World.

That Renaudot's advice in the Hudson Bay affair was eventually followed may be judged from Bernou's letter of May 2: "The answer made to the English appears excellent to me and I believe that Mr. de Callières may have inspired it, since it is exactly what you have thought and what you wrote me."

With this final link in the chain of evidence, we can join the Bernou-Renaudot story with that of Preston, for De Callières' answer to the English, in the form of a proposal, has been preserved.

* * *

Henry Savile, who had preceded Preston at Paris, wrote frankly to his successor that his domestic, Gédéon Godet, had asked to be recommended to Preston for service. The recommendation given, however, was hardly calculated to trouble Godet's modesty.[17] Nevertheless, Preston took Godet into his service and soon learned that Savile was quite correct in his estimate of Godet. At least twice before the Radisson episode engaged his attention Preston found himself obliged to get Godet out of prison. The latter blamed everything that went wrong on the fact that he was

[17] Graham MSS, May 15, 1682.

"of the Religion," a contemporaneous expression meaning that he was a Protestant. He had been, and perhaps still was, an *avocat au Parlement de Paris,* a term for which there is no English equivalent. It may be translated literally as "an advocate at the parliament of Paris," the highest court of justice in France. The position was one of honor and distinction. At one time he must have had a fair fortune, if we may believe Lord Preston, though he had lost most of it by 1683. It was Godet, apparently, who kept Preston informed of many events and personalities in France. "This person," Preston wrote, "is capable enough of the employ having acquaintance wth all the Comis of the Ministers here & alsoe accesse to them & admission to their Bureaux. He is descended of a Good family & hath lost a considerable charge because of his Religion." [18]

It was this person who succeeded in seducing Radisson back to the English interest. A Frenchman who may have had peculiar opportunities to know the facts, states that Godet was bribed with the promise that his daughter should wed Radisson, if Godet led Radisson back to his English allegiance.[19] This story seems worthy of credence for several reasons: (1) Radisson did marry Godet's daughter in 1685; (2) Godet in 1684 was moving heaven and earth to provide for his daughters; and (3) when Radisson and Margaret Charlotte Godet were married, it was by the order of the Bishop of London, the very prelate to whom Preston wrote a letter of introduction for Godet when the latter went to London.[20]

Preston presented his first petition to the French court on January 11, 1684. The reply was that "the King . . . had commanded . . . to remit the whole affair into the hands of Monsr de Seignelay." Preston then tells how Radisson

[18] Graham MSS, Preston to Jenkins, May 10, 1684.
[19] Tyrrell, *Documents Relating to Hudson Bay,* p. 242, quoting Bacqueville de la Potherie, *Histoire de l'Amérique Septentrionale* (Paris, 1753).
[20] Graham MSS, Godet to Preston, September 1, 1684; Preston to My Lord Bishop of London, May 10, 1684.

"hath been in Paris these 5 days." Des Groseilliers, he adds, "a person whose story is very well known in those countries" arrived on a merchantman, rather than in the frigate bearing Radisson.

> They are both dispatched from Monsr de la Barre with instructions for his and their own defence. A friend of mine [*Godet?*] who hath seen the former since his arrival and discoursed with him tells me that he finds him much alarmed with the charge which is given against him. . . . I am told privately that a relation of the moment of taking possession of Port Nelson in the name of the English by those very Des Grozelieres and Radison may be found amongst the papers of Prince Robert [*Rupert*]. This doubtless would be very useful to us, and it would be of consequence to have it here if by any means it can be found.[21]

Radisson and Des Groseilliers' alarms led them, it would appear, to petition De Seignelay at this time. Radisson presented his memorial through the Marquis de Belleroche.[22] In it he recited his story from the time he left the service of the Hudson's Bay Company, making much of his wife's hardships and of the jewels she had been obliged to pawn for him, including the "portrait of the king of England that he himself had presented to me, as well as the gold chain that he had hung around my neck." He gives Marshal D'Estrées as a reference for his veracity.

Des Groseilliers' letter goes into the details of the recent expedition, stressing particularly the rightness of his action in the matter of Gillam's vessel.[23] The reason for this emphasis was the fact that Preston had secured illicitly from Radisson and Des Groseilliers a copy of Gillam's petition to Governor de la Barre. When the fact became known to the two explorers, they were much concerned.[24] De la Barre's action in restoring the vessel to Gillam was men-

[21] Graham MSS, Preston to Jenkins, January 19, 1684.
[22] BN, Margry Papers, 9284, ff. 61, 62; it is also partially printed in [Sulte], *Collection de manuscrits*, 1:319. See *post*, Appendix 6.
[23] AC., C^{11}, 1682–1684, Vol. 6, f. 451. See *post*, Appendix 7.
[24] Graham MSS, Preston to Jenkins, March 8, 1684.

tioned in that document. The English were not slow in perceiving the advantage that the tacit acknowledgment of the
explorers' mistake in capturing the vessel gave them. Moreover, De la Barre was soon to be severely berated for his
action by De Seignelay.[25]

This is the only document by Des Groseilliers' hand
known to be in existence. It shows him a man of better education than Radisson, if it may be assumed that he himself
was the author. Requests and petitions were often made out
by men like Bernou. One other interesting fact about this
document is that it may throw some light on Des Groseilliers' young manhood. To prove how silly it was for England to claim Port Nelson because of English explorations
there and English settlements in James Bay, he draws the
analogy of Biencourt's colony on Mt. Desert Island, close
to Boston [!]. As well let the French of Mt. Desert Island
claim Boston, he says, as for the English of James Bay to
claim Port Nelson. His knowledge of Biencourt's and John
Winthrop's actions in Maine leads the reader to suspect
that Des Groseilliers had lived on or near the Maine coast.

Des Groseilliers ends his petition with a subtle bit of
flattery: "I hope that I shall not be blamed for having
changed the name of Port Nelson to that of Bourbon
River." He also makes an appeal to the King's religious fervor, saying that Captain Zechariah Gillam, whose vessel
had just been wrecked, was the man who had taken prisoner
the Jesuit priest, Father Albanel. The inference is that Gillam's fate was deserved.

Meanwhile Preston presented the matter to De Seignelay
on February 8 and got the reply from the minister that
"the King his master could not in justice punish Radison till
he be fully informed of the circumstances of his attempt
from the Governour of Canada to whom he had written for

[25] De Seignelay to De la Barre, April 10, 1684, in [Sulte], *Collection de manuscrits*, 1: 324, 325.

information upon this subject." [26] In other words, De Seignelay, advised by De Callières, was sparring for time, which was important in this case. On April 19 Preston writes that having learned nothing of what the King proposed to do, he demanded an audience with that monarch himself,

. . . which his most Christian Majesty was pleased to grant me privately in his *cabinet* upon Monday last. . . . He . . . told me that this affair had been often under his consideration, and that he had always ordered Monsieur de Seignelay to let me know that he would take no resolution concerning it till he had heard from his Governour of Canada, to whom he had sent to know how the action passed, and that at this time he could give no other answer.[27]

A few days later, as Preston left Paris to accompany Louis XIV on his journey to the siege of Luxemburg, he "received an advice that his Most Christian Majesty had left his orders with Monsr de Seignelay to signify his pleasure to the Governor of Canada that the French should restore the possession of Port Nelson, and of all which they had violently taken to the English." [28]

[26] Graham MSS, Preston to Jenkins, February 9, 1684.
[27] Graham MSS, Preston to Jenkins.
[28] Graham MSS, Preston to the Earl of Sunderland, April 30, 1684.

CHAPTER XVII

What Happened at the Half Moon
Tavern

Radisson had made the trip to Hudson Bay on the pledge
of the Canadian merchants to pay him and Des Groseilliers
a quarter of the furs obtained in Hudson Bay. Unfortunately the *fermier* had intercepted the furs at Quebec. So
the merchants who had planned to evade the tax ran into
difficulties. The case was sent to the King to decide, De la
Barre openly supporting the merchants. On April 10, 1684,
however, Louis XIV issued an ordinance at Versailles ordering all merchants or inhabitants of New France, who
might secure furs at Hudson Bay, Percée Rock, or other
places, with the single exception of Acadia, to take them to
Quebec and pay one fourth to the *fermier*.[1]

Thus did Radisson's hopes go glimmering. He was too
astute to believe that he would get his quarter from De la
Chenaye and that merchant's partners. Just at this time
Radisson received letters from William Young, one of the
members of the Committee of the Hudson's Bay Company.
No copies of these letters are known to have survived, but
it is obvious from references to them by Radisson, Young,
and the Company, that they offered great inducements to
Radisson to return to the Company's employment. Indeed,
Young himself later referred to them as "3 or four Insinuating Letters . . . acknowledging the Comp[ies] former severities" and containing "Large promises, that he should
bee Extreamely well Received & Rewarded by the Com-

[1] See Edouard Richard's supplement, Canadian Archives, *Report*, 1899, p.
80.

pany." [2] The Half Moon Tavern in Cheapside saw the plotting of the Committee to get Radisson back into service. Sir James Hayes, William Young, Sir Edward Dering, and Richard Cradock (Craddock) were the conspirators. "And there it was ordered that Mr Young bee desired to write to Mr Radison & corespond with him, Towards bringing him over & Reconcileing him selfe with the Comp^a." [3]

Meantime Preston in France was surely conniving with the Company. A letter of his written on May 25 adds a touch or two to the story. "Thō within ten days after my audience [*with the King*] Monsr de Seignelay went to Thoulon, so y^t I could not have an Opportunity of seeing him, yet I judge this from the uneasinesse in wch I found Radison & his friends some dayes after sev^{ll} proposalls were made to me from him & des Grozeliers all wch I seemed to slight because I durst not indeed trust them." [4] Radisson himself tells that these "proposalls" were to return to the English, to go to Hudson Bay for them, and to recapture Port Nelson together with all the furs there, for them.

Preston's letter adds the link that has long been missing in the story of what turned the trick for the English cause.

At last two dayes before I leaft Paris, two Gentlemen in whome I have a Confidence came to me from them [*Radisson and Des Groseilliers*] wth ye Proposition enclosed & did indeed avow to me y^t those persons had been hardly treated in words by Monsr de Seignelay, before his departure, & y^t they believed y^t he had told them y^t the King his Master would not avow their action, nor suport

[2] H.B.Co. Archives, A/6/2, ff. 66, 67, "Coppy of Willm Young Esqr his letter to the Committee Dated ye 20th Decemb^r 1692." See *post*, Appendix 10.

[3] The entry immediately preceding this excerpt is: "Radison being arrived & gott to Paris . . . was forced to skulke & hide him selfe, upon which wee are Easely ap^t to beleive, he writt to some freind in England to Interceed for him to the Comp^a. . . . And Esqr Young is the first that acquaints Sr James Hayes . . . who forthwith Adjourned the Comittee to the halfe moone Tavern in Cheapeside & tooke along with him for more privacy onely Mr Young Sr Edw Dering & Mr Cradock." H.B.Co. Archives, A/6/2, ff. 68–71, "The Comittees Answer to Esqr Yonges Letter," March 8, 1692/3. See *post*, Appendix 10.

[4] Graham MSS, Preston to Sir James Hayes, May 25, 1684.

them in it, tho' they would not directly owne it. The morning when I left Paris I had that account which I gave to my Lord of Sunderland of this King's ordering Radison and des Grozelieres to withdraw the French with their effects from Port Nelson, but not having it from any minister of this Court I durst not write it positively. Since my being here [*Valenciennes*] I have asked Monsr de Croissy if he had any order from the King his master concerning it, he answered No, but Monsr de Seignelay, in whose hand the business naturally was, might have one. Till his return, which must be within 12 or 14 days, nothing more can be known. In the mean time I think the proposal inclosed may be worthy of the consideration of the company, and I must add that it cometh to me from the hands of those who are assured that it will be made good. The time which they desire for putting the habitation and fort which they have seized into the possession of the English company seemeth long, but you will be a better judge of the reason which they give for it than I am.

Obviously Lord Preston did not know on May 25 that Radisson had already returned to England. His letter inclosed the proposition that Renaudot had made. It is still attached in copy to the copy of his letter that Lord Preston filed among his own papers. Radisson's affidavit that it was François de Callières who dictated it is in existence.[5] The proposition reads in modern English:

To end the troubles between the French and the English nation in the matter of the settlement made by Sieurs des Groziliers and Radisson in Hudson Bay, and to prevent a possible bloodshed in the retention of this post, the expedient which seems best and most advantageous for the English Company would be for Sieurs de Groziliers and Radisson to return to their said establishment and for them to be given a passport by the English Company, which should allow them to withdraw the Frenchmen in the garrison there with all their possessions within eighteen months from the day of departure, since it is impossible to go and come in one year on account of ice, which blocks the entrance and obliges them to winter there, by which passport Sieurs de Groziliers and Radisson would restore

[5] An abbreviated contemporary "Translation of Monsr Calliere's Direction to Mr Radisson for restoring Port Nelson . . ." is in PRO., Amer. & W. I., Vol. 539. See also "Mr Radison's Affidavitt made before Sir Robt Jeffery the 23^d August 1697," as already cited.

to the English Company the settlement made by the two men in that country, for the Company to enjoy hereafter without molestation.

The matter of damages is then discussed.

Radisson tells us that up till the very moment when he left for England the French court was laying plans for him to return to Hudson Bay. From other sources it is possible to see that court bending every effort toward getting off De la Salle to the successful establishment of his great inland colony.[6] Eighteen months would see his plans well matured. The French court knew, as well as Radisson, that it was perfectly possible to go to Hudson Bay and return in one season. Radisson, indeed, left the very month this note was penned and was back in London in October.[7]

It was part of Renaudot and Bernou's plans to make Radisson and Des Groseilliers useful in their scheme for De la Salle. In the spring of 1684 two squadrons were being fitted out at Brest, one for Canada and the other for the mouth of the Mississippi. This latter one was reported, however, to be taking De la Salle back to Canada to complete his work via that country. The aim was to keep the Jesuits in ignorance of the real plan. Renaudot's correspondence shows how desperately De la Salle and the court tried to keep the truth from the public, foreseeing the resistance of the Jesuits, which did appear as soon as De la Salle got away and the truth was out. Preston writes from Paris that Des Groseilliers is to accompany De la Salle; Bernou writes of the great assistance that Radisson will be

---

[6] Bernou's letters to Renaudot give the best account of these efforts at secrecy.

[7] "They [*the French minister's answers*] are rather dilatory and given with a design to gain time that they may see how things will turn, and if a fairer pretext may be formed to keep what those adventurers of Canada have by violence put themselves in possession of. The reason of this is obvious; for Radison and des Grozelieres have not failed since their arrival here to represent to these ministers all the advantages which the French nation may draw from this King's being master of the territory which belongeth to the English company, which will put the whole castor trade into the hands of his subjects." Preston's letter of May 25, 1684.

to Louis Hector de Callières, now that the latter has been made Governor of Montreal.[8] Everything seemed to be going so well for Bernou and Renaudot's plans: De la Salle amply supported by the court and safely on his way to Louisiana; De la Barre censured and ordered to return Fort Frontenac to De la Salle; four Recollect missionaries sent to Louisiana despite the prohibition of the Bishop of Paris; Hector de Callières on the first rung of the ladder leading to the governorship of Canada; and the Hudson Bay episode brought to a peaceable solution that would appease the anger of the Duke of York, their hope for the future of Catholicism in England.

Then they learned that Radisson had slipped off to England to restore immediately the Bay post and all that went with it to the Hudson's Bay Company! It is small wonder that both abbés were profoundly disgusted.

* * *

It is Godet who gives the clue as to what happened after Lord Preston left Paris. On May 22 he wrote to Preston from Windsor: "After a delay of ten days at Dieppe, I finally arrived at London last Thursday. . . . I came here with the man whom you know, who has been very well received by His Royal Highness and by his Company. You will be thanked on their behalfe." [9]

On May 22, old style, or June 1, 1684, new style, Sir James Hayes wrote from Whitehall to Preston, acknowledging Preston's letter of May 25 from Valenciennes: [10]

We have already found the Effects of yor L^{ps} warme applications on our behalf at the Court of France in a manner wch we did not expect; For about fortnight since, Radison came over hither in the company of a French Gen^t one Monsr Goodett (I think they call him) a servant of yor L^{ps} and rendred himself to me and another

[8] Preston to Sunderland, June 17, 1684, in Graham MSS; and Bernou to Renaudot, May 16, 1684, in BN., Renaudot Papers.

[9] Graham MSS.

[10] Graham MSS.

member of our H. B. Comittee to whom he was formerly knowne, and after a little conversation wth him, we thought fitt to carry him to Windsor and present him to his R^{ll} Highnes[s] and to advise wth him (as o^{r} Governo^{r}) if we might againe take him to serve ye Comp^{a} as he desired . . . and ye last weeke he sayled hence upon one of our vessels for Port Nelson.

It is obvious that every one assumed that Preston had persuaded Radisson to go to England, and a little later the Viscount was to receive high praise and substantial thanks from the Hudson's Bay Company.[11] But Godet's correspondence shows that Preston knew little about the journey and could not have been completely instrumental in bringing it about. On October 16, 1684, Godet wrote to Preston: [12]

I believed that having written you so many of the circumstances of the Radisson affair and remarked among other things that Mr Dablancourt could testify of what I write you, you would recall that I have done nothing without telling you about it and securing your approval. I even recall right now, Sir, an episode which will complete my justification, for surely you do not forget it. It is the fact that having had the honor of taking leave of you a half hour before you left to go to join the King in Flanders, I returned to you to say that I had just received a note from Mr Dablancourt, which advised me that Radisson had decided to go over into England with me and that he was to come to see me to take steps with help to effect that course. You told me, My Lord, that you were glad of it and you did me the honor to add that he was doing so from friendship with me and that I would be doing my full duty to His Royal Highness and to the Company to take that man to this country. I swear, My Lord, as I hope for pardon in Heaven, that the case is as I have stated. . . . But I affirm that I am telling you the truth in the matter of the information I gave you before leaving, and you even found it good that I should tell Sir [Leoline] Jenkins

[11] "Sr James Hayes is Desired to invite My Lord Preston to an Entertainement & the Warehouse keeper is ordered to Deliver Mr Jarvis Byfield as many black beaver skins of No. 53, as will make his Lordship a covering for his bed which is to be made up and presented his Lordship as a present from the Company." H.B.Co. Archives, A/1/8, entry of January 9, 1684/5. On January 19 the sum of seven pounds and fifteen shillings is mentioned "as spent upon the Ld Preston in an Entertainment at Fontack house."

[12] Godet to Preston, October 6/16, 1684, in "Godet's Letters," ff. 191–194, in Graham MSS.

—which I did the same day, having opened my dispatches just for that purpose. I mention this again today, My Lord, because Sir James Hayes mentioned it to me four or five days ago at Whitehall, and if I am so unlucky that you have not changed your mind on this point, I shall be in despair. If you believe me capable of such lack of consideration and of doing such a thing without your consent, there is nothing more for me in your esteem and no hope that you will ever have the least confidence in me.

Godet was hoping for a recommendation from Lord Preston to a post that he wanted to fill for the English government, a fact which accounts for all the groveling and complaint in this letter. Eleven days after Godet penned this letter Radisson returned to England from Hudson Bay and Godet was jubilant. An undated letter to Preston shows that Godet was under "great reproach" in the interim "in the affair of Sieur Radisson," "the gentlemen of the Company having looked upon me as a vagabond," "not even acquainted with you." [13] But Godet had "wherewith to confound them," by Radisson's return "with forty thousand beaver skins"; and in crowing over his opponents and detractors Godet has preserved the story of the fear that possessed the Company all through the summer of 1684. "There was nothing but disquietude over the conduct and fidelity of Sieur Radisson, whom these gentlemen distrusted greatly," he writes. From other sources also—such as Bridgar's biased narrative recounted to the Committee upon his return from New England with a lurid tale [14] of Radisson's duplicity and cruelty, and Governor Bradstreet's letter of warning of what De la Barre was planning [15]—it is possible to see the Committee verging on a state of nerves. But

[13] "Godet's Letters," ff. 225–228. Radisson returned to England on October 27, 1684.

[14] H.B.Co. Archives, Small Minute Book, 1683 to the end of 1684, entries of July 5 and 11, 1684.

[15] "A Narrative of the French Action at Port Nelson which was presented by Sʳ James Hayes to the King at Winchester 25 September 1684" in H.B.Co. Archives, A/6/1, ff. 51, 52.

why, the reader is surely justified in asking. The answer, pieced together from many bits of evidence, lies in the unexpected course that events took.

Radisson in Paris had found himself in an awkward position, about to be sacrificed to the plans of another explorer, De la Salle, and the men back of De la Salle's project; and to the greed of the King, the Jesuits, and others who profited from the fur trade in Canada. Being friendly with Godet, who had become a friend in his own interest, Radisson realized that he could get to England on Godet's passport. Godet saw a chance to make the Company and the English court believe that Lord Preston had made all the arrangements through Godet, and Godet would thus gain recognition for his other schemes. Only a few days intervened between Radisson's arrival in England and his departure for Hudson Bay. Then came the realization to the Company and the court that Preston either knew nothing about Radisson's return or had had no confirmation of Radisson's scheme from the French King, and that absurd confidence had been reposed in a man notorious for his ability to change allegiance.

From the agreement that Radisson made with the Company, and from his last will and testament, it is plain that his chief concern was the furs that he knew would await him at his nephew's post on Hayes River.[16] If he had to lose a quarter of his furs as a French subject, he probably argued, it would be much more to the point to return to his English allegiance, drive a hard bargain with a Company in extremities, and pose as a benefactor to them. Sir James Hayes expressed Radisson's feelings about the French as follows: "I find he thinks himself to have been illtreated by the French, for whom he undertooke the conduct of the late voyage for Port Nelson, and hath gott nothing by it but materialls

[16] For Radisson's agreement with the Company, see *post*, p. 220; for his last will and testament, see *post*, Appendix 16.

for a very Romantique Novelle entertaining enough." [17]

How little Preston knew of the details of Radisson's journey to England is apparent from the fact that it was Hayes who told the story to Preston, not vice versa, as one would expect.

When he tooke ye resolution of returning for England, he Concealed himself some dayes before he left Paris in ye Sanctuary of yor Excell^ys house there, from whence he came to Diepe and there tooke his passage, leaving his Bro^r des Grosiliers at Paris for whom in his treaty wth us he hath made some termes also, in case he comes over to us. . . . Ye last weeke he sayled hence upon one of our vessells for Port Nelson where he hath undertaken w^thout hostility to reduce the French he left behind him, and to render us the quiet possessio^n of y^t place and to be our f^tful serv^t to his end; and to conciliate Credit he hath taken an Oath of Fidelity to ye Company (wch by our Constitution we have power to administer) and hath left behind him a small parcell of French gold to erect a monum^t to his memory, in case he should fayle in ye present Expeditio^n.

Surely Sir James had a sense of the dramatic, what with his appreciation of the "Romantic Novelle" and the monument to be erected to a lost cause. Sir James had had his moments, too, if we are to believe the stories of his under-sea adventures.[18]

The terms of Radisson's agreement with the Company were that he was to receive

. . . the wages of £50 per annum and the Benefitt of haveing two hundred pounds in the Capatall Stock of the Comp^a during his Life and good behaviour in the Service, and that he should have £25 to Sett him out for the present expedition for p^t Nelson—and that his Brother Grosillier who is now in France if he comes over Shall have 20^s a week for his support dureing his abode here to Ingageing also to be faithfull to the Interest of the Company for the future.[19]

[17] Sir James Hayes to Lord Preston, May 22, 1684, in Graham MSS, volume entitled "Parliamentary Chamber of London The Press Hudson's Bay and New England Tangiers and Algiers," ff. 125, 126.

[18] Hayes to Preston, May 22, 1684, as cited in Note 17; and Mood, "Hudson's Bay Company Started as a Syndicate," pp. 57, 58.

[19] H.B.Co. Archives, A/1/2, entry of May 12, 1684.

How pleased the Company was with Radisson in May, 1684, is evidenced by several occurrences. The Committee ordered a silver tankard costing ten pounds and fourteen shillings, to be presented to him before he sailed.[20] They also wrote to one Morgan Lodge at the debarkation port to furnish Radisson, on board his vessel, "with 3 or 4 doz^n of Poultrey with what other fresh provisions he shall desire." Radisson did not interpret this largesse in any niggardly fashion. The bill that Lodge presented amounted to ten pounds, five shillings, and eight pence! [21]

To Captain John Abraham, the Governor at Port Nelson, a letter of instructions was written on May 14, which contained an announcement of Radisson's place of trust and responsibility. Abraham was cautioned: "We therefore expect that you treat him with all respect as one in whome we have entire confidence & trust & that you follow his advice in reduceing the French Factorey & in makeing our settlement in & aboute Port Nelson." By the same letter Radisson was also made one of Abraham's council in the general management and government of the area.[22]

To Captains William Bond and John Outlaw a letter of the same date, which was not to be opened till the entrance of Hudson Strait was reached, stated: "We doe therefore require you to treat him with Respect & to cause all others under y^r Command to doe the like, he being now sent upon this Expedition by the order of his Royall Highness & the allowance of his Majesty." [23]

[20] H.B.Co. Archives, A/1/2, entry of May 21, 1684.
[21] H.B.Co. Archives, A/1/2, entries of May 15 and May 28, 1684, and A/6/1, f. 43.
[22] H.B.Co. Archives, A/6/1, f. 44, the Committee to Captain John Abraham, May 14, 1684.
[23] H.B.Co. Archives, A/6/1, f. 45.

CHAPTER XVIII

The Great Affair

In 1685 Radisson wrote accounts of his two most recent trips to Hudson Bay, covering his exploits of the years 1682–1683 and 1684. Both documents have survived in their original French form and one is preserved also in contemporary translation.[1] From the eagerness with which they were read in England and France it is possible to judge how deep an interest in travel literature existed in both countries. The surprising thing is that, conscious as Radisson was of anything dramatic in his activities, he did not, like Father Hennepin, bring out a book about them. Probably he had just that object in mind, if Sir James Hayes's remarks, already quoted, may be inferred to have originated with Radisson. Radisson was dead and practically forgotten, however, when two centuries later six of his narratives appeared for the first time in print. How pleased he would have been with the mild furore they created!

The narrative for the trip of 1684 is shorter than that of any of Radisson's other travels. The reason is not far to seek: the trip itself lasted only five months. The *Happy Return* set sail from Gravesend about May 20, 1684, in company with two other vessels operating for the Hudson's Bay Company.[2] They kept together till the straits were reached, but afterwards Radisson did not catch sight of the companion

[1] For discussions of the location and origin of the several Radisson travel narratives, see Radisson, *Voyages,* p. 23; and Canadian Archives, *Report,* 1895. The French manuscript of the trip of 1684 is found in the British Museum, Sloane MS 3527.

[2] H.B.Co. Archives, A/1/2, entry of May 28, 1684; and Sir James Hayes to Lord Preston, May 22, 1684, Graham MSS, "Parliamentary Chamber . . . Hudson's Bay . . . ," ff. 125, 126.

vessels. This fact worried him, for he knew that his strategy required that he be the first to talk with his nephew. So, near his destination, he left the vessel for a shallop, or long boat, and made haste to Hayes River. There he landed to pick up clues of Jean Baptiste Chouart. He soon discovered them, learned that Chouart had already seen two English vessels, and had gone with the news to his new establishment farther up Hayes River on the spot now known as Rainbow Island. Before attempting to find Chouart, Radisson decided to sail around the spit of land separating Hayes River from the Nelson. There he found two Company vessels, Captain Outlaw's and the frigate that had spent the winter at Port Nelson. The men on the frigate were able to tell him of the events of the autumn and winter succeeding Radisson's departure from Port Nelson in 1683. Most of the story, however, he learned later from his nephew.

Almost immediately after Radisson and Des Groseilliers' departure in 1683 the latter's son with his handful of Trifluvien adherents, Elie Grimard, Jean Baptiste Godefroy, Nicolas Aigron de la Mothe, Claude Duval *dit* Boucher, Antoine Doyon, ———— Collynie, and another, had discovered two English vessels at Port Nelson.[3] A hostile feeling manifested itself immediately between the two groups of men and was reflected in the Indians' attitude. The English prevailed on a savage to attempt to kill young Chouart. In a hand-to-hand combat the Frenchman overcame his wily enemy and won the respect of the Indians, who either saw or soon heard of the incident. Indeed, Chouart's adopted "brother" followed the would-be murderer and killed him; and the "brother's" tribe took it further upon themselves to descend upon the place where the English had by this time built a fort, to attack them, and to kill some of them. Ex-

[3] The names of the companions have been secured from later events, notably the denization records of several of the men and the entries relative to contracts for a later voyage in the minutes of the Hudson's Bay Company. See *post*, p. 228.

pecting retaliation from the English for this act, Chouart
and his party decided to place themselves beyond danger
in case of attack. Accordingly, they proceeded up Hayes
River and built an establishment above the rapids, where
enemies would have great difficulty in reaching them. To
protect themselves further the Frenchmen prevailed upon
several of their Indian allies to pass the winter with them in
return for food and other provisions.

The winter passed without incident except for the wounding of one of Chouart's men by an Indian in the service of the
English; and by a visit that Chouart made to the English
fort. In the spring, after the river was free from ice, the
Indians of the interior came down to visit the Frenchmen.
Among them were many Assiniboin and Cree, "descendants
of the great Christionaux of the old acquaintance of my
uncle." In this one phrase is the sole reference by Radisson
to his earlier visit to these tribes, some twenty years before.
That it was so many years is evidenced by the further statement that the Assiniboin chief decided to remain until Radisson should return, wishing "to make it appear that he[*the
Indian*] had been worthy of the present that the Governor
of Canada had made to him formerly in giving tokens of his
zeal to serve the French." Radisson's last visit to them as
a French subject of the Governor of Canada had been in
the year 1660.

If we are to believe Radisson's report of Chouart's story,
the Indians were planning to wipe out the English on the
first pretext that should arise, and only Radisson's arrival
thwarted this scheme. On the other hand, the little French
group were reaching the end of their supplies and must soon
leave or submit to the English, unless the help arrived which
they expected from Canada and which did arrive a few
days after Radisson had carried them all back to England
with him.

As soon as Radisson found his men, he prevailed upon his
nephew and the others to submit to him and go over to the

English Company. It was Radisson's plan to leave Chouart and his best interpreter in the country. Radisson's letter of instructions empowered him to use his discretion in the matter. However, Governor Abraham overruled Radisson's orders and commanded all the Frenchmen to go at once to England in the Company's returning vessels. This irked Radisson exceedingly, for he stood very much on his dignity, and he believed it injured in this affair.

During the short space of time that Radisson was in Port Nelson, his nephew and the latter's men brought out from caches many thousands of furs and skins, and with surprising speed and industry loaded them on the vessels that were returning to England. Sails were set on September 4, 1684, and were furled in the Downs on October 23, if we are to accept Radisson's dates. In this instance they must be substantially correct, for the Company's records report him back in England in late October.

As Radisson's vessel sailed out through Hudson Bay two vessels from Canada bearing relief to Chouart and his men entered. Neither party saw the other. Thus closely did Radisson come to having his gold converted into a monument to his memory.

The two Canadian vessels made their way to Port Nelson and anchored in Hayes River, guided by Pierre Allemand, who had been there before with Radisson.[4] It is possible that Des Groseilliers' ability as a guide and knowledge of the region were also utilized by this expedition from Canada. It would be quite in keeping with his character to be aboard one of the two little vessels, for he is reported to have died in the Bay about this time.[5]

[4] "Journal of Father [Antoine] Silvy from Belle Isle to Port Nelson," in Tyrrell, Documents Relating to Hudson Bay, pp. 37–101.

[5] Radisson states in his lawsuit against the Company in the 1690's that Des Groseilliers died "in the bay," but the date, 1683 or earlier, is impossible. See Nute, "Two Documents from Radisson's Suit Against the Company," pp. 41, 43. For a reference of 1695 to Des Groseilliers at Sorel, see Gagnon, Essai de bibliographie canadienne, 2:333. P. François X. Charlevoix says that "it is certain . . . that Chouart died in Canada." Histoire générale de la Nouvelle

The French found an English flag flying where they had expected to see Bourbon lilies on a field of white. Inquiry brought to light the story of Radisson's trip, of which they had had no inkling up to that moment. Their feelings can best be left to the imagination—especially their vain regrets for many valuable pelts now in British bottoms well out on the Atlantic. The journal of the Jesuit of the party, Père Silvy, tells the story of the ensuing winter, when Frenchmen and British once more glowered at one another at Port Nelson, even as during the winter of 1682–1683. The English Company, petitioning the King in November 1685, stated

. . . that they [*the French*] have againe in the moneth of Septemb^r 1684, with two shippe and above 50 men by the Commissions of Mons. De la Barr late Governor of Canada entered a river where y^r Petitioners had made a settlement nere Port Nellson and in hostile manner set upon the Factorey and dureing ye last winter Did intercept & Divert their Trade with the Indians to the Damage of above 10000 [*pounds*].[6]

Meanwhile in England a feeling of overpowering relief and exultation replaced the Company's gnawing uneasiness, when Radisson appeared in London after a night's hard posting from the first port where he could disembark. In an otherwise businesslike and staid recordbook of Company matters his exploit is referred to extravagantly as "this great Affaire." [7] There is no hint in this volume of any other kind of feeling among the members of the Company, but Radisson's own account, written during the ensuing winter, mentions the offense that most of the Committee took "because I had had the honour to make my reverence to the King and to his Royal Highness" immediately upon arriving in England.

France, 1:481. Father Le Jeune states that he died at Sorel before 1698. See Louis Le Jeune, *Dictionnaire générale . . . du Canada,* 1:721 (Ottawa, 1931). Father Hennepin says that William Blathwayt told him in 1697 that Des Groseilliers was still living in England. See *ante,* p. 184. Was Hennepin confusing Radisson and Des Groseilliers?

[6] H.B.Co. Archives, A/6/1, ff. 60, 61.

[7] H.B.Co. Archives, Small Minute Book, 1683/4, entry for October 27, 1684.

Since it was William Young once more who presented Radisson to royalty, the suspicion is strong that Young, like Sir James Hayes and Lord Preston, was in close correspondence with the Duke of York, and so not in good odor with the Whigs of the Committee. "These same persons," Radisson goes on, "continued even their bad intention to injure me, and, under pretext of refusing me the justice which is due to me, they oppose themselves also to the solid and useful resolutions that are necessary for the glory of his Majesty and the advantage of the Nation and their own Interest." Radisson and the man who saved him from oblivion, Samuel Pepys, could sympathize with each other for the persecution that reached them through their attachment to James, Duke of York.

Perhaps some further light is thrown on this obscure point by a sentence in Sir James Hayes's letter to Lord Preston written on May 4, 1685: "neyther can I at this tyme give you an account of what hath happened concerning Radison, but in gen^{ll} that he is not in y^t esteeme wth our new Govern^r as I did fear he would." [8] The new governor was John Churchill, soon to be the great Duke of Marlborough, and, in May, 1685, still a devoted follower of the new King, James II. The latter had been obliged, of course, to give up his post as Governor of the Hudson's Bay Company, when he ceased to be Duke of York and ascended the throne in February, 1685. However, he kept firm control of the Company through the new Governor and saw that Churchill sponsored the royal protégé, Radisson. Young maintained his interest in Radisson long after James became a royal nuisance in France; and Churchill showed some concern for the explorer's welfare even after the Revolution of 1689.

Radisson, Chouart, and the other Frenchmen passed the winter of 1684–1685 in London. What an experience it must have been to a young man like Jean Baptiste Chouart, who had been born in an outpost of the French empire,

[8] Graham MSS, volume "Hudson's Bay," f. 127.

cradled to the fierce music of Iroquois war whoops, and educated to wilderness craft rather than to booklearning and courtliness! The Hudson's Bay Company books show that the Frenchmen were subsidized that winter by the corporation and to all appearances well provided for. It was one of the coldest winters within the memory of living men in London, and very stormy. In April, 1685, came the coronation of the King. The procession, fireworks, crowds, and general excitement must have impressed the Canadians.

Radisson's advice was asked on the minute points of Indian trade goods that he knew so thoroughly. Ice chisels, guns, flints, fishing nets, all had to be examined thoroughly by him before the cargoes were stored away in the ships' holds ready for another venture into arctic waters. Finally it was a question whether Radisson, his nephew, and the other Frenchmen were to enter the service of the Company and return to Port Nelson. The Committee's letter of instructions to Radisson had promised much for them, if they acceded to Radisson's wishes in Hudson Bay. On March 11, 1685, Radisson appeared before the Committee and "exhibited propositions in the behalfe of his Nephew Gosliers and the rest of the French men." [9] The matter was held over till the next committee meeting on March 13. Then the Committee voted to entertain "John Baptiste Gosliers" for four years at one hundred pounds a year, his salary to commence as soon as he should take the oath of allegiance to the Company. He was also to receive one hundred pounds to outfit for service and "in lieu of all pretenses [claims] & Demands whatsoever." Elie Grimard and Claude Duval were to enter the service under contracts for four years. The first year each was to receive thirty pounds; the second year the salary was to be thirty-five pounds; and the third and fourth years the sums were to be forty and forty-five pounds

---

[9] The data on the offers to the Frenchmen and their response are to be found in H.B.Co. Archives, A/1/8, under the dates given in this paragraph and in the succeeding ones.

respectively. Nicolas Aigron de la Mothe was also to sign up for four years, but he was to begin with thirty-five pounds and the increase for each succeeding year was to be five pounds. At a meeting on the sixteenth of March still another Frenchman was voted acceptable for the service. This was Antoine Doyon. His salary was to begin at twenty-five pounds and the increase for the three succeeding years was to be five pounds annually.

Finally, on March 30, the Committee discussed the momentous problem of who was to be appointed governor at Port Nelson.

It was resolved & it is now Ordered that Mr John Bridgar shall goe Governour in the Comp^a service of Port Nellson for 3 yeares at and under the Sallery of one hundred pounds per Annum and that Mons. Piere Radison shall be Entertained as Superintendent and Director of ye Trade there.

Probably the Committee ended this conference highly pleased with themselves for having thus settled all their problems of governor, superintendent of trade, interpreters, and special assistants—on paper. Actually nothing had been decided, as they were to learn soon enough.

On April 10 it was reported that the four Frenchmen—but not Radisson—had refused to take their oaths of fidelity, and so,

This Committee Doe therefore make that agreement void & Order that Mr Richard Cradock & Mr Sam: Clark be Desired to treate and agree with them as well as they can and give Reporte to the Committee of their Proceedings and they are Impowered by this Committee to assure Mr Piere Radison Mr John Bridgar shall not goe Governor to Port Nellson.

It might have been known from the start that Radisson would refuse to work with a governor whom he had captured and who was his sworn enemy.

When the two negotiators reported on April 21, the scale of salaries had been reduced considerably in every instance except Radisson's. Just why Jean Baptiste Chouart refused on April 10 to accept one hundred pounds per year and one hundred pounds gratuity and on April 21 accepted eighty pounds as salary and eighty pounds as gratuity is hard to say. A similar reduction was agreed upon in the case of the three other Frenchmen. Was the oath of fidelity the stumbling block? Or did Jean Baptiste refuse to give up his claim to the furs with which he had unwittingly enriched the Company?

Lord Churchill's name and influence were explicitly brought into the affair on May 11. On May 4 the other Frenchmen had signed their contracts, but Radisson had held out for his own terms. By May 6 the Committee, getting anxious over the near approach of the time when the vessels must leave for Hudson Bay, "after a long Debate" on the "propositions" of Radisson, presented, as usual, by William Young,

. . . came to these Resolutions, That dureing the time he shall be out of England in the Companies service he shall have £100 per annum and in case it shall appeare he shall doe the Comp^a any Extraordinary service in the Settlement of their Trade; he shall finde ye Company very bountifull to him at his Returne; and in case he dyed in this Expedition the Comp^a will pay unto his wife £300: provided the Comp^a be sufficiently secured from all Claymes & Demands whatever which his Heires or Executors can or may pretend unto from the Hudsons Bay Company.

On May 8 Radisson had attended the committee meeting and rejected this offer without further ado. Again Young acted as intermediary when it became necessary to report to Radisson that the Committee had voted to stand by their decision. Nothing was being accomplished. The knot must be broken. So Lord Churchill was called to the meeting of May 11.

Mr Radisons Propositions, and the Committees Resolutions upon them at the Committee the 6th May instant, were now read to the Right Honourable John Lord Churchill Governor, who did Judge the

Committee Resolutions very reasonable; but did with all desire that if Mr Radisons wife accepted not of £300: in money in case of the Decease of her husband in the next Expedition, that she may have Liberty to Elect to her selfe, the benefit of £100: stock in the Capitall Stock in lieu of the said £300:—dureing her life; which the Committee did agree to, And thereupon Mr Radison was called in, and acquainted with the Resolutions of the Committee, with which he was very well sattisfied & contented.

Nothing was said about giving up Radisson's claims (for furs) on the Company.

Thus we must believe that Radisson felt that his wife was not adequately provided for in case of his death; or that the claim for furs was the stumbing block; or that Churchill, representing, as every one knew, the King's wishes, saved the faces of all concerned in the matter. Since Radisson had just married for the second time, it may well be that his father-in-law, Gédéon Godet, learned in the law, was behind the scenes directing Radisson's movements and decisions.[10]

After Radisson had agreed to the Governor's compromise measure, the four Frenchmen were required to be bound, "one for the other for their Fidelity to the Comp^a and Mr Radison to be bound in a bond of £300:—that they shall goe the Voyage." In addition, Young had to give his bond of two hundred pounds that "Mr Radison shall goe the Voyage." It would be interesting to know why William Young from 1684 until his death considered himself and was considered by the Company as Radisson's protector. Even the Company professed to be in the dark, for its rejoinder in a chancery case of 1694 states explicitly: "these Defend[an]ts say that they are informed that the said Mr. Young is and has been for some time very intimately ac-

[10] Radisson's first wife must have died shortly before his return from the Bay in 1683. He married again in 1685. The marriage of "Peter Espritt Radison of this parish & Margarett Charlote Godet of the same," is recorded in the register of marriages for St. Martin's in the Fields, Shrove Tuesday (March 3), 1685. The ceremony was performed on license received from the Bishop of London. At the request of the author this information was found in the parish register by Alice M. Johnson of the staff of the Hudson's Bay Company's archives, who has also been very helpful on other occasions.

quainted with the Complt [*Radisson*] and pr[e]tends to be very much his Freind but for what reason these Defendts know not." [11]

That Jean Baptiste Chouart had every intention of going to Hudson Bay when he declined the Company's proposition on April 10 is evident from a letter to his mother that he wrote the following day. In it he states that he is going to the Bay in a month or six weeks. Meantime marriage proposals are being made to him, but he does not listen. He is being watched, he writes, to prevent his escape from the country. It has never been his plan to take the English side, he explains, but he has been misled by his uncle's tortuous ways; he plans not to tell his uncle of his intention to desert the English. He closes his letter with references to Daniel Greysolon, Sieur Du Lhut, and to Péré, whom he expects to see very soon.[12]

It is apparent, therefore, that Des Groseilliers' son in-

[11] Nute, "Two Documents from Radisson's Suit Against the Company," p. 49. Sir Edward Dering's docket book, which he kept as one of the keepers of the privy seal, throws a little light on a William Young, who appears to have been the man of that name on the committee of the Hudson's Bay Company. On February 10, 1669/70 was made "A graunt to Wm Young esqr of ye custody of the middle parke als[o] the North Parke & the haw warren of Hampton court . . . and also ye custody of Bushy Barke . . . and also ye office . . . of Keeper of Hampton Court . . . . formerly held by the Duke of Albemarle." British Museum, Additional MS 38,862. The use of "esquire" after the name was ordinary in the Hudson's Bay Company's references to their William Young. His will, at Somerset House, gives a little more information. He was "William Yonge of London of the Parish of St Andrews Holbourn Esqr." He mentions "joynt Stock of the Mines in Cardiganshire," part of which he bequeathed to "Christs Hospitall in London in Trust for the benefitt of the poor Children of that Hospitall." The rest of the shares were to go to his grandchildren, his daughter being Barbara Goodall, wife of Thomas Goodall "of Grays Inne Esqr." He also mentions in his will "my Brother and Sister Goodall and . . . their Sisters Mrs Pattison and Mrs Pilson," and "my sister Mrs Susannah Goodall." He refers to his stock in the "Hudsons Bay Company and in the Affrican Company," and "in the Company for raising water by Fire known by the name of Captain Thomas Savery's invention." The will was published June 14, 1703. It was proved January 5, 1708. It is printed *post,* Appendix 16.

[12] AC., C11, A7, ff. 255–257. This letter mentions the return of Médard Chouart to New France prior to November 2, 1684, and his plan to move from Quebec. See also Note 18.

tended to desert the Company as soon as he could after getting to the Bay, and to reach Canada by way of Du Lhut's new post on Lake Nipigon. He knew from Philippe Gauthier, Sieur de Comporté, an important merchant and provost marshal of New France, who was in France, that Du Lhut had been sent to the region between Lake Superior and Port Nelson with dispatches directed to young Chouart.[13] What he did not know was that Jean Baptiste Péré and his two companions, La Croix and Des Moulins, though successful in descending the Albany River to an English post on the Bay, had been captured there very shortly after Radisson had left for England in 1684 with his nephew and the other Frenchmen. How far Radisson had been aware of Du Lhut's plan when he tried to leave young Chouart at Port Nelson in 1684 is not know. Fortunately for the Company, Radisson's wishes had been overruled. So Péré had found not one of his Frenchmen in the Bay when he arrived.

Later in April Chouart also wrote to De Comporté that he would join the latter "by the route you indicate." [14] De Comporté, therefore, was the one who was mapping Chouart's course. It was he, too, who had sent out the relief expedition intended for the Frenchmen in the Bay in 1684. By the time Chouart wrote this letter he seems to have reached the belief that Du Lhut's men, or at least some of them, had perished en route to the Bay, for he writes as much in this letter. Chouart's two letters, to his mother and to De Comporté, were sent to De Seignelay with the recommendation that Chouart and the other Frenchmen be paid to return to the French interest.[15] The new Governor of Canada, De Denonville, was instructed by De Seignelay to hasten his departure from France and effect the rehabilita-

[13] L'abbé Ivanhoë Caron, ed., *Journal de l'expédition du Chevalier de Troyes à la Baie d'Hudson, en 1686,* p. 86 (Beauceville, 1918).

[14] Jean Baptiste Chouart to De Comporté, April 29, 1685, in AC., C^{ll}, A7, ff. 255–257; and [copies of] De Denonville to [De Seignelay], March 31, 1685 and May 20, 1685, in the same file, f. 28.

[15] See De Denonville's letter of May 20, 1685, in the preceding note.

tion of these men and their post in the French interest.[16] On March 31 De Denonville wrote to De Seignelay that he had just received a letter from London stating that young Des Groseilliers, "nephew of that rascal of a Radisson," had made two attempts to escape to France and had been stopped on both occasions. "He lets me know that he will join me as soon as he possibly can; that his uncle has decided to seize our posts in Hudson Bay and for that purpose will embark the end of the month; that he himself will escape with all his Frenchmen and betake themselves overland to Quebec." [17] Very appropriately did the Hudson's Bay Company take every precaution to prevent any slip in their plans for these men. Perhaps they even discovered the schemes afoot and for that reason the men accepted lower salaries.[18] De Denonville proposed a reward of fifty pistoles to any one bringing Radisson to Quebec. This sum was authorized by the minister, De Seignelay, and from that time Radisson had a price on his head. He himself mentions it on several occasions.

[16] De Seignelay to De Denonville, May 31, 1685, AC., C^ll, B, Vol. 11, f. 49.
[17] See Note 14.
[18] A copy of a pertinent letter by De la Chenaye on this matter is in BN., Margry Papers, 9284, ff. 111, 112. Most of the documents cited in Notes 12, 14, 15, and 16 may also be found in the Margry Papers.

CHAPTER XIX

"Your Loveing Friends"

Whatever these Frenchmen of Chouart's may have planned secretly, they were destined to serve out their time in Hudson Bay in the Company's service. They left London late in May, 1685. The Company again ordered fresh provisions for the three chief officers going out, Bridgar, Missenden, and Radisson, but its largesse was not to be taken advantage of this time: Mr. Lodge was to spend not more than three pounds apiece for them, instead of the ten pounds that Radisson had spent the preceding trip. However, a special courtesy was paid to Radisson in the shape of a hogshead of claret, "such as Mr Radison shall like & approve of." [1]

The voyage did not begin auspiciously. Pirates were rumored to be cruising in the Channel and a slight delay was occasioned by the news. However, the vessels soon went on and nothing untoward occurred until they were all in Hudson Straits. Then the *Perpetuana Merchant,* a ketch of sixty tons, owned and commanded by Captain Edward Hume, was attacked and taken by two French vessels. De Comporté and his company in Canada had sent them to take provisions to Radisson's Canadians. They had spent the winter harassing the English at Port Nelson, and were now on their way to Canada.[2] In one of them was Father Silvy, whose diary describes the encounter with the *Perpetuana* and mentions that Captain Hume gave him the in-

[1] H.B.Co. Archives, A/1/8, entry for May 22, 1685. A later entry, that of July 31, gives the cost of the claret to the Company as £12..8..6!

[2] H.B.Co. Archives, petition of November 4, 1685, addressed by the Company to the King of England. A/6/1, ff. 60, 61.

formation that the frigate bearing Radisson had already passed.[3] This news must have dashed the hopes of the French, who were expressly trying to catch Radisson. A day or so later another of the English vessels hove into view and was ordered by a cannon shot to halt. This must have been Captain Richard Lucas' vessel. He refused to surrender and escaped. The following day the last of the Company's vessels, the *Success,* bearing John Bridgar to his new post as sub-governor at the Bottom of the Bay, appeared and chased the French vessels, which took shelter in a land-locked harbor. The English vessel came and anchored near-by and made some attempt to recover the ketch. The French fortified themselves on a rocky point and finally Bridgar came under a flag of truce to converse. Pierre Allemand, Radisson's former pilot, was sent by the French to interview him. Bridgar inquired why Allemand's vessel had seized the ketch, since there was no war between France and England. Allemand mentioned the seizure of the French post by Radisson. Straightway Bridgar let loose a volley of tirades against Radisson, "whom he called a traitor and a thief and swore he would kill him wherever he should find him." [4] It would appear that Radisson had been well advised not to go to Port Nelson if Bridgar were made governor there. Realiz-

---

[3] "Journal of Father Silvy," p. 72, and *passim.* The journal seems to show that two of Radisson's Canadians were captured with the ketch and taken back to Quebec. See page 71. See also Edward Hume's affidavit in the introduction to Tyrrell, *Documents Relating to Hudson Bay,* pp. 15, 16. Mr. Tyrrell seems under the misapprehension that the French in the two vessels were planning to loot Radisson's post, though they were unaware till they reached Hayes River that he had gone over to the English.

[4] "Journal of Father Silvy," pp. 78, 100. For a sketch of Pierre Allemand see P. G. R[oy], "Pierre Allemand," in *Bulletin des recherches historiques,* 21 : 129–133 (May, 1915). The author does not appear to know "Carte des costes de l'Amérique Septentrionalle et des terres nouvellement découvertes par Pierre Alemand dans les trois voyages qu'il a faits de Quebeck a la Baye d'Hudson Scavoir deux par mer & un par terre dans laquelle sont exatement marquez les latitudes des principaux endroits par ou il a passé presentée a Monseigneur Le Marquis de Seignelay, 1687," Archives Nationales, Service Hydrographique, 124–1–1.

PART OF PIERRE ALLEMAND'S MANUSCRIPT MAP OF HIS THREE JOURNEYS
FROM QUEBEC TO HUDSON BAY. 1687.

[Paris. Service Hydrographique, 124–1–1.]

ing that he would gain nothing by further delay, Bridgar weighed anchor, gave a salute, and passed on.

When Captain Lucas' vessel reached the Downs the next October, it had on board "one Monsieur Parry a person that came from Canada to Albany river the last winter as a Spye, whome Governor Sergeant kept in the Factory & sent him home [to England]." [5] One of De la Barre's ways of combating the new English settlements on the west side of Hudson Bay had been to send Daniel Greysolon, Sieur du Lhut, in 1684 to establish a post on the northern end of Lake Nipigon. To Du Lhut were sent dispatches that he was to deliver from De la Barre and certain Canadian merchants to Jean Baptiste Chouart. Du Lhut sent Péré, La Croix, and Des Moulins, as we have seen, along the Albany River route from his post to Hudson Bay. [6] Probably this was the first time that white men had been over that route. Shortly all French maps, especially those of Jean Baptiste Franquelin of New France, showed this river. It bore the name Perray or Péré River.

Péré and his companions had been well received at the Hudson's Bay Company's post at the mouth of the river. They had remained several days, unaware it would seem, of the two French vessels at Port Nelson. When they left, they proceeded along the shore, only to lose their canoe on the third day, when it was anchored insecurely. There was nothing to do but return to the post. This time they were arrested. Péré was held at the fort, but the other two men were put on Charlton Island and given so much freedom that they constructed a canoe and escaped to the shore. After a bit they found some Indians, who conducted them overland to

[5] H.B.Co. Archives, A/1/8, entry of October 29, 1685. In a letter of September 10, 1684, Daniel Greysolon, Sieur du Lhut, more often referred to as Duluth in English, gives an account of the reasons that took him and Péré to Lake Nipigon and how Péré went on to Hudson Bay. See Margry, *Découvertes et établissements des Français*, 6: 50–52. Pages 3–52 in that work afford the best available source material on Duluth, with many references to Péré.

[6] See Caron, *Journal du Chevalier de Troyes*, p. 86.

the French post at Michillimackinac, where Olivier Morel, Sieur de la Durantye, was in command. Péré, however, remained a prisoner till Captain Lucas' vessel reached England.[7] There he was incarcerated, and action against him was entered in Woodstreet Counter. How blunt the business conscience of the seventeenth century was, appears in the several attempts of the company officials to enlist "Mons. Perry" for future service in Hudson Bay.[8] At one and the same time they were prosecuting him for having "damnified" the Company to the extent of many hundreds of pounds sterling in Hudson Bay; and trying to get him to enter their employment and go to Hudson Bay in their service! Finally, through a legal technicality and some connivance, apparently, on the part of Company officials, inspired perhaps by the royal ex-Governor, Péré was set free and went to France.[9] There a gratuity was given him by the government.[10] He shortly returned to Canada and served with the Marquis de Denonville against the Iroquois in 1687, an expedition in which Du Lhut also figured.[11]

Meantime Radisson was in Hudson Bay, probably quite unaware of the danger from which he had escaped. On September 15 he wrote a long letter to the Committee from York Fort, the name which had just been given to the new English post on Hayes River. The letter, written in French, has not survived, but the topics touched upon may be surmised from the lengthy reply of the Committee written on May 20,

[7] Caron, *Journal du Chevalier de Troyes,* p. 109.

[8] H.B.Co. Archives, A/1/8 entries of October 30 and November 4, 1685; and "The foule Minute Booke for the Hudson's Bay Company, beginning the 6th of November 1685 & ending the—November 1686," the entries of November 11, January 8, March 3, March 19, and March 26. For Nicholas Hayward, who was interpreter for the Company, in its contact with Péré, see Gilbert Chinard, *Un Français en Virginie,* pp. 28–30 (Institut Français de Washington, Volume 5, Baltimore, 1932).

[9] H.B.Co. Archives, A/6/1, ff. 72, 73, Instructions to Governor Sergeant, May 20, 1686.

[10] Royal memorial to De Denonville, May 31, 1686, AC., B, Vol. 12, f. 25½.

[11] See an article on Péré in *Bulletin des recherches historiques,* 10:213 (July, 1904); and BN., Collection Clairambault, 1016, ff. 474–481, a *Mémoire* of June 13–August 13, 1687, of De Denonville's expedition.

1686, and signed, by "Your loveing Friends," Churchill, Edward Dering, William Young, Nicholas Hayward, and four other committee members.[12] Evidently Radisson was uneasy, particularly over Governor Abraham's attitude toward him, over the standard of trade which occupied much of his discussion in the letter, and over interference with his negotiations with Indians of the interior, whom he wanted to bring down to the Bay in great numbers for trade purposes. To effect that trade Radisson had sent his nephew "up into the Countries," where he was to spend the winter and come down with whole families of Indians the next spring. New outposts—New Severn and one to the north—were mentioned in the letter. Then Radisson passed to complaints about the poor quality of trade goods sent out the preceding summer and to suggestions for articles to be sent in 1686. Finally he asked that birch bark for canoes be sent him from the Bottom of the Bay.

The standard of trade to which Radisson referred in this letter was a very important part of the Company's policy. Radisson regarded it as all important, as his journals, especially those of 1682–1683 and 1684, show. Briefly it meant the proportion of trade goods to skins and furs. All the Company's profits depended on that ratio, and Radisson believed that he knew so much more of Indian psychology than any one else in the Bay that he alone could be depended upon to get most profit for the Company. Probably he was right, for he did have a complete understanding of the red man's way of looking at life.

It has been said that Henry Kelsey, who as a mere lad went out to the Bay with Radisson in 1684, was the first white man to penetrate inland from Hudson Bay for the Company. He performed his exploration in 1690. This letter by Radisson makes it plain that young Jean Baptiste Chouart, as early as 1685, was exploring the interior—or was he trying to get to

[12] H.B.Co. Archives, A/6/1, entry of May 20, 1686. It is printed *post*, Appendix 8.

Du Lhut's post and return to Quebec? What a pity it is that no account of his sojourn inland has been preserved. We know all too little of this intrepid youth. A further bit of information about him is found in a letter that De la Chenaye wrote to De Denonville on April 15, 1685: [13]

> He can persuade the natives of this the more easily because he has among them some adopted relatives, with whom he has traded for seven years, and who are prejudiced in his favor, so that they believe there is no man more intrepid than he; he knows how to influence their minds so well because he is versed in their ways and can get them to do anything he wants.

The last paragraph of the Company's letter to Radisson hints at earlier difficulties between Radisson and the Company, probably in the winter of 1684–1685. "Our Committee & Government now is so constituted that . . . . there is [not] any one but who is intirely your friend" is a remark which seems to say that there had been a change in the personnel of the Committee, which made it more friendly to Radisson. Was it Hayes who was unfriendly? The chief change had been the replacement of Hayes by Sir Edward Dering as deputy governor.

[13] BN., Margry Papers, 9284, ff. 111, 112.

CHAPTER XX

Neutrality or War?

By September 4 of the next year, 1686, when Radisson wrote a full account of what had been happening at Port Nelson since the preceding autumn, there was much to recount.[1] The French had arrived overland from Quebec with a contingent of soldiers under the Chevalier de Troyes; these troops had taken three English forts at the Bottom of the Bay—Rupert, Moose, and Albany; and war had begun in North America, though England and France were still at peace in Europe. Only New Severn and York remained to the English, and they would soon be targets for further French attacks.[2]

It is plainly to be seen that Louis XIV neither wanted nor expected war with England over North American colonies. How embarrassing relations between the two countries were

[1] See the Committee's letter of June 3, 1687, to Radisson in H.B.Co. Archives, A/6/1, printed in Appendix 9.

[2] The best account of De Troyes' expedition is found in his journal already cited. The expedition was an official one sent out by the express order of De Denonville of February 12, 1686. The instructions mention Radisson several times and state that the venture is an act of reprisal for the injuries he has inflicted on the French. Pierre Allemand and Father Silvy accompanied the troops, as well as three brilliant sons of Des Groseilliers' former partner, Charles le Moyne: the Sieur de Ste-Hélène, the Sieur d'Iberville, and the Sieur de Maricourt. A son-in-law of Le Moyne's, Zacharie Robutal, Sieur de la Noue, was also one of the party, a man later to be famous in the region of the Lake of the Woods and Green Bay.

It is interesting to note that as early as June 25, 1685, the French from Canada were preparing an overland expedition to oust the English from Hudson Bay. On that day Zacharie Jolliet wrote from his post, "Nemisko," about half way to the Bay, to Hugh Verner: "I am here to execute the orders of Monsieur le général [De la Barre] requiring the English to leave the Bay. . . . For a letter has just come saying the General is sending men by land to seize you. So, having had the honor to see Mr. Bayly, to drink and eat and be lodged two or three nights with him in your fort, and having lived so long a neighbor with you, now to be forced to fight to obtain that place, would be my extreme grief." H.B.Co. Archives, A/6/1, f. 122.

becoming, however, as a result of constant friction between French and English colonials in America, is just as evident. Moreover, it is almost impossible to understand how complicated the situation of colonial affairs was at the French court, unless one reads the letters of such diverse partisans as the Jesuits, the Recollects, the Jansenists, D'Estrées and the Gallican Church party, De Villermont, Beaujeu, the representatives of the Canadian Company of the North, Renaudot, the De Callières brothers, Bernou, Frontenac, and many others. It would seem that now one party won the royal ears and now another. De Villermont's correspondence with Henri Justel in England, with his Jesuit relative, Father Thierry Beschefer, in New France, and with De Comporté reveals that he was urging strong measures against the English, both in Hudson Bay and in the Illinois country. The sequel of such urging—for De Villermont was very powerful in the King's councils—was the seizure of English traders on their way to posts on the Wabash and beyond Michillimackinac; war on the Iroquois, led by Péré, Du Lhut, De Denonville, and others interested in Hudson Bay events; and reprisals, amounting to war tactics, against the English posts in Hudson Bay.

How far De Villermont was involved in the court's actions concerning Hudson Bay is revealed by the fact that on October 30, 1687, De Comporté, of the Canadian Company of Hudson Bay—he who two years earlier had been arranging for young Chouart to deceive the British company—wrote thus to De Villermont: "Our Company of the North is exceedingly obliged to you for the care you have taken of it. The governor, who took possession of Hudson Bay, chasing out the English, will have the honor to present this letter to you. . . . His name is Mr. D'Iberville." Here is a son of Des Groseilliers' erstwhile partner, Le Moyne, appearing to confound the English![3]

[3] BN., Collection Clairambault, 1016, f. 485. "D'Iberville, Monseigneur, est un très sage garçon, entreprenant et qui sçait ce qu'il faict. Ils sont huict

The letter refers to D'Iberville's plans for new attacks that he was to make on the English posts in Hudson Bay. Those attacks were made, as is well known, and York Factory went the way of Rupert, Moose, and Albany. And all this while Louis XIV was guaranteeing the English a year of peace, pending a final solution of the difficulties between the two countries in Hudson Bay! Radisson and Des Groseilliers were well schooled, if, as we suppose, De Villermont was their tutor for a period of time. Another of De Villermont's correspondents in American affairs was Riverin, who wrote him from Quebec on November 3, 1687, about the English traders in the Illinois country and of the intention that Riverin had of not observing the late treaty of neutrality concluded with England because the English supported the Iroquois.[4]

De Villermont represents, apparently, the Jesuit side of the picture. He opposed De la Salle on principle, but the explorer had also added to the journalist's wrath by rejecting the counsel of De Villermont's appointee, Le Gallois de Beaujeu, master of vessels on De la Salle's ill-fated expedition to the mouth of the Mississippi in 1684–1685. However cross-grained and paranoiac De la Salle may have been— and there is good evidence that he was both—he had enough inside information from his attorney, Abbé Claude Bernou, to recognize what Beaujeu was and why he was on the expedition. The Jesuits, working to prevent a Recollect colony in the Mississippi Valley, were naturally opposed to the presence of Tonty in the Illinois country, for he was supported by Recollects and Jansenists. Yet, when De la Barre was recalled—seemingly through Recollect influence—for having abandoned the Illinois country to the Iroquois, the Recollects were not successful in nominating the governor they

frères, enfans de feu Le Moyne, tous les mieux élevez de Canada avec les enfans de Le Ber, leur oncle, qui a toujours gouverné les deux familles." [Sulte], *Collection de manuscrits,* 1:405.

[4] See [Denis?] Riverin to Cabart de Villermont, Quebec, November 3, 1687, in BN., Collection Clairambault, 1016, f. 485.

were planning for New France, the Count de Frontenac. It was some years before their influence succeeded in renaming him governor.

The irony of the Jesuits' position was, that having urged all sorts of reasons for abandoning the Illinois country, the French court shortly found itself obliged to fall back on De la Salle's occupancy of it as proof that the French were settled there ahead of the English. For with 1685 the English attempt at invasion of that country began in earnest.[5] On January 19, 1687, Henri Justel wrote to his friend, Edmond Halley of comet fame,

Monsieur De Villermont has received letters from Canada by which he learns that the French have taken three English forts on Hudson Bay. . . . He also writes that the English have sent an expedition more than three hundred leagues to a place called Missilimakina. If this little war continues, the two established colonies in that country will ruin each other.[6]

That there were interests in England sponsoring an English colony in the Illinois country is borne out by two or three papers that have survived.[7] Moreover, the French court

[5] See an unsigned letter of October 30, 1686, written from Canada, describing English competition at Michillimackinac, in BN., Collection Clairambault, 1016, ff. 465, 466. "We regard the English of New York no less our enemies than the Iroquois and we perceive that their entire tactics tend to our destruction and to their control of all the trade. I have already told you how they appeared in eleven loaded canoes on their way to Michillimackinac. We have since learned of their arrival there." In the same collection see folios 474–481 for details of the English ventures of 1686 and 1687 into the far interior of the continent. De Denonville also wrote at this time: "their [*English*] great scheme is to settle a post on the Wabash River, where they will intercept Tonty's Illinois trade. They have attempted this establishment three times, since I came here. . . . As for Hudson Bay, if the king cannot appropriate it, he must at least secure Bourbon [*Hayes*] River." BN., Margry Papers, 9284, f. 240, undated.

[6] Royal Society MSS, H41, letter No. 108. The letter is in French.

[7] See the account of Dr. Daniel Coxe's proposal before the Royal Society, "That an advantageous settlement for the beaver-trade might be made on those [*the Great*] Lakes." The doctor promised also to give an account of the "History of this Discovery." Royal Society MSS, Journal Book No. 8 (1685–1690), p. 121, January 12, 1686/7. The account of the history of this discovery is to be found in "A Description of yᵉ Great Western Lake," "Recᵈ Mar: 1687 from Dʳ Cox" in PRO., CO., 1/64, addenda 16, 1688, document 158, pp. 396–403.

knew what was afoot, for on June 25, 1687, De Seignelay wrote to De Denonville that—the King having been informed that a company was being formed in England for the purpose of founding a trading establishment at the great lake, called "la mer douce" (Lake Huron)—he was to resume possession of it officially, and if he could do so without violence, was to prevent the proposed establishment.[8]

This last sentiment was in accord with the tenor of Renaudot's schemes. He and his party, which included both the De Callières, D'Estrées, and Bernou, besides many other influential men, were working, as usual, for continued peace with England. The Catholic cause seemed to be gaining there; there was distinct possibility that a male heir might be born to James II and thwart the plans for a Protestant successor in the shape of either of James's Protestant daughters; and France was beginning to need friends, what with the League of Augsburg directed at her, and all Protestant Europe resentful at the revocation of the Edict of Nantes. So, when James II replied to the Hudson's Bay Company's protest at the seizures in North America, "I doe assure you shall have all ye Protection I can give you," it behooved Louis XIV to tread warily.[9]

Already, in 1686, an attempt had been made to settle the differences between the two crowns as far as they touched the New World. In the French proposals for neutrality of February 7, 1686, the ninth article dealt specifically with Hudson Bay: "The commerce of Bourbon and Nelson rivers and the circumjacent country shall be common to both nations without prejudice to the rights that each claims there," and so forth.[10] The thirteenth article, however, stipulated that Port Nelson "shall be restored to the condition that it had before Radisson led the English there." In the final treaty of neutrality of November 16, 1686, however, no

[8] The minister to De Denonville, AC., B13, f. 66½.
[9] H.B.Co. Archives, A/1/84, entry for February 26, 1685/6.
[10] [Sulte], *Collection de manuscrits*, 1: 354–362.

specific mention is made of Hudson Bay.[11] The reason may be explained through certain remarks that were made by the Hudson Bay Company about this treaty at the time of the negotiations of the Treaty of Ryswick a decade later:[12]

The Case of the Hudsons Bay Comp[a] of England in Refference to the Canada Comp[a] in France. This Comp[a] in the yeare 1685/6 Complained to the late King James of their sufferings, who promised them Releife And accordingly Directions were given to his Ambassador in France to negotiate this Affaire. But dureing his Negotiation & Endeavours, the said late King (greatly favouring the Jesuits, who have the profitts of the Beaver Trade And are the Supporters of the Canada Comp[a] in France) The 12th of November privaited [*privately*] Concluded a Treaty of peace for America wth the French ambassador then resideing in England.

According to this treaty the American possessions of each king were to remain neutral even in case of war between their owners, and a commission was to settle claims. Though the two countries' commissioners met in London in 1687 and issued claims and counterclaims, no agreement was reached. Whereupon, on December 1, 1687, documents were signed to the effect that all hostilities in the New World should cease for a year, ending January 1, 1688/9 during which time proof of prior ownership might be collected by both sides.[13] In 1688, therefore, both countries began a frantic search for documents and persons that could prove priority of occupation in the Hudson Bay country. Orders were sent from Versailles to New France to resurrect all possible proofs that Frenchmen had preceded Englishmen in the Bay.[14] Contrary to France's claims during the negotiations

[11] [Sulte], *Collection de manuscrits,* 1:372–381.

[12] H.B.Co. Archives, "Copy Book of Peticoñs to his Matie and buisinesse at Court 1688–1778," ff. 30–33. The same idea is conveyed in a printed broadside, *The Case of the Hudsons-Bay Company,* in 1697 in connection with the renewal of the Company's charter. H.B.Co. Archives, Miscellaneous file, 1540–1740.

[13] The proceedings of the commissioners are conveniently published in Canadian Archives, *Report,* 1883, pp. 173–201.

[14] [Sulte], *Collection de manuscrits,* 1:418, 419.

of 1687, France could not produce evidence that Jean Bourdon had entered the Bay in 1656 and claimed it for France;
or that De la Vallière and Father Dablon were there in
1661; or that Couture was there in 1663.[15] No proof was
adduced by the French that Radisson or Des Groseilliers
had been there prior to their trip thither with the English in
1668. Radisson was in the employ of the English and could
not be reached in 1688 to make a deposition for the French
as did some of the Frenchmen whose claims were offered
from Canada. But what of Des Groseilliers? Why was he
not interviewed like other Canadians, especially as the
French statements constantly mention these two explorers
as having been the ones who told the English about the Bay?
It is hard to believe that, living in Canada, he was not asked
to tell of his early explorations beyond Lake Superior, a
territory that France considered a part of the Hudson Bay
area that she was claiming. Yet no report of his explorations
is included.

Bernou, it is true, refers to him in a document that was
doubtless written at this time, though it bears no date. After
denying that the English could have been the discoverers of
Hudson Bay, since "the two French deserters who took them
there had been there before and knew the country and its
language," it adds:[16]

These reasons are all the stronger since the right that the English
have there is reduced to having been introduced there some years
ago by two French deserters named Des Groseliers and Radisson,
which of itself proves that the country then belonged to the King,
whose sovereignty could not be transferred by these two Frenchmen
to any other king or his subjects.

[15] "Enquête faite par Le Lieut. Générale en la prévôté de Quebec," Quebec,
November 2, 1688, BN., Margry Papers, 9284, ff. 5–10. This document
shows that Guillaume Couture was still alive and made his affidavit that
neither on the trip of 1661 or that of 1663 did he reach Hudson Bay. A man
by the name of Laurent Dubose [?] swore that he was with Bourdon in
1656 and did not reach Hudson Bay. Paul Denis, Sieur de St. Simon, swore
that he went with Father Albanel in 1671 to Hudson Bay.

[16] "Memoire sur le different touchant la Baye de Hudson," BN., Collection
Clairambault, 1016, ff. 374, 375.

The truce was to terminate on January 1, 1689, but before that date a male heir had been born to James II and England had revolted. James then fled to his protector, Louis XIV of France. It is a pity that the commissioners were unable to finish their work, a part of which was to have been the establishment of a boundary between the territories of the two kings in North America.[17] No definite bounds were ever decided upon; perhaps a full year of peace as provided by the agreement of 1687 would have produced them and made unnecessary many of the later boundary disputes between England and the United States, between England and Spain, and between Spain and the United States.

[17] "The French have declared their readiness to regulate the boundaries between the two Crowns in America, and we beg your authority to treat with them for adjustment of the same." Report of the English commissioners [November], 1687, in *Cal. St. Pap., Am. & W. I., 1685–1688*, p. 464.

CHAPTER XXI

France Tempts Radisson Once More

Meanwhile, what of Radisson and his four Frenchmen in the Bay? Everything seems to have gone smoothly the first year of his contracted sojourn in the Bay as superintendent of the Company's trade. To be sure, Thomas Phipps became jealous of him, believing him to be enjoying a greater salary than himself. The Company wrote Phipps on May 20, 1686, "We will show you the mistaken grounds on which you doe assume to your selfe to demand such a sallery; first you say you heare that wee doe give Mr Raddison £200: a yeare, which as it is a great mistake so we need say no more to it." [1] But in the second year trouble developed. With the dispatches that went from the Bay to the Committee in the autumn of 1685 must have gone some criticism of Radisson, which made the Committee uneasy. To Phipps they wrote further on May 20, 1686,

> But for the trading parte at Port Nelson, and all circumstances which may conduce to the Improvemt. or Conduct of it, We doe expressly order & Command that it be left supremly and chiefly to Mr Radison, whose skill that way & knowledge of the Indians, we have a particular assurance, as well as an entire confidence in his Integrity & faithfulness.

To Samuel Missenden, the chief warehouse keeper at Port Nelson, they wrote on the same day, "And we doe require you & every one else to permitt the whole conduct of the trading parte to Mr Radison solely." [2]

As late as September 4, 1686, when Radisson wrote his second annual letter from York Factory, everything seemed

---

[1] H.B.Co. Archives, A/6/1, ff. 75–77.
[2] H.B.Co. Archives, A/6/1, f. 78.

going smoothly enough. His letter is not to be found, but the Committee's reply of June 3, 1687, breathes satisfaction.[3] The next dispatches carried news of another sort. The English refugees at York, who had fled from the French occupation of the Bottom of the Bay in 1686, caused trouble for Governor George Geyer. They, or possibly Radisson, reported Geyer to be laying up beaver furs for his own enrichment and to have suffered "intestine Differences" in his factory. The chief troublemaker was Governor Sergeant of the Bottom of the Bay, who "endeavoured to raise what mutiny & disturbeance . . . hee could." [4] Radisson must have become the target for some of the jealousy and ill will, which in the early years of occupation were as common as icebergs in the Bay colony. He told his version of the story many years later to his protector, William Young, who in turn wrote it to the Company on December 20, 1692.[5]

When he was apointed to be your Cheife Trader, to Barter your goods with the Indians, at Port Nelson, . . . some of your servants there, tempted him to Combine with them to Cheate the Comp^a of theire Beaver, and because hee did Refuse soe to doe, they tooke an ocasion to quarell with him, & his nephew, Beating & wounding them, & dureing the time of Trade, which may well be presumed to bee done on purpose, to give them an oportunity to act these villanies without his power of Observation, which he had Refused to act in Consort with them.

The Committee replied to Young in a letter that does no credit to the breeding of the writers. One sentence refers to the fact that Radisson had preferred charges against Geyer and Sinclair as soon as he reached England, but states that the Committee "accounted [them] frivolous false & malitious, noe profe being made to any one article of Consequence." [6]

---

[3] H.B.Co. Archives, A/6/1, f. 93. See Appendix 9.
[4] H.B.Co. Archives, A/6/2, ff. 5–10, Letter of Instructions to Governor Geyer of June 2, 1688.
[5] H.B.Co. Archives, A/6/2, ff. 66–67. See *post*, Appendix 10.
[6] H.B.Co. Archives, A/6/2, ff. 68–71. See *post*, Appendix 10.

A few further facts about Radisson's return came out in 1692, such as the statement that Radisson incurred the enmity of Geyer: "The Governour Ordered your Orator [*Radisson*] to be secured on board one of the Companys Shipps there and kept a close prisoner which was accordingly done and your Orator brought home a prisoner here in October one thousand six hundred Eighty and Seaven." [7]

It is a trifle hard to reconcile the Committee's criticism of Radisson in 1692 with the minutes entered in its own record books in the autumn of 1687 and the following year. Thus on October 24, 1687, the entry states that "Mr Radisson now appeared and was welcomed home and is desired to bring this Comittee an accompt of the state how he left the Factoryes." On November 16, 1687, "Mr Radisson charge against Mr Sinclair was read and hee gave Answer to severall of the same Articles, but none of his Answeres appeare cleare or ingenious soe that he is found rather Willing to Conceale then discover for the Companyes interest." On December 16, 1687, and January, 1688, Radisson, Chouart, and Elie Grimard were naturalized at the Company's order and expense. And on July 18, 1688, a sum of fifty pounds per annum was added by the Committee's action to Radisson's salary or pension. "This Comittee takeing notice that Mr Peter Esspritt Radison is by order of a Generall Court made the 26 November 1684 to have the benefitt of 200 lb Stock dureing his life and whiles hee continues faithfull in the Companyes Service, the which this Comittee finde hee hath ever Since done." [8]

Thus Radisson came home before his time was up in the Bay, but his nephew and Elie Grimard remained for two more years. Chouart seems to have served in the warehouse

[7] Nute, "Two Documents from Radisson's Suit Against the Company," p. 44.

[8] H.B.Co. Archives, A/1/9; *Lists of Foreign Protestants and Aliens, Resident in England 1618–1688*, edited by William Durrant Cooper, pp. 48–54 (Camden Society Publication, London, 1862); PRO., Patent Rolls, C66/3300, 3 James II, Pars Decima, No. 6, January 5, 1687/8.

at York Factory at first.[9] Whether he held that position for
any length of time is not clear. The Committee's instructions
of June 2, 1688, to Geyer referred to him as "Trader." [10]
The same document inquired why Chouart wished to return
to England, since his contract would not be up for another
year. It left the matter to "his own inclinations," however.
He concluded to stay and did not return to England until
the autumn of 1689. His later history has not been found.
Whether he remained in England, returned to his native
land, or went to France is not known. His connections with
the Company ended to all appearance in the late winter of
1689–1690. On February 12, 1690, an entry was made in
the minute book to pay "to John Baptista Groselier in full
of all wages £202.2.9." [11] On March 24, 1695, Médard
Chouart, Sieur des Groseilliers, then in Canada, mentioned
the attorney of his son, Jean Baptiste Chouart, as though the
latter was not in Canada.[12] Perhaps young Chouart accepted
one of the offers of marriage made to him in England, which
he mentions in one of his letters, and, like his uncle, remained
in the country of which he had been made a legal denizen.
There were Des Groseilliers among both bourgeois and
voyageurs in the trade with the Illinois country in the next
century,[13] but whether they were descended from Jean Bap-

[9] H.B.Co. Archives, A/6/1, ff. 90–92, Letter of Instructions to Governor
Geyer of June 3, 1687.

[10] H.B.Co. Archives, A/6/2, ff. 5–10.

[11] H.B.Co. Archives, A/1/12. For a reference to Chouart on his trip to
England in 1689, see D'Iberville's letter of November 17, 1689, printed in
Louis Le Jeune, *Le Chevalier Pierre Le Moyne, Sieur D'Iberville*, p. 49 (Ot-
tawa, 1937).

[12] Gagnon, *Essai de bibliographie canadienne*, 2:333.

[13] In 1775 John Baptiste De Grossillier was among the voyageurs who took
out engagements at Montreal. He was listed as a canoeman from Montreal. In
the same year two engagements cite a "Sieur J. B[te] Des Groseilliers" as a
bourgeois in the Illinois and Mackinac trade. See E. J. Massicotte, *Répertoire
des engagements pour l'ouest conservés dans les archives judiciaires de Montréal (1670–1778)*, in *Rapport de l'Archiviste de la Province de Québec pour
1932–1933*, p. 303 (Quebec, 1933) ; and engagements Nos. 57, 32, and 49 for the
years 1775, 1781, and 1783, respectively, preserved in the Public Archives of
Canada, Ottawa.

tiste, his elder half brother, Médard, or his sister (one of whose children is reported to have taken her maiden name just as one of Radisson's Canadian nephews took the title, Sieur de Radisson) is unknown.[14] A Des Groseilliers family is still living in Minnesota, to which a Timothy Des Groseilliers migrated from Canada about 1880, settling at Gentilly; and a granddaughter of Delphine Des Groseilliers, who was related to Timothy, is a Montreal correspondent of the author of this book.[15] The fate of Jean Baptiste's father is equally unknown. If the date of Médard Chouart's statement about his son, as quoted by Gagnon, is correct, the old explorer was still living in Sorel, Canada, in 1695. The objection to such a belief is Radisson's plain statement in the 1690's that his brother-in-law died "in the bay" earlier than a certain event which occurred in 1683. However, Des Groseilliers was certainly alive after 1683. Radisson may have had good reasons for wanting the Hudson's Bay Company to believe Chouart dead while the chancery court case, instituted by Radisson in the 1690's, was being adjudicated.[16] No record of Des Groseilliers' interment in Canada has been found, though, practically without exception, his family and relatives are accounted for in parish registers. This fact lends color to the belief that he probably died on some trading venture or other expedition into the wilderness. Such a death would surely be a fitting close to the man's adventurous and active career.

Meanwhile, in France, it was seen that it might be better to have Radisson on that country's side than against it. Though De Denonville's instructions to Sieur de Troyes had been specific about seizing "Radisson and any of his

[14] "Fief et Seigneurie de Volant Radisson" in Roy, *Inventaire des concessions en fief et seigneurie,* 4: 92–94.

[15] Julia Fafard Gale to Grace L. Nute, Montreal, November 2, and 14, 1937; Francis Labonte to Grace L. Nute, Crookston, Minnesota, November 9, 1937; and the Minnesota State Census, 1885, for Gentilly, in the manuscript division of the Minnesota Historical Society.

[16] See *ante,* Chapter xviii, Note 5, and *post,* Chapter xxii.

followers, wherever they may be found," in order that he might be punished "suivant la rigueur des ordonnances," [17] De Seignelay himself wrote on March 30, 1687,

The wrong that Radisson has done the colony and the injury that he would be capable of making, if he remains longer with the English, ought to force the Sieurs de Denonville and De Champigny to do everything they can, in case he cannot be seized, to make him return, and for that purpose His Majesty will allow him to compose his differences with us on such conditions as he thinks right.[18]

It was doubtless in pursuance of this scheme that "one Monsr Perry [*Péré*] of Rochelle" addressed a letter to Radisson late in 1690 or early the following year and sent it by Hugh Verner and Stephen Sinclair, two of the Hudson's Bay Company's men who had been seized by the French in the Bay and thence shipped to London via La Rochelle. The Englishmen gave the letter to the Hudson's Bay Company instead of handing it to Radisson. It must have been a document of some importance, for it was translated and "the Secretary is ordered to Lay [it] safely up in the Cantore." [19] Apparently Radisson never saw it or knew of its existence. It is more than likely that "Monsieur Perry" was Jean Baptiste Péré. In the same year, 1690, a project was afoot in France to seize Boston and New York. At that time a letter from the King at Versailles stated that

Monsieur [*Nicolas?*] Perrot knows that coast, as well as Sieur de Villebon, who is now at La Rochelle with La Motte—all three have often been in Boston and New York. There is also the man Péré, who is at La Rochelle, who knows perfectly the vicinity of New York on the land side; Péré would be very useful in this undertaking; he is well disposed.[20]

As the years of war and excitement in Europe slipped by, Radisson was gradually forgotten by the French, even though he was well informed on those very areas in the New

[17] Caron, *Journal du Chevalier de Troyes,* p. 7.
[18] [Sulte], *Collection de manuscrits,* 1 : 394, 395.
[19] H.B.Co. Archives, A/1/13, entry of January 15, 1690/1.
[20] [Sulte], *Collection de manuscrits,* 2 : 5.

World that France was trying to wrest from the English. He became an Englishman in spirit as well as by adoption, and the story of the last quarter century of his life centers entirely at London. From France two men did keep an eye on him for a time. Bernou and Renaudot occasionally mentioned him and his brother-in-law in the years immediately following his flight to England and in so doing revealed much of the story of Radisson and Des Groseilliers' relations with the two scheming abbés.[21] Thus on September 2, 1684, Bernou retaliated to some adverse statement from Renaudot by remarking, "Radisson and his brother have not deceived me any more than you. I had recognized in the former some extravagant notions, which repelled me and I, like you, renounce him forever." An extraordinarily curious reference to Des Groseilliers' cannabilism is made by Bernou in a letter of November 11, 1684. Evidently the two churchmen knew a gruesome chapter in the explorer's life that has not been opened up to later generations. On April 10, 1685, Bernou got his long-awaited chance to express to De Villermont his criticism of the Jesuit policy in the New World by citing Radisson's case as an example of poor judgment on the part of the French Court. He wrote:

What you tell me about Radisson does not surprise me. I have long noticed and regretted the slight notice that the French Court pays to its colonies. If a little attention had been paid, we could easily have made ourselves masters of the entire fur trade of North America, which would have amounted to at least three million a year, without reference to the other advantages it would have given us. But we are not the masters of it and the people who know best and who have least at stake are not consulted in those matters.

Bernou continued the same theme in a letter of April 24 to Renaudot, saying that it was a mistake to recall Radisson

---

[21] BN., Renaudot Papers, 7497, ff. 153, 154, 171, 172, 216, and 217; and BN., MSS Français, Dangeau Collection, 22,800, ff. 16, 17, 85: "You have pardoned Radisson for having pillaged his good friends, the English, under cloak of friendship; and you have pardoned Des Grosiliers, the liar, his brother-in-law, for having eaten human flesh. Our conquistador [Peñalosa] is not so pernicious."

from England and then to neglect him. "You and Mr. de Callières have done your duty as wise and zealous counsellors. May this instance bring you more credence in the future." However, Radisson was not the person to right the wrong, he continued. Radisson "is a dishonest man, not to say worse." "It may well be that the day will come when he will be a common scapegoat for both countries."

Radisson's two narratives of his trips of 1682–1683 and 1684 fell into De Villermont's hands, perhaps through Godet's arrangements, but more probably by way of Radisson himself. Evidently De Villermont offered to have them copied for Bernou, for on October 16, 1685, Bernou wrote to De Villermont:

> I should indeed have been glad, as you guessed, to have seen Mr. Radisson's two *relations;* but it would not be fair to let you pay for having copies made for me. It will suffice if you keep them for me to see when I get back. I am not surprised that Monsieur de Seignelay is prohibiting the author from returning to France. He and his brother-in-law are very unreliable and fickle. They first introduced the English to Hudson Bay and guided them thither, whereby they did their country an irreparable wrong. Nevertheless, they were pardoned and permitted to return to Canada, where they proposed to De la Chesnaye and others to make an establishment at Port Nelson. They went there, made the settlement, and then spoiled everything by pillaging the English, which might have brought on a war with that country, which demanded satisfaction, as you know. Finally, to crown their infidelity, they betake themselves once more to the English and go to put them in possession of the only post we could occupy and where these men themselves had made an establishment for France. What can one expect of persons like that, who veer with every wind, and what satisfaction could they make for the evils they have caused? For myself, I see no way, and yet you would give me great pleasure by writing me if they are making some new proposition and of what nature it can be.

Apparently in the summer of 1685 Radisson was up to his old tricks of trying out both sides to see which would pay him most.

When Renaudot in a letter to Bernou mentioned Radisson

as Bernou's trusty servant (*féal*), Bernou fairly sputtered indignation: [22]

Trusty servant yourself! It is long since that I put him down as a bad risk, for several reasons, but especially because I saw him wavering in his religion, and from time to time I had to exhort him to persevere in it. But I should indeed like to know whether in making his fine marriage he has not turned his coat [*turned Protestant*]. God forbid! for he has picked his time badly, both from a spiritual and a temporal point of view.

With James II's accession a reality by this time, it might indeed have been hazardous for a Catholic to forswear his religion in England, had Renaudot's well-laid plans for that country succeeded. The clever abbé's designs for a Catholic England have never been properly described, though his letters and papers on the subject are extant. On June 5, 1685, Bernou again asked Renaudot whether "Radisson . . . has become a Huguenot like his wife and father-in-law." [23]

[22] BN., Renaudot Papers, 7497, f. 219, Bernou to Renaudot, May 8, 1685.
[23] BN., Renaudot Papers, 7497, f. 229.

CHAPTER XXII

In Chancery

Radisson left the Bay in 1687 never to return. Fortune always seemed on his side. That year was probably the last he could have resided at York Factory in physical safety. Exciting days in the Bay followed D'Iberville's successful mission to France in 1687–1688 to secure aid for the "Company of the North" from the King. The outbreak of war between England and France in 1689 made the treaty of neutrality of 1686 a worthless bit of paper, despite all the brave talk therein of neutrality for American colonials whether or not there was war in Europe. Three English forts were seized in 1686. New Severn was taken in 1690. In 1693 the English recaptured forts Albany, Rupert, and Moose. York Factory was taken in 1694, recaptured in 1696, retaken by the French in 1697, and held by them till the Treaty of Utrecht in 1713. It was not till that treaty was negotiated that Englishmen and Frenchmen ceased to battle in Hudson Bay. Even then the affair was not permanently closed, for only with the end of the American Revolution did France cease her attempts to seize the entire Hudson Bay area. Thus the business acumen of two French explorers began a conflict that lasted almost exactly a hundred years.

Radisson settled down in Westminster, then quite separate from London, and began rearing a family. If today one strikes south on Drury Lane from High Holborn toward the Strand, he will reach the general surroundings of Radisson's residence on the left just after passing Drury Lane Theatre. At least Radisson was living in that place, Clare Court, at the time of his death.[1] Earlier, in 1697, he gave his residence as St. James's Parish in the county of Middlesex, which lies somewhat to the west.[2] In the last decades of the seventeenth century, London was just spreading beyond the walls westward toward the Court residences in Westminster.[3] Clare Court was in the Liberty of the city of Westminster, and was considered a very desirable residential neighborhood.[4] A little to the northwest was the property of John Churchill, who was to be the great Duke of Marlborough, to whom James II entrusted the protection of Radisson before the King left his kingdom ignominiously and William of Orange invaded England in 1689.

It will be recalled that John Churchill was a devoted [?] follower of James, Duke of York.[5] When the latter became King, Baron Churchill became Governor of the Hudson's Bay Company. It was natural, therefore, that James II should entrust a Catholic Frenchman to the special care

[1] Radisson's will, which mentions his residence, is preserved in Somerset House, London. It was made, sealed, and published on June 17, 1710, and proved on July 21 of the same year. See Appendix 15.

[2] Radisson's affidavit of August 23, 1697, in PRO., Amer. & W. I., Hudson's Bay, p. 539. See *post*, Appendix 11.

[3] "The gradual extension of London westwards to meet Westminster really dates from the beginning of the Stuart period, and is clearly divisible into two periods. Up to the Restoration the main development is first in Lincoln's Inn Fields and the ground immediately adjoining, between Chancery Lane and Drury Lane; and secondly in the Covent Garden area, between Drury Lane and St. Martin's Lane." Norman G. Brett-James, *The Growth of Stuart London*, p. 151 (London, 1935).

[4] "Clare Court, a very handsome open Place [*in the parish of St. Clements*] with a Passage into Blackmore Street." John Stow, *The Survey of London*, Fifth Edition by J. Strype, 2: Book 4, 108, 118 (London, 1720). Strype in his description of St. James' parish in 1708 tells of Berwick Street in it: "It begins at Peter-street, and runs Northwards as far as Tyburn Road; a pretty handsome strait Street, with new well built Houses, much inhabited by the French, where they have a Church." See Vol. 2, p. 84.

[5] "Lord Marlborough . . . . was the Lord who was entirely advanced by King James, and was the first who betrayed and forsook his master. He was the son of Sir Winston Churchill of the Green-cloth." Evelyn, *Diary*, 2:318. If Marlborough's papers could be consulted, they might very well throw some light on the London residence of Radisson, as well as on other events in his career. Until that privilege shall be accorded, it is necessary to tell the story of Marlborough's association with him from other and less authoritative sources.

of a man who was at once the King's henchman and the governor of the company for which that Frenchman worked. In addition, there seems to have been some special connection between William Young and Churchill. Young was always the go-between when the Company needed Churchill's assistance. Young's star fell, as far as the Company was concerned, with Marlborough's disgrace in 1692, and rose again with Marlborough's renown in military affairs. It would be interesting to know more of the relations of these two men.

On December 16, 1687, while Churchill was still Governor of the Company, "it . . . . [was] moved in behalfe of Mr Espritt Radison that a Gratuity or benevolence of Fifty pounds per Ann^m might be added to his Sallery for his better Subsistance till his Matie shall putt him into some ymploy to that or better value and noe longer." [6] The motion was carried. Later events were to show that the action was made at Churchill's request.[7]

For two years and a little more the Company paid Radisson one hundred pounds per year. These were prosperous years for the Company. On July 18, 1688, the Committee agreed to pay fifty pounds dividend for every hundred pounds of stock.[8] Radisson accordingly was given one hundred pounds on his two hundred pounds of stock, which had been granted him at the General Court of November 26, 1684. On September 27, 1690, a newsletter carried this item: "The Hudson Bay Company met yesterday and notwithstanding the loss of two ships have made a dividend of 75 per cent, which has doubled their accounts. They are now

[6] H.B.Co. Archives, A/1/10.

[7] "The said Fifty pounds per anm being meerly bestowed on the Complt. for the prsent out of Charity and at the request and desire of the said Earle of Malbrough . . . untill the said Earle should procure him some employment which he promised the said Company he would doe in some very short time." See Nute, "Two Documents from Radisson's Suit Against the Company," p. 48.

[8] H.B.Co. Archives, A/1/10.

the only flourishing Company in the Kingdom." [9] Yet on
October 1 of the same year the Committee "Takeing into
Consideration the Late Aditionall Gratuity of 50 [lbs] per
Ann[um] given M[r] Peter Espritt Radison . . . considering there Extrordinary charges they have been at, & are Like
to be doe Resolve that the said aditionall gratuity of 50 [lb]
per Ann shall cease & Expire at Mich[lms] Last past." [10]
However, Radisson got one hundred and fifty pounds at
this time on his two hundred pounds' worth of original stock
now trebled to be considered the equivalent of six hundred
pounds.[11]

Radisson and Young explained this action of the Committee in rescinding Radisson's fifty pounds "gratuity" as
due to Governor Geyer's influence on the deputy Governor,
Sir Edward Dering.[12] On November 23, 1691, a petition by
Radisson was read at a committee meeting, asking that the
sum of one hundred pounds be paid him as formerly.[13]
The deputy Governor then "made a Rehearsall of all Transactions of M[r] Radison from his first serveing the Comp[a]
to this day," and the committee, "considering their great
Losses," and "the vast charges they have been at & are at
da[i]ly," unanimously refused to grant the request.

So the affair rested till December 14, 1692, when Radisson appeared at a committee meeting and waited below stairs
during the consideration of his case.[14] Marlborough, no
longer governor, had signified to the Committee his interest
in the affair and minutes were prepared for his perusal. On
December 20, 1692, William Young wrote a long letter to

[9] "The Manuscripts of S. H. Le Fleming," p. 293. See also H.B.Co. Archives,
A/1/12, entry for September 3, 1690.

[10] H.B.Co. Archives, A/1/12.

[11] The vote of September 3 to treble the stock, gives the reasons therefor
and states the value of the Company's capital stock as £10,500 before the expansion and £31,500 thereafter.

[12] Young's letter to the Company. See Appendix 10.

[13] H.B.Co. Archives, A/1/14.

[14] H.B.Co. Archives, A/1/15.

the Committee on Radisson's behalf, reciting the latter's entire history and claiming that justice demanded that the Company continue to pay him the hundred pounds that had been agreed upon. It also affords a glimpse into Radisson's home life in 1692, for it states that he had at that time four or five children and was then expecting another; that he paid twenty-four pounds for rent; that he kept servants; and that he was in debt and must soon let his family go on the parish unless his salary be augmented. Young's letter was presented by Radisson himself on December 21. The Committee evaded answering at the time on the plea that the Governor was not present, but they promised to take up the case "spedily after Christmas." [15]

On January 25, 1693, the Governor's recommendation that the case be settled (presumably in Radisson's favor) was taken up at a committee meeting. It was voted that a gratuity of fifty pounds be given Radisson on condition that he relinquish all his claims against the Company and agree to receive only fifty pounds per annum henceforth. [16]

By February 1 Lord Marlborough had written in Radisson's behalf. His letter and Young's were considered at a committee meeting of that date. [17] It was voted to write letters of acknowledgment to both men, promising some immediate action. Radisson himself appeared before the Committee on February 8, but neither side yielded. [18] By February 22 a reply of many pages was ready for Mr. Young. Indeed, it is quite plain that the Committee smugly fancied that the crude and inaccurate letter which they had indited would crush Mr. Young completely. Its tone is several social levels below that of Young's letter to them. [19] One thing is very patent: the Company did not know its own history and had no easy way to recover it. Though only twenty-seven years

[15] H.B.Co. Archives, A/1/15. The letter is printed in Appendix 10.
[16] H.B.Co. Archives, A/1/15.
[17] H.B.Co. Archives, A/1/15.
[18] H.B.Co. Archives, A/1/15.
[19] The letter is printed in Appendix 10.

had elapsed since Radisson had first arrived in England, the Company in 1693 admitted somewhat grudgingly that possibly he had had something to do with the founding of the corporation; but they asked why he had left the Company after a few years of service! Young himself supplies in part the explanation for such abysmal ignorance. As he says, all the members of the Committee were new ones. A complete change of personnel had occurred, probably as a result of the "Glorious Revolution."

Still intercession went on for Radisson. On March 22 both Young and Gédéon Godet, Radisson's father-in-law, appeared before the Committee.[20] On September 14 the Governor himself interceded for Radisson.[21] But the Committee stood adamant. Finally, late in 1693, at the General Court of the year, Young moved again in Radisson's behalf.[22] This time he merely asked that fifty pounds be given Radisson in expectation of the next dividend. He described Radisson as being in a "low & meane Condition," greatly needing money. For the first time the Committee yielded a little. Young's request was granted and Radisson received the money. As we shall see, no dividend was made during the remainder of Radisson's lifetime.

If the Committee thought that they had quelled a troublesome servant, they lived to learn the contrary. Radisson seems to have known nothing of fear, either physical or social. On May 22, 1694, he instituted a suit in chancery against one of the most powerful cliques in London's economic life at that time, the Hudson's Bay Company.[23] However, it should be pointed out that he had powerful friends, Marlborough, Young, and all that these men stood for. Since it was Young who prepared the Company's case against France in the very important negotiations of 1687, he must

[20] H.B.Co. Archives, A/1/15.
[21] H.B.Co. Archives, A/1/16.
[22] H.B.Co. Archives, A/1/16, November 16, 1693.
[23] PRO., C6/303. This is printed in Nute, "Two Documents from Radisson's Suit Against the Company."

have had either unusual acumen or unusual legal training. If we but knew more of this mysterious William Yonge, or Young! With Young at Radisson's elbow advising him and writing legal documents for him, and with the Company jealously envied by large parts of the populace, the case began its long course "in chancery." Nor was it the Company's fault that it did not drag out to greater length.

Radisson's formal petition to the Lord Keeper of the Great Seal of England is dated May 22, 1694. It recited at length, and much after the style of Young's letter in Radisson's behalf, the life history of the petitioner from childhood to date. It asked for continuance of the pension of fifty pounds per year, which had been rescinded; for the payment of arrears; and for a court order that the Company's records be produced to show the exact conditions under which Radisson's agreements with the Company had been made. This last move was a wise one, since Radisson had nothing to prove even that he should get his first pension, much less the additional gratuity and some twelve thousand beaver skins. Payment for them was now claimed as having been due him since 1684, when he brought the Frenchmen and their furs to England.

Probably the Company was stunned by the audacity of this action of Radisson's. On June 6, 1694, the Committee officially recorded that it had received a copy of a "bill in Chancery preferred against them by Mr Peter Espritt Radison." [24] Arrangement was made for securing counsel in order that the bill might be answered. However, it was not until November 7 that any action was reported. Then it was announced that Sir Thomas Powys had been retained to defend "ye Motion of Radison against the Compa," that the Company's records had been investigated for evidence, and that an answer was being prepared.[25] On November 21 the answer was still not prepared for filing in the Company's

[24] H.B.Co. Archives, A/1/16.
[25] H.B.Co. Archives, A/1/16.

safe, an iron chest, to which there were two keys, kept by two individuals, and both necessary for opening the strong box.[26] So little had the seventeenth century learned to demand absolute honesty from its secretaries and treasurers.

The next day, November 22, a General Court was held and Young moved again "in Behalfe of M[r] Radison desireing that this Generall Court would Consider his Condition." The fact that Radisson was petitioning as a pauper in the court tells something of the meaning of that expression, "his Condition." A committee was appointed "to give the s[d] Esq[r] Yonge a meeting to discourse him concerning that matter." [27] Nearly six months later, April 10, 1695, the Company's answer was ready; it was sealed and delivered to Mr. Shaller, the Company's attorney.[28]

This document has practically none of the smug "smartness" of the Company's reply to Young. Perhaps by this time it had become apparent to the gentlemen of the Committee that Radisson was not to be regarded with sure equanimity. A man who had upset their calculations on several earlier occasions might do so again.

The course that the Company followed was to procrastinate, claiming that material witnesses were in Hudson Bay and could not be secured till a vessel could get there and return. On May 20, 1695, three servants of the Company, John Constant, William Fowler, and Anthony Beale, were sworn to be such material witnesses, and necessary for the Company's cause.[29] On November 6, 1695, other material witnesses were announced as being absent but necessary to the Company's side of the case.[30] That day the defendants asked the court to defer the case till the first day of the next term.

[26] H.B.Co. Archives, A/1/16.

[27] H.B.Co. Archives, A/1/17.

[28] H.B.Co. Archives, A/1/17. It is printed in Nute, "Two Documents from Radisson's Suit Against the Company."

[29] PRO., Chancery Records, volume marked, "Register of Oaths and Affidavits, Easter, Trinity, Michas, Hillary, 1695 and Easter, 1696," No. 624.

[30] PRO., Chancery Records, "Register of Oaths and Affidavits . . . 1695, 1696." No. 286.

Radisson knew just how to convince the court that the Company was merely sparring for time. On November 8 Richard Terrell appeared before the court and swore that he "hath strictly Examined the Custom house Bookes of Entrys of Shipps outward bound and Doth not find therein any Entry made by the Govern^r or Company of Adventure[r]s tradeing into Hudson's Bay or any other p^{r}sons of any Ship or Ships bound for Hudsons Bay since Christmas one thousand Six hundred and ninty four." [31] If no vessels had left, the Company was neither quite honest nor reliable in this matter of securing material witnesses for their side. At this rate all the parties to the suit would be in their graves before the witnesses could be heard and the case decided. On November 13 Radisson told the court in plain language just how he had learned of the Company's plan to procrastinate, how he had had search made at the customs-house, and even how members of the Company had admitted that no ships were intended to be sent that year to the Bay.[32]

This affair has special interest as showing Radisson's independence, even of his own counsel, who had "advised this Depon^t to nominate Comison^{rs} and joyn in Comison with the Defts." Radisson refused to do so, and started an investigation on his own account at the customs-house. He further reminded the court that he was now indebted to several persons and "hath bin Divers times Arrested & Imprisoned [*for debt*] where he had Still Continued & his Family utterly ruined had he not bin releived by Charitable Christians." William Young may very well have been one of the good Samaritans. Radisson went on to say: "If this Cause be putt of and Delayed any long^r he is in great feare all his Credito^{rs} will fall on him att once to his utter ruin without the releife of this Honor^{ble} Court." One has to admire the perspicacity of the man and his shrewd knowledge of human nature, par-

[31] PRO., Chancery Records, "Register of Oaths and Affidavits . . . 1695, 1696." No. 333.

[32] PRO., Chancery Records, "Register of Oaths and Affidavits . . . 1695, 1696." No. 334.

ticularly the easy approach to men's sympathy, even if one suspects that his condition was not quite as bad as he painted it.

Two days later the General Court was called to discuss the disaster that had befallen the Company: York Fort had fallen to the French. "Esquire Young," however, seized the opportunity to move "in Behalfe of Mr Radison." A great deal of discussion took place and then the General Court concluded to refer the subject back to the Committee. On January 19, 1696, the Court of Chancery ordered that the Company pay the money and salary claimed by Radisson, a part of the arrears within a month and the residue in six months.[33] A chance was given the Company, however, to show cause why the amount should not be paid in a shorter time.

By this time the Company had decided that it might be wise to compose their differences with their erstwhile servant. On the fifth of February, therefore, the committee reported that on

. . . the 24th of January last the Dep^t Govr Capt John Nicholson & Mr John Smith mett Esqr Young & Mr Cradock at this house In order to Compose the Diference between the Comp^a & Mr Radison & it Being agreed on both sides before they Entred on any discourse in Case they came to Noe Conclusion or agrement that w^t was discoursed here should be no prejudice to either side . . . [*the Company's representatives*] Condesended as followeth viz To pay Mr Radison in Money 150^lb & to discharge him of 50^lb hee stands debtor for in the Comp^as Bookes he giveing a generall Release to the Comp^a of all Claimes & pretences whatsoever upon which Condition he should have the Comp^as Seale to pay him dureing his Naturale Life £100: p^r ann^m Excepting those yeares the Comp^a shall make a Devidend or Devidends & then but 50^lb p^r ann^m according to his originall agrement.[34]

Evidently the Company was afraid they would also be ordered by the court to reimburse Radisson for the furs and

[33] PRO., Chancery Records, Decrees and Orders, 1696, f. 159.
[34] H.B.Co. Archives, A/1/18.

skins that he had brought back from Hudson Bay in 1684.

Apparently Radisson refused this offer, which gave him most of what he asked for. He or his counsel believed that he could get even more if he could await the results of the long-drawn-out process of English justice. In May, 1696, the court again took up Radisson's case.[35] On July 29 the court ratified and confirmed its earlier order, "unless ye Defts having notice hereof shall within 8 days after such notice shew unto this Court good Cause to the contrary." [36]

The Company took exception to the report of Radisson's counsel, William Meredith, of July 28, on which the court had based its decision, and the case was continued once more. By November 7, 1696, Radisson had petitioned the Lord Keeper and the court had ordered the case to "stand early in ye paper on Wednesday ye 11th of November Instant." [37]

By March 9, 1697, it was certain that Radisson had won his suit and the Committee ordered the Company's secretary "to pay to Mr Radison in part of the first payment ordered to be paid by the Court of Chancery." [38] The account of Radisson's receipts from the Company that is to be found in a stately volume of the Company's records for the years from 1697 to 1713 records that in 1697 the Company had already paid him during his periods of service with the Company £220.18. At the end of his life the sum was £1679.10.5.[39] Thus the Company carried out faithfully the decree of the court for approximately thirteen years and Radisson seems to have been content, at least on the score of salary. He still felt that the Company owed him a very large sum for the beaver skins that he brought to them from the Bay in 1684. He died bequeathing that claim to his heirs.

The Company had now embarked on its darkest years. Disaster followed disaster. Dividends were not declared for

[35] PRO., Chancery Records, C33, ff. 335, 336.
[36] PRO., Chancery Records, Decrees and Orders, 1696, Vol. 286, f. 487.
[37] PRO., Chancery Records, Decrees and Orders, 1696, ff. 9, 49, 50.
[38] H.B.Co. Archives, A/1/19.
[39] H.B.Co. Archives, Ledger 106, especially f. 231.

twenty-eight years. In October, 1697, Radisson, anxious lest the Company should be unable to pay him, wrote to the Company desiring "that the Comp^a would bee pleased to give their bond payable" in six months "for ye Remaind^r of the Money ordered by the Court of Chancery being 140^lb." [40] The secretary was ordered to acquaint him that they "were willing to doe him what Kindness they could in the Affairs, but that their Circumstances would not permitt them to pay the same under Twelve months." On October 28, however, such a bond, for one hundred pounds, payable on October 28, 1698, was issued to Thomas Goodall, Junior, Esquire, of Gray's Inn.[41] This was Radisson's attorney and the son-in-law of William Yonge!

[40] H.B.Co. Archives, A/1/19, under date of October 26, 1697.
[41] H.B.Co. Archives, A/1/19.

CHAPTER XXIII

On Being "Verry Usefull"

While the case between Radisson and the Company was coming to a long delayed close, England and France were patching up a temporary truce in their international difficulties. In France the clique to which Abbé Bernou, Abbé Renaudot, Frontenac, the De Callières, De Pontchartrain, De Beauharnois, and others belonged had come into at least some measure of power. Under its guidance every effort had been made to wrest Hudson Bay from the English, once war was declared. Not a little success had been achieved, largely through the prowess of Pierre Le Moyne, Sieur d'Iberville, the son of Des Groseilliers' partner in the fur trade in 1660. Louis Hector de Callières had long been governor of Montreal. Frontenac had been restored to the Governorship of Canada, a restitution so devoutly prayed for by Bernou in many of his letters to Renaudot. Louis Hector de Callières was to be Frontenac's successor in 1699, when the staunch old warrior governor died. Soon the work of claiming Louisiana for France and the Recollects, relinquished temporarily by Bernou's group when De la Salle was killed, would go forward, D'Iberville in command, against Hennepin and his French and English aids and colonists.

Late in 1694 Louis XIV was corresponding with two envoys whom he had sent to Holland to arrange a truce. One of these men, often addressed as Monsieur de Gigny, was that De Callières who had dictated a letter of instructions to Radisson in 1684 for the purpose of settling the differences between France and England over Port Nelson in Hudson Bay, lately wrested from the Hudson's Bay Company by Radisson and Des Groseilliers. De Callières was now addressed by the King on the subject of the restitution of English conquests in America.[1] Nothing was accomplished at this time in the way of peace, but De Callières became one of the official negotiators for France of the Treaty of Ryswick in 1697.

Early in 1697 the Hudson's Bay Company noted that their claims against France for the wrongs done them in the Bay were not getting proper recognition "in the French Govern[ts] affaire, wch wee hope has a favourable aspect towards the Comp[a] but wee find they [*the French*] have much favour amongst greate persons wch wee could never have thought." [2] With the "great persons" of their own side in England favoring the French, there was nothing to do but call on Radisson to bolster up the Company's claims. On August 16, 1697, the Committee understood "that there is a Person already sent into Holland from them [*the Canada fur company*]" and believed the situation was serious enough for the calling of a general court.[3] The result was that Radisson was called to the Company's assistance. The very next day, August 17,

. . . The Comittee Considering M[r] Peter Espritt Radison may be verry usefull at this time as to the Affaires betwixt the French and this Company, The Secretary was ordered to take Coach and Fetch him to the Comittee—which he did, after which the Comittee had some discours with him before Dinner, and then Adjourned to the Afternoone.[4]

After dinner discussion was resumed with Radisson.

[*The Committee*] desired an account of him of all Voyages to Hudsons Bay from his first outsett to his last arriveall from Port Nelson which he did, giveing a Perticular accompt of the Voyage he made from Canada to Port Nelson in the yeare 1682 & how he left that place, as also how he went in the yeare 1684 by the Perticular order of Mons[r] Calier now one of the French Plenipotentiaries

[1] BN., MSS Fr., 15,883, ff. 162, 181, December 6, 1694.
[2] H.B.Co. Archives, A/6/3, letter to William Young, January 9, 1696/7.
[3] H.B.Co. Archives, A/1/19.
[4] H.B.Co. Archives, A/1/19.

in Holland as also produced the Orriginall paper wch was wrote in his presence.

On the eighteenth of August the Committee "farther Discoursed Mr Radison" and considered the negotiations in Holland until eight o'clock in the evening.[5] On the twenty-third Radisson made an affidavit before Sir Robert Jeffery covering the whole course of his life, with special reference to his exploits in Hudson Bay.[6]

The Treaty of Ryswick restored all conquered places and areas to their condition and ownership at the outbreak of the war in 1689. This was a great blow to the Company, which had reconquered many of its posts in the interim. Though the deputy Governor, Samuel Clarke, and Colonel Perry had gone to Holland to plead with the English plenipotentiaries, and though great care had been exercised in drawing up the English "pretensions" [claims] in the Bay from Radisson's narratives and from the records of the Company, all that that corporation succeeded in obtaining was "that the French Commissioners should come over for England to adjust the affaire betwixt this Comp^a and that of France."[7] It should be added that William Blathwayt, the acting secretary of state, who accompanied William III on his campaigns on the continent, was very much concerned over the failure of the English commissioners to secure the return of the control of the Hudson Bay country to the English Company.[8] Blathwayt seems to have been more statesmanlike in the whole matter of the English colonies than his royal master; it was he who got in touch with Father Hennepin at this period and laid plans for the English Company that was to seize and occupy the Mississippi Valley.[9] How-

[5] H.B.Co. Archives, A/1/19.
[6] The statement is printed as Appendix 11.
[7] H.B.Co. Archives, A/1/19, November 17, 1697.
[8] Gertrude A. Jacobsen, *William Blathwayt, A Late Seventeenth Century English Administrator*, pp. 321–324 (New Haven, 1932).
[9] Grace Lee Nute, "Father Hennepin's Later Years," in *Minnesota History*, 19:393–398 (Dec., 1938); and a review by her of Father Jean Delanglez' *The Journal of Jean Cavelier*, in the *Mississippi Valley Historical Review*, 26:78,

ever, the sons of Des Groseilliers' old partner, Le Moyne, once more were a trifle in advance of the English and turned back the first contingent of English settlers in the lower reaches of the Mississippi.

In the summer of 1698 relatives of De Pontchartrain went to England as the French commissioners who were to adjust matters between the Company and France. The English commissioners were the earls of Pembroke, Bridgewater, and Portland, and two other officials. The Company was frantically busy the ensuing weeks drawing up its case. It is interesting to note that on September 14, 1698, the books and papers belonging to the Company that were turned over to Sir Edward Dering, who was preparing the Company's briefs, were "A Coppy of M[r] Radisons agrement made in Canada anno 1682 for a voyage to Hudsons Bay, the orriginall of which M[r] Radison has"; and "M[r] Radisons affidavitt, with a paper Dictated to him by Mons[r] Caleir anno 1684 in English & French." [10]

The negotiations dragged out. Radisson and Des Groseilliers' names were mentioned again and again, both by the French and the English in the voluminous records of the parleys. Indeed, the French mention that "Radisson is still in London," drawing his pension from the Company. [11]

On February 14, 1699, the Company sent a letter to William Young, who evidently had advised them to make use of Radisson in their claims against France: [12]

79 (June, 1939) showing a probable connection between Baron La Hontan, Hennepin, and Blathwayt.

[10] "A bull of Bookes & Papers belonging to the Hudsons Bay Comp[a] which were delivered by order of the Dep[t] Govern[r] and Comittee to S[r] Edward Dering K[t] for their use the 14th Septem[r] 1698." H.B.Co. Archives, Memorial Book, 1698–1719, ff. 2, 3.

[11] *Cal. St. Pap., Am. & W. I., 1699*, p. 207. Those who wish to read the claims and counter claims will find many of them in the Calendar of State Papers for 1699; and in the Archives des Colonies, C[11], Correspondance Générale, a volume of boundary regulations, 1685–1700, Vol. 1; as well as in the manuscripts of the Earl of Ashburnham in the Stowe MSS in the British Museum ("Transactions between England and France relating to Hudson's Bay in 1698 and 1699").

[12] H.B.Co. Archives, A/6/3.

As for our takeing Mr Radisons Advice in our Affayres you need not Doubt for wee doe apprehend his perticular Evidence in the Primier occupancy of those Places [*Hudson Bay*] to be substantiall, & hope will prove convinceing. And notwithstanding any former misunderstanding betwixt the Comittee & Mr Radison, the Com^tt will not be ungrateful for any service he shall doe them to the utmost of his Merit, which he may assuredly depend upon.

This letter reveals that Young was once more active in the Company's affairs after several years of silence as far as the Company's books are concerned. Apparently his great labors in 1687, under similar conditions, were recalled and his advice was sought. This letter also throws a ray of light on who he was: "Wee hope you will be mindfull of what the Dept. Govr spoke to you in the Lobby of the House of Commons, that you will be pleased to make all your freinds in the House of Lords for the passing of the Russia bill."

Young's letter had an immediate effect. Though Radisson had won a suit against the Company in 1697 and had petitioned Parliament against regranting the Company's charter in 1698 unless a clause in his favor should be inserted in it, Young's hint carried weight.[13] On February 17, 1699, Radisson was called before the deputy Governor and the Committee to be "discoursed" concerning the Company's affairs, "now goeing to be heard before the English & French Commiss^rs." [14] For his pains he got, on March 7, fifteen pounds as "a gratuity by the Comittee for the Buying him a sute of Clothes &c." [15] Moreover, on the seventeenth of March it became necessary to elect a committee man in place of the late Samuel Shepard. Young was unanimously chosen.[16] Again Radisson had a powerful friend on the Committee.

Meanwhile in France a similar dragnet was spread for all possible evidence of French occupancy of Hudson Bay before the English settled there. Some one recalled the Dutchman,

13 See *post*, Appendix 13.
14 H.B.Co. Archives, A/1/21.
15 H.B.Co. Archives, Ledger 106, f. 39.
16 H.B.Co. Archives, A/1/21.

PART OF ENSIGN DE FONVILLE'S MANUSCRIPT MAP OF NORTH AMERICA. 1699.

[Paris. Service Hydrographique, B 4040.9b.]

Van Heemskerk, who had stolen Des Groseilliers' story in
1670 and sold it to Louis XIV. Now Van Heemskerk in his
old age was looked up and requested to tell of his relative's
first trip to the "Florida of the North." [17] By 1697, however,
even the French saw through his story, and nothing was made
of it in the negotiations.

It is worth a mention that the French made no use of a
certain document of this period by D'Iberville, reviewing the
whole story of the discovery of the Bay, of English and
French claims, and of Radisson and Des Groseilliers' trips
thither. The reason is obvious: D'Iberville states mercilessly
that Englishmen were in the Bay long before Frenchmen. He
refers to remains of white occupation that he had seen, especially on Charlton Island and "at Port Nelson, three
leagues up the river, on the north shore, where two English
ships spent a winter and where the larger vessel was left . . .
These were the first Europeans that ever appeared in that
place, according to the Indians. I do not know the year."
Another comment that may be made on this memoir by
D'Iberville is that it is the only fairly contemporaneous document that gives correctly the details of Radisson's return to
France in 1683 and his seduction by Preston and Godet.[18]

The Ryswick commissioners' negotiations came to nothing,
the war of the Spanish Succession began, and the future of
the Bay and the Company remained uncertain until 1713.

---

[17] Lawrence Van Hemskerk [also Heemskerck] to De Pontchartrain, July 1,
July 29, and August 5, 1697, in BN., Margry Papers, 9284, ff. 10, 11, 30, 31, 32–
34. See *ante,* p. 125.

[18] BN., Margry Papers, 9284, ff. 113–120.

CHAPTER XXIV

Death Comes for the Explorer

In March, 1697/8, the Hudson's Bay Company petitioned Parliament for the "Continuance of a former Act for Confirmeing to the Gov[r] & Comp[a] of Hudson Bay their Priviledges & Trade." This was the signal for many groups and persons to protest against the monopoly of the Company. The Company of Feltmakers in London, the "Master Wardens & Comonalty of the Mistery of Skiners" in London; the "Merchants & others trading to New England New Yorke &c[a]"; "Severall persons Concerned in the Ship Charles, Captain Lucas [*a former Company employee*] Comander"; and others protested.[1] Some were against any charter, others were for a charter with certain insertions. Radisson joined the latter group of oddly assorted persons, petitioning, in the interest of his "four small children all borne in England," that Parliament "insert a Proviso in the Bill depending to grant the s[d] Annuity to be paid—Quarterly, & the Dividends of the s[d] Actions [*stocks*] as often as any shall become due to your Pet[r] & his Heires for Ever, dureing the Joint Stock of the said Comp[a]." [2] Though the outcry was great and rather terrifying to the Company, the corporation was able to convince Parliament that its charter should be renewed. In the renewal no mention was made of the right of Radisson's heirs to his share of the stock. He evidently feared that death might come to him before his children were grown. However, he was to live many years yet and give his family the benefit of his pension, though half of it was received, not quarterly, as he preferred, but annually.

[1] See H.B.Co. Archives, Miscellaneous File, 1540–1740; and A/1/20, the entry for March 16, 1697/8.
[2] See *post*, Appendix 13.

Late in 1700 at a committee meeting it was reported that the Company's warehouse keeper was dead. Three persons petitioned the Committee for the job, among them Radisson. To be quite impartial the Company had lots drawn. Radisson was not successful.[3] The salary was thirty pounds per year and so would not have invalidated his second pension of fifty pounds, payable by court order until he should get a job equal to or greater than fifty pounds in value.

This was Radisson's last essay to better his fortune through the Company. His last decade appears to have been quiet and uneventful. Quarter after quarter the books of the Company were inscribed, "To Peter Espritt Radisson £12..10..00." Once a year there was an entry in October or November for fifty pounds for the annual payment ordered by the court. His second wife must have died—there is no mention of a wife in his petition of 1698—and a third marriage must have been contracted, for his will mentions his dear wife Elizabeth. His second wife's name was Margaret Charlotte. Moreover, his will mentions his "three small daughters."[4] But Margaret's children could hardly have been termed "small" in 1710, for at least four of them were born prior to 1692. The will refers to "my former Wifes Children being by me according to my ability advanced and preferred to severall Trades." Such a statement infers that all of Margaret's surviving children were males. That there were no other surviving children of Elizabeth's, other than the small daughters, may be inferred from the phraseology of the will: "to apply and dispose of for the support and advancement of my said dear Wife and my three small daughters on her begotten and now Living my former Wifes Children being by me according to my ability advanced and preferred to severall Trades."

Early in 1709, Radisson's staunch friend, William Young, died, having served more than ten years as a Company com-

---

[3] H.B.Co. Archives, A/1/22, October 31, November 14, 1700.
[4] Radisson's will. See *post*, Appendix 15.

mitteeman.[5] His will mentions both the Company and Radisson. To the latter he forgave a debt of about fifty-three pounds.[6] Marlborough's sun had risen higher and higher and his victories were soon to restore to the Company all that vast empire that the Company owed in large part to Radisson. However, when that result was achieved by the Treaty of Utrecht in 1713, Radisson had been in his grave for three years.

One other friend of this period is known to us only by name and occupation. One of the two executors of Radisson's will was "my trusty and beloved Freind James Heanes of the City of London Winecooper." The other was "my beloved and dear Wife Elizabeth Radisson."

On June 17, 1710, Radisson made his will. Even as death beckoned to him he remembered the furs that the Hudson's Bay Company had owed him, as he believed and argued, since 1684. After the usual preliminaries the will states:

And Whereas I did at the desire of his late Majestie King Charles the second and his late Majestie King James the second when Duke of York and those imployed by them quitt the Interest and Service of the Present French King and imbrace the Service of their said Majesties and that of the English Nation and by my means severall Colonys in America formerly in the possession of the French were reduced into the Obedience of the late King Charles the Second and the same continue now in the possession of her present Majesty and her Subjects to the great advantage of the English Nation and in particular of the Society or Company of Hudsons Bay a great part of which transactions is in the memory of his Grace the Duke of Marlborrough to whose care I have been recommended by the late King James before the Revolution . . . And whereas besides what is due on account of the said Pension there is now above Eighteen hundred pounds due to me for other demands I justly have to the said Company I doe hereby devise and my Will is that my said Executor and Executrix . . . do pay and satisfy all my just debts and the residue to apply [to the support of] my dear Wife and my three small daughters.

[5] H.B.Co. Archives, A/1/31, entry of March 30, 1709.
[6] Young's will is filed in Somerset House. It is printed post, Appendix 14.

Sometime between June 17 and July 2, 1710, Pierre Esprit Radisson died. His will was proved on July 21, 1710. On July 2 the "Secretary [*of the Hudson's Bay Company*] is ordered to pay Mr Radisons widow as Charity the Sume of Six pounds." [7] Probably this sum was intended to help defray funeral expenses. No record of his interment has been found, though a great deal of search has been made to locate it. His widow seems never to have attempted to claim the eighteen hundred pounds from the Company.

Almost exactly a year later a Marguérite des Groseilliers was buried across the Atlantic in Three Rivers.[8] Presumably it was Des Groseilliers' widow, though possibly it was his daughter. On May 11, 1722, Elizabeth La Valée [*sic*], née Radisson, aged eighty-six years, was interred in the same place.[9] The explorer, his brother-in-law, and all his sisters were gone.

Radisson's widow survived him many years. It is sad to relate that she died in extreme poverty. On September 24, 1729, the secretary of the Hudson's Bay Company's Committee was "Order'd to pay Mrs Radison Widow of Mr Peter Esprit Radison who was formerly Employ'd in the Company's Service, the Sum of ten Pounds as Charity, She being very Ill and in great want, the said Sum to be paid her at such times as the Sec^r shall think most convenient." [10] It is worth noting, perhaps, that the next year Mrs. Elizabeth Kelsey, widow of the "late Governor at York Fort," petitioned the Company for money with which to apprentice her son.[11] Another of Radisson's old Bay acquaintances, and very likely his pupil, was gone and his widow was seeking help from the Company.

Elizabeth Radisson survived for a few years her illness

[7] H.B.Co. Archives, A/1/32.
[8] Three Rivers, parish registers, June 22, 1711.
[9] Three Rivers, parish registers, May 11, 1722.
[10] H.B.Co. Archives, Foul Minute Book, 1726–1731.
[11] H.B.Co. Archives, Foul Minute Book, 1726–1731, entry for January 28, 1729/30.

and poverty. What appears to be her interment record is found in the books of Saint Bennet Sherehog, London, under date of January 2, 1732. There it is entered that "Elizabeth Radiston" was buried that day in the churchyard.[12]

[12] *The Register of the Burials of the United Parishes of St Stephen in Walbrook, & St Bennet Sherehog in the City of London, from the Year of Our Lord, 1716* (Publications of the Harleian Society, Vol. 50, Part 2, p. 175, London, 1920).

Early Trips to Hudson Bay

Though De la Tour's trip or trips to Hudson Bay have not been proved, three Canadian historians state that he was trading there between 1646 and 1650.[1] In those same years, a refugee from his home, he was spending much time in Quebec and Three Rivers,[2] where he was associated with many persons with whom Des Groseilliers and the Radisson family had then, or were later to have relations of one sort or another: Etienne Racine, the brother-in-law of Hélène Martin Chouart, and very likely one of Des Groseilliers' companions in Huronia; Jean Godefroy, Sieur de Lintot, a founder of Three Rivers, in whose home the sister of Pierre Esprit Radisson was living; and Jean Bourdon, who headed an expedition to Hudson Bay

[1] Thomas C. Haliburton, *An Historical and Statistical Account of Nova Scotia*, 1:60 (Halifax, 1829); François X. Garneau, *History of Canada From the Time of Its Discovery till the Union Year (1840–1841)*, translated and edited by Andrew Bell, 1:169 (Montreal, 1860); [Benjamin Sulte], ed., *Collection de manuscrits*, 1:302, note.

[2] Benjamin Sulte, *Histoire des canadiens-français*, 4:143. Father Druillettes, who was sent to Boston by New France in 1651 to endeavor to get help against the Iroquois, states that on December 9, 1651, "I was led by my interlocutor and the major-general here (Mr. Quebin [*Gibbons*], a great friend of M. de la Tour and so of the governor of Quebec), to Mr. Dudley." "The major-general would be all powerful, if he had a little instruction in this war. Try, please, to have M. de la Tour write him on this subject." See *Le Canada Français*, August, 1933, which contains the "Rapport du R. P. Druillettes," which is quite different from the report in the *Jesuit Relations*, 36:82–111. It is at least curious that another would-be discoverer of the Northwest Passage arrived in Quebec on the same day as De la Tour. This was Captain Poulet of Dieppe. See *Jesuit Relations*, 28:223. On November 10, 1670, Talon wrote Colbert of this man: "The proposal made to me by Captain Poullet of Dieppe ought to be mentioned here. This man, wise by long practice and experience acquired from an early age, and become a skillful navigator, offers to undertake the discovery, if not yet accomplished, of the passage between the two seas, the Southern and Northern, either by David's Strait or by that of Magellan, which he thinks more certain. After having doubled the opposite coasts of America, as far as California, he will take the western winds, and . . . re-enter by Hudson's bay or David's strait." O'Callaghan, ed., *Documents Relative to the Colonial History of the State of New York*, 9:67–70.

in 1657, which all but succeeded.³ Though Englishmen and Danes had long been acquainted with Hudson Bay, Canadians were not able to find a way thither by sea until Des Groseilliers and Radisson in 1682 showed them a route long familiar to the brothers-in-law. Des Groseilliers may have learned that route from De la Tour, from certain New England mariners, or from actual trips that he himself made.

New England enterprise in Hudson Bay has never been studied adequately, but it seems certain that daring mariners from that area penetrated to the bay soon after English seamen gave up their interest in it in the early part of the century, when it became necessary for them to turn their thoughts to civil war. The bold exploits of Hudson, Foxe, James, Button, and others might well have been forgotten in the forties, fifties, and sixties, but for New Englanders.

In 1708, in the April and June issues of the *Monthly Miscellany, or Memoirs for the Curious,* of London, there appeared a letter purporting to have been written by a Spanish naval officer, Admiral Bartolomeo de Fonte, giving a succinct account of his discovery of a northeast passage from the Pacific in 1640. According to that letter the viceroys of New Spain and Peru, learning of a search for the Northwest Passage undertaken by men of Boston in 1639, ordered Admiral de Fonte to sail in four "Ships of Force" from the western edge of the continent to circumvent the Bostonians. He left Callao on April 3, 1640, having under his command, among others, Diego Peñalosa. Sailing and paddling north and east they finally reached an open sea, presumably Hudson Bay, where on July 17, 1640, they met in a vessel an elderly man and a youth.

They told me the Ship was of *New-England,* from a town call'd Boston. The Owner and the whole Ship's Company came on board . . . and the Navigator of the Ship, Captain *Shapley,* told me, his owner was a fine Gentleman and Major-General of the largest Colony in *New-England,* called the Massachusets; so I received him like a Gentleman and told him, my Commission was to make prize of any People seeking a North-west or West Passage into the *South-Sea,* but I would look upon them as Merchants trading with the Natives for Beavers, Otters, and other Furs and Skins.

³ Judicial Archives, Quebec, *greffe* Claude Lecoustre; parish registers in the court-house in Three Rivers, which are copies of the originals in the possession of the parishes; the marriage record of Etienne Dumais and Françoise Morin, Judicial Archives, Quebec, *greffe* Claude Lecoustre, January 1, 1648; and *A General Index to the Proceedings and Transactions of the Royal Society of Canada, 1882–1906* (Toronto, 1908), under the name of Jean Bourdon.

Appendices 283

De Fonte obtained several charts from Captain Shapley and sent a cask of wine to the owner of the vessel, Gibbons.[4] This document is considered a hoax by historians, and it is of interest to the present study only through its reference to actual men living in New England in De la Tour and Des Groseilliers' day, who are thereby reported as trading in Hudson Bay. It is easy enough to see why the Spaniards would choose to represent that they entered Hudson Bay from the West. By the papal line of demarcation, they were prohibited from entering from the Atlantic side.

Major-General Edward Gibbons was a friend and financial backer of De la Tour. There were many Shapleighs in New England in the middle of the seventeenth century. Nicholas Shapleigh of York and Charlestown was a well-known sea captain and colonial cartographer, of whom tall tales are told.[5]

Did De la Tour get his knowledge of Hudson Bay from Gibbons and Shapleigh and pass it on to Des Groseilliers? Nothing is proved, but circumstantial evidence points in that direction. There is even a possibility that Des Groseilliers went with De la Tour on one of

[4] Nellis Crouse, *In Quest of the Western Ocean*, p. 418 (New York, 1928); John G. Palfrey, *History of New England*, 2:225–227 (Boston, 1890); *North American Review*, 48:129–132; "A Letter From Bartholomew de Fonte" in Arthur Dobbs's *An Account of the Countries adjoining to Hudson's Bay*, pp. 123–130 (London, 1744); and in H. R. Wagner, "Apocryphal Voyages" in American Antiquarian Society *Proceedings*, n.s., 41 (1931), pp. 179–234. Wagner is not completely convincing in his argument.

[5] For the Shapleigh family see "The deposiecion of Mr Benjamin Gillam Eaged 45 years or thare abouts" of May 12, 1654, in the Gullison case at Piscataqua, *Maine Historical Collections*, Second Series, 4:114. Gibbons was the "younger brother of the house of an honourable extraction." See J. Scottow, *A Narrative of the Planting of the Massachusetts Colony* in *Massachusetts Historical Collections*, Fourth Series, 4:289. See also *The Voyage of Captain Luke Foxe of Hull and Captain Thomas James of Bristol, in Search of a North-West Passage, in 1631–32; with Narratives of the Earlier North-West Voyages of Frobisher, Davis, Weymouth, Hall, Knight, Hudson, Button Gibbons . . . and Others*, edited with notes and introduction by Miller Christy (London, 1894). See also page 42 of the reference in the *Maine Historical Collections* for mention of a Shapleigh in 1652. See also "A map of the Carolina coast, as explored by William Hilton and drafted in 1652 by Willian Shapley," in the British Museum and reproduced in the Massachusetts Historical Society's *Proceedings*, 20:402; and also Justin Winsor, ed., *Narrative and Critical History of America*, 5:98 (Boston and New York, 1884–1889). A Nicholas Shapleigh was living in Kittery, Maine, on May 14, 1667. See *Maine Historical Collections*, Second Series, 4:207. For a curious pronouncement of 1674 relative to the current belief that the Spaniards had found and used a channel between the South Sea and Hudson Bay, see the Royal Society's *Philosophical Transactions*, 9:208.

the latter's trips to Hudson Bay. In 1816 a London quarterly published an article mentioning Des Groseilliers (who was quite unknown as an historical character to the author) stating that "about the time" of Captain Thomas James's discoveries in Hudson Bay in 1631, Des Groseilliers had reached Hudson Bay "from Quebec for the purpose of discovery." "Landing near Nelson's River, he fell in with a wretched hut in which were six people nearly famished. They were part of the crew of a ship which had been sent from Boston, and which, while they were on shore, had been driven to sea by the ice, and was never heard of more." The author goes on with Des Groseilliers' story, through his visit to France, his introduction to Prince Rupert, and the founding of the Hudson's Bay Company. The source of information is unknown and unique, but it bears the mark of authenticity. It is not necessary to believe that the date was 1631, for the author himself is vague on the point.[6]

In 1640 a man, now at last almost certainly identified as Sir Thomas Yonge, or Young, a relative of John Evelyn the diarist, was picked up by the Jesuits in the St. Lawrence after he had made at least two trips up the Atlantic coast and its tributaries in quest of a Northwest Passage.[7] His latest trip had been up the Kennebec River and overland to a tributary of the St. Lawrence. He said that he was trying to find the Northwest Passage by way of the Saguenay River. Needless to remark, the Jesuits saw him safely out of North America before he should discover what they hoped to find. Years later a William Yonge, or Young, of whom there is slight record except in the books of the Hudson's Bay Company, was Radisson's stoutest defender among the members of that Company when he sorely needed friendship and aid. Were the two Yonges related? If so, the reason for William Yonge's sponsorship of Radisson may conceivably go back to Canadian days.[8] One historian of merit states that Des

---

[6] See *The Quarterly Review* (Oct., 1816), 26:160 (London, 1817).

[7] *Jesuit Relations,* 18:235.

[8] See *post,* p. 336. When he died in 1709, Young was a resident of the parish of St. Andrews, Holborn, London. A William Young, Esquire, was the custodian of Hampton Court and Park in 1670. See British Museum, Additional MS, 38,862, the docquet book of Sir Edward Dering, as one of the keepers of the privy seal from September 22, 1669, to April 19, 1673. Dering later was deputy governor of the Hudson's Bay Company. Young's will of 1703 mentions his stock in the mines of Cardiganshire, his Hudson's Bay Company and African Company stock, his interest in the "Company for raising water by Fire known by the name of Captain Thomas Savery's invention," and other scientific ventures.

"Captain Thomas Young, who was a gentleman of influence in London, received a special commission from the King, which is printed in the nineteenth

Groseilliers, after returning from Huronia in August, 1646, "became, at first, a soldier in the Quebec garrison, and then a pilot on the St. Lawrence." The author gives no authority for his remark and it is a trifle hard to reconcile a part of it with Radisson's explicit denial in 1697 that either he or his brother-in-law was a pilot.[9]

volume of Rymer's *Fœdera,* and dated September 23, 1633, authorizing him to fit out ships, appoint officers to explore all territories in America that he wished. . . . In the spring of 1634 the exploring expedition departed, the Lieutenant of which was Robert Evelyn [*a footnote states that his mother was Susan Young, daughter of Gregory Young of York*], a nephew of Young, and cousin of John Evelyn, the celebrated author of Sylva. . . . Early in 1635 Lieutenant Evelyn returned to England on special business, while Young continued to seek for a navigable inland passage for ships from the Atlantic Ocean to the South Sea. . . . After eighteen months passed in discoveries, and seeking an inland water route through the American continent, supposed to be somewhere about the fortieth parallel of latitude, Young proceeded to England, and asked that the King would grant permission for him and his associates to enjoy the right to such inland countries as they might discover." Edward D. Neill, *English Colonization of America,* pp. 261–263 (London, 1871). See also *Cal. St. Pap., Dom.,* *1635–1636.* Fulmer Mood has furnished the author with many references to Young and his discoveries. See also *ante,* p. 227, for another mention of Young, when he ascended the Kennebec River in 1640.

[9] *Jesuit Relations,* 28:319, Note 32. Sulte, *Histoire des canadiens-français,* 5:5, note, says that Chouart's marriage contract of November 16, 1646, states that he was "at present a soldier of the Quebec garrison." The contract seems to be no longer in existence. "Desgroziliers & Radisson were neither of them Pilotts or Marriners," is the statement in "The Narrative of M[r] Peter Espritt Radisson in Refferance to the Answer of the Comm[rs] of France to the Right and Title of the Hudson Bay Company," in the PRO., S.P., Amer. & W. I., Vol. 539, under date of June 5, 1699. It is printed in Appendix 11 of this volume.

Extract of Mr Thomas Gorst's Journall in the Voyage to Hudsons Bay begun the 31th day of May 1670 [1]

May 31th The Rupert commanded by Capt Zachariah Guillam together with the Wyvenhoe under command of Capt Robert Newland set saile from Ratcliffe.

June 9 Wee Anchored in the Downes, & sailed thence Westward Lat: 50^d 2: [*June*] 13 Wee passed the Lands end and Silly Islands 59^d: 45' July 20 Wee saw Ice & ye 29th fell in 60: 43' with abundance of it 1870 miles to the Westward of Silly Lat: 61^d 20' Augt 7th Wee passed the Island Resolution & entered the Streights being 1938 miles West of Silly

Lat. 63: 1' [*August*]	16 Wee passd by Cape Charles
	17 by Cape Wolstenholme & Digg's Island
	18 The 2 shipps parted Wee steering So: West for Ruperts River & Capt Newland West for Port Nelson
59^d 43'	20 Wee passed by some small Islands called Bakers dozen
	28 Sailed by Beare Isle in Lat 54^d 28'
51^d 36'	29 Wee saw ye West maine full of wood & Low Land
	30 Wee saw Point Comfort about 14 leagues short of Ruperts River (& about 2930 miles from Silly)
	31 Wee Anchored there. The Capt Mr Foster, Mr Goosberry & I went ashore killd some Fowle & stayd all night, in the morning 2 of the Natives of the Captaines old Acquaintance came to us called Noah & his Brother

[1] "Gorst's Journal to Hudson's Bay in 1670, n⁰ 11" in the Guildhall Library, London. Printed by permission of the Guildhall Library, owners of the copyright.

Sep^t 1 came six Canoes more with Men Women and children

5 The Long boat was sent out to sound the River & at her returne the Boatswain brought word that the house was standing as they left it & that at ⅔ flood there was neare 2 fathom Water over the Barr.

7th Wee weighed & stood for the River & came aground upon the Barr at ¾ floud but got very well off in an houre.

Septemb^r 8th By sailing and warping wee got up the River & Anchored before Charles Fort in 2½ fathom at low Water. The Capt & 4 more goe a shore & kill 8 geese. An Indian called Damaris comes to us & quickly after went to call his Companions from the Woods where they were hunting.

9 Wee get the Cargoe a shore

10 Unrigg the Vessell & the Capt killd 27 geese [*Here was added later:*] & every day after we killd more or lesse untill ye cold weather sent them more southerly

12 All hands goe to worke to make a Dock for ye ship over against our house. The Carpenter in ye mean time goes to ye wood & cutts Timber to build the Captain a new house The Indians come to us a pace & are willing to Trade.

19 The Dock being finished Wee get in ye ship wth a high Tide

20 Wee rummage the Hold get out the Beere & bury it under ground to preserve it from freezing that wee may not want for our homeward bound Voyage. And the Beere which Wee spent upon the place wee brewd there having malt along with us from England for that purpose. All hands are every day at worke about the new house some getting of Osier or thatch, others thatching the house (at which the Capt & Mr Foster were Principall Artists), Some fetching clay for morter, others bricks from ye ship for a chimney, & no one exempled [?] or backward in carrying on the worke.

27 The Indians set up their Wigwams or Hutts which is almost in the manner of a Tent, covered with Moose & Deere skins dress'd, close of all sides & a hole at ye top for ye smoke to vent it selfe at. Their bedds are bowes of pine & spruce which are much like ye English Ferne & their Bever coats serve them for sheets blanketts & Ruggs. Those Tents they make bigger or lesser at pleasure, sometimes I have known 16 or 18 men women & children pigg

all together, much like ye Irish but onely that here are
no cowes nor hogs to keep them company although indeed these poor wretches are scarce fit for any better society. Septemb^r 29th Some of ye Natives brought store of
fresh fish as Pikes which are very large   Some I have
seen 6 foot long, with attickemeck or scaly fish of ye big-
ness of a perch. There is also fresh Sturgeon very good &
Salmon trout plenty enough. They themselves feast cheifly
on dryed moose and Beaver, bread they have none nor
any thing in stead of it. The bones of those beasts they
use to bruise & boile & ye fat arising thence they skim off
& keep like butter, which they call cockamo & serves for
sauce to all their delicate dishes—heretofore they used to
boile their victualls in some of ye skins of those beasts
they feed on, but now they find the better convenience of
our English kettles. Their dishes are made of the out-
most rind of Birch which they work so close together that
they will hold water as well as our wooden platters. When
they eat they sit upon ye ground which serves them for
Tables stooles & Table cloth; Trenchers they use none
& their own tawny bodies serve for napkins, which are so
much more beautifull by how much they are the more
greasy.

When the weather grew colder they removed their Wigwams from
us some leagues into the woods for ye better conveniency of killing
Deere & wild fowle with which they often came & supplyed us, as
also with some share of hares in winter as white as Snow.

The men are much about our stature, & borne in a manner as
white as ye English but with grease & paint they spoile their Skins
& make themselves look very deformed. The Women differ not from
them in habit, onely that the Cape of their coats hang down behind
Somewhat like a monks hood whereas the men weare theirs close to
their necks. Also ye mens haire hang long & for ye most part down-
right, but ye womens are generally plaited.

Our English houses consisted of three roomes a peece & as many
severall floors. The Cellar held ye beer wee brewd there for our dayly
drinking, together with the Beefe Pork and Butter. The Chamber
held our dry Provisions as bread, flower, peas & Oatmeale and on the
ground floore was our kitchin, Dyning roome & Lodgings—which
were Standing Cabbins such as are used in his Maties shipps. The
houses themselves are built of Timber cut into Sparrs set quite close
to one another & calked with Mosse instead of Okam to keep out y^e

wind & yᵉ weather. Thatched with a ranke sort of grasse growing in
yᵉ marshes much like yᵉ Saggs [?] wᶜʰ are every where in our English brookes. Wee had a large Chimney built of bricks which wee
carryed along with us, & wee spared not ye wood, that Country affording enough to keep alwayes Summer within, while nothing but
Ice & snow are without doores. Wee had also erected a good Oven &
feasted our selves at pleasure with venson pasty.

October 12 Both the houses being in a manner compleated Severall
of Our Company are sent into the woods to provide fewell for yᵉ
winter which now begins to come on a pace.

Afternoon a Great Boat makes into Ruperts River, being the longboat of yᵉ Wyvenhoe. in her Mʳ Radison & 3 more who relate their
misfortunes. That at Mansfeilds Island presently after they parted
from us their ship struck upon some rocks & was in great danger of
being lost. That at Port Nelson they also run aground, & found no
entrance in to yᵉ River there. That 2 of their men were dead & the
Captain & severall of them sick. That yᵉ Ship now rode at point
Comfort.

[October] 13 Next morning Capᵗ Gillam, Mʳ Foster & 6 more
went out in our owne boat & I with 4 more in yᵉ Wivenhoes boate
Wee run aground upon yᵉ barr & were forced to stay till the Flood
brought us off, though it were bitter freezing weather, so cold that yᵉ
water thickned & stuck to Our Oares while wee were rowing.

October 14ᵗʰ Capᵗ Newland dyed at 10 in yᵉ morning

16 Capᵗ Gillam Instructed yᵉ Wivenhoes boatswaine what to doe
with the ship, & himselfe with his own Boat returned for Ruperts
River. Wee set saile also with yᵉ ship & next day came safe to an
Anchor ½ a mile below yᵉ place where yᵉ Prince Rupert was in Dock.

18 Capᵗ Newland was buryed by our new house like a Soldier
wee gave him some Gunns from both yᵉ Shipps & followed his corps
to yᵉ grave in Armes.

20 Capᵗ Bayly begins a Dock for yᵉ Wivenho at which work our
shipps Company are aiding, & wee get some of their Provisions &
Cargoe into Our houses.

22 Wee leave the ship & ly ashore at our new Quarters. yesterday
snowd hard & now lyes 4 feet thick on yᵉ ground.

24 Capᵗ Newlands things were exposed to sale at yᵉ Mast on
board yᵉ Prince Rupert.

28 That shipps Company set up their Wigwam covered in stead of
skins with old sailes the cold weather being too far advanced to admit
of yᵉ building another house.

Novemb 20 The River was quite frozen over being a mile and ½ from Side to Side

23 The Indians brought us a young Deere wch they had killed & [sic] ye woods & they used afterwards to bring us fresh Venson & truck it for our peas which they love extreamly but hate beef & pork & every thing which tasts of ye salt

Decemb^r 17 Wee caught a white Fox & afterwards severall other of that & other colours.

25 being Christmas day wee made merry remembering our Freinds in England, having for Liquor Brandy & strong beer & for Food plenty of Partridges & Venson besides what ye shipps provisions afforded.

January 16. Capt Gillam fell ill of ye Scurvy, which is there the onely dangerous disease, but quickly recovered.

29 Mr Radison went to Moose Cebee a broad River about 18 leagues off the banks wherof are well furnished with streight & tall Trees of Pine & Spruce fit for Masts, some of them being near 60 inches circumference.

March 14 he returned from thence but could give no accompt of the depth of ye River it being frozen over all ye while, & that was ye place where afterwards ye Governo^r went along with him & traded with ye People of that place & from thence had all ye Beaver which was brought home in ye Wivenho, which neverthelesse wee beleeve would have been brought to Ruperts River if no body had went thither to fetch it.

The first of this month I left Capt Gillam & listed myselfe with ye Governour Bayly among those who were designed to stay in the Country having a great desire so to doe, & I am sure many other would have been willing if the Governo^r had commanded them.

Warm weather comes on apace

31 Wee sowd Peas & Mustardseed which came up well enough for ye time wee stayd there & no doubt but all sorts of rootes would have grown very well if Wee had been furnished with seed. Wee kept theire some hens & hoggs which lived & did well enough

Aprill 18 Mr Manning & Mr Walker were sent to ye other side of Ruperts River for convenience of killing ye wild fowle especially Geese which in ye spring come hither in great numbers, but by ye later end of May or beginning of June Fly more Northwards & breed in ye lands & Islands about the Streights.

May 16 The weather begins to grow hot & ye mosquitos to be very busy

22 The River was quite cleere of Ice

30 Wee launched ye Shallop wee had built there & the Gover-
no^r named her the Royall Charles

June 28 Wee broke ground from Charles Fort

July   1 Wee weighed & left Ruperts River & came to an Anchor at
Point Comfort, where wee cut wood for our Voyage & prepared for
our return homewards.

 5 The Governo^r with severall others whereof I was one went
in ye Shallops to make further discoveries. Upon an Island wee found
an old wigwam not built by Indians, but suppose it rather to bee y^e
place where poor Hudson ended his dayes. From thence wee sailed
among severall Islands & land upon Charleton ye place where Capt
James of Bristoll wintered.   wee found severall barrell boards, Trees
sawne, & ye bones of some persons supposed to be ye same he buryed
there

 11 Wee returned to ye Ship.

 24 Weighed from Point Comfort & steered homewards

 30 in Lat 55^d: 0' wee come amongst Ice & from that time were
scarce ever free from it untill wee got quite cleere of Hudsons Streights
being near 300 leagues together.

Augt 14 Wee passd Digg's Island

 16 by Cape Charles

 Lost sight of Capt Gillam & could never come at him againe
untill wee found him in ye River of Thames

 27 Wee passd Buttons Isles in 61^d 27' being quite cleere of the
Streights & shaped our Course directly for England

Sep^t 30 At 6 in ye morning Wee saw Silly Islands &

Octob^r 2 Arrived safe at Plymouth

[*On the reverse side of the last sheet:*] Mr Paul Mercer gives this
Accompt of the Wivenhoe after she was parted from the other, & bound
for Port Nelson.

Augt 19th That they run aground upon a small low Island lying
even almost with ye Water about a league to ye Eastward of Mansfeilds & got not off without danger & damage. Mansfeilds Island is
high barren land having nothing upon it but snow undisolved. It is in
length about 26 leagues. Y^e So: end lyes in 61^d 30': 31'   They arrived
before Port Nelson in Lat 57^d: 0': but by reason of foggs & contrary
winds could not find ye right channell to get in.

Sep^t 14 They attempted it but run aground & were in much danger
ye wind blowing wth great violence, however ye Vessell came off with
ye losse of some Anchors & Cables.

The Tide rises & falls here, about 11 or 12 foot   there is very fine
Marsh land, & great plenty of wood about a mile beyond the Marshes,

yet not very large. There were ye remaines of some of ye Natives Wigwams & Sweating houses & some peeces of dressd Beaver skins, & they supposed the Indians had not long been gone from that place further Southward or higher into the Country. There is no want of food being great store of wild fowle Rabbets & Deeres. There was then upon the ground Straw berryes, Goosberryes, large red currans huckleberryes & Cramberryes. The weather beginning to grow cold apace & ye men being tired & disheartened with fruitlesse labour, Upon a Consultation it was resolved on as most fit, to saile to Ruperts River where they arrived & Anchored ye 17th October.

[*Endorsed:*] Gorst's Journal to Hudson's Bay in 1670. N° 11

APPENDIX 3

Radisson's Petition of 1677 [?] [1]

Radisson ayant acquis une particuliere connoissance de la plus grande partie de Lamerique Septentrionale tant par les voyages quil a faits dans toutes les terres comprises dans la nouvelle france que par le Seiour quil a fait ~~parmis les anglais dans les~~ au Nort et au Sud du mesme pays parmis les anglois lesquels il a quitté pour obeir aus ordres quil en a recus et satisfaire a linclination quil a touiours ue de servir sa patrie

prend la liberté de Representer que la Nouvelle france est un pays dune si grande estendue, si beau si fertile et si bien scitué quil semble que dieu lait reservé pour augmenter la puissance de la france et loger une partie du people dont elle est tellement remplie quil se repand de tous costes et principalement dans les estates voisins ou lon voit que les francois se vont establir tous les iours ne pouvant pas trouver de lemploy dans leur patrie

Le voyage de la nouvelle france est court et facile et lon ny est pas exposé aus maladies qui ont touiours fait perir une partie de ceux qui vont s'establir du coste de la ligne equinoctiale [2]

Le Climat ~~est~~ fort temperé et tout pareil a celuy de france particulierement au midy de la riviere de St Laurent, il produit ~~les naturels fruits~~ ou est propre a produire tout ce que peut la france comme on la vue par plusieurs experiences mais il a cela de plus quil surpasse la france en beaucoup de choses principalement en fourrures et en poissons de mer et deau douce en quoy il nya point de pays au monde qui lesgale

Cependant il est arrivé tant par les guerres civiles et estrangeres qui sont presque touiours agité la france que par les desordres du gouvernement du Canada [3] et les massacres que les Iroquois y faiserent ~~que~~ continuellement, que cette Colonie ne fait que languir depuis son establissement jusqu'a ce que S. M. apres avoir donné la paix a lancienne france en a fait ressentir les douceurs a la nouvelle en subuigant les Iroquois   depuis ce temps la par les soins de son ministre les habitans y

[1] An unsigned, undated manuscript, BN., Collection Clairambault, 1016, ff. 649–650.

[2] [*In the margin:*] lestendue en est tres vaste au couchant et au midy et

[3] [*In the margin:*] les entreprises de nos voisins sur le mesme pays

293

ont multiplis a veue [?] doeil et iusqu'au nombre ~~de plus~~ de 8 a $\frac{M}{10}$ ames mais par le malheur ord^{re} a la pluspart des francois qui ne suivent iamais de nouvelles routes si on ne leur trace le Chemin on a veu que depuis que des occupations plus pressantes ont empesché S. M. et ses ministres de les conduire commes par la mains ~~qu~~ ils ont cessé daug-menter en nombre et on ~~est~~ commencé de diminuer en Richesses.

La Cause nen est pourtant pas difficile a deviner, les 1ers françois qui allerent a la descouverte de ce pays esperoient dy trouver de grandes richesses mais ils ny rencontrerent que des fourrures dont le commerce nestant pas fort considerable ne les attira pas a sy establir comme auroient fait des mines dor et dargent ils y faisoient un voyage tous les ans sans y laisser personne, mais au commencement de ce siecle lon craignit que les estrangers ne nous vinssent enlever ce commerce et le pays mesme comme ils nous en avoient pris beaucoup dautres en divers endroits de lamerique on savisa de sy fortifier et dy former une Colo-nie, mais sans autre veue que de fournir aisement a la subsistence des habitans lorsquils ne passoient pas le nombre de mille ou 1200 a Cause que les anglois qui avoient chasse diverses fois les francois des costes de lacadie et de Quebec mesme et les courses continuelles des iroquois avoient empesché les habitans de multiplier davantage, de sestendre et de rechercher les richesses du pays

Mais ce qui est estonnant cest que depuis que la paix a este faitte avec les Iroquois et que les francois se sont augmentes iusqu'au nombre de pres de $\frac{M}{10}$ ames ils ont touiours suivy les mesmes brisees et se sont at-tachés uniquement aus Castors de telles Sorte que les profits de ce commerce diminuent tous les iours par le grand nombre et lavidité de ceux qui sen mesloient ils ont este contrains de se repandre au loin daller au devant des Sauvages de les aller chercher jusques dans leurs habitations de les achepter plus cher tous les iours a lenvis les uns des autres et den faire par ce moyen connoistre aus Sauvages le prix et la veritable valeur ~~de telle force~~ tellement que comme ce desordre alloit a la ruine de ce Commerce et mesme a la destruction entiere des castors de la Chasse, on fut obligé il y a pres de 3 ans de faire une compagnie pour le commerce des pelleteries laquelle connoissant la quantité que lon en devoit et pouvoit [?] debiter raisonnablement a reglé la traitte des Castors a la verite mais na pu toute fois remedier aus necessites de la Colonie, qui languira touiours au lieu de saugmenter et dont les plaints recommenceront tous les ans sans quon en puisse trouver dautre Cause que la petitesse du commerce du Castor et laveuglement et la foiblesse des habitans et cest ce que ie Crois pouvoir prouver demons-trativement.

Il est certain que les habitans nont presentament que deux moyens

pour subsister scavoir la Culture de la terre et les pelleteries, le 1er
peut servir a les nourrir avec layde de leurs bestiaux de la Chasse et de
la pesche quils font touiours de leurs habitations, mais il leur faut
outre cela du vin du tabac de leau de vie du sel des habits et de toute
sorte de hardis et dustensils   le commerce du bled ny peut presque rien
contribuer tant a cause que les lieux quils habitent ne sont pas les meilleurs du Canada que parcequil y a beaucoup dhabitans qui nen ont pas
iusque la fin de lannee et quainsy le pays ne scauroit de longtemps estre
en estat d'en fair commerce. Les pelleteries ne peuvent pas non plus y
suffire dautant que la Compagnie a veu par experience quelle ne pouvoit
debiter qu'environ 60000^{tt} Castors qui se vendent sur les lieux que
3^{tt} P [?] mais quand elle pouvoit en vendre $\frac{M}{100}$ et que les habitans
gaigneroient 20 P sur chacun ce ne seroit que $\frac{M}{100}$ de profit qui pourroient a la verité faire subsister commodement 100 ou 200 familles au
plus mais non pas 2 ou 3000 familles qui sont presentement establies
dans la nouvelle france et dont il y en a beaucoup qui au lieu dattirer
de Nouveaux habitans voudroient estre dans leur ancienne patrie
    ainsy ie Crois quil est evident que tant que les habitans sattacheront
comme ils font uniquement aus pelleteries il faudra necessairement que
la Colonie languisse et perisse peutestre tout a fait ou delle mesme ou
par la guerre que luy pourroient faire quelque iour les ennemis de lestat
ausquels elle ne seroit pas en estat de faire resistance, il faudroit a mon
avis laisser ce commerce tel qui est et sans y faire beaucoup de reflection
a la compagnie qui pourra peu a peu faire des avances aus habitans pour
faire des commerces beaucoup plus importans et ausquels ils ne songent
seulement pas et cest a cet aveuglement aussy bien que leur foiblesse
que iattribue toutes les miseres de cette colonie.
    Il faut remarquer icy pour impliquer ma pensee quil y a des richesses
immenses et inepuisables dans la nouvelle france qui la rendront asseurement si lon y travaille avec application le plus puissant pays de lamerique
en toutes manieres.   ces richesses sont de deux sortes les unes sont dans
les eaux et les autres peuvent estre tirees de la terre
    Les premieres consistent dans la pesche qui est sans difficulté la plus
abondante et la plus riche qui soit au monde ~~la plus riche pesche qui soit~~
[*illegible*] ~~est asseurement   celle de la morue~~ Celle de la Morue, verte
et seche, est sans dout la principale et la plus importante   on connoit
assez la bonté et la commodité de ce poisson   le grand debit qui sen fait
dans toute leurope et dans une partie de lamerique on scait quil y a
tous les ans pres de 600 vaisseaux employez a cette seule pesche et
quelle produit plusieurs millions a ceux qui sy occupent, en sorte que
ie ne crois pas quil y ait au monde un commerce dune seule chose si
considerable que celuy la   il doit appartenir aus francois preferablement

a toutes les autres nations par plusieurs raisons   ils ont este le premiers qui sen sont meslés, ils y travaillent davantage que toutes les autres nations ensembles et ce poisson ne se trouve presque que dans le golfe S^t laurent et sur les costes de Lacadie du Cap Breton et de lisle de terreneuve qui toutes appartiennent a la france a lexception peutestre de la Coste orientale de terreneuve ou il y a des anglois establis.

Mais outre cela on trouve presque par tout un nombre infiny de Saumons que lon pourroit saler et fumer [4] de truittes saumons desquelles iay mangé en france et qui se sont trouvees excellentes et dignes de la table dun prince   on les avoit apportees de plaisance qui est en la Coste meridionale de terreneuve. il y a une quantité inepuisable desturgeons dune grandeur extraord^{re} et si gras quil sera necessaire de les mettre sous la presse comme font les anglois. On en liveroit tant de Caviar que lon voudroit   ce sont des oeufs deschargés salés que les hollandois tirent de Moscovie et dont ils font un grand commerce   il y a aussy beaucoup de maquereaux tres bons et des bars dun pied et demie a 2 pieds de long que les anglois salent et transportent aus isles et en europe ces sortes de poissons produisent de grands profits aus estrangers qui mesmes en apportent en france une grande quantité et en tirent par ce moyen beaucoup dargent qui nen sortiroit pas

On peut aussy pescher beaucoup de baleines dans le golfe et sur la Coste de labrador, des vaches marines dont on tireroit quantité de dens de cuirs et dhuiles de poisson, des loups marins dont les peaux se vendent tres biens et dont lhuile est bonne a manger estant fraische et excellente pour brusler quand elles est vieille [?] dautant quelle ne iette aucune odeur et demeure touiours claire sans avoir presque aucune lie, et des marsouins dont on peut tirer quantité dhuiles et que lon trouve dans la riviere de S^t laurant et ailleurs ie ne larle pas des anguilles [5] lon pescheroit et saleroit en grand nombre si les habitans estoient en plus ~~grand nombre~~ nombreux et plus a leur ayse.
Cependent les francois ne profitent pas comme ils devroient de toutes les pesches qui seules seroient capable denrichir

TRANSLATION

Radisson, having acquired a peculiar knowledge of the greater part of North America both through the journeys that he has made in all the regions comprising New France and through his sojourn to the north and to the south of that country among the English, whom he has

[4] [*In the margin:*] dont des gens [*word illegible*] cent poissons un seul coup desquoy charger un Chaloupe ~~dun coup de filet~~
[5] qui lemportent sur toutes les autres ny des autres poissons de mer et deau douce

quitted in obedience to orders received and in order to satisfy his perennial desire to serve his fatherland,

takes the liberty of showing that New France is a country so vast, so beautiful, so fertile, and so well situated that it appears that God has reserved it to increase France's power and to shelter a part of the populace with which she is so overflowing that they extend in all directions, but principally in neighboring countries, where Frenchmen are seen to be establishing themselves continually, not being able to find employment in their own country.

The journey to New France is short and easy and one is not exposed during the passage to the illnesses which are forever causing a part of the emigrants to equinoctial countries to perish. Its extent is very great to the west and south and the climate is very temperate and similar to that of France, particularly in the region south of the St. Lawrence. It produces, or is capable of producing, everything that France can produce, as several experiences have revealed, but in certain respects it surpasses France, particularly in furs and in salt-water and fresh-water fish, for which it has no equal in the world.

Yet because of civil and foreign wars, which have agitated France almost constantly, and because of disorders in the government of Canada, the undertakings of our neighbors on the same continent, and the constant Iroquois wars, that colony has only languished from its first establishment until His Majesty gave peace to Old France and made its enjoyment felt in New France by subjugating the Iroquois. Since that time, through the cares of his minister, the inhabitants of that country have multiplied in the twinkling of an eye to eight or ten thousand souls. But through the customary misfortune of Frenchmen, who never seek out new ways if some one will lead them along old ones, it is noticeable that since more pressing business has prevented His Majesty and his ministers from leading them as by the hand, they have ceased to increase in number and have begun to lose their wealth.

The cause for this is not difficult to guess. The first Frenchmen who explored that country hoped to find there great wealth, but they found only furs. The trade in them not being very great, they were not led to go there to settle, as they would have done if there had been mines of gold or silver. They went there year by year and left no one there; but at the beginning of this century it was feared that foreigners would filch this commerce and even the country itself from us, as they had done in several other instances and in other places in America. It appeared advisable to settle a colony there, but without other aim than to furnish an easy subsistence to some thousand or twelve hundred habitants. They could not increase beyond those figures because of the

English, who chased the French several times from the shores of Acadia
and from Quebec itself; and because of the Iroquois, who prevented
the habitants from further increasing, of extending themselves, and of
searching out the riches of the country.

But it is astonishing that since peace was made with the Iroquois
and the habitants have increased in number almost to ten thousand
souls, they have followed the same course and devoted themselves entirely to beaver skins, so that the profits of that trade are diminishing
daily through the great number and the cupidity of those who engage
in it. They are forced to spread out into distant regions, to go to seek
the Indians in their homes, and to buy more dearly every day in emula-
tion of one another, thus showing the natives the true value of trade
articles. So this trade was being ruined and the complete destruction
of the beaver trade was being achieved three years ago when it became
necessary to form a fur-trade company, which, knowing the quantity
of furs that could be reasonably marketed, has regulated the beaver
trade, it is true, but which has not been able in all instances to remedy
the ills of the colony. It has ever languished instead of improving. Its
complaints are heard every year without any one's being able to find
the cause of the poverty of the beaver trade other than the blindness
and the feebleness of the habitants. It is that which I believe I can prove.

It is certain that at present the habitants have only two means of
support: agriculture and the fur trade. The first can keep them alive
with the aid of their stock, the fur trade, and fishing, which they continually prosecute from their dwellings; but in addition they must have
wine, tobacco, brandy, salt, clothes, and all sorts of equipment and
tools. Trade in wheat can contribute almost nothing, because the regions
they inhabit are not the best in Canada and because some of the people
themselves lack wheat by the end of the year. Thus the country can
hardly export any. Furs, in the same way, cannot suffice, especially
since the Company has seen that it cannot market more than 60,000
pounds of beaver, which sell on the spot at only three livres. But when
it could sell 100,000 and the habitants got 20 livres for every pound,
that was only 100,000 profit, which in truth could comfortably support 100 or 200 families at the most, but not 2,000 or 3,000 families,
the number now established in New France, many of whom would
prefer to be in their fatherland rather than trying to influence others
to go to New France.

Thus it is evident, I believe, that as long as the habitants rely solely
on the fur trade, the colony must languish and perhaps fail, either of
itself or through a war that some day their enemies may inflict on them
and which they will not be in condition to resist. It is necessary, in my

opinion, to leave that trade as it is and without further concern about it deliver its care over to the Company, which can make, little by little, some advances to the habitants. Other trades, much more important, which they give no thought to now must be undertaken. It is to this blindness as well as to their weakness that I attribute all their distress.

To indicate my thought I must remark that there are immense and inexhaustible resources in New France, which, if properly worked, will render it the most powerful country of America in every respect. These resources are of two kinds: one in the water and the other to be taken out of the soil.

The first consist of the fisheries, which are easily the most abundant and the richest in the world. That of the cod, both fresh and dried, is without doubt the chief and most important. The value and uses of that fish are well known, as well as the great market for it in all of Europe and in parts of America. It is known that every year close to six hundred vessels are employed in this fishery alone and that it produces many millions to those who are engaged in it, so that I believe that there is no commerce of any other single article in the world equal to it. It should belong to the French for several reasons. They were the first to engage in it; they have developed it more than all other peoples together; and this fish is found only in the Gulf of St. Lawrence and off the shores of Acadia, Cape Breton, and Newfoundland, all of which belong to France with the exception, perhaps, of the eastern side of Newfoundland, where the English are settled.

But in addition there are infinite numbers of salmon everywhere, which can be salted and smoked. [*Two*] hundred of these fishes can be caught at a time, filling a longboat with one netful. There are salmon trout, which I have eaten in France and which are considered excellent and worthy of the table of a prince. They have been taken at Plaisance, which is the southern shore of Newfoundland. There is an inexhaustible number of sturgeons, of extraordinary size and so fat that it is necessary to put them in a press, as the English do. From them one gets as much caviar as desired. That is the eggs of the sturgeon, salted, such as the Dutch get from Muscovy, which is a great trade for them. There are also many mackerels, very fine, bass a foot and a half to two feet in length, which the English salt and transport to the West Indies and to Europe. These kinds of fish offer great profits to foreigners, who even take them to France in great numbers and by this means withdraw much money, which should not leave the country.

Whales can also be caught in the Gulf and on the coast of Labrador; walruses, from which are obtained quantities of teeth, leather, and fish oil; seals, whose hides sell very well and whose oil is good to eat, while

fresh, and excellent to burn when it gets old, since it gives off no odor
and always remains clear with almost no dregs; and porpoises, from
which one can get quantities of oil, and which are found in the St.
Lawrence and elsewhere. I make no mention of eels, which surpass all
the others. They could be secured and salted in great numbers, if the
habitants were more numerous and more secure.

Yet the French do not profit as they should from all these fishes,
which alone are capable of enriching. . . .

[Notes for Radisson's Petition in Bernou's Handwriting] [6]

la pesche de la morue qui augmenteroit les barques et matelots tous les
francois le devenant, qui se nouriront du pays la Compagnie et autres
envoyant des vaisseaux et marchandises qui nauroient qua charger des
baleines dans le golfe et coste da labredor ou aussy vaches marines cuirs
huiles dans des marsouins dont de lhuyle dans la riviere S^t laurens, loups
marins partout dont peaux et huiles   truittes saumones amirables costes
de labredor et de terreneuve plaisance dont mangé en france excellens
caviar ou eufs desturgeons infinis

maquereaux saumons et esturgeons infinis trop gras mais bons par un
moyen quon scait mettre sous la presse, anguilles, petites morues frayans
au bord que lon ne prend que depuis un an. Le bar iusqua 2 pieds que
les anglois salent et autres pesches que lon peut trouver

Cela peupleroit lacadie et terreneuve rendroit quebec florissans riche
et puissant, les anglois amassent tous les ans le sel que nos vaisseaux
trouvent toutes sortes de bois pour bastir vaisseaux et le mastes de beaux
mats pour de l'eau les saj [?] a esté fait par un vaisseau de guerre basty
pour le roy et autres bastimens marchands, vendre et mener en france
planches courbes mats goudrons, merrein, cercles bois a bastir eschalats
du bardeau a couvrir &c potous en quantité

chanvre en quantité, lin, fil dorties du pays que lon file plus fort que
de Chanvre et fin comme le lin peaux de dain et de bufles meilleurs
que celles dont on son se sert que les sauvages mesme apprestent bien,
Cornes, poils de bufle fins et longs fourrures non Comprises dans la
Concession de la Compagnie, dours loutres renards beaux quelques
noirs, martes, loups &c

la terre produit de tout vin bled fruits gibier & poissons infinis partout
mines de Charbon de terre sans fouir au Cap breton et ailleurs mines
de bon fer partout, de plomb esprouves dont le transport feroit faicte
par les moyens quon scait, de Cuivre dont on a veu plusieurs pieces
et eschantillons, quelques pierres pretieuses dont on avoit lessay et

---

[6] An incomplete manuscript, BN., Collection Clairambault, 1016, ff. 390, 391.

turquoises qu'on a veu a des sauvages, et dor mesme

Gloire immortelle   ialousies

Les anglois 300 vaisseaux   les mines sepuisent non les productions
avantages communs par tout bois fer &c, moyens de faire la pesche et
enrichir la compagnie   comparaison des anglois   demandes et offres
de M^r radisson   passage p^r la Chine par terre ou mer

Pour ce qui regarde la terre les richesses de ~~mais pour me mieux
expliquer~~ il faut remarquer que lon peut diviser La nouvelle france
en orientale et occidentale   La 1ere Comprend tous les pays qui sont au
deia du meridien de Montreal et la 2e tous ceux qui sont audela ou
a Louest du mesme meridien

La nouvelle france orientale est tres propre a estre habitee [*ici suit
un résumé des avantages précedents*] a legard de la Nouvelle france
occidentale on la peut considerer en deux manieres   les parties septen-
trionales sont les plus riches du monde en pelleteries parmy lesquelles
il y en a plusieurs qui ne sont pas comprises dans la concession de la
Compagnie au moins jusqua present comme les peaux dours de loups
de martens dhermines de Renards parmy lesquelles il y en a de noires
tres fines et tres pretieuses comme aussy de Castors noirs &c   il y a
enfin quantité de mines de fer [*en marge:* parler des mines de Cuivre
et autres que lon croit y estre et que lon decouvrirait a loisir] quel lon
croit excellent et qui seroit une grande richesse pour le pays   Les
parties de la nouvelle france occidentale qui regardent le Sudouest et
le sud ont aussi quantité de belles forets mais on ny trouveroit pas la
mesme facilite pour le transport que dans lorientale mais en recompense
outre les pelletries ord^res

TRANSLATION

the cod fishery, which would increase the barks and sailors, especially
the French, who would be sustained from the country, the Company,
and others sending vessels and merchandise, who would have only to
load with whales in the Gulf and along the coast of Labrador—whence
also walruses (hides and oil) teeth, seals, from which oil—in the St.
Lawrence, porpoises everywhere, from which skins and oil—salmon
trout, admirable, coast of Labrador and Newfoundland—Plaisance—
some eaten in France—admirable—caviar or sturgeon eggs—innumerable—mackerel—salmon and numberless sturgeons—very fat but good
through a method that is known of putting them in a press, eels, little
cod spawning on the shores—cannot be taken until a year old. bass up
to two feet which the English salt and other fisheries that can be found

That would settle Acadia and Newfoundland, render Quebec prosperous, rich, and powerful. Every year the English collect the salt

that our vessels find—all kinds of lumber for building vessels and masts, fine mast poles for the water [*illegible*] has been made by a war vessel built for the king and other merchant ships, to sell and take into France boards, ship knees, masts, pitch, staves, hoops, building wood, hop poles, shingles, &c., stakes [*?*] in great quantity

much flax, linen, nettle fibre of that country that can be spun stronger than flax and fine as linen—deer and buffalo skins better than those we use, which the Indians even tan very well, horns, fine, long buffalo wool, furs not included in the Company's concession, bears, otters, foxes, sometimes beautiful and black, martens, wolves, &c.

the soil produces all kinds of wines, wheat, fruit, game, and numberless fishes   everywhere coal mines without going to Cape Breton and elsewhere, mines of good iron everywhere, essayed lead, whose freight could be taken care of by known methods, copper, of which several pieces and samples have been seen, some precious stones that have been essayed, and turquoises that have been seen on savages, and even gold

IMMORTAL GLORY   JEALOUSIES

The English—300 vessels—the mines are giving out—not the products —resources common everywhere—wood, iron, &c.—means of conducting the fisheries and enriching the Company—comparison with the English—requirements and offers of Mr. Radisson—passage to China by land or sea

As for the soil—its riches   It is necessary to observe that New France can be divided into east and west. The first includes all the country this side of the meridian of Montreal and the second all to the west of that meridian

East New France is very proper for settlements [*here follows a résumé of preceding advantages and resources*]. As for west New France, it can be considered in two ways. The northern parts are richer in furs than any other region in the world. Among these furs are many not included in the Company's concession—at least not to the present time. Such are the pelts of bears, wolves, martens, ermines, and foxes, among which are some very fine and precious furs, as well as black beaver skins. Finally there are many iron mines [*in the margin:* speak of copper mines and other kinds that are believed to be there and that one could explore at leisure] which are thought to be excellent and which would prove to be great wealth for the country.

The portions of west New France which face southwest and south have quantities of fine forests, but one does not find there the same ease of transport as in the east, but on the other hand, besides ordinary furs [*this is the end, but one may conjecture that the author was on the point of adding:*] there are cibola hides.

Pierre Esprit Radisson to [Claude Bernou], January 1, 1678 [1]

De la grenade le 1 Janvier 1678

Monsieur

Lhonneur que vous m'avé fait Me Commandant de vous escrire les particularitez de nostre voiage me fait prendre la hardiesse de vous adresser ces lignes souetant du mellieurs de mon coeur estre capable de vous en faire une naration plus polie pour vous en donner le récit dans un mellieur stil   vostre bonté me pardonnera comme elle a esté a me rendre tous les bons offices que juse peu prétendre dun perre   continué cette charité en y invittant ceux qui saproche des pouvoirs   dieu en sera vos[e] récompance et obligeres le plus sensible de tous les hommes a recognoistre vos favoeurs

Le 27. Septembre nous avons quité Brest dou jus lhonneur de vous Escrire la liste des vessaux qui composse cette escadre   le mauvais tempt nous contregnit de rentre le lendemain. Le 3 oc[bre] nous mime a la voille lovoiant jusque au 10. sur les cost de france le vent estant favorable sans discontinuer nous a fait voir le 18 lisle de porto santo et le lendemain celle de madera   sans ancrer avons poursuivy nostre Route au S. Sr.   le 20 m[r] le v. admiral a ressolu danvoier un brulot a la martinique pour faire partir insesament les navire de Roy qui y estois pour nous venir atendre en veue de la barbada et nous cependant aller a lentreprize du Cap de Vert habitée par les holandois pour le trafique des negres et cuires de boeuf   nous avons passé lisle gomera le 22.   en suite celle de parma distance de laut. 10. ou 12. L   sur la soirante avons veu celle de fero   Tout ses isles a babort excepté celle de madera qui nous demeroit a stribort ainsi que porto santo   Nous estions soubs le tropique le 26. ou lon a batizé ceux qui ny avois passé   le vent continuant bon mais plus fort que lordinaire le 28. le signal nous estant donné daler recognoistre un navire qui sest trouvé anglois alant en guinée   apres le salut ordinaire da la mer forcant de voille avons Ratrapé nostre flote le 29 par la hauteur de 16[d] 30[m] le vent tres fort plusieurs poissons vollans au tours de nos vesseaux quelques uns tombe dedans

---

[1] Autograph letter signed, BN., Collection Clairambault, 1016, 376, 377.

le dernier du mois sur les 5 heurs du Soir en veu du Cap vert et le premier dece^bre avons doublé y celuy Cap avec un petit vent de norouest le courant nous porte au S. audedans dud. Cap a quelque 7 L de la il y a une petite isle nommée gorée et celle dont il est question nous avons aproché avec pavilion dholand,—Excepté 2 qui portois celui dangl^e cest une isle denviron un lieu de tour il y avoit 2 fort lun sur le plus haut qui commandois celuy de bas qui est sur la pointe du nort ou est la dessante Elle est tres forte a des hom^s qui la saurois defendre il mirent leur pavilion sur leurs 2 forts et ma pancée est quil recognurent bien nostre finte par le signal quils firent nous rangame le plus proche que nous pume ou nous voiant les enemis nous tirerent quels coups de canon voisy la blancheur des lis arborée partout voyant quils ne sétoit point mépris continuèrent a tirer sans tuer personne nous mouillame lancre a la porté du canon sans tirer [?] un seul coup le landemain conseil fut pris que 5 de nos vesseaux aprocherois le plus pres qué faire le poura les ayant sommé a ce rendre ou autrement point de cartier leurs responces fut quils avois juré fidelité a leur prince et quils le voulois defandre Mais peu de tempt apres ils envoierent leur chirugien a bort quy tesmoignoit par sa posture la crinte de ces Confraires il demandoit un peu de tempt a advisser lon le renvoie sans responce lon fait armer toutes les chaloupes de quelques 500 ho^s pour la dessante qui ce rende a bort de lamiral, et les vesseaux destinés pour laproche ce mete soubs voile et vont se ranger a leurs poste ordonné Javois fait demander a Monsr le Conte destrée de me permetre la desante par Monsr de Chambly en calité de volontaire quoy qua brest il mavoit fait la grace que de parler fort a mon advantage et plus que je ne merite a Monsr lintendant qui mordonna le poste et la ration des gardes de la marine, sa responce fut par le mesme mien bien faiteur quil me reservoit pour des chose plus considerable Je ne fais que soueter lhonneur de ces commandement et me rendre digne de les execequter Ce ne sera pas par manque de coeur ny de bonne vollonté Je gardé le Cort qui estoit lun qui avoit recu le commandent ils commence la baterie du fort danhaut ce qui nous fit voir quil avois abandonné celuy denbas quoy que le pavilion y restat nous numes pas tiré 300 coups de canon quils amenerent et arborerent pavilion blanq un coup ayant donné dans leur magazin a poudre leurs fit crindre quun autre coup ne leurs fut pas sy favorable et quil naurois point de cartier fit sortir le gouverneur du fort et senvenir sembarquer sur un basteau pour venir a bort a porter les clefs et ne point atendre la dessante et voyant que lon tiroit toujour a cause quils ny avoit personne pour abatre le pavilion dholande qui estoit au fort denbas avant de partir il y enfoya un ho^e pour labatre nostre bateau et quelq. autre y furent ausy tost et trouverent le canon encloué les poudre jesté dans la siterne et les canons des montés M^r le conte donna ausy tost ses ordre quelque heurs apres lun en fut prendre possesion en ordre trouverent 40 p. de c. 130 h^s bien fait et bien armés au fort de bas il y avoit 29 piece de c. 2 de 30^tt de bal, 24 18 jus 3 les autre onze a celuy den haut quelque 60 negres autant de beste a corne 5000 livre et la valeur de 200000 escus de marchandize sest la croyance du publique avant que dentreprendre aucune chose lon envoya a Rufix ville des negres pour les assurer que nous ne venions que pour destruire nous enemis et qua vers eux nous voulions conserver une inviolable amitié la responce de ce prince more fut autant obligente quon la pouvoit soueter et quantité de ces gens nous aporter des petite commoditez laction estant fait ayant pris ce qui ce pouvait prendre brulé et demoly les forts avons fait voille nostre flotte ocmanté de deux petit batiment de 4 p. de c. chaque Nous avions cent et tant de prisonniers pour le gouverneur sa demande luy fut octroyé davoir la liberté de sen aler a un fort holandois a vingt lieux de la en terre ferme avec 10 ou 12 des siens dans un petit bateau et quil ne serviroit de 18 mois Je laurois oblige de servir au plutost Sur lisle lon construit 5 chaloupe que lon atire pour les autres exceputions Le 12 estions en veue de S^t jago et la nuict densuivant celle de fugo qui jestoit force feu de la avons directé nostre route ouest nayant aucune hauteur a elever pour la barbade le premier de septembre veue de la d. isle y avons envoié un bateau et le fils du gouverneur ang. de S^t cristof quelque gens armés vinrent les recevoir au bort de leau pavoisant leur pavilion et voyant que nous ne fesions pas le semblable tirerent leurs espée sur les nostre lon leurs en demanda la cause ils dirent que nous ne leurs rendions le salut ny a fit [?] que ce la pour accorder le differant il cera bien tost fait ils arestre par belle paroles et par finesses 3 jours pour avoir le tempt davertir ceux de tabago lon peut juger de leurs volonté pour la france le 6 avons veu tabago et le 7 avons mouillé a 3 L. du fort des le soir mesme lon a disposé 500 h^s pour sasurer de la dessente qui na point este disposé [?] Le 8 300 h^s ont suivy lon recu la nouvelle par un petit batiment arivé a cette Isle il y avoit quelque jours venue de Martinique qui en passant par devant le havre avoit veu 2 navire de guerre 2 flute et 2 autre batiment et une kache englosse qui a eu 400 esque pour venir advertir A la veu de nos vesseaux les enemis avois mis un pavillion sur une hauteur a ½ L. de leur fort qui avoit donné signal de combien il voiet de voil il ne nous manqoit plus que 2: 2: nous ayant joins a la barbade le lendemain de nostre arivé avec le brulot que lon avoit depeché vers madera pour les advertir il avois bien 200 h^s des troupes des Isles et 200 de plus qui sont arivé dans les 2

autre apres laction qui commanca par la marche des troupes Mr le
Conte de blenay vice Roy ce ces lieux commondoit conjointment avec le
Conte destrée lon fut camper a une lieue du bort le leau en destachant
quelque 50 h⁵ pour aler des le soir recognoistre la posture des enemis
quelque francois ce vienne rendre qui tous diversement font leurs raport nous revenons le soir au camp ayant veu le fort et le enemis fort
afferer a le fortifier des quil eurent cognoisance de nostre desante il quit-
erent la hauteur 5 ou 6 h⁵ qui pouvois estre enportant leurs pavilion
nous ny trouvame que le baston lon fit quelque prisonnier qui confirme
la resolutions que leurs compatriotes ont de le bien deffandre lon fait
marche a la pointe du jour et lon campe sur la hauteur en veu du fort
demeurant 3 jour sans rien entreprendre faisant venir provision munitions et 2 mortiers qui furent en estat de jouer le 12 par un dimanche
lenemy navois point tiré quoy quil nous vie partout nous promener 2
jour avant leurs prize lon avoit envoyé 2 trompete les sommer binker
qui commandoit fort sivile dans son procedé voiant que lon comandoit
au francois de sortir les asura de sa protection les faisant souvenir
du passé ce qui les fit crier vive le prince dorange ils pouvois estre 60
h⁵ il les asura que sy il estoit obligé de capituler il periroit ou ils serois
compris les premier Mais quil avoit un avis a donner a Monsʳ le vice
amiral qui estoit de ne point perdre de tempt et que dans 4 jour la
moitié de ses troupe perirois de fatigue et le mauvais climat de lIsle la
pluie estant continuelle presque sur nostre dos que cela le facheroit qun
fils de Marechale de france ut une segonde disgrace quareste il luy
estoit bien obligé de lhonneur de sa visite que sy le bonheur des armes
luy en vouloit encore les francois ne serois pas sy maltrestez que lautre
fois et quils ne manquerois pas de chemize quil avoit de tout en a
bondance pour les regaller les trompete de retour lon ce dispose
sur le midy les bombe estant prete et inpatience francois de voir des
curieux fit que plus de 500 h⁵ parurent ensemble le enemis comman-
cerent a tirer quelque coups de canon sans effect. la curiausité passerent
a plussieur 1½ heure apres lon leurs envoye une bombe qui nala jusqua
fort ils firent des grans saluts avec leurs chapeaux par bravade il
le pairont bientost lon tire une carcase qui tombe audela et dans leau
du marest setoit lheur du diner Binker nous voulut faire raison
faisant préparer son mortier et buvant a la santé de son prince avec
tout ses officiers nostre troisième coup le boulet tomba estant directé
par un pouvoir divin au milieu de leur fort persant 3 plancher et la voute
de brique ou estoit leurs poudre setoit un effroyable dessert ils navois
jamais esté servy dun telle fruit 22000ᴴ de poudre fit sur ses mizéra-
ble un furieux effect pres de 300 h⁵ les modérés dize 200 h⁵ et quelque
uns 4 a 500 homˢ y ont pery. 2000 grenades et tous les canons prenant

feu laire paroissoit un goufre denfer à ¼L. ce nest que bras teste
jambe et corps enpies des monstre vivant que lon voit remuer le feu
ayant grillié quantité de ces mizerables la fumée disipée lon ne voit
plus le fort le reste eschapée du naufrage qui pouvir marcher fuit ce
spectacle dhoreur le long du bort de leau crignant la fureur francois par
le point de Cartier cõme on leurs avoit dit Mais ils eprouve que le
francois victorieux est clement plus que nation de monde et sest marque
de gloire pour ces peoples qui on lhonneur destre noz subgets du plus
clement et du plus invinsible et heureux Roy du monde que dieu benise
de plusieur millier de victoire ce sont mes voeux pour une gloire
imortelle que je luy souete Jespere quil me continura ses bontez par
bontes de vous autres noble ames mes patrons. Je vit tomber la bombe
et eus lhonneur de crier le premier vive le Roy lon desent prontement
au mieux que le chemin le pouvoit permetre en bataille a la bort ceux
qui ne pouvois fuire crier la vie bon francois lon les assure de toute
benignitéz a la vue dun traitement sy doux plusieurs prene courage
et vont avertire leurs camarade de cette clemence de france qui ussent
sy moderement des victoires plus de 300 revi[e]ne 2 heur apres sy le
francois est bon il est charitable lon les plain lon les soulage lon
voit un p. jesuite et un pere blanq courir aux agonisant leur faisant
crier Jesus Marie dont plusieur proferois le S^t non du profond du
coeur Je leurs servy a quelque uns dinterprete pour leur faire entendre
ce que ces pp leur disoit Monsieur le vice ad^l ayant donné ses ordres
les soldats pilaire le reste du debris autant que le feu le pouvoit permetre quelque grenade prirent feu qui tua 1 ou 2 des nostres a ce que
lon ma dit estant proche de m^r le Conte qui estoit venu des premier
sur le lieu tous les jours il ce vient rendre des holandois et mesme des
francois qui font raport de leurs infortune ils on recu la liberté exsepté un nommé laforest leurs Capitaine qui est au forts et dun coquin
qui fut erré au fort le jour avant la prize leurs disant que les francois
avois une machine que lon [bon ?] recevroit [?] carcase estonné de ce
qui ne pouvoient imaginer ce que setoit le enemis lui fire demander
ce quil avoit de quiter sa patrie i fit responce quil mouroit de fain
comment cela peut il estre ayant ton sac plein de pain il se remit dans
les troupe mais les holandois le montrere Je vous ay dit le lavertisement
quils avois eu le soir mesme de nostre arivée il firerent en diligence partire
une grand flute chargée deau de vie de toille et autre chosse pour aler a
corosole et de la a la nouvelle espaigne nous trouvame 2 baterie au
desoubs du fort qui deffendoit le port la premiere de 9 p. de 20^{ll} de bal le
2nd de 5 de 18 Et le costé du fort qui regardoit la Merre de 16 p. chaqun
de 8^{ll} de balle et triple palisade et le qui regardoit le bois dyceluy il y
avoit une manier de rampart defendu de 3 p. de 18^{ll} tous les ho^s qui

estois dedans bien armés darme offensive et defensive de toute les
main dans le port il y avoit un des navire du Roy le presieux que
lholandois esperoit envoier a corosole ils ny avois mis que 36 p. de C.

un de leurs navire nomé le defenseur monté de 48 dont 22 estois de fonte
le seule navire qui leurs resta de location dernier en terre estoit il eschoué
setoit leur amiral de plus une flute de 12 p. et un petit veseau quils
avois mit a s^t domingue sur les francois de 6 a 8 p. pour lautre plus
petit un nomé Rasmus famue corcerre ce sauva dedans ou plustost
setoit mis dans un bateau crignant que le fr ne le poursuivit dans le
plus grand et par ce stratageme ce sauva a terre ou il avoit envoié le
jour presedent quelque vivre et munition et arme lon la cherché en
vain lon a fait embarquer tout le Canon exsepté 12 p. que lon a fait
crever requerant trop de tempt a les faire ambarquer le tout etant
embarque et le reste destruit et donnant ordre de raporter les 2 p. de
C. que lon avoit mis a terre au lieu du debarquem^t nous avons fait
voile a la grenade dou vostre tres humble serviteur vous escrit et vous
prie que sy vous les trouvé digne de la faire metre au net pour la faire
lire a ces noble amis a qui je suis comme a vous

tres humble et oblige serviteur

P. E. Radisson

[*P.S.*] Monsr de Cambly vous salue et ce porte bien grace a dieu
Dieu vous continue en santé Exquzé la presipitation qui nest de ma
cognoissance que veritable de ce que jay veu [2]

TRANSLATION [3]

Grenada, January 1, 1678.

Monsieur,

The honor that you did me to command me to write you the details
of our voyage makes me so bold as to address you these lines, wishing
with all my heart that I were able to give you a more polished account
so that my narrative would have a better style. Your kindness will
pardon me as it formerly did in being kinder to me than I could have
expected a father to be. Continue to be so understanding, recommending the same course to those who are close to the ones in authority.

---

[2] Various persons have been of assistance to me in deciphering Radisson's
handwriting and phonetic spelling, including the Reverend Father Albert
Tessier of Three Rivers, Canada; Monsieur Aug. Radisson of Lyons, France;
and the Reverend Father Archange Godbout of Montreal. The responsibility
for the rendering given above, however, is entirely my own.—Author.

[3] It is impossible to read some passages certainly and to translate others
with complete assurance. Readers conversant with the French language will
perceive readily the difficulties that the translator encountered.

God will be your recompense and will oblige the most understanding of all men to recognize your services.

On September 27 we left Brest, where I had the honor to send you the list of the vessels that compose our squadron. Bad weather forced us to return the next day. On October 3 we set sail tacking about until the tenth on the coast of France. The wind being favorable without falling enabled us to catch sight of Porto Santo on the eighteenth and the next day we came in sight of Madeira. Without anchoring we continued our route south southwest. On the twentieth the Vice-Admiral decided to send a fireship to Martinique to order the immediate departure thence of royal vessels at that place to Barbados, there to await us whilst we went on to carry out our plan for Cap Vert, which is inhabited by the Dutch, who traffic there in Negroes and hides. We passed the island of Gomera on the twenty-second and that of Parma [*La Palma*] soon after, a distance of 10 or 12 leagues. Towards evening we caught sight of the island of Ferro. All these islands lay to port except that of Madeira, which as well as that of Porto Santo, was on our starboard side.

We were at the Tropic on the twenty-sixth, where all were baptized who had not passed it before. The wind continuing fair but stronger than usual on the twenty-eighth the signal was given for us to go reconnoiter in the matter of a vessel which proved to be an English craft on its way to Guinea. After the usual salute of the sea, crowding on sail, we caught up with our squadron. On the twenty-ninth at latitude 16° 30′, the wind very strong some of several flying fish about our vessels fell within.

The last of the month about five o'clock of the evening we came in sight of Cap Vert and the first of December we doubled it by means of a little wind from the northwest. The current bore us south of the said cape for some 7 leagues to a little island named Gorée. This island we approached under a Dutch flag—with the exception of two vessels which carried the English flag. It is an island about a league in circumference. There were two forts, the higher one commanding the lower, which is on the northern tip where we made our descent. It is very strong for men who know how to defend it. The Dutch put their flag on their two forts and my belief is that they recognised our ruse by the signal that they gave. We came up as close as we could. Then our enemies fired some shots. Behold at once the lilies on their white fields, raised everywhere. Seeing that they were not mistaken they continued to fire, but without killing any one. We anchored a cannon shot away without firing a single shot. Next day a council was held with the plan that five of our vessels should approach as close as possible and summon the enemy to yield or else no quarter would be given. Their reply was that they had sworn fidelity to their ruler and that they wanted to defend him. But a little time afterwards they sent their surgeon on board, who by his attitude showed the fears of his associates. He asked a little time for counsel. We sent him back without reply. We armed all the long boats with about five hundred men for the descent and these came on board the flagship. The vessels planned for the approach got under sail and went to their appointed places. I had requested Count D'Estrées to permit me to make the descent with Monsieur de Chambly in the capacity of volunteer, although at Brest he had had the kindness to speak strongly in my favor and more than I deserved to the intendant, who ordered me to the position and rations of the marine guards. His reply was from my same good benefactor, that he was keeping me for more important things. I could do nothing but honor these commandments and try to be worthy of executing them. I shall not lack enthusiasm and interest. I guarded the contingent which was the one that had received the command. The upper fort battery opened fire, which made us perceive that the lower fort had been abandoned, although the flag still flew there. We had not fired three hundred rounds when they ran up a white flag, a shot having entered their powder magazine, which made them fear that another shot might not be so favorable to them and that there would be no quarter. So the Governor of the fort set out and embarked on a boat to come on board, bearing the keys, not wanting to await our attack and seeing that we kept on firing because there was no one to pull down the Dutch flag still flying on the lower fort. Before leaving he sent a man to pull down that flag. Our boat and some others were there immediately and found the cannon spiked, the powder thrown into the cistern, and the cannons dismounted. The Count immediately gave his orders. Some hours after we had taken possession in due order. We found 40 pieces of cannon, 130 men well supplied and armed. At the lower fort there were 29 pieces of cannon, two of 30 pounds, 24 of 18. One had three, the others eleven. At the upper fort there were some 60 Negroes, as many horned cattle, 5,000 pounds and the value of 200,000 écus of merchandise. It was the general belief that before undertaking anything else we should send to Rufisque some Negroes, who should assure the ones there that we were coming only to destroy our enemies and that toward them we should preserve an inviolable friendship. The reply of this Moorish ruler was as agreeable as one could wish and many people brought us small articles.

The deed having been done, having taken what we could, burned and demolished the forts, we set sail with a fleet augmented with two small vessels of four pieces of cannon apiece. We had a hundred and as many prisoners [?]. As for the Governor, his request was granted him of being at liberty to go to a Dutch fort twenty leagues distant inland, accompanied by ten or twelve of his men in a little boat; and of not having to serve for eighteen months. I would have made him serve sooner. On the island five long boats were constructed in preparation for other activities.

The twelfth we were in sight of Santiago and the following night in view of Fogo, which belched forth flames. From there we directed our course westward, having no land to raise before reaching Barbados. The first of September we had sent a boat there and the son of the English governor of St. Kitts. Some armed persons came to receive them at the water's edge, draped in flags, and seeing that we did not do likewise drew their swords on our men. We asked the cause and they said that we did not return their salute and that was all that was necessary to patch up the trouble [?]. It will soon be done. We were kept there by fine words and finesse for three days, so that time might be gained for warning Tobago. One may judge therefrom of their sentiment towards France. On the sixth we saw Tobago and on the seventh anchored three leagues from the fort. In the evening of the same day we made five hundred men ready to be sure of the landing, which was not disputed. On the eighth three hundred men followed. The people of Tobago had got the news through a little vessel sent out some days earlier from Martinique, which, passing before the harbor, had seen two ships of war, two flutes, and two other craft and an English ketch, which had received 400 écus for coming to warn them. When they caught sight of our vessels the enemy placed a flag on a height a half league from their fort, which gave the signal of how many sail they could see. We lacked now only two, two having joined us at Barbados. The day after our arrival, with the fireship that had been sent from the vicinity of Madeira to warn them, they had 200 men in Island troops and 200 more who had been secured from the two vessels that had arrived. After the action, which commenced by a march of the troops of the Count of Blenay, Viceroy of these places, commanding with the Count D'Estrées, camp was made a league from the edge of the water while some fifty men were sent to reconnoitre and determine the enemy's position. Some Frenchmen came to report, each in his own way. We returned that evening to the camp having seen the enemy's fort and the enemy greatly agitated and fortifying themselves. As soon as they learned of our descent they left the height, five or six men carrying off their flag. We found there only the bastion. We took several prisoners, who confirmed their compatriots' resolution

to defend the fort at all cost. The march was taken up at daybreak
and camp was made on the height in view of the fort. Three days were
passed doing nothing but bringing up provisions, munitions, and two
mortars which were in condition to be used. The twelfth, a Sunday,
the enemy did not fire, though we could be seen everywhere. We went
along for two days without taking them. Two trumpeters were sent
to summon them to surrender. Binker, who was in command, was very
civil in his actions. Seeing that he was commanded in French to leave,
he assured them of his protection, recalling to them the past, which
made them cry out, "Long live the Prince of Orange." There were
perhaps sixty men. He assured them that if he were obliged to capitulate, he would die where he was first taken, but that he had some
advice to give to Monsieur the Vice-Admiral, which was not to lose
time and that within four days half of his troops would perish of
fatigue and the bad climate of the island. The rain would be constant,
almost on our very backs. That it would irritate him [D'Estrées]
as a Marshal of France, to endure a second disgrace; that he [Binker]
was much obliged for the honor of his visit; that if success in arms
should crown his efforts, the French would not be mistreated as in
the other instance and that they should not lack for shirts. That he
had everything in abundance with which to regale them. The trumpets
for return sounded about midday. The bombs being ready and the
French impatient to see what was to happen, some five hundred men
assembled. The enemy commenced to shoot some cannon without result. The curiosity of some ceased. An hour and a half later we sent
them a bomb which did not quite reach the fort. They made elaborate
salutes with their hats in sheer bravado. They will soon be repaid. A
carcass was shot which fell beyond in the water of the swamp. It was
the hour for dinner. Binker wished to give us satisfaction and was preparing his mortar and drinking to the health of his Prince along with
all his officers, when our third blow struck. The bullet fell, directed by
a Divine power, in the midst of their fort, penetrated three planks and
the brick roof of their powder magazine. It was a terrible dessert. They
had never been served such fruit before. Twenty-two thousand livres of
powder made awful havoc with those wretches. Close to three hundred
of them perished. The moderates say two hundred and some claim four
or five hundred were killed. Two thousand grenades and all the cannons taking fire the air seemed like an abyss of Hell for a quarter of a
league. There was nothing but arms, legs, and intertwined bodies that
one perceived to writhe. Flames roasted many of these wretches. When
the smoke cleared away there was no longer a fort to be seen. Those
who escaped and who could walk fled this scene of horror along the

edge of the water, fearing the reprisal of the French, according to remarks on lack of quarter that had been made to them. But they learned that the French as victors are the most clement people in the world and that it is a mark of glory for these people to be the subjects of the most merciful, the most invincible, and the happiest King of the world, whom may God bless with numberless victories. These are my prayers for an immortal glory that I wish him. I hope that he will continue his kindness to me through the goodwill of you noble souls, my patrons.

I saw the bomb fall and had the honor of being the first to cry "Long live the King!" We went down as quickly as the road would permit in battle array to the shore. Those who could not flee cried, "Our lives, good Frenchmen!" They were assured of clemency. Seeing such mild treatment many of them took courage and went to tell their companions of this French mercy, thus extended in victory. More than three hundred returned two hours later. If the Frenchman is good, he is charitable. These men were commiserated, they were comforted. A Jesuit and a White Father were seen to run to those in anguish, crying to them the names of Jesus and Mary. Several of them uttered the holy name from the depth of their hearts. I assisted them by interpreting to several, trying to make them understand what the reverend fathers were saying to them. Monsieur the Vice-Admiral having given his orders, the soldiers pillaged the ruins as much as the fire would permit. Some grenades took fire and killed one or two of our men, according to what I was told, being near to the Count, who had come among the first on the ground. Every day some Dutch came to give themselves up, and even some Frenchmen, telling of their misfortunes. They received their liberty except a man named La Forest, their Captain, who was at the fort, and a rascal who had deserted to the fort the day before the conquest, telling them that the French had a machine which [*word illegible; possibly,* would receive] carcasses. Astonished at what they could not imagine, the enemy asked him why he abandoned his country. He replied that he was dying of hunger. How can that be? Your sack is full of bread. He lost himself among the troops, but the Dutch pointed him out. I have written you of the warning that they had had the very evening of our arrival. They hastened to send off a large flute loaded with rum, cloth, and other things, for Curaçao and from there to New Spain. We found two batteries below the fort, defending the port, the former of 20 lbs. the second of 18. The side of the fort that commanded the sea of 16 pieces of 12. The four bastions of the fort, which was star-shaped, was furnished with three pieces, each of 8 lbs. and a triple palisade; and the one that looked out over the woods had a sort of rampart defended by three pieces of 18 each and all the men within it armed with offensive and defensive weapons. In the port there was one of the King's ships, the *Precious,* which the Dutch hoped to send to Curaçao. They had sent there only 36 pieces of cannon. One of their ships named the *Defender,* mounted with 48, of which 22 were cast, the only ship remaining for hire [?] back in the interior was wrecked. It was their flagship. In addition there was a flute of 12 pieces and a little vessel which they had sent to Santo Domingo against the French, of 6 or 8 pieces. As for the other smaller vessel, a famous corsair called Rasmus, saved himself therein, or rather, he put himself in a boat fearing that the French would follow him in the large one and by this stratagem saved himself inland, where he had sent the preceding day some provisions, arms, and ammunition. We sought for him in vain. We embarked all the cannon except 12 pieces, which we destroyed as requiring too much time to put on board. With everything embarked and the rest destroyed we gave orders to bring on board the two pieces of cannon that had been landed. We set sail for Grenada, from which place your very humble servant is writing you and begging you, if you have found in this letter anything worthy, to make a fair copy to be read to your noble friends, to whom I am as to you the very obedient, humble servant,

P. E. Radisson

[*P.S.*] Monsieur de C[h]ambly greets you. He is well, thanks be to God. May God keep you in good health. Excuse my haste. I have written, as far as I know, only what I have seen.

APPENDIX 5

Radisson's Petition of 1681 [?] [1]

Esprit de Radisson

Mémoire de Radisson sur les découvertes et Commerce de l'Amérique septentrionale.

L'Amérique septentrionale est plus à la bienséance des françois que d'aucune autre nation de l'Europe, a cause de la commodité qu'ils ont de pénétrer jusques à 6 our 700 lieues vers l'ouest et le sud ouest par le moyen du fleuve St Laurent et des grands lacs où il prend sa source.

On peut conjecturer quelles sont ses richesses, tant par celles de L'Amérique méridionale que parcequ'il n'y a jamais eu de grands pays sur la terre garni de montagnes où il n'y ait présentement ou n'y ait eu autrefois de riches mines d'or ou d'argent.

Mais il y a lieu de croire que comme ces richesses se sont toujours trouvés dans les parties occidentales de l'Amérique, telles que sont la nouvelle biscaye, la nouvelle galice, le Pérou et le Chili, on ne les trouvera vers le nord qu'a mesure qu'on s'avancera vers le couchant, d'où l'on a apporté divers échantillons, de cuivre, d'argent et de cuirs de Cibola, mais ou ne saurait s'en éclaircir a fond que par les moyens des découvertes.

On les peut pousser vers le Sud, ou sud ouest vers l'ouest et vers le nord.

Pour le premier il semble que M. de la Sale fait ce qu'il faut pour cela puis qu'on apprend qu'il s'est embarqué à l'entrée du lac Erie dans une barque de 50 ou 60 tonneaux pour aller au bout du lac des Ilinois et de là par la grande rivière du Mississipi vers le Golfe de Mexique dans des lieux où il n'y a aucun Européen établi à 150 lieues aux environs et où il ne sera éloigné selon toutes les cartes que d'environ 250 lieues des mines d'or et d'argent de la nouvelle Biscaye qui sont les plus riches de la nouvelle Espagne et où les Espagnols sont plus faibles qu'en aucun autre endroit, de sorte qu'il y a beaucoup d'apparence que M. De la Sale fera de grands établissements dans ces beaux

---

[1] BN., Collection Clairambault, 1016, ff. 647, 648, and also in modern French copy in BN., Margry Papers, 9284, ff. 50–53.

et vastes pays pourvu qu'il ne lui arrive point de malheur imprévu et qu'il soit un peu soutenu.

La descouverte des pays qui sont du costé du Coucher se peut faire par 2 endroits différents, le premier par terre allant depuis Montréal par le chemin que prennent les Outawacs jusques au Saut Ste Marie qui est la décharge du lac Supérieur, et de là allant au bout du même lac d'où l'on pourrait aller chercher la mer occidentale ou de Californie à travers le pays des Nadouessious chez lesquels le Sr Radisson a fait quelques voyages et a appris des sauvages qu'il y avait un très grand lac dans leur pays qui s'étendait vers le sud ouest jusques auprès de la mer dans laquelle ils lui ont dit qu'il se dégorge, ce qui est d'autant plus vraisemblable que dans tout le rest de l'Amérique la partie orientale est incomparablement plus large que l'occidentale et qu'aussitôt que l'on est arrivé au lieu où les eaux courent vers le couchant on se trouve fort près de la mer.

Cette même descouverte se peut faire en partie par mer en s'établissant dans la baie d'Hudson, d'où il n'y a pas loin par terre pour arriver chez les Nadouessious d'où l'on continuerait la route vers la mer du couchant de la manière qu'il a été dit ci-devant.

Il ne faut pas plus de 15 hommes sages et bien choisis pour exécuter cette entreprise, tant pour éviter la dépense que pour maintenir l'ordre parmi eux et leur pourvoir trouver partout les vivres nécessaires.

La 3e decouverte qui est celle du Nord est d'une passage pour pénétrer par mer au delà de l'Amérique, lequel passage les Anglais et les Danois ont jusques à présent cherché inutilement, parceque comme il n'y avaient aucune retraite, ny établissment, ils étaient contraints de s'en retourner presqu'aussitôt qu'ils y étaient arrivés.

On éviterait cette inconvénient en s'établissant dans un endroit situé dans la partie occidentale de la baie de Hudson dans lequel le Sieur Radisson a fréquenté et d'où l'on partirait dans une bonne double chaloupe ou brigantin de 12 à 15 tonneaux pour visiter toutes les côtes en allant vers le nord et par ce moyen, on s'éclaircirait dans deux ou trois ans de la possibilité de ce passage et au cas qu'il n'y en eut point on pourroit de là tenter la découverte par le pays des Nadouessious.

À l'égard du commerce il est indubitable qu'il deviendra très considerable à mesure que ces grands pays se peupleront, tant par les mines que l'on découvrira presque infailliblement que par les cuirs de Cibola, manufactures, denrées, &c

Mais pour ne parler que de celui qui est déjà établi, c'est à dire de celui des pelleteries, il deviendrait très-considérable si les françois le faisaient seuls dans toute l'Europe le débit des fourrures, loutres et castors qui en viennent ce qui arriverait indubitablement si on pouvait, comme on le peut même sans esclat, exclure les Anglais de ce Commerce.

Surquoi il faut remarquer qu'il n'y a que 3 portes par où les pelleteries sortent de l'Amérique septentrionale desquelles il est aisé aux françois de se rendre maîtres; savoir: la rivière de St Laurent, la N^elle York et la baie d'Hudson.

Les françois sont maîtres de la 1ere par les colonies que l'on a établies sur les bords de ce grand fleuve.

Il est aisé de fermer la seconde en peuplant la côte septentrionale du lac Ontario et l'entrée du lac Erie, y bâtissant 2 ou 3 forts pour mettre ces colonies hors d'insulte, par ce moyen il arriverait:

1.º que l'on briderait les Iroquois et on les empecherait de diminuer et même d'interrompre quelquefois la chasse des sauvages nos alliés.

2.º Comme les Iroquois n'ont presque point de pelleteries chez eux et qu'ils les vont chercher au Nord de ces lacs d'où ils les rapportent en traversant ces mêmes lacs vers l'endroit où ils s'approchent le plus l'un de l'autre et où ils sont les plus étroits, il arriverait que trouvant les françois dans leurs panages, ils aimeraient mieux leur vendre leurs pelleteries que. . . .

TRANSLATION

Esprit de Radisson

Radisson's memoir concerning discoveries and commerce in North America.

North America is more advantageous to the French than to any other European country because of the ease with which they can penetrate six or seven hundred leagues to the west and southwest by means of the St. Lawrence River and the Great Lakes, its source.

One can guess its wealth as much by that of Central America as by the fact that there has never been a great country on earth possessing mountains, which does not have or has not had at some time rich mines of gold or silver.

But there is reason to think that as these riches have always been found in the western parts of America—such as New Biscay, New Galicia, Peru, and Chile—they will be found now according as one goes west, whence are brought various samples of copper, silver, and Cibola hides, but one can be sure only by exploration.

One can explore toward the south, toward the southwest, toward the west, or toward the north.

In the first direction it appears that M. de la Salle is doing all that can be done, since we learn that he has embarked at the entrance of

Lake Erie on a bark of 50 or 60 tons to go to the end of Lake Illinois and from there by the great Mississippi River towards the Gulf of Mexico into those regions inhabited by no Europeans for a distance of 150 leagues or thereabouts. There he will be not farther distant, according to all the maps, than 250 leagues from the gold and silver mines of New Biscay, which are the richest of New Spain and where the Spaniards are weaker than in any other spot. So that there is a strong likelihood that M. de la Salle will make some large establishments in those beautiful, vast countries, provided that no evil befalls him and that a little support is given him.

The discovery of countries to the west can be made in two different ways: the first by land, starting from Montreal, by means of the route followed by the Ottawa to Sault Ste Marie, which is the outlet of Lake Superior; thence to the end of that lake, whence one can go to find the Western Sea or the California Sea across the country of the Nadouessioux, among whom Sieur Radisson has made some expeditions and learned from the natives that there was a very large lake in their country, extending southwestward to the sea, in which they told him it empties. This is the more credible because in all the rest of America the western part is incomparably larger than the eastern and as soon as one reaches the area of westward-flowing streams, one is very close to the sea.

This same exploration can be partly accomplished by sea through colonizing Hudson Bay, whence it is not far by land to the country of the Nadouessious. Thence one would continue the route to the western sea in the way described above.

No more than fifteen wise, well-chosen men would be required to execute this undertaking, both in order to save expense and to maintain order among them and provide necessaries off the land.

The third exploration, which is the northern one, is by way of the sea passage through America, which passage the English and the Danes have thus far sought in vain, because they have no base, or factory. Thus they are obliged to return almost as soon as they get there.

This obstacle could be obviated by establishing a settlement in a place in the western part of Hudson Bay, which Sieur Radisson has often visited and from which one could leave in a good double longboat or brigantine of 12 to 15 tons, in order to visit all shores northward and by this means one could make sure in two or three years' time of the possibility of effecting this passage. In case one could not find such a passage, one could thence try discovery through the country of the Nadouessious.

As for commerce, it is undeniable that it will become very great as the country settles, not only through the mines that will surely be discovered, but also through the Cibola hides, manufactures, foodstuffs, etc.

But to speak only of what is a fact, that is to say, of the fur trade— it would become very great, if the French had the sole European market for furs, otters, and beaver, which would be the case, if one did, as one could do inconspicuously, that is, exclude the English from this trade.

Whereupon one may remark, that there are only three ports whence furs leave North America and of which it would be easy for the French to be in control: the St. Lawrence River, New York, and Hudson Bay.

The French are masters of the first through their colonies on the banks of that great river.

It would be easy to close the second by peopling the north shore of Lake Ontario and the entrance to Lake Erie, and by building there two or three forts to protect the colonies. Thus it would result:

(1) That the Iroquois would be subdued and prevented from lessening and occasionally preventing altogether our native allies' hunts.

(2) That as the Iroquois have no furs in their own country and go hunting north of those lakes, bringing back their furs across those same lakes near the place where they come closest together and are narrowest, they would find the French on the shores and would prefer to sell them their furs that . . . .

APPENDIX 6

Radisson to M. le Marquis de Belleroche, at Paris, December, 1683 [?] [1]

Monsieur Radisson vous supplie de représenter, s'il vous plaist, à Monseigneur le Marquis de Seignelay, qu'il y a neuf ans qu'obéissant au commandement de Monseigneur Colbert, j'ay quitté 200 lbs sterling de pension et l'entrestient de ma famille chez le Chevallier Kerke, mon beau père, qui a presque abandonné sa fille, ma femme, dans la croyance qu'elle avoit embrassé, la Religion Catholique, et dont je suis absent depuis ay longtems, que Sa Grandeur nous avoit faict promettre employ à nostre arrivée, que par ses ordres nous avons faict un voyage en Canada où nous avons consommé plus de 400 lbs, que ma femme a esté obligé de s'en retourner chez son père, s'estant sauvée de son païs à son insue, que depuis, soub Monsiegneur le Maréchal d'Estrées, j'avois faict le campagne de Guinée et perdu plus de 2000 ₶. au naufrage de l'Isle d'Aves, qu'à mon retour, Sa Grandeur m'avois faict donner 1000 ₶. pour faire revenir ma famille, que sans crainte javois passé en Angleterre où le père de ma femme s'estoit opposé à ma volonté, voulant déshériter sa fille d'un bien considérable sy elle me suivoit, ne m'ayant laissé voir mon enfant; que depuis ce tems là, je n'avois recu que de ce, que ma femme m'avoit envoyé jusques à la dernière de ses bagues, que javois esté contraint de vendre le portrait du Roy d'Angleterre que luy mesme m'avoit faict présent, comme la chaine d'or qu'il m'avoit mis au cou. Que le dernier voyage que mon frère et moy venions de faire estoit une preuve de nostre zèle, fidélité et expérience. Que je supplie Sa Majesté d'avoir pitié de ma famille pour prouver ma fidélité à Dieu et ay celle, le priant le reste de mes jours qu'il la comble de ses bénédictions.

Monsieur Le Maréschal d'Estrées peut je m'assure rendre bon témoignage de ce que je vous réprésente et vous serais obligé de mon bonheur et du salut de ma famille qui priera Dieu pour vous   Depuis neuf ans j'ai constamment refusé les offres Etrangères et celles de mon beau père

[1] BN., Margry Papers, 9284, ff. 61, 62.

Monsieur Radisson begs you to represent, if you please, to My Lord the Marquis of Seignelay, that in obedience to the order of My Lord Colbert nine years ago I left a pension of two hundred pounds sterling and the support of my family at the home of Sir [*John*] Kerke, my father-in-law, who almost disowned my wife, his daughter, in the belief that she had become a Catholic and from whom I had been absent a long time; that His Lordship had promised us employment upon our arrival; that by his order we made a trip to Canada, where we used up more than four hundred pounds sterling; that my wife was obliged to return to her father's home, having left her country without his knowledge; that since that time I have been on the Guinea campaign under My Lord the Marshal D'Estrées, losing more than two thousand *livres* in a shipwreck on the island of Aves; that on my return His Lordship had one thousand livres given me to bring my family here; that without fear I went to England, where the father of my wife opposed my design, threatening to disinherit his daughter of a large patrimony if she followed me and not allowing me to see my child; that since that time I have lived only on what my wife has sent me, even to the last of her jewels; that I have been obliged to sell the portrait of the King of England which he himself presented to me, as well as the gold chain that he hung about my neck; that the last trip that my brother and I have just made was a proof of our zeal, fidelity, and experience; that I beg His Majesty to have pity on my family in order that I may prove my fidelity to God and to him, begging Him the remainder of my days that He will crown him with all good things.

Monsieur the Marshal D'Estrées can testify, I feel sure, that what I tell you is the truth. You will be rewarded by my happiness and the well-being of my family, who will pray to God for you. For nine years I have consistently refused foreign offers and those of my father-in-law.

APPENDIX 7

Des Groseilliers' Petition [January, 1684] [1]

Monseigneur

Je suis obligé de dire la verité pour ce qui regarde ma Conqueste et celle de mon frère qui est la mesme chose, courant tous les deux le mesme hazard dans les païs Sauvages. J'ay esté obligé de faire mon devoir comme fidelle françois en ce qui concerne mon establissement et touschant la prise d'un vaisseau qui n'avoit nulle commission, lequel s'est jetté entre mes mains, voyant qu'il n'en pouvoit échapper et en a agy fort honnestement avec moy; mais ayant appris qu'il y avoit encore un aultre vaisseau, il a esté obligé de se deffier de nous. Il s'est amorcé de luy mesme par la visite qu'il m'a rendue dans mon fort, accompagné de quelques aultres, mais ayant une parfaicte connoissance de la malice de cette nation, je connus bien qu'il ne venoit à aultre dessein que pour sonder:—et l'ayant regallé l'espace de trois semaines, voulant s'en aller librement, je l'ay arresté et conduict dans une chambre et mesme déclaré que je les arrestois prisonniers, tant pour la sureté de ma vie que de la sienne mesme.

Aussytost mon frère se prépara et se mit en campagne pour aller prendre son fort et son vaisseau. Ce qui fut exécuté dans un moment sans répandre une goutte de sang, quoyqu'ils fussent armez jusques aux dents. Ce que mon frère sachant, il les a pris par son adresse en peu de tems et m'envoya dans l'instant tous les prisonniers qui m'ont donné beaucoup de peine à les garder; ayant pris plus de canons que d'hommes. Tous leur dessein et leur entretien n'estant que de trouver le moyen de nous tailler en pièces, tous leurs couteaux estant affilez et pointus comme des lancettes. Et c'est à tort de m'accuser comme ils le font, leur aultre vaisseau qui est allé à la drive n'a esté transporte que par les Glaces, ce qui n'est pas difficile à croire puisque les Glaces ont brisé les deux miens, et du débris de l'un j en ay remonté l'aultre. Ils me l'ont demandé à achepter et pryé de le renvoyer dans les fonds de la baye de l'Est où je les avois posté auparavant et où il y a huict ou dix ans que je les ay quitté. Ce que jay faict et je leur ay donné du tems assez pour venir dans la rivière d'où ils prétendoient me chasser, puisque

---

[1] AC., C^II, Vol. 6, f. 203, 451. Partly printed in [Sulte], *Collection de manuscrits*, 1: 314–316.

je suis estably et prist possession du lieu et mes maisons et magazins faicts et mesme garnison dans la place dont mon fils est le commandant, joint que leur fort est à près de deux cens lieuës de là, où je les ay posté; leurs prétentions sont vaines. Nous avons Pentagouët, fort de l'Acadie, qui appartient aux François, et à douze ou quinze lieuës de nous au surouast il y a habitation angloise qui s'appelle Pémécuid, et entre eulx et nous, il y a une baye nommée St George où il y a de très belle nature et grande eau. Mons. de Biencourt, estant habitué au mont désert, prosche Pentagouët, a envoyé pendant plusieurs années son brigantin en traitte dans le lieu mesme où les Anglois sont postez à présent, qui est la ville de Baston, Nouvelle Angleterre, qui n'est que à trente ou quarante lieuës de la colonie des François, dont M. de Biencourt est commandant, où ils n'avoient point droit d'aller se mettre, puisque ce lieu appartient à la France.

Le Roy d'Angleterre a envoyé Winthrop, 1er Gouverneur de la Nouvelle Angleterre, de laquelle il a pris possession, où il y a à présent une grande ville, bastie en bois, et 200 navires, et la France a bien droit de disputer ce terrain qui vaut beaucoup mieux que l'aultre cy dessus qu'ils demandent. Nous avons eu autrefois une habitation à la coste de l'Amérique entre le cap de Virginie et de la Floride, qui s'appeloit le Port Royal, et les Anglois y sont habitez à présent et le nomme Caroline, et un aultre attenant le cap de Fer; cependant, ils n'ont pas eu droit de s'en emparer   il est vray que les Espagnols nous ont chassé.

J'espère que lon ne me blamera point d'avoir changé le nom de Port Nelson pour le nommer la Rivière Bourbon; lorsque je m'en suis emparé personne ne s'y est opposé et je suis avant les aultres plus de 15 jours, et estant estably et ne songeant que à mon repos d'hyver, l'Anglois y est venu et entré dans le port. Nous luy avons faict commandement de s'en retirer, ce qu'il auroit mieux faict, parce que les glaces n'auroient pas envoyé son navire à la dérive. Il nous a laissé 15 hommes à terre auxquels je puis dire avoir sauvé la vye les ayant assistes de poudres armes et vivres sans compter ceux qui sont venus de rendre a moy suivant leur declaration que jay par écrit et signée d'Eux, et il est certain que les d. deux vaisseaux ne nous ont montré aucune Commission et celui qui est allé a la Drive est le mesme qui avoit pris le père Albanel Jesuist et les mesmes Officiers sans aucun sujet n'avoit point d'autres armes que son brevière ils l'ont garde 18 mois dont le Roy d'Angleterre a été mecontent dans la prise de ce bon pere il n'y a que Dieu qui en puisse pretendre des Dommages et intérests, parce qu'il alloit pour la conversion des aames. Il est vray que les Anglois ont esté 2 ou 3 fois dans la rivière du Port Nelson pour y traitter mais ils n'y ont pourtant faict aucune habitation n'y traite dont il ne faut pas s'étonner parceque nos françois sont hyver et Este dans cette Riviere et Lacs et ou l'Anglois pretend avoir droit nous n'en sommes éloignez que de deux lieues au travers les terres et la riviere ou nous sommes nous a été donnée par les sauvages pour la Commodité de leur negoce.

TRANSLATION

My Lord,

I am constrained to tell you the facts about my conquest and that of my brother, which is the same thing, both of us running the same risks in the Indian countries. I was forced to do my duty as a loyal Frenchman in all things relating to my colony and the seizure of a vessel with no papers that fell into my hands. Seeing that the master could not escape, he acted very well by me; but having learned that there was yet another vessel, he felt obliged to oppose us. He accepted our bait and paid us a visit, accompanied by some of his men; I, knowing full well the deceit of that nation, realized that he came for no other purpose than to spy out our situation. Having entertained him for three weeks, he was about to depart, when I stopped him. Leading him into a chamber, I myself announced that they were my prisoners, as much for my safety as for theirs.

My brother immediately got ready for an expedition to take his fort and his vessel. That was accomplished in very little time without the spilling of a drop of blood, though they were armed to the teeth. Knowing that fact, my brother took them by his skill in a very short time and sent me the prisoners immediately. They gave me much trouble to guard, having more cannons than men. All their idea and talk being merely to find a way to tear us to pieces, they sharpened their knives till the points were like needles. And it is wrong to accuse me, as they have done, of the loss of their vessel, which was lost only by the ice. That is not hard to believe, since the ice broke our two vessels in pieces. From the remains of one I repaired the other. They asked to buy it of me in order to send it to the Bottom of the Bay, to the East Main, where I built them a fort formerly. I left that place and them some eight or ten years ago. I did what they asked and gave them time enough to take possession themselves of the river from which they now claim they have a right to chase me. I was settled there and had taken possession of the place, and my houses and magazines were built and even the garrison was settled, of which my son was the commandant. In addition, their fort is almost two hundred leagues from that place where I was established. Their claim is preposterous. We own Pentagouët, a fort in Acadia, which belongs to the French. A dozen or fifteen leagues from us to the southwest is an English settlement called Pemequid, and between them and us is a bay called St. George Bay, where there is a fine region and good water. Monsieur de Biencourt lived on Mount Desert, near Pentagouët, and for several years sent his boat to trade in that place where the English are settled today, which is called Boston in New England. It is not thirty or forty leagues from the French colony, where Monsieur Biencourt commanded, to the place where the English have no right to be, for it belongs to France.

The King of England sent Winthrop, the first governor of New England, to the place and he took possession. At present there is a big city there, built of wood, and two hundred ships. France has a good right to claim it and it is worth infinitely more than this place that the English are now demanding. Formerly we had a colony on the American coast between the Virginia cape and the Florida one. It was called Port Royal. The English are now settled there and call it Carolina. There is another settlement near Cape Fear. Yet they had no right to take possession there. It is true that the Spanish drove us out.

I hope that I shall not be blamed for changing the name of Port Nelson to Bourbon River. When I took possession of it there was no one there to dispute it and I was there fifteen days ahead of all the others; I was already established and thinking only of my plans for the winter, when the English arrived and entered the port. We ordered them to withdraw and it would have been much better for them if they had done so, for the ice then would not have destroyed their ship. That left fifteen men on shore, of whom I may truthfully say that I saved their lives, having given them powder, arms, and provisions. That does not include the men who came to give themselves up to me by their own volition, which I have in writing, signed by them. It is certain that the two vessels showed us no commissions and the vessel that was lost was the one that took Father Albanel, the Jesuit priest. The same officers were on it. They took him without cause. He was unarmed except for his breviary. They kept him eighteen months. The King of England was displeased at the seizure of the good father. Only God can say what was lost thereby, for he went there to convert souls. It is true that Englishmen have been in the river of Port Nelson two or three times to trade. But then, that is nothing, for our Frenchmen have been in that river and in the lakes, and where the English claim to have a right, we were distant only two leagues across country; and the river where we were located has been ceded to us by the Indians, so that they may have a convenient place for trading with us.

APPENDIX 8

The Committee's Letter of May 20, 1686 [1]

London, 20 May, 1686

Mr Raddison,

We are heartily glad of your arrivall at Port Nellson the last yeare in Capt. Bond, by whose Returne we recd yours of the 15 Septemb[e]r last from Yorke fort & thanke you for the large account you give us of all things, but we are sorry that you should finde any occation which should make you uneasie. We have had two many Instances of the weakness & Imprudent carriage of Mr Abraham as Governor but as We Determined the last yeare, soe we have now perticulerly called him home, hoping Mr Phipps is w[i]th you in his Command, but if Mr Phipps be not there, Our order is that Mr Abraham doe nevertheless returne home, & We have apointed Mr Geyer from New Severne to take the Governement upon him, & Mr Missenden to goe Chiefe there with Mr Welsh for his Trader, And in Port Nellson we resolve to have no Second or Dept. Governor, Geyer being sufficient to command the Fort & Factorey and your selfe to manidge & superintend the trading parte. But if Mr Phipps be there & will stay there, then Mr Missenden remaines second in Port Nelson & Mr Geyer continues at New Severne.

The Invasion of the French from Canada in 1684 with them two Barques was very unhappy to us especially when our Factorey at Port Nellson was so ill provided of fortification & prudent & resolute men to Defend it, which if we had had there they might not only have Defended themselves but also have dislodged the French & prevented their intercepting 12000 Beavers from us, but they not only did that, but in their departure also intercepted our little ship the Perpetuana Merchant & carryed her & all her men to Quebeck wth them, for which & other Injuries and Depredations we hope we shall have an opertunity to reckon wth them. We heare they threatned a Returne the next yeare, but we rather wish it then feare it, because if they come againe we hope we shall finde that courage & fidelity from all our men as shall make them refund what they stole away wth advantage.

---

[1] H.B.Co. Archives, A/6/1, ff. 78-82.

For our Standard of Trade we leave it wholly to your manidgment, as you shall finde occation & reason to bring it downe without loosing the Indians, for Indeed as you yourselfe observe, our charge is so great, our losses many & the fall of beaver here in Europe so considerable daily, that unless there be amends made by your Trading there to greater proffitt & a larger Income of Trade, our expence will Devour us, but we have a confidence in your prudent conduct in trading to our best Advantage and in procureing a Trade & in inviteing the great Nations downe who have ye best Furrs. We have therefore writt expressly to our Governor to be communicated to the whole Councell, that in matter of Trade & in all the Designes & methods which you shall project or take for prosecuting our Trade, no man whatsoever shall oppose or controul you, but therein readily give you all the Assistance they are able & hereby we hope you shall be encouraged, and we receive the fruits & benefit of your good success, as this yeare (God sending our shipps thither & back againe in safety) we doe not Doubt but to receive from you a very ample Cargo.

We will also that you be permitted by the Governor & every one else, to dispose such presents as you shall thinke fitting to the Captaines of the Nations to further our Trade & oblige them to bring their Families Downe

We are very glad that you had sent your Nephew up into the Countries, whome you expected not Downe till aboute April, from which Expedition we promise our selves a good account, & that by his Endeavors great number of Indians will be brought downe to our Factories to trade at the proper seasons

And for New-Severne we have great hopes it will prove a Considerable factorey, & that it will be no Impediment to Port Nellson, but rather that they will prove mutuall helpes & strengthenings to one another Wee understand likewise that there is a little New Factorey begun detached from Port Nellson, all which we have had in our consideration in our supply of goods & provisions this yeare.

Our Guns are all English guns, the best though they cost us ye Dearer, which you will know how to make use of in ye trading of them, & our tobacco is all the same as last yeare, and the right sort of Brazeele tobacco which they so much desire

We have also sent you Indian Corne, Daggers, & all things according to your Demand & particulars tooke care to furnish you.

Our powder is also the best, & our shott, kettles, & all sorte of commodities we hope to content, moreover according to your advice we have sent two great guns of 23 lb weight a peece mounted upon ship carriages proper for the plat-forme with sufficient ball and chayne shott, the better to defend our Fort, wich guns will more than reach cross the River.

We cannot Imagine how we should be abused in the just weight of our Provissions, our beefe peeces not to weigh above ¼ of what yey should weigh, we wish it could be discovered to us, however, we have tooke that care that we thinke the like abuse cannot be put upon us this Voyage.

We have writ to the Bottome of the Bay to send you Barke of Birch Trees from thence for making Canoes according as you desire. We desire you to encourage & encrease our trade of Martin skins & all other small furrs as much as you can possible, for yey turne better to account here than beaver, & are in great request here, the Canada Comp^a have 30 & 40 thousand Martin skins returned and if some course were taken to encourage the takeing of yem our Countrey affords plenty enough of them & we might have as many returnes.

We heare there are also very many Ermines about Yorke Fort where you are, they also wold doe very well if you can catch yem to sende us what you can home

We have sent a few tinne Kettles this yeare to Port Nellson, as we have also done to our other Factories for a tryall how yey will please the Indians, being extreame light of carriage & we thinke may be as serviceable to them as the heavey brass & copper kettles   pray write us your opinion of them.

We hope we have made every thinge easey to you, at least we doe resolve to doe it, if any thing be yet deficient, resolveing to cast our whole hopes of a great & flourishing trade upon you & your contrivance; & therefore we have commanded ye whole guidance of the trading parte to be left entirely to your conduct & manidgment. And as we will have none to blame if we faile of a glorious trade but your selfe, so in the happy success of it, you will not only finde your owne account & advantage together with us, but we shall alwaies enlarge our selves towards you in such waies of acknowledgment as shall be fitting & Due to your prudence & Industrey.

And for as much as the perfection of any thinge is not attained of a sudden, but is the worke of some tyme, & from solid and wise foundations growes up by degrees to a flourishing state, wee shall extreamely desire that besides the two yeares which you agreed to stay at Port Nelson, you would be so kinde to our affaires & to your owne Int. as to resolve to stay one yeare more, that so you may have a competent & sufficient tyme to doe yose great things for this Company which you have promised to our Gratious King & to us, & which * in the meane tyme for your encouragement to goe on cheerefully in

all waies of advanceing our honour & profitt, We thinke it not amiss
to put you in mind, that your particular Interest is fixed & safe here
at home And that our Committee & governement now is so constituted
that you must doe your Faith great violence if you beleave that there
is any one but who is intirely your friend & will in all occations be
ready upon your good Success in our affaires to embrace you with all
respect, affections & gratitude

Your loveing Friends

Churchill Govern^r

* & which we beleeve you alone
to be capable to bring to pass

Ed: Dering Dept. Governor
John Huband
Wm Younge
Richard Cradock
Sam: Clarke
Nicho Hayward
Ste. Pitts

The Committee's Letter of June 3, 1687 [1]

1687, June 3

Monsr Espritt Radisson

Wee accept verry kindly yor ample Narrative of the state of the Comp^{as} affaires ever since you have been in those parts, by Yo^r Letter of the 4th Septemb^r and should have answered every paragraph were you not designed to returne for England this yeare, therefore are resolved to Wave those matters till wee see you, when wee shall gladly hearken to yor advise in what ever may relate to the well Carryeing on of our Trade and makeing of Further Settlem^{ts} in the interim you may read in our Gen^rall Letter what at p^rsent Wee can Recollect most necessary to be observed and Wee hope and expect before yor departure you may bee extreame usefull to us on Adviseing and directing what is best to be done, for the French haveing dispoyled us (as wee are Informed) att the Bottome of the Bay disables us how to make any certaine Calculation how to provide for those parts soe must leave such things to be determined by the Governo^r and the rest of the Councell beleiveing you may have received a perfect relation of every particular action that has happened for questionlesse our men were sent either to New Severne or Port Nelson else if they have failed of arriveing att either of those places we have Just reason to Fear they are all utterly lost 'twill therefore require yor greatest care and prudence to Consider how to Steere matters as in probability may be most safe and Advantageous. Wee have ordered that you have the great Cabbin for yor accomodation and that the Comander that brings you home does use you with great respect and kindnesse, wee have alsoe p^rsented you with a Quarter Caske of Clarrett to drinke in yor Voyage, and Ordered the Governo^r to be extreame kind and Courteous to yor Nephew and the other French men that stay behinde, being desireous that all of you doe plentifully participate of what Favours wee can showe. You must remember to leave in Writeing with our Governo^r such admonitions and advices as you can deeme any wayes Conducible to the well Carryeing on of the Companyes affairs in yor absence and

---

[1] H.B.Co. Archives, A/6/1, f. 93.

you may assure them from us that all such goods with whatsoever else
may be thought necessary for the Briske carryeing on of the Trade
and the Comfort of all our People shall the next yeare bee certainely
sent them soe heartily wishing you a Prosperous Voyage and safe arriveall to us Wee remaine

Yo^r assured Loveing Freinds

Churchill Govern^r

E Dering Dep Govr

&c^a

3^d June 1687

Coppy of Willm Young Esqr his Letter to the Comittee Dated ye 20th Decemb^r 1692 [1]

Gentellmen,

I am verry sory yo^ur Benevolence to Mr Radison moves soe slowley, dureing his great necessity, since he was soe Kindly Recomended to you by our Late Govern^r the Earle of Marleborough. I presume the onely Reason is, because the Majority of the Present Committee are strangers to him & his former Concernes with the Comp^a I hold myselfe obleiged, therefore to doe him Right, by giveing you his Caracter, in as few words as I am able.

Mr Radison was borne a French man, he was Educated from a Child in Canada & spent all his Youthfull yeares in hunting & Commercing with the Indians in the Countries Adjacent to Hudsons Bay: By Reason whereof, he became absolute Master of theire Language, theire Customes & methods of Trade.

Mr Radison being at New England about 27 or 28 yeares past, mett there with Coll. Nichols the govern^r of New Yorke, & was by him persuaded to goe for England & proffer his service to King Charles the Second, in order to make a Settlement of an English factory in that Bay.

Att his arrivall here the said King, giveing Creditt to his Reasons for that Undertakeing, granted to Prince Rupert, the Duke of Albemarle, & others, (the same Charter we doe still Claime by,) thereby Constituting them the Proprietors of the said Bay: Under which Authority he the said Radison went Imediately, & made an English settlement there according to his promise.

Att his Returne to England, & the said factory being settled, the King publickly acknowledged his great service to the Nation, & presented him a Medall with a gold Chaine to weare, in Token of his favour.

Some years after when the Comp^a denied him maintenance & Rejected his service, he went to Canada againe, the Place of his Education,

---

[1] H.B.Co. Archives, A/6/2, ff. 66–67.

and as he Tould the Comp^a Before he went, he was Compelled to doe, haveing no other place of Abode.

Being at Canada & wanting maintenance, he was Easely persuaded to Joyne, with his Countreymen the French, & to Conduct an Expedition into the Bay, which for the Present seemed to the Prejudice of our Company, though it hath since redounded much to theire Advantage.

When he was arrived in the Bay, he was soe well Knowne to all the Indian Captaines, with whose Assistance & Intelligence, Joyned with his owne Courage & Conduct, he easeily destroyed, our Comp^ies factory, as also he did a New England factory planted above us, in the Port Nelson River

This New England Factory being settled above us, would have been a Thorne in our sides, & would have Intercepted our Trade with the Indians nor could wee have easeley (if att all or Justly) removed them, they being settled in that River, before our settlement there made.

Dureing that Winter Mr Radison used violence to none of the English, but sustained them with victuals, & gave them powder & shott, when theire Shipp was Cast away, & they were destitu[t]e of Booth, & when the Indians offered him a great Present, to suffer them to Destroy all the English, he utterly Refused it, & gave them a Shipp to carry them away.

After this Mr Radison settled the french factory much higher in the same River (above the fall) where Considering his alliances with the Indians, it was out of the Power of New England or Old England to destroy them & Imediately went him selfe to France.

Mr Young that yeare being a member of the Hudsons Bay Comittee, with Leave obtained from Sr James Hayes (then theire Deputy Governour) did write 3 or foure Insinuating Letters to the said Mr Radison then at Paris, acknowledging the Comp^ies former severities to him, and to allure him to Returne againe into the Comp^ies service, did make him Large promises, that he should bee Extreamely well Received & Rewarded by the Company

After the Exchange of 3 or 4 Letters, Mr Radison unexpectedly arrived at London as much to the surprise of his Correspondent Mr Young, as the Rest of ye Comittee, for he durst not write a Word of his Intention, Least his Letters should have been Intercepted, which he said would have cost him his Life.

Att his arrivall, the Comp^ies ships were Ready to depart, for the Bay, soe y^t he had butt just time to Kisse the Kings hand at Windsor, and Likewise, the Duke of Yorkes, who was then Governour of the Comp^a they Booth Recomended him to the Comp^ies Care & Kindness, by theire Comands, to Sr James Hayes, then the Deputy Govern^r

& also directed that he should bee made an English man, Least by any Casualty he should fall into the hands of the French, which in his absence was performed.

Before he went in the Comp^ies shipps to the Bay, the Comp^a gave him Two originall actions in the Comp^ies stock & 50^lb per Ann subsistance money, with Large promises of future Rewards, if he should performe what he undertooke, & doe them any Considerable service: & then he went away with the Companies servants.

Arriveing at Port Nelson, he Imediately put the Comp^ies Agents into the Entire possesion of that River, he brought away all the French into England, and all the Beaver & other furs which the french had Traded & gave them to the Comp^a without demanding any share for them selves. Though some men are of oppinion, since they were the product of theire owne Labours, they had a Right to it all, which was sold for seaven thousand pounds.

Att this time also he was Kindly welcomed to England by the King, who againe Recommended him to the Comp^a as a person much deserveing there Kindness, & then the Comittee presented him with 100 guneys, and Entered an order in theire Bookes, that he should have 50^lb per ann. more, added to his former 50^lb till the King should give him a place, & then the Last 50^lb to Cease & determine.

He never had any place given him. Y^t Sr Edw Dering when Deputy Govern^r had power to Influence the Comittee, to take away the said 50^lb againe, & he hath not Received it the space of Two yeares & halfe Last past, soe y^t he hath at Present but 50^lb per Ann to mainttaine him selfe, & wife & 4 or 5 Children and servants, & of which 50^lb 24^lb goeth for house Rent.

I did omitt to acquaint you in its propper place that when he was apointed to be your Cheife Trader, to Barter your goods with the Indians, at Port Nelson, & was sent thither onely for that purpose, some of your servants there, tempted him to Combine with them to Cheate the Comp^a of theire Beaver, and because hee did Refuse soe to doe, they tooke an ocasion to quarell with him, & his nephew, Beating & wounding them, & dureing the time of Trade, which may well be presumed to bee done on purpose, to give them an oportunity to act these villanies without his power of Observation, which he had Refused to act in Consort with them.

Thus Gentelmen I have given you the History of Mr Radisons Transactions in the fewest words I could possible, If there bee any Errors (besides my scrawling hand which I cannot helpe) I begg your pardon. God is my witnes there is none to my Knowledg. Therefore I doe humbly & heartily desier you to Continue & pay him the 100^lb per Ann. & the arrears from the time that any part of it was stopt, for the Reasons following,

1st   Because all persons that know his story, (that Ever I met with) except Sr Edw Dering, thinke it most Just & Reasonable.

2   Because he had noe place given him in Lew of the 50^{lb} per Ann. stop^t from him: & that is his great Losse, for it cannot bee Imagined, that any place to bee given him by the King, could bee worth soe Little as 50^{lb} per Ann.

3   Because of his great fidelity to the Comp^a who in more than Twenty years service, was never Taxed for defrauding them to the vallew of a skin, notwithstanding his many temptations.

4   Because he did never Capitulate with the Comp^a but thankefully accepted what they were pleased to give him.

5   Because he hath been Extreamly affronted & misused by y^r Servants in ye Bay, & made a prisoner on the water in the time of Trade for noe other Reason, Because he would not confederate with them, to cheate the Comp^a of theire goods

6   Because the Comp^a have Received from Port Nelson since he delivered them that factory, furrs neare the vallew of 100000^{lb}.: which wiser men then, myselfe, beleive had all been lost, & theire whole Interest in the Bay (I meane as to the Comp^{ies} present Posession) If he had not come over to the Comp^{ies} service when Invited.

7   Because the 2 originall actions & the 100^{lb} per Ann revert to the Comp^a againe at his death: & what Reward is that Considering his services, for a man who hath Crost the seas between England & America 24 times, & is growne old in the service of the Comp^a

8   Because it is Impossible he can maintaine a Wife & servants & 4 or 5 Children with £26: in London with meate & drinke & Clothes.

9   Because his debts are soe great, through Necessity, not Ill Management, y^t he must bee forced to shift for him selfe, & Leave his wife great with Child & 4 or 5 children more on the parrish, if you Releive him not.

10   Because he cannot sell any of his 2 actions to sustaine his great necessities because they are onely for his Life.

11   Because King Charles who gave us our Charter, gave him also a Token of his favour in the Medall & gold chaine, & gave soe many Kind Recomendations to the Company

12   Because the french have sett a price upon his head on pretence that he is a Traytor to his Countrey: soe y^t if he goes home, he must bee Chop^t to peices, & if he stayes in England, he must starve, without y^r favourable Assistance

13   Lastly Gentelmen, give me Leave to Remember you, what I should

not have done but to serve Mr Radison, viz   That as he was the Imediate author of the Comp^ies present prosperity, soe I myselfe was the first mover that Induced him to it, & without me he had never come back to theire service, nay when I wrote to Invite him, the Comittee Ridiculed me for the attempt, But when it Succeeded to theire Admiration, I had the Honour to have the Thankes of the Comittee, & some friends moved y^t I should bee presented with a gratuity for my good service, But I utterly Refused any, as Knowing I did nothing but my duty, y^t if you thinke I deserved any, I humbly desier you will give it to Mr Radison, in his greate & pressing necesity, & I begg it as heartily as I would begg a Morsell of Bread for Myselfe, If I were Ready to Starve, and will ever acknowledg it as the greatest as well as the Justest Kindness you can doe to

Y^r most obedient servant
Will Yonge.

The Comittees Answer to Esqr Yonges Letter [2]

In answer unto Esqr Yonges Letter to the Committee dated ye 20th Decemb^r Last The Three or foure first paragraphs, are a history of Mr Radisons Birth Education & Travels, which wee doe not Gainsay. And Beleive hee might bee some wayes Instrumentall in ye first Settlement at the Bottome of the Bay, and y^t King Charles did order him a Medall & gold Chaine at his first Returne, And wee doubt not but those Hon^lbe Persons in the Comittee then, did verry well Reward him for the service hee did them.

Yet Mr Yonge in the next parragraph saith the Comp^a denyed him Mainetenance & Rejected his service, But wholey omitts the Reasons thereof, which If wee could bee soe happy as to Know, wee should bee better able to Judg, whether twere the Comp^ies Unkindness or Radisons desert.

Wee doe Understand that about the yeare 1681 or 1682 y^t Mr Radison & his brother Gooseberry did enter Into an other Contract with the Company & Received of them 50^lb & soone after without any service don them, they absconded & deserted theire service & went for France & thence to Canada.

And the next yeare following as Mr Yonge saith, they did Confederate with theire Countreymen, & Joyned with them in An Expedition to Port Nelson, being animated thereto by the Report Mr Abram had given the Comp^a of the Situation & great hopes & probability of

2 H.B.Co. Archives, A/6/2, ff. 68–71.

that Place to Prove the best factory in the Bay. And accordingly Radison arrived in Hayes River, & haled up his Two Barkes Wherein they came, as high as they could for feare of the English, whome Radison Knew would bee there y^t yeare. There the French about the fall built a small Hutt, which is the fortification y^t Mr Yonge saith neither the Power of old nor new England could Remove, haveing neither gun or any workes made about it, a place merely to sleepe in, & manned onely with 7 frenchmen

This Expedition of Radisons Mr Yonge saith tho it seemed then Prejudiciall to the Comp^a yet since hath Redounded much to the Comp^{ies} Advantage, But how that can bee wee Cannot apprehend,

For in the next Line almost hee saith Radison had such Correspondency with & Knowledg of the Indian Cap^{ts} that Joyned with his owne Courage & Conduct, hee soone destroyed the Comp^{ies} Settlement, as also y^t of New England. And ye^t is also pleased to say, y^t the New England Settlement, was soe firme & strong, that the Power of Old England, could not destroy it, & y^{et} Mr Radison makes nothing of it, but upon second thoughts, wee beleive Mr Yonge will bee of another opinnion, therefore wee answer Nothing att all to it.

But as for the old England Settlement, it was onely a house Mr Bridgar had Built to Lodg in & keepe the goods dry, without Gun or any Workes, or one Corne of powder, for Old Gillam in the Comp^{ies} Shipp, arrives verry Late (the Reason wee will give you afterwards), And as soone as arrived at Port Nelson River, hee Landed his Beefe porke shott & Iron ware &c^a that would take noe harme by Lying open, (because there was noe house built there) and before Old Gillam could have an opertunity to Land more goods, the Ice came soe thick upon him, y^t drove his Shipp to Sea & was never heard of afterwards. A Just Reward of his perjury and perfidiousness to ye Comp^a as you will heare heareafter.

You have heard of a New England Settlement, made & Taken by Radison, it came thus. Old Gillam hereing from Mr Abram, what an Advantageous place this Port Nelson might prove And the Comendations hee gave it, (And not without cause as it proves) And haveing Entered into service of the Comp^{as}, at the same time his son being here: he sent him for New England, wth Recomendacons for Equiping out an Expedition to Port Nelson, telling him hee would give him opertunity to gett in Before him, & to make a Settlement first above the Comp^a, which would (hee Thought) prevent the Comp^{ies} Settlement. Whereupon Young Gillam sailes for New England, and Equips a Shipp, and tooke with him Trading goods & provisions accordingly, & sailes for Port Nelson & accordingly arrives there Before his father, and Settles him selfe, in the most Advantageous place. This was not done neither without some Jealousey that Old Gillam & his son & Radison had Laid this plott Togeather in Old England to frustrate the Comp^ies Intentions, for Radison being first arrived ~~at Port Nelson River, comes~~ there, & heareing there was an English shipp arrived Presently after, hee by Intelligence heares of young Gillams arrivall att Port Nelson River, comes downe to him & then makes a Confederacey with young Gillam to defend one another, And If Possible to surprize & seize the Comp^ies Shipp & goods, which also succeeded, for Old Gillam comeing in soe Late with designe to Lett his son first arrive, & hee being driven out to sea & Lost, which Radison heareing of, came downe & without much Resistance, Bridgar haveing noe powder, hee seized upon Bridgar & the few men with him & his goods & carries them to the fall or neare thereto, where there Barkes Lay, & Lodged them on board a Barke good p^rt of the Winter without fier or Clothes, And whereas Mr Yonge saith Radison used the English verry Kindly, giveing them victuals & powder, in the first place they had such quantites of salt provisions that they needed none, and Mr Bridgar sath hee offered Radison 25^lb Ster: & more for one Barrell of Powder to Kill fresh provisions with, butt was deneyed him and Instead of Shewing them Kindnesse, hee tooke all they had & burnt theire house.

Radison haveing Bridgar & all his men & goods secure, he makes a second visett to young Gillam, in all Love & flattering friendshipp, & Tempts him to take a Walke into the woods, where Radison Laid an ambush for him, & there young Gillam is seized, who by a Stratagem is Carried to his men and forced to Betray his men shipp & goods to the french, in feare of his Life which most Certainly hee had Left if hee had Refused to doe, & heare young Gillam has his Reward & Radison has posession of all. But how Kindly hee used the English Lett the World Judg.

By this seizure as you have heard Radison is Capacitated to make Large Returnes, which hee doth for canada, not onely off Furrs but of Europian Comodities, to a Considerable Vallew.

Accordingly hee sailes for Canada in the next fall in young Gillams shipp takeing Bridgar & young Gillam with him prisoners, & shipps all the English men both from Old & New England in one of his old and Toren Barkes to the Bottome of the Bay, & in goeing downe, they mett with one of our shipps Returneing for England from the Bottome of the Bay, where all those men Lay upon the Comp^as hand for $\frac{12}{M}$ time, the other Barke of Radisons, was toren in peices by the Ice, soe y^t had not Radison seized upon young Gillams Shipp he and his French

men had all Certainely perrished, Except could have Travelled overland for Canada (& then must have lost all theire goods behind them)
But that was Imposible.

Now sailes Radison for Canada in young Gillams shipp with a
Large Cargoe of furrs & other goods taken from the English to a
great vallew, Leaveing also with his nephew Gooseberry a whole yeares
Trade of Europian comodities which produced that verry Cargoe M^r
Radison came with for England and made his peace with the Comp^a
in ann° *1684*

Radison Being arrived at Canada, Bridgar makes his complaint to
the government at Quebeck & Enters prossess against Radison, for his
Ill usage & Robbing of the English of all they had, which was highly
Resent^d by them in soe much y^t hee durst not show his head there, but
skulkes away and goes for France, upon which Bridgars action falls;
the Person offending not being to bee found.

By this time our shipps arrive from the Bottome of the Bay in England, By whome the Comp^a had Intelligence of the Prankes Radison
had plaied at Port Nelson, whereupon the Comp^a made an adresse to
King Charles, who gave order forth with to his Ambasad^r in France
to give in a Memoriall to the French King, which is don & prest verry
hard for Restitution &c^a. Radison being arrived & gott to Paris,
heares thereof his name being in the English Ambasad^s memoriall, hee
was forced to skulke & hide him selfe, upon which wee are Easely ap^t to
beleive, he writt to some freind in England to Interceed for him to the
Comp^a. And Esqr Young is the first that acquaints Sr James Hayes
the Deputy Govern^r then in Comittee, who forthwith Adjourned the
Comittee to the halfe moone Tavern in Cheapside & tooke along with
him for more privacy onely Mr Young Sr Edw Dering & Mr Cradock,
& there it was ordered that Mr Young bee desired to write to M^r
Radison & corespond with him, Towards bringing him over & Reconcileing him selfe with the Comp^a whome wee conceive was Easely
persuaded thereto, Considering the Condition he was in, & accordingly
he came for England and all misdemeanors forgiven, upon promise
that he would Restore what hee could Especially what was traded by
the 7 Frenchmen at Port Nelson, and that he would bring the French
men for England, & Leave our men in possession of Hayes River.

Whereupon Mr Radison appeares before the Comittee and Enters
into a new Contract, the Comp^a Giveing him the Benefitt of 200^lb
stock & 50^lb sallery for Life, and thereupon hee sailes for Hayes River
& as soone as he arrives there hee acquaints his nephew Gooseberry
& the Rest, what Entertainment hee had met with at Canada, as also
in France, and how necessitated to make the Best termes hee could

with the Comp^a to save his neck & theires to. They forth with came downe bringing with them all they had Traded, But whether more or Lesse twas the product of the goods they had Taken from the English, when Radison arrived here the Comittee gratified him & his French men verry Libarally, & maintayned them a whole yeare & Tooke as many of them into the Comp^{ies} service as would Returne, at verry high wages his nephey haveing 80^{lb} per Ann & the Rest in Proportion, the meanest 30^{lb} per Ann. in Expectation that they should doe some Extrordinary service, which they all promised, by Travelling & bringing downe new Nations of Indians to Trade with us, & Increased Mr Radisons wages to 100^{lb} per Ann dureing his Service abroad

Whereupon Radison his nephew Gooseberry & 4 or 5 more Returned to Port Nelson the next yeare and stayed there 2 years, But instead of doeing the Comp^a Extrordinary Service, our Govern^r there found not that they did any better service then our owne men, at 10 or 12^{lb} per Ann. for they never would Travell nor was the Increase of Beaver or other skins anything the more for them, nor any service in any manner done the Comp^a by them more then was done by our owne men.

Whereupon after Two years stay, back they Returned, & arriveing here, there wages were p^d them, & they acknowledged, they never in theire Lives saw soe much of their owne before. Mr Radison at his Returne, hee Exhibits a long scrowle of 40 or 50 Articles against Governo^r Geyer & Sinclar, of High Treason & wee Know not what, but upon serious Examination of, the then Comittee they were accounted frivolous false & malitious, noe profe being made to any one article of Consequence, Tho Mr Radison had persuaded one Mr Misenden to come over with him, who left his charge as Deputy Govern^r & Cheife in New Severn, haveing promises from Radison, if would witness to some articles he should by the Interest hee could make in the Comittee, Returne Govern^r of the Bay: But what profe hee made & how Rewarded is notoriously Knowne, for y^t hee was discarded the Comp^{as} service & never to bee Imployed more.

And this wee may observe by the way, that notwithstanding Mr Radisons Complaint that Govern^r Geyer & others Fell out with him & his nephew because they would not Joyne with them in cheating the Comp^a of theire Beaver, y^t wee have ever since Mr Radisons Returne, had verry large Increase, & much better Beaver than Ever, & have not to this day heard of any wrong done don [sic] us in y^t nature.

But, on the other hand, wee have found Govern^r Geyer soe discreet, Judicious & carefull in ye Comp^{ies} affaires, that wee never heard the Governm^t there was ever in such good hands Before. And had the

Comittee hearkened to the Importunacy of M[r] Radison in calling him home, wee have Reason to fear our Trade would have come to nothing. If wee had not Lost all. But y[t] If Radison has any Charge against Govern[r] Geyer, wee doubt not butt in a few monthes time hee may speake to him face to face, & may bee ashured hee shall bee Impartially heard before y[e] Comittee. one thing more wee take Leave to Observe by the way, That had not the Comittee Interceded & stopt the proceedings of M[r] Bridgar, at M[r] Radisons Returne in 1684 from y[e] Bay, hee had Certainely given him a great deale of Trouble & put him to Expence too; If it had not gon farther, for Takeing all hee had away from him at Port Nelson.

And soe the Like of young Gillam, but that the Comp[a] Threatened him If he medled with Radison the Comp[a] would fall upon him, for Trading into theire priveleges, & soe stopt him, whereas they were both sencible Enough that Radison had done all what hee did at Port Nelson, without any Comission from y[e] French King or Canada Company either, how hard it might have gone with Radison wee say not.

As for the 50[lb] gratuity M[r] Radison received, Its Knowne to most that that was not Intended to Continue halfe soe Long as twas paid, But some Reasonable time the Earle of Marleborough might have to promote him to some place Equivelent, But we understand from my Lord the Reasons why it could not bee done, wee are well satisffied therein, But Because it could not conveniently be done by My Lord, wee doe not thinke the Comp[a] are one Jott the more obleiged to pay him the gratuity, for the Comittee never promised any place, & should not hee gett one till Domes Day shall wee bee therefore obleiged to give him yearly the gratuity wee think not, and If his gratuities should bee proportionable to his Expences it may come to 500[lb] per Ann as well as one.

That King Charles was soe Kind as to Welcome him home &c[a], Wee Apprehend had the good King Knowne of his Behaviour to this Comp[a], & to others his subjects, hee would have banished such a fellow his presence & Court.

And Last of all, That the Comittee now Cannot bee of M[r] Yongs opinnion as to M[r] Radison in all things, wee crave pardon for, wee cannot helpe it, as all men are not alike in face are they neither alike in minde & Judgment. Besides the Information wee have Received about this affaire wee have Reason to beleive it, Being from persons still in Being, and are Ready to Testifie the Truth of the above Narrative & answer   As for the Reasons y[t] added for the Continuance of the 50[lb] Gratuity, The most of them are answered by the foregoeing narrative & Answer   Y[t] wee say

1.   That Whereas its Afirmed all that have ever heard the story of Mr Radison Except Sr Edw Dering, thinke it most Reasonable & Just, wee must begg y^r pardon for that, for wee never heard one member of the Comp^a that had y^t opinion but Mr Yonge, & wee thinke Its most Reasonable, that those y^t give should Know why they give, & ought to dispose of theire owne as they thinke best, nor will a gratuity or Charity admitt of Compulsion.

2.   That tho hee never has had any place nor never should have one given him, Thats noe Reason to Continue the gratuity. If soe it would not bee a gratuity but a due debt, which wee cannot permitt, being noe Contract in ye Case, nor promise hee should have a place.

3.   As for Mr Radisons Fidelity to the Comp^a wee grant that wee doe not finde him accused for stealeing or purloyning theire goods, but Breach of Trust & Contracts leaveing the Comp^ies service after had Received theire money, wee doe find him guilty off.

4.   Tho its said he never did Capittulate with the Comp^a wee find that hee did Capitulate as per the minute the 6 May 1685.

5.   Wee cannot beleive the Comp^ies servants did ever abuse or affront Mr Radison because he would not Consent with them in Cheating the Comp^a of theire Beaver, for y^t the persons hee accused were never found guilty since Mr Radisons departure nor before, & y^t Every yeare since the Comp^a have Received a Considerable Increase of Beaver & other goods in Returne.

6.   That the great quantities of goods wee have Received has been since Mr Radisons departure out of the Bay, soe y^t hee could not bee the occasion of ye Increase, & that hee came into the Comp^ies service, was more to serve himselfe then any Respect or Love he had for the Comp^a

7.   Wee grant that booth the 200^lb stock & 50^lb sallery revert to ye Comp^a after his death, & y^t was the agrement made with him as above said, nor know wee of above 4 times at most of the 24 that hee went to the Bay in ye Comp^ies service.

8.   Its not our busines to Enquire how Mr Radison mainetaynes his Wife & famuly [sic] wee have not onely p^d him what hee Contracted with us for, But have given him such large gratuities & guifts that hee has Received of the Comp^a about 1000^lb in Eight yeares time, but how he spends it, is not ouer [sic] busines to Enquire after.

9.   Wee know not, nor can wee take cognizance how Mr Radison contracts his debts, hee Knowes best, what hee does, & that he will Leave his Wife & children upon the Parrish Lett them Looke to that.

10.   Wee agree with Mr Yonge, that the 2 actions are but for his Life and therefore cannot sell them, & this Mr Radison Knew when

hee made the contract with the Comp^a Else did not understand him selfe. Butt wee know hee thought it the Best Bargaine he ever made in all his Life time & soe it was.

11.   That the King was pleased to give him a medall & chaine of 25 or 30^lb thats noe argument for us to give him 1000^lb, & wee know that was contrived too. But wee are all of opinnion that Capt Edgcombe deserved a gold chaine & medall much better then Mr Radison.

12.   If Mr Radison dares not Returne home hee may stay here. If had behaved himselfe faithfull & constant either to English or Frenc[h]e hee might have gone where he would

13.   Wee must Begg pardon that wee cannot bee of Mr Yonges opinnion, that Mr Radison should bee the founder of the Comp^a nor the Author of our prosperity, as he is pleased to say. But on ye other hand, has been verry falce & perfidious to the Comp^a, & has been the ocasion of vast Expences to the Comp^a, & has put many Inconvienienceys upon them, which noe man but him selfe could doe, & that the Comp^a, notwithstanding have been Extreame Kind to him and all the french men hee has Recomended to theire service, tho never soe Ill deserveing, which has not amounted to Lesse then 500^lb in gratuities & Extravagant charges about them, ocasioned by Mr Radisons Recomendation, when in Truth, when wee came to make use of them, they never would Travell or doe any thing more then one of our owne people of 6 or 8^lb p^r ann   That Mr Radison may bee an object of our pitty, If in soe meane a condition as Represented to us; which wee can scarcely beleive, being has been so high in his capitulation, thinkeing wee must either give him what hee demands, or else will accept of nothing. Lett him doe his pleasure, But wee must tell him wee will not admitt of any capitulation for our own Benevolence or Charity & will be Judges what best to give & to whome.

And to conclude wee thinke wee have noe Reason to depart from the opinnion of the Comittee that Retrenched the 50^lb Gratuity. Y^t at the Instance of the R^t Honble the Earle of Marleborough wee were Induced to Gratifie Mr Radison with one 50^lb, but finding him so Imperious & scornefull of soe small a sume as he Esteemes it, wee Lett him know we have more deserveing objects to Bestow it upon.

Signed

By order of the Comittee of the

Hudsons Bay Company

Wm Potter Secretary

Hudsons Bay House the
8th of March 1692/3

Mr Radison's Affidavitt made before
Sir Robt Jeffery the 23^d August 1697.
Left with Y^e English Commiss^ers
the 5th June 1699.[1]

Peter Espritt Radisson of the Parish of St. James In the County of Middlesex. Esqre Aged Sixty one Yeares or thereabouts Maketh Oath that he Came Into England In the Yeare one thousand Six hundred Sixty five, And In the Yeare 1672 [2] married one of the Daughters of Sir John Kirke & In the Yeare 1667. this Deponent with his brother-In-Law Madard Chowar De Grosilliers were designed for a Voyage in the Service of the English in Hudson Bay, which they undertooke this Deponent Goeing on board the Shipp Eagle, Then Comanded by one Captain Wm. Stanard, was hindered being Disabled at Sea by bad weather So Could not Compleate the S^d Intended Voyage; but the S^d Grosilere proceeded In another English Ship Called the NonSuch & arrived In the Bottome of Hudson's Bay In a Certaine River there which Capt Zachary Gilham Comander of the Shipp (as the S^d Grosiliere told this Deponont) then named Rupert's River in Hon^r of His Highness Prince Rupert who was (Cheifly) Interested In that Expedition, & that the S^d Captain Gilham then alsoe built a ffort, there Which he called Charles ffort In honor of his then Matie King Charles the Second & this Deponont Alsoe Saith that In the Yeare one thousand Six hundred Sixty Eight He, This Deponont went From England In order to another voyage to Port Nelson in Hudson Bay In an English Shipp Called the Waveno then Comanded by the S^d Captaine Stanard, but this Deponont was then Alsoe obstructed & could not Accomplish the Intended Voyage that Yeare Also but returned Into England & at his Returne found the S^d Grosillier Safely Arrived with the S^d Gilham, In England, & in the yeare one thousand six hundred sixty nine this Deponont went In the S^d Shipp the Waveno then Commanded by one Capt Newland & arrived at Port Nelson & went on Shoare

---

[1] This was copied from the transcript in the Public Archives of Canada: Hudson's Bay Memorial Book, No. 701, pp. 81–86. The transcript is inaccurate. The original is in PRO., Amer. & W. I., Vol. 539.
[2] 1667 has been erased.

there with the English (which was the first time that he, this Deponont
or any other French to his Knowledge or that he ever heard of went
to that Place) & there the English left some Goods there to trade with,
& from thence the S^d Shipp went to the Bottome of the Bay where he
wintered with the S^d Grosilliere who went thither that Yeare with
the Ship Rupert, then Comanded by the S^d Zachary Gilham and the
Place where they wintered was In Rupert's River at Charles' Fort &
In the Yeare one thousand six hundred & Seventy the S^d Grosiliere was
sent In An English Barke Comanded & Navigated by English Men
from the Bottom of the Bay to Port Nelson, & there the English left
them Some Goodes to trade with the Indians & this Deponont alsoe
Saith that there were Noe French in Any of the S^d Shippes or Barke,
during the S^d Voyages save this Deponent & the S^d Grosiliere & a
French Chirurgeon & this Deponent Alsoe Saith that he continued In
England till the Yeare one thousand Six hundred Seventy three: &
there arising Some differences between the Hudson Bay Company of
England & this Deponent, He, this Deponont went into France & In
the Yeare one thousand Six Hundred Eighty two there were Two
Barkes fitted out at Canada Chiefly at the Expense of one Monsr
Lachenay of Quebeck, one where of was Comanded by this Deponent
& the other by this Deponont's S^d Brother Grosiliere who Sailed from
Canada to Hudson's Bay & arrived in Hayes River there and that
Yeare this Deponent with the other French with him tooke Port Nel-
son & an English Vessall which came from New England comanded
by one Benj: Gilham & the S^d Zachary Gilham was In the River of
Port Nelson wth a Shipp of the English Comp^{as} To trade there, but
was cast away haveing first landed Severall Goods there & put on
Shore one Mr John Bridgar whom the English Comp^{ie} had sent as
there Governour to that Place Whome this Deponent Carried the
Next Yeare To Canada & disposed of Severall of the other English
some to New England, & others to the Bottome of the Bay, & this Deponent then Gave the Name of Bourbon to the Said Port Nelson &
the Name of St Therese to the River Called Hayes River but before
that time this Deponent well Knew that the English Called the Said
Place Port Nelson & this Deponent Alsoe Saith that In the Yeare one
thousand six hundred Eighty three he came from Canada to Paris by
the order of Monsr Colbert who soon after Dyed. And this Deponent
being At Paris was there Informed that the Lord Preston Ambassador
of the King of England had given in a Memoriall to the Ministers of
His Most Christian Maj$^{tie's}$ Court against the Action of this Deponont at Port Nelson & after this Deponent had been severall times
with the Marquis de Seignlay & Monsr Calliere (now one of the Pleni-

potentiaries for His Most Christian Maj^{tie} at the Treaty of Peace)
on the Occasion aforesaid & this Deponent then found that the French
had quitted All pretenses to Hudson Bay & thereupon He this Deponent At Paris In the Month of Aprill In the Yeare one thousand
Six hundred Eighty four In the Chamber of the S^d Monsr Calliere He
this Deponent with his owne proper hand but of the Special Direction
of the S^d Monsr Calliere did write the Paper here unto Annexed beginning with these words (Viz) Pour terminer les Differends qui Sont
Entre les deux Nationes Francois & Anglois au Susjest de l habitation
fait par les Srs Desgroziliere & Radisson Dans le Baie De Hudson Etc.
And Ending with these words. En Raportan le d^t Inventorie En
Quendrant Acc^s Proprietare Anglois le mesme Effect in Valeur) all
which the S^d Mon^s Calliere dictated to this Deponent from Whose
Mouth this Deponent accordingly writt the Same & this Deponent
Alsoe Saith that the S^d Monsr Calliere then Acted In the S^d Affaire
by the direction of the S^d Marquis de Seignlay then Superintendent of
the Sea Ports or Maritime Affaires in ffrance & there upon this De-
ponent was Comanded by the S^d Monsr Calliere to Address himself to
the S^d Lord Preston to obtaine a pass from the English Hudson Bay
Comp^{ie} to Goe to Port Nelson to withdraw the French from thence
And to restore the Same to the English, Who he Saide Should be Satisfied for the Wrong & Damages Done them by this Deponent. And this
Deponent Knoweth that there was one thousand Livres offered by the
S^d Lechaney to the S^d Benj Gilham & the Deponent alsoe Saith that
after his Arriveall In England he went In one of the Hudson Bay
Companys Shipps to Port Nelson; and withdrew the French that were
there from that Place— And the Said Place was then put into the pos-
session of the English Hudson Bay Compie & the French that were
there were brought in to England & were there soe kindly treated &
Entertained that Severall of them Entered into the S^d Comp$^{ie's}$ Service
And continued therein for about foure Yeares.

Pierre Esprit Radisson

The Narative of Mr Peter Espritt Radisson in Refferance to the Answar of the Comm^rs of France to the Right and Title of the Hudson Bay Company.[1]

It cannot be made appeare that the ffrench were the first Discoverers of Hudson Bay or that they ever made any Settlem^ts but since 1682 and that without any Order Commission or Pass or that they Sett up any Trade there save Onley that the Savages came from the Bottom of the said Bay to Tadousac. If that may be Admitted Then Suppose England Traded first to France doth it therefore belong to France. The first Acts of Hostility went down by the French, consequently the English were there first.

The French are in Right not to Insist on the Voyages for that they never made any but since 1682 by Sea Those which they made in Canada and Newfoundland are not Disputed nor those to the Coast of Labradore which are 3 or 400 Leagues Distant from the Bay however it is very Observable that they should Allow the English went thither to Seeke a passage into the South Sea, they having moreover wintered Traded built Houses and lost Severall Ships there which must Indisputably give them the Right thereof they having put up the Arms of the Kings of England from Time to Time Their Charts and Mapps will confute the ffrench.

It cannot be Denyed but that althô a Settlement hath been Interrupted Yett it is a better Title then where none hath been and it is often Found that persons are punished wth the Same punishm^ts that they Dessigned for Others and there is a greate difference Between Publick Colonies and a private One.

If the ffrench would maintaine their Rights to Carolina New England and the Netherlands &c they must then have been the first who tooke the same from the Kings of Spaine whose pattent or Grant from the Pope of all America (at the first discovery had no Limitation or Bounds.

[1] This was copied from the transcript in the Public Archives of Canada, Hudson's Bay, State Papers, M394B, pp. 61–70. It was inaccurately transcribed for the Archives.

If the Old Authors give no Limitts to Canada to the North It is Evident that it being above 1000 Leagues (According to their Report) in the Lakes of the West the Proximity thereof to the English Colonies upon the Coast of America which are much nearer may give matter of disputeing the right of Possession or Usurpation and if the Kings of France could give Letters of Corporation or Charters of New France and the Bay and particularly in the yeare 1628 They Ought alsoe to have Obliged the ffrench who rec^d Canady by Capitulation of the English to pay what was agreed on which they never did Contrary to the Hon^r and Good Faith of Nations but Messrs Kirke who Delivered the same up by Order of the King of England had noe Concerne or right in the Bay in Question and it can be proved that whilst the said Kirks possessed Canada Other English men Sailed into the Bay and Continued the Capture & possession as Others had done.

The 5th Answar Serves for the 6th and to this 7th Paragrapha the first would be Sufficient However we Answar that men Travil with the Language very easily. But as to those 120 Leagues mentioned in the French Answar they must be Reckoned above 250 leagues by reason of the Forests Falls Boggs and Rapid Streams which put them In danger of drowning and are allmost Unpassable to the Savages who can hardly goe and come in One Summer and then at that time the Savages would not have permitted the French if they had been Able to prevent it & as to their Acknowledging the Sovereignty they have no More than a propriety for the presents they have need of would give themselves up this day to God if they had Knowledge of him and tomorrow they would give themselves to the Devil for a pipe of Tobacco and they would even deliver up their Inheritance for the Like things. And they received at each place where the English have been settled theire presents for takeing possession whosoever hath Known those Savage Nations doth Understand the Same things.

The English doe not give out anything that is false neither doe they Equivocate desgroziliers & Radisson were neither of them Pilotts or Marriners but were Entertained in Service by the English. The French having refused them for such Reasons as makes the Right of the English Appear the Two abovenamed after such signall Services done for Canada it self which was allmost ruined were Unjustly pillaged and Deprived of their Livelyhood & were fforced to seek their livings elsewhere not being under any Engagem^t to any person. If the first was an Inhabitant the Other was a freeman but he would not Ingage in the Service of the English untill the returne of A Vessell sent to Kbec to know if they would doe them Justice. If Zach^y Gilham did not arrive at the Bottom of the Bay before 1663 He built the said Fort

Charles upon the ruines of a House which had been built there above 60 yeares before by the English and the said D'Grozilier Served them only as Interpreter Amongst the Savages.

The French hav^g never had any Fort or House it will be very difficult to prove that ever they were there King Charles the 2nd Might very well grant Charters of Letters of Possession to his Subjects who had built Several above 60 or 70 yeares before.

One is often caught in the Snare prepared for Others the Cevil warrs of England did not Hinder the English noe more then the French to Attempt Upon all Europe but the Engagements which ffrance had wth King Charles the Second ought not to have been greater then those which they Ought to have with King William both being Oblidged to maintaine the Right of their Crowne & of their Subjects, And the Ship pretended is yet to build And the Master and Pilot to be Borne, which they Alleadge was in the Bay in the Yeare 1695.

A Merch^t called La Chaney of Kebec being at Paris in 1681 did Secretly (for Fear it should be Known by the English) by himself propose to the said Radisson to Undertake a Voyage to Hudson Bay and to Imbarke at Kebec to hinder all Suspition the said Radisson himself being discountenanced and Out of Favour wth the Marq^s d'Seignlay for having Demanded Some thing of the Rights of Sr John Kirke for the surrender of Canada to the French in 1632 He undertooke to goe thither and came privately into England to Informe himself in what State and Condition the Eng^h Comp^a was and then he went Over to Kebec where the Governour the Marq^s de ffrontenac refused him a pass & forbid him Expressly from Undertakeing Such a Voyage for that Such Designes would Disturb the Union between the Two Kings and that it was the Right of the English, whereupon the said Merch^t desired that Mr Radisson wou'd goe Back into France to which the Governour Agred but the said Radisson was sent by the said Merch^t to Winter at Accadie with Orders to be at the Mouth of the River of St Lawrence in the Spring of the yeare 1682 whither the said Merch^t sent him a very bad Barke ill maned and Worse Furnished with Necessaries laden wth sorry refuge Goods that had been for the Most part of them in the ware houses above 20 years which barke was Accompanied by another Barke Much Worse then the first freighted by three Merchants without any Order or pass who Joyned and came to An Agreem^t with the said Merchant above named which the said Radisson can shew under their Hands and the said Groziliere was on Board and if the Two Brothers were pardoned for having Served Strangers the Fault of having Abused them was thereby Acknowledged & they Shewed themselves faithfull Subjects by giving up their

Fortunes to the promisses made by the Jesuite Albenel who made 2 Voyages for that purpose into the Bay and afterwards Brought to England the said Radisson can produce the Letter which the said Jesuite left in the Bay and was Delivered to him by the Savages and this said Radisson doth Dessire that the Contradiction of these Two Last Articles may be Examined.

The Day before the Arrival of the Two French Barkes before mentioned they being Off at Port Nelson they went into one of the Branches to the Southward of the said Port devided by a Neck of land of about half a Mile from the Breach to the Northward where the English from New England had put in & 8 or 10 dayes afterwards the Capt having killed his Supracargo And caused Sev^l Gunns to be fired at his being Buried the said Radisson did thereby Dis-cover him and went to Visset him and the Next day they parted good friends Radisson coming back to the River on the South where he had built Two Small Houses One Called the St Ann & the Other the St Peter being the Names of their Two Barkes he saw a Ship coming in wth the English Coulours belonging to the Hudson Bay Comp^a having a Govern^r on Board wth a Commission to Settle there The said Radisson went on Board alone & Told them that he had been there a yeare with 300 French Men & 3 Ships perswading to goe to some Other Place but the Season would not permitt it being the End of September about 6 or 7 Weaks Afterward the Ship was Destroyed and lost by the Ice by reason they durst not come into a River for Feare of the ffrench & there remained 18 Men on Shoar all winter with a small Quantity of Provisions, Radisson Invited the Capt from New England to his House where he came & afterw^{ds} he took his Fort and his Ship which he with the Men Belonging to him Carried to Kebec and gave the Other Men a Barke built of the Materials of the Two Barks brought from Quebec to carry them to the Bottom of the Bay Except the Comp^{as} Governour Mr John Bridgar whom he Carried to Kebec in 1683 leaveing 8 French Men in the said River They went to Monsr de laBarr who was then Governour of Canada who Caused them to Restore the English Ship and made Offer of Satisfaction for the Damages were done which being to little the English would not Accept and Returned all of them to New England.

The French will always Endeavor to Disguise the Truth of the Matter which Occationed the said Radisson to Returne to England which shall be proved to their Shame and that he doth not Deserve those ill Names that are given him. If the English do not give him all his Due he Expects the whole by the Justice of his cause.

It may be that in 1687 Messrs de Barrillon & Bonrepos after the

Complaints of the Company might make Complaints again against the Company but King James maintained his subjects then in their Rights and no less is hoped from King William.

If the French had not Surprized the English at the Bottom of the Bay the same French would all have perished wth ffamine & if the Losses are Compared that of the ffrench is but a Chimara or an Imagination in Comparisson of that of the English which is but Tuto Greate to be only pretended as may be seen by the Inventorie made at that Time, When the said Radisson recd the 8 ffrenchmen who came to him in the very moment That they could subsist no Longer.

This is an Answar to the 16th Article and Consequently to the Rest We Defy the French to shew any Commission given for Makeing any Company for a Settlem^t in any part of the Bay but since 1683 only which was given by Monsr de la Barr then Governour of Canada And we Certainly say that he gave no pass tell 1684 which was to 5 or 6 Merchants of Kebec thinking to Maintaine the Post which Desgroziliers & Radison had made because they Wintered there in 1682.

Mr Baley the English Governour went with Radison in 1669 to Port Nelson in the Ship Rupert Capt Newland Comd^r Carrying English Coulors, Out and were Driven thence only by a Terrible Storme in which they thought to Have lost their Lives and Ship. In 1672 Monsr Desgroziliere was there Under English Coulors in the ship called the Employm^t who likewise Tooke possession thereof for the English being then in their Service.

APPENDIX 13

To the Honble the Knights Citizens & Burgesses in Parliam^t
Assembled
The Humble Peticon of Peter Esprit Raddison [1]

Humbly Sheweth

That your Petitioner is a Native of France who wth a Brother of his (since deceased) Spent many Years of their youths among the Indians in and about Hudsons Bay, by reason whereof they became absolute Masters of the Trade & Language of the said Indians in those Parts of America

That about the yeare 1666 King Charles the Second Sent yor Pet^r & his s^d Brother wth two Ships on purpose to Settle English Colonies & factorys in the s^d Bay wch they Effected soe well to ye said Kings Satisfaction that he gave Each of them a Gold Chain & Medall, as a Marke of his Royale favour & recomended them to the Comp^a of Adventurers of England tradeing into Hudsons Bay to be well Gratified & Rewarded by them for their services aforesaid

That since the Death of your Pet^rs Brother the s^d Comp^a have Settled on your Pete^er six actions in the joint stock of ye s^d Comp^a and one hundred pounds p^r annum dureing your Petit^rs life.

That your Pet^r is now 62 yeares of Age (being growne old in the Comp^as Service) & hath not recd any Benefitt of the s^d six shares in the Comp^as Stock for more than 7 yeares last past & hath had nothing but the said 100^lbs per Ann to maintaine himselfe & four small children all borne in England

That dureing the late Reign's a Price was set upon your Petit^rs head by the French & severall attempts were made upon him to Assassinate him & that for Noe other reason but for quiting his owne Country & Serving the Comp^a

That your Pet^r dares not returne to his Native Country for the Reasons afores^d & seing all his subsistance depends on the said Comp^a

---

[1] H.B.Co. Archives, Misc. File, 1540–1740, under date of March 11, 1697/8. See also in the same file *The Case of the Hudson's Bay Company*, a printed sheet of the year 1697 or 1698.

& is shortly to Determine wth the life of your Pet^r and his four small Children must Consequently fall to be Maintain'd by the Alm's of the Parish altho the Comp^a hath had many Thousand pounds Effects by his procurement & some that he conceives he had himselfe a good Tytle to

Your pet^r therefore most humbly prays that this Honble House will Comiserate the Condition of your Pet^{rs} said Children—and whereas he hath now the said six Actions & 100^{lbs} per ann only for his life, that you will Vouchsafe to insert a Provisoe in the Bill depending to grant the s^d Annuity to be paid—Quarterly, & the Dividends of the s^d Actions as often as any shall become due to your Pet^r & his Heires for Ever, dureing the Joint Stock of the said Comp^a and yor Pet^r shall for Ever Pray &c^a

Peter Esprit Radison

William Yonge's Will [1]

IN THE NAME OF GOD AMEN

I William Yonge of London of the Parish of St Andrews Holbourn
Esqr do hereby make null and revoke all former Wills and do make
this my last Will and Testament in manner and form following vizt
Imprimis my Soul I bequeth to God its Almighty Creator and my Body
to the Earth from whence it came in a firm expectation of a happy
Resurrection at the last day when my Saviour shall come to judge the
world I desire decently to be buried where I shall happen to dye
with the least expense and charge immaginable for the Ease of my
Executor and my Grandchildren Item all my Right Title and Interest which I now have and hereafter shall have at the time of my death
in the joynt Stock of the Mines in Cardiganshire and elsewhere in
the principallity of Wales I give and bequeath the same even all my
blanks shares and Interest in manner following vizt the first Five hundred pounds that shall become due from them after my decease I bequeath to the Masters and Governours of Christs Hospitall in London
In Trust for the benefitt of the poor Children of that Hospitall and I
desire Sr Humphry Mackworth and Mr William Shiers our Secratary
will see it faithfully paid accordingly And after the said Five hundred
pounds shall be fully satisfyed and paid I give and bequeath all my
remaining Right Title and Interest in the said Mines and premises to
my Grandchildren which already are or shall hereafter be begotten
on the Body of my daughter Mrs Barbara Goodall by Thomas Goodall
of Grays Inne Esqr her present Husband share and share alike whether
they be Males or Females And if any of them happen to dye unmar-
ried my Will is that their shares shall inure and goe to the augmenta-
tion of the survivors shares And I will that never any of my Blanks or
shares shall at any time be sold but that an equall distribution of the
profitts ariseing annually from the premises be made respectively to my
said Grandchildren as aforesaid Item I bequeath to my Brother and
Sister Goodall and to their Sisters Mrs Pattison and Mrs Pilson to
each of them Five pounds And to my Sister Mrs Susannah Goodall I

---

[1] Yonge's will is filed in Somerset House, London.

farther bequeath all my Pictures in the staircase and elsewhere in her present dwelling house Except my Family Pictures which I give to my daughter   Item I give to such of my Servants that shall live with me at the time of my death to each of them Five pounds   Item I give to Mr William Shiers our Secretary at the Mine Adventure office Five pounds for his trouble in paying the Five hundred pounds to the Masters and Governors of the Hospitall aforesaid   Item I give and Forgive to Mr Peter Esprit Radisson all the Money he oweth me which I think is Fifty Three pounds   Lastly I do give and bequeath all my Lands and Fee farms Rents also my Stock in the Hudsons Bay Company and in the Affrican Company and also my whole Interest and Joynt stock in the Company for raising water by Fire known by the name of Captain Thomas Savery's invention and also my Interest in Mr Neales Million Lottery and the Malt Lottery together with my Interest in a Pattent granted to Mr Hadley which I bought of Doctor Wall and also all other my Goods Leases of Houses or Lands and Chattles whatsoever I give and bequeath to my Son in Law Thomas Goodall of Grays Inne Esqr whom I hereby make and appoint the sole Executor of this my last Will and Testament   This Testament was written with my own hand when I was in perfect health and sane memory it was Stamped with two Stamps according to Law and was afterwards Signed Sealed and published this Fourteenth day of June in the second year of the Reign of our gracious Soveraign Queen Anne and in the year of our Lord Seventeen hundred and Three 1703. Will: Yong. Signed Sealed and published in the presence of us W: Mackworth Tho: Breton Wm Shires J^no Llewellin Clerke to Mr William Shiers Secretary to the Company of Mine Adventurers [*Proved January 5, 1708*].

Radisson's Will [1]

IN THE NAME OF GOD AMEN

I Peter Radisson of Clare Court in the Liberty of the City of Westminster being at present sickly in Body but of perfect Sense and memory and being mindfull of my mortallity with hearty sorrow for my Sins recommending my Soul to Almighty God and trusting for salvation through the meritts of my blessed Saviour As touching my worldly Estate and substance doe make this my last Will and Testament in manner following vis^t Imprimis I do give and devise unto my trusty and beloved Friend James Heanes of the City of London Winecooper and to my beloved and dear Wife Elizabeth Radisson all my reall and personall Estate and other my Goods and Chattles and worldly substance whatsoever And I doe make and ordain them Executors of this my last Will and Testament And Whereas I did at the desire of his late Majestie King Charles the second and his late Majestie King James the second when Duke of York and those imployed by them quitt the Interest and Service of the present French King and imbrace the Service of their said Majesties and that of the English Nation and by my means severall Colonys in America formerly in possession of the French were reduced unto the Obedience of the late King Charles the Second and the same continue now in the possession of her present Majesty and her Subjects to the great advantage of the English Nation and in particular of the Society or Company of Hudsons Bay a great part of which transactions is in the memory of his Grace the Duke of Marlborrough to whose care I have been recomended by the late King James before the Revolution And Whereas in regard to my Services the said late King Charles the Second ordered the said Company of Hudsons Bay (to whose benefitt the same did more particularly redound) to pay me a yearly Pension and other gratuities to which order the said Company did chearfully condescend with publick acknowledgments of the benefitt they had by my means And whereas besides what is due on account of the said Pension there is now above Eighteen

[1] Radisson's will is filed in Somerset House, London, No. 167 under the letter *R* for 1710.

hundred pounds due to me for other demands I justly have to the said
Company I doe hereby devise and my Will is that my said Executrix
and Executor shall have and recover the same and the full benefitt
thereof And shall also have and recover all other debts and demands to
me due from any other persons whatsoever And my Will is that out
of the said debts my said Executor and Executrix do pay and satisfy
all my just debts and the residue to apply and dispose of for the support
and advancement of my said dear Wife and my three small daughters
on her begotten and now Living my former Wifes Children being by
me according to my ability advanced and preferred to severall Trades
And I do revoke all former and other Wills and devises by me made
for or concerning the premises And now have to this my last Will and
Testament putt my hand and seal this Seventeenth day of June 1710
Seventeen hundred and Ten Peter Radisson. Signed Sealed and published by the said Peter Radison as his last Will and Testament this
17th day of June 1710 the words besides what is due and the word for
being first interlined Per Champourrain Julian Bromley her mark.

BIBLIOGRAPHY

This bibliography is for use in conjunction with the footnotes of the chapters. Its primary aim is to list printed material alphabetically, so that the full name of an author and the full title and date of publication of his work may be determined easily. These data are given fully only in the first citation. An abbreviated form is used for later citations.

Manuscript sources are listed very briefly in this bibliography. Thousands of documents were consulted in the larger collections in Paris, London, Three Rivers, Quebec, and elsewhere. Obviously only a mention of most of these collections is possible. Footnotes usually give sufficient data to identify documents that are actually quoted or used to establish specific facts. Hundreds of other manuscripts, however, have been used for background or for reinforcement.

MANUSCRIPTS

Paris

Bibliothèque Nationale
    Collection Clairambault
    Fonds Français—22,593–22,822, especially 22,800 (Dangeau Collection)
    Mélanges de Colbert
    Nouvelles Acquisitions
        7483–7497—Papers of Eusèbe Renaudot
        560–563—Papers of Nicholas Thoynard
        9255–9510—Papers of Pierre Margry
Archives des Affaires Étrangères
Archives des Colonies
Archives Nationales
Dépôt des Cartes et Plans de la Marine. Service Hyrographique

Other Places in France

Avignon
    Palace of the Popes—Vital Statistics of Vaucluse
Carpentras
    Archives Municipales
    Bibliothèque de Carpentras
Charly-sur-Marne
    Office of the Mayor—parish registers

LONDON

British Museum

Many manuscripts were consulted in this institution, but few are cited in footnotes. The Royal, Stowe, Egerton, Sloane, and Additional MSS were those most productive of data. The parchment map of Hudson Bay, prepared by John Thornton in the middle 1680's for the Hudson's Bay Company, and much sought for by that Company, was noted in Additional MSS 5414. 20. It is very large. Other maps by Thornton were also useful.

Friends' Reference Library, Friends' House

Here, among the archives of the Quakers of England, are most of the documents that throw light on Charles Bayly, the first governor of the territory of the Hudson's Bay Company in Hudson Bay.

The Guildhall Library

The Hudson's Bay Company Archives

These archives, in process of classification, are voluminous. They are housed in basement rooms of Hudson's Bay House, 68 Bishopsgate. They are invaluable for the careers of Radisson and Des Groseilliers from 1665 to 1710. Several main series were used: the minute books, the ledgers, the letterbooks, and miscellany. Practically no original correspondence for the period under consideration is now extant. They are utilized for the purposes of this book by the kind permission of the Governor and Committee.

The Public Record office

Colonial Office: Board of Trade, Colonial Papers, America and West
    Indies, Colonial Entry Books
State Papers—Domestic
Admiralty Papers—Navy Board
Treasury Papers and Books
Privy Council
Chancery Papers

Royal Society of London

Journals, register books, class papers, general manuscripts

Somerset House

Wills of several persons mentioned in this volume are filed in this depository

OTHER PLACES IN ENGLAND

Cambridge

Arthur Bryant, engaged in writing his biography of Samuel Pepys, inspected the manuscripts in the Pepysian Library, Magdalene College, for the author, but he was unable to find in that great collection any references to Radisson and Des Groseilliers. The library was closed for repairs when the author herself went to use the papers.

Longtown, Cumberland

The papers of Viscount Preston are preserved at Crofthead on the estate of Sir Fergus Graham, near Netherby Hall, the ancestral home of the Grahams. They include numerous pieces for the period of Lord Preston's service as envoy extraordinary at the court of Louis XIV. For a true account of Radisson's return to an English allegiance in 1684 they are the finest data available.

Oxford

Bodleian Library

The papers of Samuel Pepys contain Radisson's narratives as well as some other data of value. The Tanner and Rawlinson papers were most used.

All Souls College Library

This library has some useful seventeenth-century manuscripts and newspapers.

Ottawa

Public Archives

The Public Archives of Canada contain transcripts of many of the manuscripts listed in this volume as being in Paris, London, Montreal, Quebec, and Three Rivers. The author has found many errors of transcription in using them and so has usually ended by using the original documents.

Montreal

The Old Court-House

There are many depositories of seventeenth-century manuscripts in this city, but those of most value for this study have been found in the Old Court-House. They are difficult to find and use.

The Gagnon Collection

This collection is now a part of the Library of the City of Montreal.

Quebec

Palais de Justice

The judicial archives in this depository are a large and important body of records, including *greffes* of seventeenth-century notaries and copies of early church records. They are indexed and calendared to a considerable extent. The spelling and writing will cause difficulty for those untrained in the use of sixteenth- and early seventeenth-century documents.

Museum of the Province of Quebec

The most important documents used in this depository were the volumes of Three Rivers local archives, supplementing similar records in Three Rivers. For brevity's sake in the footnotes in this volume the Quebec series are distinguished from the Three Rivers series by the use of (Q) after the citation. Many of these documents are fragile with age and difficult to handle and decipher.

THREE RIVERS [1]

Palais de Justice

The *greffes* of notaries, prévôté archives, copies of church and parish registers, and many other invaluable local records are preserved here from the early seventeenth century. Some are in French, some in Latin, and nearly all are written in the style of handwriting that was dying out in France by the third quarter of the seventeenth century.

BOSTON

State House

The court records of the Colony of the Massachusetts Bay in New England are preserved in the State House, Boston. They are well preserved and easily accessible. They indicate considerable intercourse between the inhabitants of New England and New France at the time of Radisson and Des Groseilliers' sojourn in Boston, but not a single specific reference to the two Frenchmen has been found.

CHICAGO

Chicago Historical Society

The Schmidt Collection contains a number of interesting and valuable manuscripts relating to the early French period in Canada. They may once have been a part of a famous notary's *greffe* in Three Rivers and Quebec.

Newberry Library—Ayer Collection

This depository owns a magnificent portolan atlas once owned and inscribed by Radisson.

SAINT PAUL

St. Paul Seminary

Cyprien Tanguay sent copies of Canadian manuscripts and results of his own investigations at one time to a correspondent of this seminary.

[1] Trois Rivières is the French name of this city.

Minnesota Historical Society
The author, as curator of manuscripts in this institution, has collected here many photostats and transcripts of French and English documents relating to Canada and the two subjects of this volume. In addition, she has made a very large personal collection, which will doubtless go eventually to the Minnesota Historical Society. The papers of Edward D. Neill also contain valuable copies of seventeenth-century documents.

WASHINGTON

The Library of Congress
Found here are transcripts or filmslides of some of the documents used by the author in Europe, as well as some other material.

NEWSPAPERS

London [before February 1, 1666, the *Oxford*] *Gazette*. 1665 to date.
The file consulted in the preparation of this work is in the Harvard College Library, Cambridge, Massachusetts.

BOOKS AND PERIODICALS

ACHARD, FÉLIX ET DUHAMEL, L., *Inventaire-sommaire des archives départementales: Vaucluse* (Paris, 1878).

Acts of the Privy Council of England, Colonial Series, edited by W. L. Grant and J. Munro, 6 vols. (Hereford, 1908–1912).

ADAIR, E. R., "Dollard des Ormeaux and the Fight at the Long Sault," in *Canadian Historical Review*, 13: 121–138 (June, 1932).

ANDREWS, CHARLES M., *The Colonial Period of American History: The Settlements*, 4 vols. (New Haven, 1934–1938).

The Beaver, see Hudson's Bay Company.

Boston, Record Commissioners, *Ninth Report* (*Births, Baptisms, Marriages and Deaths, 1630–1699*) (Boston, 1883).

BOYLE, ROBERT, "Experiments and Observations Touching Cold," in his *Works*, 2: 228–403 (London, 1744).

BRAY, WILLIAM, ed., see EVELYN, JOHN.

BRETT-JAMES, NORMAN, *The Growth of Stuart London* (London, 1935).

BRYANT, ARTHUR, *The England of Charles II* (London, 1934).

———, *Samuel Pepys*, 3 vols. (New York, 1933–1939).

BROWN, HARCOURT, *Scientific Organizations in Seventeenth Century France* (*1620–1680*) (History of Science Society, New Series, Vol. 5, 1934).

Bulletin des recherches historiques, ed., Pierre-Georges Roy, monthly publication (Lévis, 1895———).

BURNHAM, GUY M., *The First House Built by White Men in Wisconsin* (Ashland, Wis. [1931]).

Calendar of State Papers, Colonial Series, America and West Indies (1574–1711), edited by W. N. Sainsbury, J. W. Fortescue, and C. Headlam (London, 1860–1924).

Calendar of State Papers, Domestic Series (1547———), edited by Robert Lemon and others (London, 1856———).

Calendar of Treasury Books (1660–1689), edited by W. A. Shaw, 8 vols. (London, 1904–1923).

CAMPBELL, HENRY C., "Radisson and Groseilliers. Problems in Western History," in *American Historical Review,* 1: 226–237 (New York, 1896).

Le Canada Français, a monthly publication appearing as the organ of La Société du Parler Français au Canada and published by Laval University (Quebec, 1918———).

Canadian Archives, annual *Report* (Ottawa).

CARON, IVANHOË, *Journal de l'expédition du Chevalier de Troyes à la Baie d'Hudson, en 1686* (Beauceville, 1918).

CASSON, FRANÇOIS DOLLIER DE, *Histoire de Montréal* in *Mémoires de la société historique de Montréal,* 4:[3]–272.

CHARLEVOIX, FRANÇOIS XAVIER DE, *Histoire et description générale de la Nouvelle France avec le journal historique d'un voyage fait par ordre du Roi dans l'Amérique Septentrionale,* 2 vols. (Paris, 1744).

CHINARD, GILBERT, *Un Français en Virginie* (Institut Français de Washington, Vol. 5, Baltimore, 1932).

CHRISTY, MILLER, *The Voyages of Captain Luke Foxe of Hull, and Captain Thomas James of Bristol in Search of a North-West Passage . . . ,* 2 vols. (Hakluyt Society Publications, London, 1894).

CLÉMENT, P., *Lettres, instructions, et mémoires de Colbert,* 3 vols. (Paris, 1865).

COOPER, WILLIAM DURRANT, ed., *Lists of Foreign Protestants and Aliens, Resident in England, 1618–1688* (Camden Society Publications, London, 1862).

———, *Letters to and From Henry Savile, Esq., Envoy at Paris, and Vice-Chamberlain to Charles II and James II* (Camden Society Publications, London, 1857).

CORLIEU, A., *Géographie du Canton de Charly-Sur-Marne* (Château-Thierry, 1879).

COX, LEO, "River Without End," in *Canadian Geographical Journal,* 13: 86 (Ottawa, June, 1936).

CRANE, VERNER W., *The Southern Frontier, 1670–1732* (Duke University Press, 1928).

CROSS, MARION E., ed., trans., *Father Louis Hennepin's Description of Louisiana Newly Discovered to the Southwest of New France by Order of the King* (Minneapolis, 1938).

CROUSE, NELLIS M., *Contributions of the Canadian Jesuits to the Geographical Knowledge of New France, 1632–1675* (Ithaca, 1924).

———, *In Quest of the Western Ocean* (New York, 1928).

DAMPIER, WILLIAM, *Voyages*, see MASEFIELD, JOHN, ed.

DELANGLEZ, JEAN, S. J., *Some La Salle Journeys* (Institute of Jesuit History Publications, Chicago, 1938).

———, *Frontenac and the Jesuits* (Institute of Jesuit History Publications, Chicago, 1939).

———, *Hennepin's Description of Louisiana, A Critical Essay* (Institute of Jesuit History Publications, Chicago, 1940).

DEPPING, G. B., *Correspondance administrative sous le règne de Louis XIV*, 4 vols. (Paris, 1850–1855).

Dictionary of American Biography, edited by Allen Johnson and Dumas Malone, 21 vols. (New York, 1928–1937).

DOBBS, ARTHUR, *An Account of the Countries Adjoining to Hudson's Bay* (London, 1744).

DODD, WILLIAM E., "The Emergence of the First Social Order in the United States," in *The American Historical Review*, 40: 217–231 (January, 1935).

DUNN, WILLIAM E., *Spanish and French Rivalry in the Gulf Region of the United States, 1678–1702; the Beginnings of Texas and Pensacola* (Austin, 1917).

English Pilot, see FISHER, WILLIAM

EVELYN, JOHN, *Diary and Correspondence of John Evelyn, F.R.S.*, edited by William Bray, 4 vols. (London, 1857).

EXQUEMELIN, A. O., *The History of the Bucaniers of America*, 2 vols. (London, fourth edition, 1741).

FISHER, WILLIAM, *The English Pilot, The Fourth Book* (London, 1689).

FOX, GEORGE, see PENNEY, NORMAN, ed.

GAGNON, PHILEAS, *Essai de bibliographie canadienne*, 2 vols. (Montreal, 1895, 1913).

GARNEAU, FRANÇOIS X., *History of Canada from the Time of Its Discovery till the Union Year (1840–41)*, translated and edited by Andrew Bell, 3 vols. (Montreal, 1860). There is a later edition by H. Garneau (Paris, 1925), but the older editions, including the French, were used by the author.

GREGORICH, JOSEPH, *The Apostle of the Chippewas: The Life Story of the Most Rev. Frederick Baraga, D.D., the First Bishop of Marquette* (Chicago, 1932).

HACKETT, C. W., "New Light on Don Diego de Peñalosa," in *Mississippi Valley Historical Review*, 6: 313–335 (December, 1919).

HALIBURTON, THOMAS C., *An Historical and Statistical Account of Nova Scotia*, 2 vols. (Halifax, 1829).

HARING, CLARENCE H., *The Buccaneers in the West Indies in the XVII Century* (New York, 1910).

Harleian Society, *Publications.* Volume 50 is *The Register of the Burials of the United Parishes of St. Stephen in Walbrook, & St. Bennet Sherehog in the City of London, from the Year of Our Lord, 1716* (London, 1920).

HARTMAN, CYRIL HUGHES, *Charles II and Madame* (London, 1934).

HENEKER, DOROTHY A., *The Seigniorial Régime in Canada* ([Montreal], [1927]).

HENNEPIN, LOUIS, *Description of Louisiana*, see CROSS, MARION E., ed.

———, *Nouveau Voiage* (Utrecht, 1698).

Historical Manuscripts Commission (The Royal Commission on Historical Manuscripts), *Reports* (London, 1870———). The seventh and twelfth reports were of special value for this study.

Hudson's Bay Company, *The Beaver*, a quarterly magazine (Winnipeg, 1920———).

JACOBSEN, GERTRUDE ANN, *William Blathwayt, A Late Seventeenth Century English Administrator* (New Haven, 1932).

JOSSELYN, JOHN, *New Englands Rarities* (London, 1672).

Journal des Sçavans, continued as *Journal des Savants* (Paris and Amsterdam), Vol. 1–169 (1655–1753).

Jugements et délibérations du conseil souverain de la Nouvelle-France, 6 vols. (Quebec, 1885–1891).

KARPINSKI, LOUIS C., *Historical Atlas of the Great Lakes and Michigan* (Lansing, 1931).

KELLOGG, LOUISE P., *The French Régime in Wisconsin and the Northwest* (State Historical Society of Wisconsin, Madison, 1925).

KIRKE, HENRY, *The First English Conquest of Canada; with some Account of the Early Settlements in Nova Scotia and Newfoundland* (London, 1871).

LE JEUNE, LOUIS, *Le Chevalier Pierre Le Moyne, Sieur D'Iberville* (Editions de l'Université d'Ottawa, 1937).

———, *Dictionnaire générale . . . du Canada*, 2 vols. (Ottawa, 1931).

LELAND, WALDO G., *Guide to Materials for American History in the Libraries and Archives of Paris* (Washington, 1932).

Maine Historical Society, *Collections*, Second Series, Vol. 4 (James Phinney Baxter, ed., *Documentary History of the State of Maine*, Portland, 1889).

MARGRY, PIERRE, *Découvertes et établissements des Français dans l'Ouest et dans le Sud de l'Amérique Septentrionale*, 6 vols. (Paris, 1879–1886).

MARIE DE L'INCARNATION, *Lettres de la Vénérable Mère Marie de l'Incarnation, première supérieure des Ursulines de la Nouvelle France*, edited by Dom Claude Martin (Paris, 1681).

———, *Lettres de la Révérende Mère Marie de l'Incarnation*, édition Richaudeau, 3 vols. (Tournal, 1876).

———, *Marie de l'Incarnation, Ursuline de Tours: Ecrits Spirituels et Historiques*, 3 vols. (Paris and Quebec, 1929–1935).

MASEFIELD, JOHN, ed., *Dampier's Voyages by Captain William Dampier*, 2 vols. (New York, 1906).

Massachusetts, *Records and Files of the Quarterly Courts of Essex County, Massachusetts*, 8 vols. (Essex Institute, Salem, 1911–1921).

———, *Records of the Governor and Company of the Massachusetts Bay in New England*, edited by Nathaniel B. Shurtleff, 5 vols. in 6 (Boston, 1853, 1854).

———, *Suffolk Deeds*, 5 vols. in 6 (Boston, 1880–1906).

———, *Records of the Court of Assistants of the Massachusetts Bay, 1630–1692* (Boston, 1928).

Massachusetts Historical Society, *Proceedings* (Boston, 1791———).

———, *The Winthrop Papers*, Part IV, in *Collections of the Massachusetts Historical Society*, Fifth Series, Vol. VIII (Boston, 1882).

MASSICOTTE, E. J., *Répertoire des engagements pour l'ouest conservés dans les archives judiciaires de Montréal* in *Rapport de l'Archiviste de la Province de Québec pour 1932–1933* (Quebec, 1933).

MILLER, E. T., "The Connection of Peñalosa with the La Salle Expedition," in *The Quarterly of the Texas State Historical Association*, 5: 97–112 (October, 1901).

Minnesota History, formerly *Minnesota History Bulletin*, published by the Minnesota Historical Society (St. Paul, 1915———), especially Vols. 6, 7, 13, which contain several articles on Radisson and Des Groseilliers.

MOOD, FULMER, "The London Background of the Radisson Problem," in *Minnesota History*, 16: 391–413 (December, 1935).

———, "Hudson's Bay Company Started as a Syndicate," in *The Beaver*, 52–58 (March, 1938).

MORTON, ARTHUR S., *A History of the Canadian West to 1870–71* (Toronto and New York [1939]).

MOULIN, H., "Les deux de Callières (Jacques et François)," in *Mémoires de l'Académie de Caën*, Vol. 38 (1883).

NEILL, EDWARD D., *English Colonization of America* (London, 1871).

NEWTON, ARTHUR P., *The European Nations in the West Indies, 1493–1688* (The Pioneer Histories, London, 1933).

North American Review (Boston, New York, 1815——).

NUTE, GRACE LEE, "Radisson and Groseilliers' Contribution to Geography," in *Minnesota History*, 16: 414–426 (December, 1935).

——, "Two Documents from Radisson's Suit Against the Company," in *The Beaver*, December, 1935, pp. 41–49.

——, *The Voyageur's Highway* (Minnesota Historical Society, St. Paul, 1941).

O'CALLAGHAN, EDMUND B., ed., *Documents Relative to the Colonial History of the State of New York Procured in Holland, England and France*, 15 vols. (Albany, 1853–1887).

OLDMIXON, JOHN, *The British Empire in America* . . . , 2 vols. (London, 1741).

PALFREY, JOHN G., *History of New England*, 5 vols. (Boston, 1890).

Papier terrier de la Compagnie des Indes Occidentales, see Quebec (Province).

PENNEY, NORMAN, ed., *A Journal or Historical Account of the Life, Travels, . . . of . . . George Fox* (Cambridge, 1911).

POTHERIE, BACQUEVILLE DE LA, *Histoire de l'Amérique Septentrionale*, 4 vols. in 2 (Paris, 1722).

Quarterly Review, (London, 1809——).

Quebec (Province), *Archives de la province de Québec: Papier terrier de la Compagnie des Indes Occidentales, 1667–1668*, edited by Pierre-Georges Roy (Beauceville, 1931).

——, *Archives de la province de Québec: Ordonnances, Commissions etc. etc., des Gouverneurs et Intendants de la Nouvelle-France, 1639–1706*, edited by Pierre-Georges Roy, 2 vols. (Beauceville, 1924).

——, *Rapport de l'Archiviste de la Province de Québec*, annually, from 1920–1921 to date (Quebec).

——, *Archives de la province de Québec: Inventaire des insinuations du conseil souverain de la Nouvelle-France*, edited by Pierre-Georges Roy (Beauceville, 1921).

——, *Inventaire des concessions en fief et seigneurie fois et hommages* . . . , edited by Pierre-Georges Roy, 6 vols. (Beauceville, 1927–1929).

RADISSON, PIERRE ESPRIT, *Voyages of Peter Esprit Radisson, Being an Account of His Travels and Experiences Among the North American In-*

dians, from 1652 to 1684, edited by Gideon Scull (Prince Society Publications, Boston, 1885).

ROBSON, JOSEPH, *An Account of Six Years Residence in Hudson's-Bay, from 1733 to 1736, and 1744 to 1747* (London, 1752).

RONCIÈRE, CHARLES DE LA, *Une épopée canadienne* (Paris, 1930).

ROY, J. EDMOND, "Jean Bourdon," in *Bulletin des recherches historiques,* 2: 2–9, 21–23; also in booklet form (Lévis, 1896).

————, *Rapport sur les archives relatives à l'histoire du Canada* (Ottawa, 1911).

ROY, PIERRE-GEORGES, ed., see Quebec (Province).

————, *La famille Godefroy de Tonnancour* (Lévis, 1904).

Royal Society of Canada, *Proceedings and Transactions* (Ottawa; Montreal, 1882————).

Royal Society of London, *Philosophical Transactions,* First Series, 1665–1886.

RYLANDS, W. HARRY, ed., *Grantees of Arms Named in Docquets and Patents to the End of the Seventeenth Century* (Harleian Society Publications, Vol. 66, London, 1915).

SCOTTOW, J., *A Narrative of the Planting of the Massachusetts Colony in 1628,* in *Massachusetts Historical Collections,* Fourth Series, Vol. 4, pp. 279–330 (Boston, 1858).

SCULL, GIDEON D., ed., *The Evelyns in America* (Oxford, 1881).

————, ed., *Voyages of Peter Esprit Radisson.* See RADISSON, PIERRE ESPRIT.

SEMMES, RAPHAEL, *Captains and Mariners of Early Maryland* (Baltimore, 1937).

SHAW, WILLIAM A., *Letters of Denization and Acts of Naturalization for Aliens in England and Ireland, 1603–1700* (Huguenot Society of London Publications, Vol. 18, London, 1911).

SMITH, JOSEPH, *A Descriptive Catalogue of Friends' Books or Books Written by Members of the Society of Friends,* 2 vols. (London, 1867).

STOW, JOHN, *A Survey of London,* fifth edition by J. Strype, 2 vols. (London, 1720).

[SULTE, BENJAMIN, ed.], *Collection de manuscrits contenant lettres, mémoires, et autres documents historiques relatifs à la Nouvelle-France,* 4 vols. (Quebec, 1883–1885).

SULTE, BENJAMIN, *Histoire des canadiens-français, 1608–1880,* 8 vols. in 4 (Montreal, 1882).

TANGUAY, CYPRIEN, *Dictionnaire généalogique des familles canadiennes,* 7 vols. (Montreal, 1871–1890).

TANNER, J. R., ed., *A Descriptive Catalogue of the Naval Manuscripts in the Pepysian Library at Magdalene College, Cambridge,* 4 vols. (Navy Record Society Publications, London, 1903–1923).

THWAITES, REUBEN GOLD, ed., *The Jesuit Relations and Allied Documents,* 73 vols. (Cleveland, 1896–1901).

TYRRELL, J. B., ed., *Documents Relating to the Early History of Hudson Bay* (Champlain Society Publications, Vol. 18, Toronto, 1931).

UPHAM, WARREN, "Groseilliers and Radisson, the First White Men in Minnesota, 1655–56, and 1659–60, and Their Discovery of the Upper Mississippi River," in *Collections of the Minnesota Historical Society,* X, Pt. 2, 449–594 (St. Paul, 1905) with bibliography.

WAGNER, HENRY R., "Apocryphal Voyages to the Northwest Coast of America," in *Proceedings of the American Antiquarian Society,* New Series, 40: 179–234 (Worcester, April, 1931).

WARREN, WILLIAM WHIPPLE, *History of the Ojibways Based Upon Traditions and Oral Statements* in *Minnesota Historical Collections,* Vol. 5 (St. Paul, 1885).

WINSOR, JUSTIN, *Narrative and Critical History of America,* 8 vols. (Boston and New York, 1884–1889).

WINTHROP, JOHN, see Massachusetts, *Collections of the Massachusetts Historical Society.*

INDEX

371

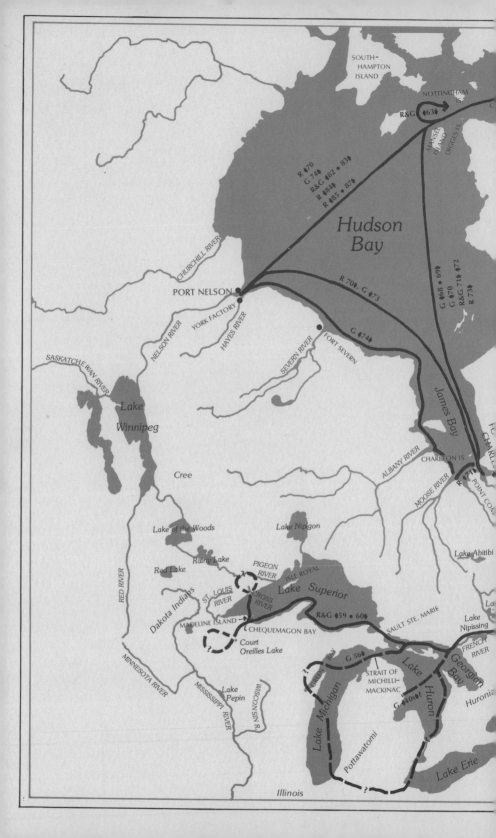